THE NAPA VALLEY BOOK
The Insider's Guide for Visitors and Residents

Wineries, restaurants, hotels, sightseeing,
historic attractions, shopping, recreation, tours,
and much, much more

Mick Winter

Westsong Publishing
Napa, California
www.westsongpublishing.com

THE NAPA VALLEY BOOK

The Insider's Guide for Visitors and Residents

Mick Winter

Published by
Westsong Publishing
PO Box 2254
Napa CA 94558
www.westsongpublishing.com
nvbook@westsong.com

Much of this material originally published as *Napa Valley in a Nutshell*, copyright © 1996 by Mick Winter.

First print edition published 2003 — ISBN 0-9659000-1-0
Updated 2004

Cover design by Nancy Shapiro

Printed in the United States of America

Cover photos (courtesy of):
    Hot air balloon (Napa Valley Conference and Visitors Bureau)
    Wine Train (Napa Valley Wine Train)
    Wind machines in vineyard (Napa Valley Vintners Association)
    Trail ride (Napa Valley Trail Rides)
    Grape cluster (Wine Institute)
    Sculptures at Artesa Winery (Gordon Huether)
    Welcome sign (Napa Valley Conference and Visitors Bureau)

Dedicated to Kathryn, with gratitude for her encouragement;
to all those who fight—and fought—to preserve
the beauty of the Napa Valley;
and to Joanna, because it's her home.

Acknowledgments

Thanks to Stuart Bockman, Sharon Dellamonica, Lowell Downey, Paul Franson, Louis Gottfried, Ginger Gregory, Eve Kahn, Paulette Litz, Laura Madonna, Shauna Marshall, Curtis Phillips, and Joanna Winter for their contributions to this book. To Tashi Wangdu, whose excellent work saved me from having to key in the entire content of the original version. To Nancy Shapiro for her eye-catching cover. And to Patty Winter and Sarah Martin for their invaluable editing. Any remaining glitches are totally my responsibility.

We welcome feedback

If you have comments, suggestions or other feedback about this book and its information, please let us know at:

nvbook@westsong.com

or drop us a line at:

Napa Valley Book
PO Box 2254
Napa CA 94558

Promotional Copies of this Book

Quantity purchases are available with your business name, logo and marketing message on the cover for use as corporate gifts or promotional tools. For more information, email

nvbook@westsong.com

Buy the eBook

You've bought the book! Now buy the eBook!

It's filled with color photographs and over 700 active hyperlinks to Napa Valley websites. Put it on your home computer, laptop or PDA.

For more information on the ebook, or to buy additional copies of this book, visit: www.napavalleybooks.com

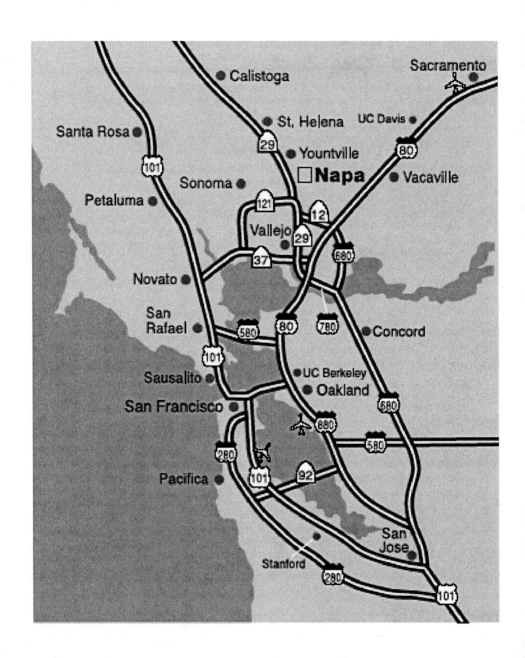

San Francisco Bay Area

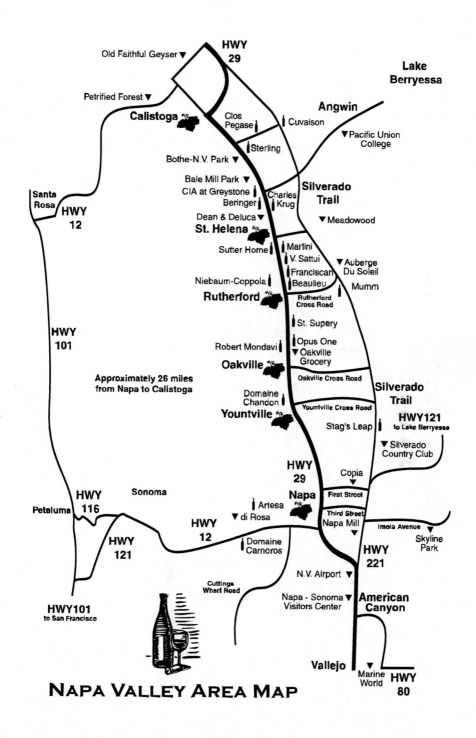

NAPA VALLEY AREA MAP

Table of Contents

Welcome to the Napa Valley   1
Towns and Regions of the Napa Valley   21
   American Canyon   21
   Carneros   22
   Napa   25
   Yountville   50
   Oakville   56
   Rutherford   58
   St. Helena   61
   Calistoga   72
   Angwin   81
   Pope Valley   82
   Chiles Valley   82
   Lake Berryessa   83
   Silverado Trail   84
   Scenic Drives   89
   Just Outside the Napa Valley   90
Lodging and Spas   93
Things to Do   109
Napa Valley Cuisine   109
Recreation and Outdoors   127
Romantic Tips   140
Kids' Favorites   140
Gay Information   141
Night Life   141
Downtown Napa Walking Tour   143
Hill and Mountain Biking   147
Wine   151
Winery List   188
Local Information   199
Relocating to the Napa Valley   209
Napa Valley Trivia   211
Wedding Planning   217
California State Historical Landmarks   221
History of Napa County   225
Napa County Statistics   233
Index   235

Welcome to the Napa Valley

Hello—and welcome.

If you're here for only a day or two, as are 90% of the visitors to our valley, you don't have time to visit every one of the more than 250 wineries, or to eat at each of our fine restaurants. And then there's shopping, hiking, golf, ballooning, spas, music, gliding, entertainment and more.

To make your visit easier, we've listed what we feel are the very best, most unusual, most interesting, most enjoyable and most varied Napa Valley experiences. The rest is up to you.

The first half of the book offers a section on each town or region, moving south to north up the valley and then dealing with surrounding areas. Each section includes wineries, resorts, restaurants, shopping, events and sightseeing attractions. You'll find lodging and spas, recreation and other activities and information in their own sections further on in the book. There's also a section on local information that is particularly helpful to new residents.

The last major section is on wine and covers grapegrowing, winemaking, wine tasting, and the wines of the Napa Valley, as well as a glossary of wine terms, tips on pronunciation of wine names, and answers to frequently asked questions about wine.

A big thanks to our volunteer panel of Napa Valley residents for their suggestions on what to include in the book. Their collective wisdom was of great help.

Of course, just because something isn't included in the book, doesn't mean it isn't worth seeing. Almost all wineries in the Napa Valley make wine that's well worth tasting. We've focused on wineries that are perennial visitor favorites and that are open for drop-in visitors. We've also included some others that have a unique quality or offering we felt you would enjoy.

The same with restaurants. We may be a small rural area, but we're blessed with a large number of truly first-class restaurants.

Here again, we've listed the best known, and added others known largely only to locals, but there are many others that deserve your patronage.

Because this guide has no paid advertising, you can be sure that all of the listings are based totally on what we believe is their value to you, the visitor to the Napa Valley. We hope we're able to make your visit more enjoyable, whether it's for a day, a weekend, or longer.

We should also add that local residents have found the book as valuable as visitors have. That was our intent. We wrote it because it was the book we wanted on our *own* bookshelf. We probably refer to it for information as much as anyone does. We're pleased that other residents are doing the same.

We welcome any comments, suggestions and recommendations you have. If you found one of the listings unsatisfactory, we definitely want to know. And if you discovered a place or activity you feel should be included in the next edition, we want to know that, too. You can email us at *nvbook@westsong.com* or drop us a line at:

Napa Valley Book
PO Box 2254
Napa CA 94558

Thanks for buying the book. We wish you great enjoyment as you visit our home—the beautiful Napa Valley.

Mick Winter
Napa, California

Getting There

Air

There is no scheduled air service to the Napa County Airport but visitors with private planes can fly into Napa Valley Airport.

Napa Valley Airport

2030 Airport Road Napa CA 94558
707.253.4300

Located 6.5 miles south of the city of Napa, Napa Valley Airport is a general aviation airport operated by the County of Napa. It was originally established by the U.S. Army in 1942 as the Napa Auxiliary Air Defense Field. The Army turned it over to the county in 1945. It can accommodate aircraft up to a Gulfstream V. Its FAA-manned control tower is operated seven days a week from 7 a.m. to 7 p.m.

Pilot info: Napa Airport (KAPC), N38-12.8°-W122-16.8° VAR-16°E Elev. 33 ft. 18R-36L Length 5931' x 150', 6/24 Length 5007' x 150' Unicom 122.95 Oakland Center 127.8 Tower 118.7 Ground 121.7

AIRPORT SHUTTLES

Evans Airporter

4075 Solano Avenue Napa CA 94558
707.255.1559, 707.944.2025 (upvalley)
www.evanstransportation.com

Evans has frequent, regularly scheduled trips to and from both San Francisco and Oakland Airports with a stop at Vallejo. Their local terminal is at the north end of Napa just off Highway 29. Evans is how those of us who live here usually get to the airport.

ABC Transport Express

707.259.0363

Locals are starting to use Sacramento Airport as well. Currently transportation is provided five times a day between Napa and Sacramento by ABC Transport Express.

HELICOPTER

Wine Country Helicopters

2030 Airport Road   Napa CA 94558
707.226.8470
www.winecountryhelicopters.com

Helicopter transportation to/from Bay Area airports, wineries, resorts. Also tours and various commercial services such as aerial photography.

Water

Few visitors come to the Napa Valley by water, although if you have a small boat it's possible to motor up the Napa River as far as the city of Napa.

MARINA

You can also stop south of the city of Napa and dock your boat in the Carneros region at the Napa Valley Marina.

Napa Valley Marina

1200 Milton Road
(Off Cuttings Wharf Road)
Napa CA 94559 707.252.8011
www.napavalleymarina.com

FERRY

BayLink Ferries

877.64-FERRY
www.baylinkferry.com

BayLink offers a very enjoyable ride that takes you from the San Francisco Ferry Building to Vallejo, which is about 20 miles south of Napa. It's about a one-hour trip with a great view of San Francisco, the Golden Gate and Bay Bridges, Angel Island, and areas you'll never see when driving. From Vallejo, you can take the Napa Valley Transit bus to the valley, but this is not yet a highly traveled method. Someday, there will be train service between the Vallejo ferry terminal and Napa, but it's not here yet.

CRUISE SHIPS

American Safari Cruises
888.862.8881
www.americansafaricruises.com

American Safari offers three- and four-night luxury cruises of the wine country, including up the Napa River with visits to Napa Valley art museums and wineries. The 120-foot yacht Safari Quest sleeps 21 guests. Fare includes all on- and off-yacht meals, wines, liquors, excursions and other activities. You'll see the wine country from a perspective few have seen, and even get a chance to go kayaking if you wish.

Cruise West
2401 4th Avenue, Suite 700
Seattle, WA 98121
800.888.9378 Fax: 206.441.4757
www.cruisewest.com

A private cruise line with low-draft ships that sail up the lower Napa River to dock in the Carneros area. Ships hold about 100 passengers. Three and four-night cruises let passengers visit wineries in both Napa and Sonoma Valleys.

Land

You can reach the Napa Valley by car, tour bus, Greyhound bus, or Amtrak bus (from the Amtrak train station in Martinez, about 30 minutes away.)

BUS

Greyhound
800.231.2222
www.greyhound.com

Greyhound now has bus service between Napa and San Francisco, the state capital in Sacramento, Sonoma and Santa Rosa in Sonoma County, and Lakeport in Lake County. The bus stops at the downtown Napa transit center on Pearl Street behind Mervyn's department store.

Buses leave at 11:05 a.m. for San Francisco, 1:05 a.m. and 5:45 p.m. for Sonoma and Santa Rosa, 5:35 p.m. for Sacramento and 5:45 p.m. for Lakeport.

Buses arrive from Sacramento at 1:05 p.m., from San Francisco at 5:45 p.m., from Santa Rosa at 11:05 a.m. and 5:35 p.m. and from Lakeport at 11:05 a.m.

TRAIN

Amtrak
800.USA.RAIL
www.amtrak.com

Amtrak buses to and from the Amtrak train station in Martinez stop at the downtown Napa transit center as well as at the Wine Train station.

AUTO

Since over 90% of our visitors come by car (or tour bus), we'll focus on driving to the Napa Valley.

Via Golden Gate Bridge
Drive north over the Golden Gate Bridge on Highway 101 and continue through Marin County almost to Novato. Take the Napa 37 East turnoff to the east and continue following the signs to Napa. The trip takes just under an hour in good traffic, considerably more at rush hour. But as a visitor you shouldn't be driving at rush hour

The Golden Gate Bridge connects San Francisco with Marin County to the north (Photo courtesy of Wine Institute)

anyhow. Enjoy the views, the cows, the vineyards, the oak trees. It's by far the most scenic way to drive to the Napa Valley.

Shortly before you reach the Napa Valley, you'll pass (on the right side of Highway 12/121—the Carneros Highway) *Domaine Carneros* winery.

Continuing east, you'll see a sign for "Napa River Resorts" on the south side of the road. The sign has been there a long time, and transportation officials have no idea why it's there, since there are no resorts and have been none in recent memory. (There are, however, a number of homes, vineyards and wineries as well as the *Napa Valley Marina* and *Moore's Landing* restaurant.)

A short time after passing the "resort" turnoff, you'll find yourself at Highway 29, the main highway running north-south in the valley. Turn left (north) toward Napa and Calistoga.

Via San Francisco-Oakland Bay Bridge

Take the Bay Bridge east towards Oakland, then head north on Highway 80 (although it says "East") towards Sacramento. If you're staying in downtown San Francisco, driving to the Napa Valley is usually quicker over the Bay Bridge than going over the Golden Gate Bridge. Going up the East Bay isn't pretty, but it's fast.

Once through Vallejo, turn off Highway 80 at the exit marked "Napa" and head toward the Napa Valley. North of the town of American Canyon you'll pass the inter-

section of Highway 29 and Highway 12. At the southeast corner of this intersection, across from the Napa County Airport, is a large three-story stone building nestled among oak trees that looks like it just has to be winery. It isn't. It's a medical malpractice insurance company—*The Doctors Company.* Sorry; no wine, no visitors, and no picnicking.

On the other (west) side of Highway 29 is the Napa Valley Airport (*www.mynapa.info/departments/airport*). The largest facility there belongs to Japan Air Lines. JAL provides basic flight training for almost all its pilots at this airport. More than 150 student pilots are undergoing training at any given time.

Continuing north on Highway 29, you'll come to a fork. You can either go right onto Soscol Avenue (forking off to the right just before the traffic light) and on into the downtown area of Napa, or stay on Highway 29 and pass over the Southern Crossing (George F. Butler Bridge) and continue north on Highway 29 toward Calistoga. (Along Highway 29 there are a number of exits into the city of Napa.) If you follow the "Calistoga" sign and stay on 29, you'll cross over the bridge and be able to look down on the meandering Napa River.

You'll also see a group of large satellite dishes. This "dish farm" is the Napa Teleport belonging to PanAm Sat (www.panamsat.com), that provides global video and data broadcasting services via satellite. The network reaches 98 percent of the world's population, and distributes entertainment and information for cable television systems, TV broadcast affiliates, direct-to-home TV operators, Internet service providers, telecommunications companies and corporations.

PanAmSat carries an average of 7,000 hours a month of news, sports and special events for such clients as A&E, CNN Discovery, Disney, Dow Jones, BBC, AOL Time-Warner, Fox, HBO, NPR, MTV,

Reuters, Direct TV, Deutsche Welle, British Telecom, Hughes Network Systems, and Japan Telecom.

Continue on over the bridge and you're now in the Napa Valley.

Getting Around

DRIVING TIPS

The California Highway Patrol points out that most roads in Napa County are two-lane and require extra caution. Common accidents include head-on collisions, and running off the road over the embankment or into a tree. Drivers need to be aware of bicyclists, particularly on the winding country roads that bikers love. If you're pulling a trailer, be especially aware of how much clearance you have when you pass a bicyclist.

Although we recognize the competition is tough, we believe the city of Napa has some of the worst drivers in California, maybe even in the country. (Note: If you're from Boston, you win.) So some helpful hints.

When the red light turns green, it does not mean you can safely enter the intersection. It means you can *legally* enter the intersection. Look both ways to make sure that no vehicles are continuing to drive through.

If you are a pedestrian, work on the assumption that no driver will even look for you, let alone see you. Actually stopping for you is out of the question. Crosswalks and green lights mean nothing. It isn't that drivers are out to get you. It's just that they're not interested in your existence. Cross a street only when you are sure it is totally safe.

First Street in downtown Napa is one-way. This does not mean you need look in only one direction before crossing the street. It is not unusual for a car to be traveling in the wrong direction. (In all fairness,

this is almost always a tourist. This is one thing locals seldom do.)

In California, unless otherwise indicated, it is legal to make a right turn on a red light after stopping and checking that it is safe to make the turn. In Napa, the stopping and checking parts are usually ignored. The custom is to just turn; slowing down only enough to keep the car from tipping over.

Cars at an intersection, unless there is a left turn signal, must yield to oncoming traffic before making a left turn. The decorative broken glass and plastic at many intersections should give you an idea of how closely this quaint law is followed.

In summary, assume that at every intersection, no matter what color the light, vehicles are likely to turn left right in front of you or to attack you from either or both sides. Assume the worst and you should survive to happily enjoy your visit.

Two-lane highways lead into Napa County from both the east (Highway 12) and west (Highway 12/121). Both can be dangerous. Highway 12 from the east travels from Highway 80 through Jameson Canyon to Highway 29. Most of the stretch through the canyon is two-lane. Do not try to pass on the two-lane section, and watch out for cars coming toward you that try to pass. Many accidents on this highway are head-on and fatal.

Highway 12/121 is the "Carneros Highway," and it is two-lane all the way from Highway 37 in Marin County to Highway 29 in Napa County. The last stretch, from the turnoff for the town of Sonoma over the hills to Napa, deserves particular caution. Avoid passing, and be particularly cautious when you come over the hill at the Napa/Sonoma County line. There is a passing lane for cars going uphill, which is occasionally used by cars going the other way downhill. Again, many accidents on this highway are head-on and frequently fatal.

Once you've survived the drive to the Napa Valley, you'll find the country driving pleasant. Stay sober, take your time, and you should enjoy driving along Highway 29. Just be careful turning off, and onto, Highway 29, particularly when it involves a left turn.

The main caution is driving along the Silverado Trail, which runs along the east side of the valley. Locals use this road to avoid tourist traffic and get somewhere in a hurry. As a result, the average speed on this road is considerably higher than that on Highway 29. This leads to accidents on the Trail that are more often fatal than those on Highway 29. Use caution, take your time, don't bother passing, and watch out for passing cars coming towards you. If you decide you want to drive the Trail at sightseeing speed, please pull over occasionally to let the line of cars (there will be one) behind you go by.

Traffic Information

For online traffic information for the entire San Francisco Bay Area, including the North Bay and Napa Valley, we recommend:
www.sfgate.com/traffic/

CalTrans
Caltrans, the State of California's Department of Transportation, has up-to-the-minute online information on state highways. Here's information on Highway 29, which runs north-south through the Napa Valley.
www.dot.ca.gov/hq/roadinfo/sr29

For toll-free information on significant delays on California State Highways, call 1.800.427.ROAD (7623).

Caltrans District 4
www.dot.ca.gov/dist4/
Information on District 4, which covers the entire Bay Area including Napa County.

511
www.511.org

Toll-free hotline from all area codes in the San Francisco Bay Area that provides complete Bay Area public and private transportation information, including up-to-the-minute traffic information on 37 freeways, eight bridges and all major roads. Includes information on public transit, paratransit, carpools, vanpools, parking and biking. Just dial 511 from your cell phone or land phone.

Napa County Transportation Planning Agency
707.259.8631
www.nctpa.net

The NCTPA web site provides information on transit and paratransit throughout Napa County. This includes these services:

VINE (County-wide bus system)
Downtown Napa Transit Center
1151 Pearl Street
Napa CA 94558
707.255.7631 800.696.6443
TDD 707.226.9722

VINE Go (Paratransit)
Napa 707.252.2600
Upvalley 707.963.4222
American Canyon 707.556.8221

American Canyon Transit
707.648.7275

Calistoga HandyVan
707.963.4229

St. Helena VINE Shuttle
707.963.3007

Yountville Shuttle
707.944.1234

TaxiScrip Program
707.255.7631

Flood Control Construction
www.napatraffic.info

Current traffic information for the city of Napa connected with the Napa River Flood Control project construction.

AUTOMOBILE RENTAL

If you didn't arrive by car, you can rent one in Napa.

Budget
407 Soscol Ave Napa CA 94559
800.527.7000

Enterprise
230 Soscol Ave Napa CA 94559
707.253.8000

Hertz
686 Soscol Ave Napa CA 94559
707.265.7575

TOUR/LIMOUSINE SERVICES

If you don't want to drive, you can take a guided tour or rent a limousine.

California Wine Tours

800.294.6386
www.californiawinetours.com

Five-hour Napa Valley tour and tasting $49/person.

Antique Tours Limousine Service

707.226.9227
www.antiquetours.net

Fully restored 1947 convertible Packard limousines.

Classic Limousine

572 Lincoln Avenue, Napa CA 94558
707.253.0999 800.259.8401
www.classiclimousine.50megs.com

Limos include a 1949 Packard and a 1969 Silver Cloud Rolls Royce.

Esperya

101 Old Vine Way   Napa CA 94558
707.255.7517
www.winecountryesperya.com

Guided tours of the valley customized to your preferences

Group Outings

4225 Solano Avenue #575
Napa CA 94558
Fax 707.226.8652
www.groupoutings.com

Limos include a town car and 120" stretch limousine. A special tour offers barrel tastings and discounts at top wineries.

Napa Valley Off-Road Tours

3266 Silverado Trail   Napa CA 94558
707.257.6680
www.napaoffroad.com
$150 per person

Wine tasting, vineyard tours, lunch, off-road excursions, private visits to wineries, all in a comfortable Pinzgauer all-terrain vehicle that seats 10 visitors.

TAXIS

Taxi service is available throughout the valley, but only by telephone. It's very unlikely you'll be able to wave one down on the street. These two services offer vehicles that are much more luxurious than the average.

Black Tie Taxi

707.259.1000 888.544.8294
www.blacktietaxi.com

Taxi Cabernet

707.963.2620
www.taxicabernet.com

WINERY SHUTTLE

Napa Winery Shuttle

707.257.1950
www.wineshuttle.com

The shuttle is a great service if you'd like to spend the day touring and tasting and have someone else do the driving. The shuttle, which leaves from most Napa Valley hotels, travels on a fixed route, stopping at seven well-known wineries. You can get off and on when and where you wish. Because they stop at each location every 30-40 minutes, you can do a tasting, then conveniently catch the next shuttle to the next winery.

If you get hungry, the shuttle also stops at two upvalley restaurants for lunch. Price, which does not include winery tasting fees or food purchases, is $38 per person, which includes unlimited stops per day. Plus they'll pick up your wine at the winery and deliver it to your hotel.

WINE TRAIN

Napa Valley Wine Train

1275 McKinstry Napa CA 94559
707.253.2111   Fax: 707.253.9264
www.winetrain.com

For detailed information, see the Wine Train listing in the Napa section.

About the Napa Valley

The Napa Valley is in Northern California at the northeastern tip of San Francisco Bay (actually called San Pablo Bay up that far), about an hour's drive north of San Francisco. To the west is the Sonoma Valley, to the north is Lake Country, and to the east is the Sacramento Valley. The Napa Valley is actually just one of many valleys in Napa County, but it's by far the largest and best known. The valley itself is about 30 miles long and ranges from one to five miles in width.

Napa County has a population of about 125,000 people, including five incorporated cities. North to south, they are: Calistoga, St. Helena, Yountville, Napa and, at the southern end, American Canyon.

Angwin, Deer Park, Pope Valley, Rutherford and Oakville are communities with post offices but aren't actual towns.

The county's primary industries are wine-grape growing, wine production and tourism. Thanks to stringent and ongoing efforts by a number of dedicated agriculturalists, environmentalists, elected officials, and concerned citizens, and the support of the vast majority of the voters, there is little development in the unincorporated area of the county. Most commercial and residential development is in the cities. This preserves a huge amount of agricultural land, allowing Napa County to avoid the urban sprawl that has affected almost all other San Francisco Bay Area counties. The result is an attractive place for residents to live and for tourists to visit.

NAPA RIVER

The Napa River is one of four navigable rivers in California and one of only three surviving free-flowing rivers. It's a major source of freshwater to San Francisco Bay, and offers excellent fishing for striped bass and sturgeon. There's even peaceful canoeing right in the heart of the city of Napa.

A local organization, "Friends of the Napa River" (*www.friendsofthenapariver.org*), was formed to preserve the river, which has a tendency to frequently flood downtown Napa. Of course, building a city on a flood plain wasn't a great idea to begin with, but now that it's here, citizens decided to create ways to save both the river and the city by turning out a river that's developed and flood-safe, yet still natural and free-flowing.

Voters approved a bond issue and construction is underway now to restore the river to a more natural state, as well as one that will not flood populated areas.

For more information on the Napa River, see the separate section later in this book.

MOUNT ST. HELENA

That extinct volcano you see at the north end of the valley–Mount St. Helena–is not extinct. But don't worry; it isn't a volcano either. Despite the beliefs of many locals, it's just a mountain, in fact the highest part of the Mayacmas Mountains (frequently misspelled "Mayacamas"—in fact so frequently, that we'll use that spelling in this book) that also extend into Sonoma, Lake and Mendocino Counties. It is, however, one (and the highest at 4,343 feet) of the four dominant mountains of the San Francisco Bay Area. Mount St. Helena at the north, Mount Hamilton at the south—near San Jose; Mount Diablo at the east—near Concord; and Mount Tamalpais at the west in Marin County.

Even if Mount St. Helena was never a volcano, there is a great deal of geyser activity just below it in the hot springs town of Calistoga, and to the northwest in an area known as The Geysers, currently used as a source of thermal energy.

HISTORY

The original inhabitants of the valley were the Wappo. The name Wappo was given by the Spanish and probably derived from the Spanish word "guapo" meaning "handsome." The natives were here at least 4,000 years before the Spaniards arrived. In 1831 there were an estimated 10,000 to 12,000 Wappo living in the valley. Most later lost their lives to cholera and smallpox, as well as to attacks by white men. There are still surviving Wappo in Napa, Sonoma and Lake counties.

The first American settler in the Napa Valley was George Yount. He arrived in 1831, became friends with General Mariano Vallejo, and was given an 11,000-acre Mexican land grant. He built the first wooden structure in the county, a two-story Kentucky block house. He also planted the first grapevines in the Napa Valley. The vines were from Mexico; it was not until 1860 that the higher-quality European winegrapes were introduced.

The wealth of post-Gold Rush San Francisco created a huge demand for wine, and by 1891 there were 619 vineyards throughout the valley. Many of wines produced were receiving awards in European wine competitions. The wineries survived economic depression and the disease of phylloxera but were no match for Prohibition, the United States' "Great Experiment" of declaring alcoholic beverages not just immoral but illegal.

Prohibition closed almost every Napa Valley winery. The few that survived provided medicinal wine or sacramental wine for churches. Vineyards were ripped out to be replaced by prune and walnut orchards.

Prohibition ended in 1933, but it was not until 1951 that a new winery was finally built in the Napa Valley. It was Stony Hill, a small family winery that is still actively producing excellent wine. Sixteen years later, in 1967, the next winery opened. It is a much larger winery, located in Oakville. Its founder, Robert Mondavi, launched a wave of winery construction—and wine promotion—that has not yet stopped.

Since that time more than two hundred wineries have been built, as the Napa Valley was rediscovered as a premium wine region, recapturing its earlier pro-Prohibition fame. Today there are more than 250 wineries throughout Napa County.

Napa County is one of the 27 original counties that were established on February 18, 1850 and therefore part of California when it became a state on September 9, 1850. In 1861, Lake County, including Clear Lake, was formed from the northern part of Napa County. Some additional land was given to Lake County in the 1860s but returned back to Napa County in 1972. In addition, some land in Solano and Sonoma Counties was also added to Napa County in 1855.

NAPA VALLEY TODAY

Today the Napa Valley is one of the most popular tourist attractions in California, and world-renowned for its wines. The fame of its wineries is matched by the reputation of its restaurants. Combined with the beauty of the area, and the gentleness of its climate, they provide a vacation holiday without equal anywhere in the country.

Although many locals bragged for years that the Napa Valley received as many visitors as Disneyland, the reality is that Disneyland has about 14 million visitors a year and the Napa Valley nearly five million.

Five million is enough—particularly because most of them come during the summer, "Crush"—the harvest in September and October, or the Mustard Festival in the early spring. Come visit us in the off periods and you'll find far fewer people and have much more time to chat with winery staff.

The valley is beautiful all year long, just different from season to season. The wine and food are always delicious.

BEST TIME TO VISIT

Winter tends to be the quietest time of the year in the Napa Valley, although February and March are now lost to the Mustard Festival (www.mustardfestival.org). This festival was initiated because restaurants and lodging facilities weren't getting enough business during the slow months. (It also meant they had to lay off staff during this time.) This is a beautiful season with mustard flowers in the vineyards and early-blooming trees.

The quietest time is November, December and January—except over the Christmas holidays. It's easier then to get a room reservation and, who knows, you may even be able to get a reservation at the French Laundry. Many hotels and bed and breakfast inns offer lower rates from November through March.

Summer is very busy, as are September and October during "Crush."

WHO COMES TO THE NAPA VALLEY?

(Courtesy of the Napa Valley Conference and Visitors Bureau)

Nearly 80 percent are couples. Over 60 percent have no children at home, including young couples with no children and older persons whose children have left home.

Age of Visitors

25-44 - 54%		45-54 - 17%	
55-64 - 14%		Over 65 - 8%	

Mean household income of visitors is $53,600 (more than double the $24,000 national average).

Education

At least some college	80+%
College graduate	43%
Master's Degree	21%

Home Town

Northern California	31%
Southern California	5%
East Coast	17.5%
Midwest	17.5%
Southern U.S.	17.5%
International	11.5%

Led by:

> Canada
> Germany
> United Kingdom
> Japan

Average Daily Spending

Day visitor: $150
Overnight visitor: $300.

Annual visitor spending: $712 million

Number of local tourism employees: 9,000

4.7 million annual visitors (of which 1.7 are business visitors), including 3.0 million day only, and 1.7 million overnight. Average length of stay for overnight visitors is 2.9 days.

Year-Round Visitation

January-March	27%
April-June	17%
July-September	38%
October-December	17%

Most Visited Attractions

(Courtesy of the Napa Valley Conference and Visitors Bureau)

St. Helena—Main Street, Beringer Winery and Culinary Institute of America

Calistoga—Lincoln Ave, Sterling Vineyards and Old Faithful Geyser

Rutherford—Niebaum-Coppola Winery, Beaulieu Vineyards, St. Supéry Wine Discovery Center

Oakville—Robert Mondavi Winery and Oakville Grocery

Yountville—Domaine Chandon Winery and Washington Street restaurants

Napa—Premium Outlets and Napa Town Center (Napa Valley Visitors Center)

Top Reasons Why People Come for a Leisure Visit

(Courtesy of the Napa Valley Conference and Visitors Bureau)

Visit winery	81%
Just relax	69%
Sightsee	56%
Shop	49%
Picnic	28%
Historical site	25%
Hike/camp	18%
Spa/mudbath	17%
Art gallery	11%
Wildlife viewing	6%
Bicycle ride	6%
Golf	5%

CLIMATE

In short, it's Californian—very Mediterranean. It's a great place to be a grape, and a very good one to be a human. The Napa Valley is far enough inland to escape most of the fog that lingers along the California coast during summer. Yet, unlike California's Central Valley, it's close enough to the ocean to take advantage of the cooling effect of that fog.

It can get hot in the summer, but usually not too hot. We can expect a week or two during the summer when the temperatures are around 100° F, usually in July or August, which are the hottest months. The southern end of the valley, where the city of Napa is located, is cooler. It's closer to the northern tip of San Francisco Bay, known as San Pablo Bay. Winds come through the Golden Gate, move upward and cool off the southern end of Napa County as far as Yountville. They also come over the hills from the west and Sonoma County's coast.

North of Yountville the valley doglegs to the left (west). The late afternoon wind from the bay doesn't make the turn, so the St. Helena and Calistoga areas tend to be much warmer. During the summer, the temperature upvalley can be ten to twenty degrees (F) warmer than in the Napa area.

In the winter, it rains—but not a lot. The county's average annual rainfall for the entire year is less than 24 inches, with over half of that in December, January and February. And it's not unusual to have temperatures in the 70s and 80s (F) around Christmas time.

The western side of the valley—the Mayacamas Mountains—gets more rain, apparent by the redwood and fir forests and numerous streams and waterfalls. The eastern side of the valley—the Vacas Mountains (named for the Vaca family that settled here in 1841)—tends to be more desert-like in many areas, with scrub brush and even cactus.

Average Temperatures by Season (°F)

	MAXIMUM	MINIMUM
Spring	78°	64°
Summer	92°	81°
Fall	85°	74°
Winter	72°	61°

Average Temperatures by Month
City of Napa

Located at 38.30°N 122.28°W. Height 6m / 19 feet above sea level.

MONTH	FAHRENHEIT	CELSIUS
Jan	46.8	8.2
Feb	50.5	10.3
Mar	52.9	11.6
Apr	56.1	13.4
May	60.3	15.7
Jun	64.9	18.3
Jul	66.9	19.4
Aug	66.6	19.2
Sep	65.8	18.8
Oct	61.3	16.3
Nov	53.6	12.0
Dec	47.7	8.7
Year	57.7	14.3

City of St. Helena

Located at 38.50° N 122.46° W. Height 68m / 223 feet above sea level.

MONTH	FAHRENHEIT	CELSIUS
Jan	46.0	50.2
Feb	50.2	10.1
Mar	52.3	11.3
Apr	56.3	13.5
May	62.4	16.9
Jun	68.0	20.0
Jul	71.1	70.7
Aug	70.7	21.5
Sep	67.6	19.8
Oct	61.7	16.5
Nov	52.3	11.3
Dec	46.6	8.1
Year	58.8	14.9

Average Rainfall for Napa County

MONTH	MM	INCHES
Jan	117.3	4.6
Feb	84.8	3.3
Mar	79.5	3.1
Apr	50.2	2.0
May	13.6	0.5
Jun	5.9	0.2
Jul	0.4	0.0
Aug	3.1	0.1
Sep	6.0	0.2
Oct	32.6	1.3
Nov	72.3	2.8
Dec	132.9	5.2
Year	599.3	23.6

Weather Report

For current weather conditions in the Napa Valley, and the forecast for the following week, we recommend:

www.sfgate.com/weather/

Click on "Napa" on the map.

The Best and Worst of the Napa Valley

Best Things about the Napa Valley

1. The natural beauty of the valley
2. Wonderful weather
3. Outstanding restaurants
4. Superb wines
5. The relatively slow pace of small town life
6. Friendly people
7. The ease of finding a parking place and the low traffic compared to the rest of the Bay Area
8. Closeness to San Francisco
9. County-wide cooperation on important issues
10. The proximity of both beach and mountains

Worst Things about the Napa Valley

1. Expensive restaurants
2. Expensive wines (and the markup on wine in most restaurants)
3. The traffic on Highway 29
4. Ugly ego-driven "houses on steroids" on top of hills and ridges
5. High cost of housing
6. Low wages
7. Snobs (See 1, 2 and 4)
8. Box chain stores in the city of Napa
9. City of Napa's terrible planning, (lack of) design review, and even worse traffic engineering
10. Wealth disparity and the disappearing middle class.

Best Ideas that Actually Happened

1. Ending Prohibition

2. Agricultural Preserve. In 1968 Napa Valley vintners and other community leaders enacted the country's first Agricultural Preserve, protecting over 30,000 acres of open space

3. "Measure A". Vote of the people in 1980. It saved agriculture in the Napa Valley by restricting growth in the unincorporated areas to 1% a year, with 25% of that having to be affordable housing. (The affordable housing never happened, but at least it further restricted the expensive housing)

4. Measure J. Vote of the people in 1990. This further protected agriculture by requiring all currently agricultural-zoned land to be rezoned to non-agricultural use only with the approval of the voters

5. Flood control on Napa River - Vote of the people in 1998 that approved a bond measure to restore much of the Napa River to its natural state, increase and protect wetlands, prevent frequent flooding of homes and businesses through the valley, and help revitalize the downtown Napa business area.

Of course there's a downside, too. Many small businesses and low-income residents are being displaced, a few property owners will make a lot of money, and the slow and easy character of downtown Napa is likely to be significantly changed. Whether that's for the better remains to be seen.

In fact, we can't yet tell whether this was a really good idea, a really bad idea, or somewhere in the middle. In the meantime, we'll list it under "Good Ideas", but keep a space open for it under "Worst Ideas That Actually Happened."

Worst Ideas that Actually Happened

1. Stopping passenger train service between Napa and Calistoga in 1929. Long-gone are the days when you could take the train from Calistoga all the way to Napa and then take the ferry to San Francisco.

2. Prohibition

3. "Redeveloping" downtown Napa by tearing down most of its historical buildings.

4. Allowing Wal-Mart, Home Depot, Target and other box stores into the valley.

5. Building "trophy homes/homes on steroids" on top of hills and ridges in the valley.

6. Bulldozing thousands of beautiful old valley oaks and replacing them with vineyards.

Worst Ideas that were Fortunately Avoided

1. Building a freeway on the east side of the Napa Valley. (This one still pops up occasionally.)

2. Making Highway 29 a four-lane freeway all the way up the valley and into Lake County.

3. Expanding the city of Napa to a population of 198,000 by the year 2000. (Or

558,000 by 2020.) Fortunately we're only at 72,000, which many feel is bad enough.

4. Cementing the Napa River in the city of Napa area in order to prevent flooding. This was another brilliant idea from the Army Corps of Engineers, who brought us the now dead Los Angeles River (but whose reputation was saved by their support of the Napa River project).

Top Misconceptions about the Napa Valley

1. Mt. St. Helena is an extinct volcano. (It's not extinct because it never was a volcano.)

2. Mt. St. Helena is the highest point in Napa County. (It's the highest point in *Sonoma* County, 4,343 feet.) The highest point in *Napa* County is Sugarloaf Mountain, 2,988 feet, northeast of Calistoga.

3. Napa Valley gets more tourists than Disneyland. (Napa Valley gets less than 5 million visitors, Disneyland approximately 14 million. This was a rumor promoted by the local daily newspaper and the chamber of commerce.)

4. Robert Mondavi Winery was the first winery built in the Napa Valley after Prohibition. (The first one was Stony Hill, built in 1951. Mondavi was the second, opening in 1967.)

Most Uniquely Napa Valley Things to See and Do

1. Artesa Winery (Carneros)
2. Bale Grist Mill Historic State Park (St. Helena)
3. Beringer Vineyards (St. Helena)
4. Bothe-Napa Valley State Park (Calistoga)
5. Bridgeford Flying Services or Wine Plane (Napa County Airport)
6. Buy a good bottle of wine (everywhere)
7. California State Historical Landmarks (throughout the county)

8. Veterans Home of California (Yountville)
9. Calistoga spas (Calistoga)
10. City of Napa walking tours (Napa)
11. Copia—American Center for Wine, Food and the Arts (Napa)
12. DiRosa Art Preserve (Carneros)
13. Downtown Calistoga (Calistoga)
14. Eating in a good restaurant (everywhere)
15. French Laundry (Yountville)
16. Greystone—Culinary Institute of America (St. Helena)
17. Hot air balloons (Yountville)
18. Napa Valley Museum (Yountville)
19. Niebaum-Coppola Winery (Rutherford)
20. Old Faithful Geyser (Calistoga)
21. Petrified Forest (Calistoga)
22. Robert Louis Stevenson State Park (Calistoga)
23. Robert Mondavi Winery (Oakville)
24. Scenic drives (throughout the county)
25. Sharpsteen Museum (Calistoga)
26. Silverado Museum (Calistoga)
27. Sterling Vineyards Airtram (Calistoga)
28. Wine Train (Napa)
29. Wine-tasting fund raisers (all towns)

Best Things That You Probably Don't Have Back Home

1. Hot air balloons
2. Mud baths
3. The French Laundry
4. Internationally known wineries
5. Small towns filled with gourmet restaurants
6. Vineyards instead of subdivisions
7. Copia
8. Culinary Institute of America at Greystone
9. The Wine Train
10. Napa Valley Opera House
11. Uptown Theater (once it's open)

Best Broadway Show Set in the Napa Valley

"Most Happy Fella." 1956. Music, lyrics & book by Frank Loesser based on Sidney Howard's "They Knew What They Wanted." Ran for 676 performances. Cast: Robert Weede, Jo Sullivan, Art Lund. Best known song: "Standing on the Corner (Watching All the Girls Go By)."

Best TV Melodrama Set in the Napa Valley

"Falconcrest." Starring Jane Wyman (first wife of former president Ronald Reagan), and a bunch of others. The winery shown in the series was Spring Mountain Winery, which still exists.

Best Books on Napa Valley Politics

Napa: The Story of an American Eden and the more recent *The Far Side of Eden: The Ongoing Saga of Napa Valley.* Both books are by James Conaway and both are available at Napa Valley bookstores, as well as at www.napavalleybooks.com.

They describe the players and events in the ongoing land-use battles in the Napa Valley. Grapegrowers, vintners, developers, politicians and environmentalists all appear in fascinating detail. Not everyone liked how they were portrayed in the books, but they all read them. We highly recommend both books if you'd like to know the behind-the-scenes story of life in the valley.

Photo Opportunities

You can take beautiful photographs anywhere in the Napa Valley. Here are some of the most popular locations for photos.

1. Artesa Winery (Carneros)
2. Beringer Vineyards (St. Helena)
3. Culinary Institute of America -

Greystone (St. Helena)
4. DiRosa Preserve (Carneros) - outside only.
5. Old Faithful Geyser (Calistoga)
6. Robert Mondavi Winery (Oakville)
7. Sterling Vineyards (Calistoga)
8. "The wine is bottled poetry sign"

The welcome sign quotes Robert Louis Stevenson–who was actually talking about France. But he liked the Napa Valley, too.

Between Yountville and Oakville on the west side of Highway 29. There's another one on the east side of Highway 29 between Calistoga and St. Helena.

Websites

VISITOR INFORMATION

Napa Valley Online

www.napavalleyonline.com

The most comprehensive online guide to the valley.

Napa Valley.com

www.napavalley.com

Official site for the Napa Valley Conference and Visitors Bureau and several chambers of commerce.

Napa Life

www.napalife.com

Napa Valley Register columnist Paul Franson's excellent guide to wining, dining and events in the valley.

American Canyon Online

www.americancanyon.com

Online site for the American Canyon community.

NEWS

Napa Sentinel

www.napasentinel.com

Napa's weekly newspaper.

Napa Valley Register

www.napanews.com

The valley's only daily newspaper, based in Napa and founded in 1863. Website includes the latest edition as well as searchable archives going back to January 2001.

St. Helena Star

www.sthelenastar.com

St. Helena's weekly newspaper, founded in 1874, offers an online version of the latest edition, along with searchable archives going back to May 1999.

Weekly Calistogan

www.weeklycalistogan.com

Online version of Calistoga's weekly newspaper that has been publishing for over 120 years. Searchable archives back to September 2003

WEBCAM

Copia

www.copia.org/pages/webcam.asp

Copia—The American Center for Wine, Food and the Arts—is located alongside the Napa River in the city of Napa. The home page of their website includes a link to this webcam overlooking their gardens.

Napa Valley Today

www.wineviews.com

The webcam of award-winning Napa Valley photographer Charles O'Rear shows a St. Helena Cabernet Sauvignon vineyard. O'Rear's latest book is *Napa Valley, The Land, The Wine, The People.*

Tour Ideas

Here are some ideas for "off-the-shelf" drive-it-yourself tours. The attractions in each tour are similar; only the length of time varies—from a quick journey through the valley to a more leisurely one or two-night stay. They focus on places that can handle large numbers of drop-in visitors. Ideally you'll have even more time to visit, and you'll be able to put together your own personalized tour, based on the hundreds of listings you'll find in this book.

The *I'm Just Passing Through*

If you're just passing through the Napa Valley, heading north or south to get somewhere else, try this tour. It's set up for those driving south to north through the valley. Simply reverse it if you're heading in the other direction.

However you approach the valley from the south, head north on Highway 29. Continue north till you come to Yountville. Take the Washington Street turnoff, turn right at the stop sign, then immediately left at the next stop sign. Continue into town, staying on the left at the fork. You'll find yourself at Vintage 1870, 40 shops in a three-story brick building on the west side of Washington Street. Stop, park, shop and/or have lunch. (If there's no time, just keep on driving through Yountville and pick up the directions in the next paragraph.) You can eat lunch at Pacific Blues at Vintage 1870, just south across the street at Piatti's, just north of Vintage 1870 at Compadre's, or at the north end of town at the Napa Valley Grille.

After lunch, continue north on Washington Street. Turn left at Madison Street (there's a stop sign there) to Highway 29. At the traffic light, very carefully turn right on the highway and head north. Approximately two miles ahead, just past Oakville, you'll see Robert Mondavi Winery on the left. Go into the left turn lane, then head into the winery. Park in the visitors' area. If there's time, take a tour. Otherwise just taste a few wines (there's a charge for tasting), take a few photographs, and head north again. Be careful as you make a left turn onto Highway 29.

A few miles further north and you'll be in Rutherford. On the right, just past the Rutherford Cross Road and the Rutherford Grill restaurant, pull into the Beaulieu Vineyard (BV) parking lot. Taste a few complimentary wines from this more than 100-year old winery. If you have the time, and the next tour is soon, take it. It's an excellent tour of wonderfully wine-smelling cellars and aging areas.

After BV, head north and drive through the town of St. Helena. Admire the quaintness of the town and overlook the fact that having a main highway through your quaint town is a traffic nightmare. Continue through town, taking pictures out the window as you pass Beringer Vineyards and the Culinary Institute of America at Greystone on your left just north of town.

Continue a few more miles till you reach Calistoga. Turn right on Lincoln Avenue and drive into the heart of Calistoga's main shopping area. Here you can window shop, have an ice cream cone or cold beer (it's not all wine here), or, if you've suddenly decided you're not in so much of a hurry, visit a spa and have a mud bath and massage. Your *I'm Just Passing Through* tour is over and you're on your own.

The *Five-Hour*

Head up Highway 29 until you're just north of Oakville. Visit Robert Mondavi Winery on the left (west) side of the highway. Take a tour, taste some wine. It's the first of the major new Napa Valley wineries; that is, it opened in 1967, the first large winery built in the valley after Prohibition. Since Mondavi, several hundred others have appeared.

Leave Mondavi, turn left on Highway 29 and continue north. Just past the Rutherford Cross Road, turn right into Beaulieu Vineyard. This is the true monarch of the valley, built in 1900 and famous for its wines, particularly its Cabernet Sauvignon. Taste a variety of their complimentary wines, then tour the winery and experience the 100-year-old buildings. This place looks and smells like a winery. It's wonderful.

After BV, keep your car in the parking lot and walk into the Rutherford Grill for lunch. Good food, extremely varied menu, and very casual and comfortable. Good place for kids, too.

After lunch, continue to the north on Highway 29 and go into St. Helena. Wander around, enjoy the window shopping, maybe even buy something. There are top-notch stores for all tastes.

Leave St. Helena and head back south. If you still have time, you can visit another winery, shop at Vintage 1870 in Yountville, or visit Moët et Chandon's Domaine Chandon sparkling wine facilities (also in Yountville but on the west side of the highway).

We mentioned the view? It 's everywhere. Highway 29 is an incredibly scenic highway and you'll see wineries and vineyards galore on the entire stretch.

Enjoy.

The *First Timer-All Day*

Most first-time visitors tend to start at the bottom of the valley and work their way north, generally visiting wineries on the right-hand (east) side of the road. We suggest you skip the crowds and drive directly (but enjoy the view) to Rutherford. Visit Beaulieu Vineyard (outstanding wines, historic winery facility, excellent tour guides), then drive through St. Helena to Sterling Vineyards (beautiful winery, self-guided tour, and an air tram ride up and down the hill—there is a charge) just south of Calistoga.

After Sterling, drive to Calistoga, walk around town, and have lunch. Then do a leisurely drive back downvalley, drive through St. Helena (stop for a little window shopping if you wish), then visit Robert Mondavi Winery just north of Oakville. Mondavi is perhaps the best known winery in the Napa Valley. The tour is optional; take it if you have time and are interested in yet another winery tour.

After Mondavi, continue south on Highway 29 to Yountville and visit shops in Vintage 1870 (40 shops in an historic building formerly a winery/distillery built in—yes—1870). Be sure to leave town by 3:30 or 4:00 to miss most of the traffic.

If you want to have dinner in the valley, stay in Yountville and cross Highway 29 on California Avenue at the south end of Yountville. Just before the entrance to the Veterans Home, turn right into Domaine Chandon. Chandon has an optional tour and excellent sparkling wine. They're usually open till 6 p.m. They also have an outstanding restaurant. You may get lucky and find they have a table available for dinner.

Or, after your pre-dinner sparkling wine, go back into downtown Yountville and have dinner at one of the many outstanding restaurants in town. (Yountville probably has more good restaurants per capita than any town in California.) By the time dinner is over, you can head home, secure in the knowledge that you've missed the worst of the traffic.

The *Overnight*

The Napa Valley Conference and Visitors Bureau would like you to stay overnight because that way you'll leave more money in the valley. We suggest that you'll find it a good idea for your own reasons, too.

By staying at least one night, you'll be able to enjoy a leisurely dinner, stroll around whichever town you're staying in, and go back to your hotel or B&B for a good night's sleep without having to fight the traffic leaving the valley. The next morning you can enjoy breakfast, shop, visit another winery or two, and then drive out of the valley ahead of the pack of day visitors.

Which part of the valley should you stay in? It really doesn't matter. You're just minutes from wineries no matter where you stay. And the various towns are separated by about a ten-minute drive, so distance isn't much of a problem. Some towns, such as Yountville and Calistoga, offer many rooms right in the downtown area, so you can spend most of your time afoot. But you'll still have to drive to almost all wineries, no matter where you stay.

If you book a B&B room far in advance of your trip, you should be able to stay anywhere you wish. If you're trying for a last-minute reservation, or you're already in the valley and need a room right now, you may have your best luck with one of the large hotels in the city of Napa.

We suggest that each time you visit the valley, you stay in a different town, so that you can get to know one locale well on each trip.

The *Midweek Weekend*

Weekends don't have to mean Saturday and Sunday. If your schedule allows, we suggest that you spend two nights in the middle of the week in the Napa Valley. You'll find far fewer visitors, a greater chance of getting a room in one of the more popular inns and, at some hotels and B&Bs, cheaper room rates as well.

Two nights gives you one full day when you can either kick back and totally relax, or fill the day with dining, wine tasting, shopping, even golf or tennis if you wish. If you want to relax, we suggest you book a room at a place that has a swimming pool, so you can lie in the sun with a book and a glass of wine. If you want to fill your day with activities, you might consider a B&B located right in one of the downtown areas, so you can walk in minutes to shops and other entertainments.

Read the various town sections of this book and pick a place that seems to offer what you seek. If you're looking for a full-service spa, as well as shops, restaurants and near-by wineries, Calistoga is the place to stay. St. Helena offers a good variety of shops and restaurants, as well as some of the Napa Valley's oldest and best-known wineries. Yountville is famous for its restaurants, and its many shops include those at the historic Vintage 1870 building.

The city of Napa offers hotels and B&Bs, excellent restaurants, museums, historical buildings and Victorians, and such visitor favorites as Copia and the newly renovated Opera House. In Napa you'll also find movie theaters and other amenities that only the largest town in the valley can offer.

Wine Bars/Tasting

If you'd like to sample wines from a variety of wineries, but your visiting time is limited, consider *wine bars*. Wine bars offer you the opportunity to taste a number of different wines.

In the past year, the number of wine tasting bars in the Napa Valley has greatly increased. They provide an easy way to taste wines from a number of different wineries. Since they're not operated by the wineries, there's a charge. But they're convenient and offer you a chance to try a variety of hard-to-find, limited-production wines.

You'll find more information under each wine bar's listing in the appropriate town section of this book.

American Canyon

Napa-Sonoma Visitors Center

Calistoga

All Seasons Bistro, Wine Bar and Wine Shop

Napa

Back Room Wines
Bombay Bistro/Corks
Bounty Hunter
JV Wine & Spirits
Napa General Store (Napa Mill)
Napa Wine Merchants
Vineyard Outlet (Napa Premium Outlets)
Vintner's Collective
Wine Spectator Tasting Table (Copia)
Wineries of Napa Valley (Napa Town Center)

Oakville

Napa Wine Company

St. Helena

Artisan Wine Tasting
Cantinetta Wine Bar at Tra Vigne
Tasting on Main

Yountville

Vintage 1870 Wine Cellar

NOTES

Towns and Regions of the Napa Valley

Town are listed south to north, starting with the southernmost town of American Canyon. Wineries and other attractions that are located on the Silverado Trail are listed in the *Silverado Trail* section, rather than by their respective towns. St. Helena Highway is also known as Highway 29

Unless otherwise stated, restaurant prices are for dinner entrées only. Most restaurants charge a corkage fee if you bring your own bottle of wine. Fees range from $5-$50, with most from $10-$15.

Bed and breakfast inns are listed in the Lodging section later in the book. All prices provided for restaurants, lodging, transportation, attractions, wine tastings and all other activities are subject to change at any time. Seldom downward. Varietals listed for wineries are also subject to change depending on availability. To find out current winery tasting hours, which vary by season and other factors, we suggest you pick up one of the many free advertising-focused tabloids available at locations throughout the valley.

American Canyon

American Canyon is Napa County's newest and second-largest city, incorporated in 1992. For those who drive north up Highway 80, it's the "gateway" to the Napa Valley.

Comfort Inn

3800 Broadway
American Canyon CA 94503
707.643.3800
80 rooms - $99 and up

A new addition to American Canyon's lodging options.

Greenfield Winery

205-B Jim Oswald Way
American Canyon CA
707.552.0362
www.greenfieldwinery.com

American Canyon's only winery, with sales and tasting. Located at the end of Green Island Road one mile off Highway 29. Chardonnay, Merlot, Cabernet Sauvignon, Syrah. Exceptionally low prices. Also produces Manzanita Canyon, Stratford, and Cartlidge & Browne labels.

Marshall's Farm Honey

159 Lombard Road
American Canyon CA 94503
707.556.8088 800.624.4637
www.marshallshoney.com

DIRECTIONS: From Napa go south on Highway 29 toward Vallejo. The next road after Green Island Road is Napa Junction. Turn right on Napa Junction, then take the first right onto Lombard Road. You'll see the honey-colored buildings and the little red barn.

Natural and organic gourmet honey from over 650 beehives at 100 locations throughout the San Francisco Bay Area. From wildflower to eucalyptus to lavender to berry to orange blossom. Over 50 delicious varieties, depending on the season.

Napa-Sonoma Wine Country Visitors Center

101 Antonina Drive
American Canyon CA 94589
707.642.0686 800.723.0575
Fax: 707.642.4610

Tourist information, wine tasting, delicatessen, light meals and souvenirs. They can also arrange for last-minute lodging. Tasting bar offers a sample of four wines. Usually they'll include a dessert wine as well.

The Visitors Center is the first wine-related location for visitors coming from the East Bay. They have information on the

Sonoma Valley, too, but naturally we think you should visit *our* valley. It's still the place for wine and beauty.

Paintball Jungle

Eucalyptus Drive,
American Canyon CA 94503
707.552.2426
www.paintballjungle.com
Admission $20

Open every Saturday and Sunday from 8:30 am to 4:00 pm., weekdays by arrangement for private groups. Admission charge includes goggles and face mask. Gun rentals start at $20/day. Paintballs and CO2 refills average $20-$40/day.

American Canyon Paintball Jungle is located in a flat, lush Eucalyptus grove just minutes from Six Flags Marine World in Vallejo. Its 50 acres of playing fields include forts, bunkers, a speedball course, a teepee village, and team practice fields. It's considered to be one of the finest paintball playing fields in the country.

Restaurante La Strada

6240 Napa-Vallejo Highway
American Canyon CA 94503
707.226.3027
Northern Italian – Entrees $12.95-$19.95

A new restaurant on the site of the former Tonelli's Steak House, on the east side of Highway 29 between American Canyon and Napa. It's owned by the same people who have La Strada in San Pablo, off Highway 80 towards Oakland.

Specialties include veal scaloppini, la strada (veal with eggplant and mozzarella in a light tomato sauce), carciofi (with artichokes, mushrooms and bell peppers), picatta, polo marsala, petrale alla Fiorentina, and gamberi bordolese (sautéed with garlic, rosemary and white wine.)

Carneros

The Carneros Region, with a climate similar to that of Burgundy in France, is a prime area for growing Pinot Noir and Chardonnay grapes.

Grapes have been grown in the Carneros since the 1830s, and the first Carneros winery, Winter Winery, was built in 1870. In the 1870s and 1880s, phylloxera destroyed almost all vineyards in the area, except the Stanly Ranch. In 1929 Beaulieu Vineyard and Louis M. Martini Winery began purchasing Carneros grapes, and in 1942 Martini purchased 200 acres of vineyard on the Stanly Ranch and later began planting Pinot Noir and Chardonnay.

The next key event was in 1960 when Rene di Rosa established Winery Lake Vineyard. The next year Beaulieu purchased 142 acres and planted Pinot Noir and Chardonnay. As the success and fame of di Rosa's grapes spread, more and more wineries purchased Carneros land. In 1985 the Carneros Quality Alliance (www.carneros.com) was formed, and it now has 29 winery members in the Carneros area of both Napa and Sonoma Counties, and over 40 vineyard members.

The Carneros is an uncrowded area with excellent wineries, low rolling hills and superb bicycling roads—if you stay off the highway.

Acacia Winery

2750 Las Amigas Road, Napa CA 94559
707.226.9991

DIRECTIONS: From Highway 121/12 turn south on Duhig Road. Follow Duhig for 1.5 miles, then turn left onto Las Amigas Road. Acacia is 100 yards up Las Amigas on the left.

Acacia has been producing wine in the Carneros since 1979. Now part of the Chalone Wine Group, it continues to focus on single vineyard wines.

Artesa Winery

1345 Henry Road Napa CA 94558
707.224.1668 Fax: 707.224.1672
www.artesawinery.com

DIRECTIONS: Go south from Napa to Highway 12/121 and turn west toward Sonoma. Turn right on Old Sonoma Road at Mont St. John Winery. Go one block, then turn left on Dealy Lane, Proceed due west on Dealy Lane, which becomes Henry Road where the road curves beyond Carneros Creek Winery. Turn left into Artesa's driveway. (Not easy, is it? But it's worth the drive.)

Artesa Winery, owned by the Codorniu Family of Spain, features art by Napa artist Gordon Huether. Photo courtesy of the artist.

In 1872, the Codorniu family of Barcelona created the first *methode champenoise* sparkling wine in Spain. 120 years later they came to the Napa Valley to create premium, distinctly California sparkling wine. They now primarily produce still wine here. The winery, initially named Codorniu Napa, blends into the surrounding landscape and is as beautiful as their wine as delicious.

The view from the winery towards San Pablo Bay and the lower Carneros is gorgeous, as is the landscaping. But it's the art that truly sets it apart from other wineries. The stained glass and sculpture (inside and outside) by local—but internationally known—artist Gordon Huether (www.gordonhuether.com) is exquisitely beautiful. We won't attempt to describe it, because we can't do it justice, but we're sure you'll be entranced by it.

Bouchaine

1075 Buchli Station Road, Napa CA 94559
707.252.9065
www.bouchaine.com

Directions: From Highway 121/12 turn south on Duhig Road. Follow Duhig for 1.5 miles, then turn left onto Las Amigas Road. Turn right (south) on Buchli Station Road. Bouchaine is on the right.

Founded in 1981, Bouchaine is the oldest continually operated winery in the Carneros, producing primarily Chardonnays and Pinot Noirs.

Carneros Inn

4048 Sonoma Highway Napa CA 94559
707.299.4900.
www.thecarnerosinn.com
86 cottages including 10 suites - $375 - $1200

A brand-new resort in the Carneros District located on the Carneros Highway (Highways 12/121) a short ways west of Highway 29. Cottages offer between 975 to 1800 sq. ft. of indoor/outdoor space, and include private patio and garden with gas-fired heater, wood-burning fireplace, high-speed Internet connection, bathroom with soaking tub, shower and heated slate floors, and a large-screen flat-panel television with DVD player.

Other features include the inn's private dining room, a full-service spa, swimming pool, bocce ball, croquet, and the Boon Fly, a café and wine bar, as well as over 1,000 sq. ft. of meeting space. The complex also offers 24 homes at prices ranging from $1,000,000 to $1,800,000.

Carneros Lodge

www.carneroslodge.com

Adjacent to Carneros Inn. A proposed upscale resort with 25 rooms and a conference area.

Di Rosa Art & Nature Preserve

5200 Carneros Highway 12/121
Napa CA 94559
707.226.5991 Fax: 707.255.8934
www.dirosapreserve.org

DIRECTIONS: Drive south of Napa on Hwy 29. Turn right onto Carneros Hwy 121/12 toward Sonoma, and continue 2.5 miles. The di Rosa Preserve is on the right, just beyond Domaine Carneros winery.

Rene di Rosa was a trailblazer in developing vineyards in the Carneros region. His Winery Lake Vineyard was legendary for its Chardonnay grapes. He now focuses full-time on his art collection, over 1000 works created in the greater San Francisco Bay Area during the latter part of the 20th Century. The art varies from stunning to whimsical (such as the late Veronica di Rosa's cows) to outrageous, and the environment is absolutely beautiful. There's also a gift store.

Reservations are required and tours can accommodate up to 25 people. Hours and days of operation are subject to change. Admission is $12 per person. Wear comfortable clothing because you'll be wandering around in what is also a nature preserve.

Domaine Carneros Winery

1240 Duhig Road
Napa CA 94559
707.257.0101
www.domaine.com

The Chateau for this sparkling wine producer was inspired by Chateau de la Marquetterie, the historic 18th century Champagne residence owned by the principal founder of Domaine Carneros, Champagne Tattinger of Reims, France. It's open from 10:30 a.m. to 6:00 p.m. daily. Their tour includes a DVD presentation in

Domaine Carneros Winery greets visitors along the Carneros Highway.

English, French, Spanish, German and Japanese.

Etude Wines

1250 Cuttings Wharf Road Napa CA 94559
707.257.5300
www.etudewines.com
Directions: Turn south off the Carneros Highway about one mile west of Highway 29.

Tony Soter is consulting winemaker to a number of cult wineries. Now he's opening his own winery facility where he'll continue to produce his own label with its focus on Pinot Noir and Cabernet Sauvignon. It's at the site of the former RMS Brandy distillery.

Madonna Estate Winery/ Mont St. John

5400 Old Sonoma Road, Napa CA 94559
707.255.8864
www.madonnaestate.com

Madonna Estate is on Old Sonoma Road just west of Highway 12/121 before it meets Highway 29. The Bartolucci family has been growing grapes organically for their estate wines for 80 years, originally in Oakville and now, for the last 30 years, in the Carneros. You'll enjoy all their wines, but keep in mind that their Johannisberg Riesling, Gewürztraminer and Muscat di Canelli are available only at the winery.

Moore's Landing

6 Cuttings Wharf Road Napa CA 94559
707.253.2439
American/Mexican - Entrees $7.25-$12.49

Lunch every day except Monday. Also dinners Friday and Saturday, and brunch Saturday and Sunday from 9 a.m. At the very end of Cuttings Wharf Road (turn south off Carneros Highway).

A funky right-on-the-Napa-River lunch and (sometimes) dinner spot that's a favorite of locals. Great tostada ceviche. Also burgers, sandwiches, enchiladas, burritos. It's particularly popular for weekend brunch on the deck overlooking the river. Pull right up in your boat, if you have one. A hangout for Carneros wine folks.

Napa Valley Marina

1200 Milton Road
(Off Cuttings Wharf Road) Napa CA 94559
707.252.8011
www.napavalleymarina.com

DIRECTIONS: From Napa go south on Highway 29, turn west on Highway 12/12. Go 1.4 miles and turn left (south) on Cuttings Wharf Road. Go 1.8 miles and veer right onto Las Amigas Road. Go .6 miles and turn left onto Milton Road. Go another .6 miles to marina.

The Napa Valley Marina, surrounded by vineyards in the Carneros region. Photo courtesy of Kathryn Winter.

200 deep water slips, storage, chandlery, sales. In the heart of the Carneros wine country, and just 9 miles up the Napa River from San Pablo Bay.

Saintsbury

1500 Los Carneros Avenue Napa CA 94559
707.252.0592
www.saintsbury.com

DIRECTIONS: From Highway 121/12 turn south onto Los Carneros Avenue, then left onto Withers Road. Saintsbury is off Withers Road between Los Carneros and Cuttings Wharf.

Richard Ward and David Graves have been making Pinot Noir and Chardonnay in the Carneros since 1981. They were convinced the Carneros could produce excellent Burgundian wines. Critics who've tasted their wines agree.

Napa

The City of Napa is the county seat and was founded in 1848 by Nathan Coombs. The word "napa" is of Indian derivation and has been translated as "house," "motherland," "fish," or "grizzly bear." The most likely is that it is derived from the Patwin Indian word "napo" meaning "house".

During Gold Rush days, cattle and lumber were mainstays of the local economy. Today the economy is based on wine and tourism. More than 72,000 people live here.

Adobe House Restaurant

376 Soscol Avenue Napa CA 94559
707.255.4310
Caribbean – Entrees $10.75-$21.95

Napa's oldest and most historic building, the Adobe House was built in 1840 by Don Cayetano Juarez, whose land-grant Rancho Tulocay spread out over 8,800 acres east of the Napa River. It's located at the intersection of Soscol Avenue and the beginning of the Silverado Trail.

The menu offers everything from fajitas, enchiladas and steaks to *lumpia* (Filipino spring rolls) and Jamaican Curried Short Ribs. It's also a great place for a mojito. Watch your head when moving from room to room. Doorways were lower in the 1840s.

Alexis Baking Company & Café

1517 Third St. Napa CA 94559
707.258.1827
American with a wine country flair - Lunch
entrees $9.00-$10.00

The "ABC" is one of Napa's most popular coffee and lunch spots. Highly recommended. For breakfast, try Alexis Handleman's scrambled eggs with potatoes and tomato-basil toast. If you're lucky, she'll feature her grilled vegetable sandwich at lunchtime. Don't miss the unique—and uniquely labeled—bathrooms.

Allegria

1026 First Street Napa CA 94559
707.254.9917
Northern Italian - Entrees: 10.95-$23.95

Northern Italian food with an elegant décor. Located in an historic bank building in Downtown Napa next to the plaza (where the much-despised Clocktower formerly stood). Friends say it has the best tiramisu they've ever tasted. Outdoor dining on the plaza.

Alpacas of Napa Valley

3233 Dry Creek Road
Napa CA 94558
866.431.8978 707.257.2226
www.alpacasofnapavalley.com

Open seven days a week by appointment only. Visits can include shearing days, Alpaca husbandry and petting Alpacas. Alpaca wool products are available including sweaters, shawls, baby blankets, fiber and yarn, and even an entire Alpaca (or more) if you'd like to breed them.

American Center for Wine, Food and the Arts (see Copia)

Andretti Winery

4162 Big Ranch Road   Napa CA 94558
707.255.3524   888.460.8463
www.andrettiwinery.com

Open daily for tasting. Founded in 1996 by famed race car driver Mario Andretti. Cabernet Sauvignon, Merlot, Sangiovese, Chardonnay, Sauvignon Blanc.

Anette's Chocolate & Ice Cream Factory

1321 First Street Napa CA 94559
707.252.4228
www.anettes.com

Ice cream fountain (they make more than 25 flavors), candy factory, wine-flavored truffles, sugar-free chocolates. They ship UPS almost everywhere. Anette is maintaining a 50-year tradition and the quality is outstanding. Try Brent's Chocolate Wine and Liqueur Sauces.

Angèle Restaurant

540 Main Street Napa CA 94559
707.252.8115
www.angele.us
French Country - Entrees $12-$19

A French Provençal country farmhouse restaurant and bar run by Claude Rouas and his daughters Bettina and Claudia. Rouas founded the *Auberge du Soleil* inn and restaurant in Rutherford and *Piatti's* in Yountville. Located at the Napa Mill in downtown Napa. Outdoor dining available overlooking the Napa River.

Back Room Wines

974 Franklin Street, Napa CA 94559
707.226.1378 877.322.2576
www.backroomwines.com

DIRECTIONS: Between First and Second Streets in Downtown Napa.

A wine shop and tasting bar. Winetasting by the half-glass or glass, as well as artisan cheeses and charcuterie. Tasting flights of six wines are also available.

Bay Leaf Restaurant

2025 Monticello Road
Napa CA 94558
707.257.9720
www.bayleafnapa.com
American Cuisine with French/Italian – Entrees
$13 - $32

DIRECTIONS: Drive east on Trancas Street, which becomes Monticello Road. Drive one-tenth mile past the Silverado Country Club/Atlas Peak Road turnoff. Restaurant is on right just past Vichy Avenue.

A restaurant near Silverado Country Club with a focus on top-notch service. Extensive wine list with a large selection of half-bottles (why don't more restaurants do this?). Offers a comfortable bar, outdoor dining when weather permits, and free valet parking. Entrees include pizza, pasta, Beef Wellington, lamb shanks, pork and veal loins. Comfort food with a flair.

Beaded Nomad

1238 First Street Napa CA 94559
707.258.8004.

An incredible selection of beads of all size, shapes, colors and materials. Truly unique! Ready to purchase earrings, necklaces and other jewelry as well.

Belle Arti

1040 Main Street, Suite 1040
Napa CA 94559
707.255.0720
Sicilian - Entrees $9-$23.50

The valley's first Sicilian restaurant (most of the others are *northern* Italian, primarily Tuscan). At Belle Arti you can enjoy the lighter and more simple Sicilian style, with an emphasis on seafood. You'll also find an excellent selection of Sicilian wines, which you're unlikely to find elsewhere in the valley. Pity, since the Sicilians have been making wine for more than 2,000 years, they've had time to get it down.

Dining indoors and outside on the patio overlooking Napa Creek. Belle Arti opened and instantly became one of the very best Italian restaurants in the valley.

Bistro Don Giovanni

4110 St. Helena Highway (Highway 29)
Napa CA 94558
707.224.3300
www.bistrodongiovanni.com
Italian/French Country - Entrees $13-$24

DIRECTIONS: From Napa take Highway 29 north. After passing the Salvador Avenue traffic light, continue for about 300 yards and turn right into the first driveway. The road turns right but veer left into the restaurant parking lot.

Overlooking vineyards and the hills beyond, Bistro Don Giovanni captures the essence of Italy with all the charm and elegance of the Napa Valley. Excellent menu featuring pizzas, pastas, grilled dishes (try the seared salmon with buttermilk), and exquisite salads (we like the spinach salad with Stilton cheese and fresh beets). We recommend the terrace on a warm wine country evening, surrounded by the gardens that supply many of the herbs and vegetables for your meal.

Bombay Bistro

1011 First St. Napa CA 94559
707.253.9375
Indian - Entrees $9-$15

An Indian restaurant that's been very popular since the day it opened. Classic curries, Tandoori, and vegetarian. Dining indoors and on the patio.

Bounty Hunter Rare Wine & Provisions

975 First Street Napa CA 94559
707.255.0622 800.943.9463
www.bountyhunterwine.com

Mark Pope focuses on rare, limited-production wines, primarily from California but including wines—and wine paraphernalia—from throughout the world. He's in the historic Semorile Building, constructed in 1888 and located between Main Street and the river. Mark also offers a wine bar and *charcuterie* for tasting and fine snacking. Open until 2 a.m. Friday and Saturday nights, the Bounty Hunter has become a lively and popular hangout

Bridgeford Flying Services

Napa Valley Airport Napa CA 94558
(Halfway between Napa and Vallejo)
707.224.0887
www.bfsnapa.com

Tours of Napa Valley, Lake Berryessa, the Golden Gate Bridge and San Francisco Bay, and the Marin and Sonoma Coasts. Cessna Skyhawk (1-3 passengers) or Cessna Centurion (4-5 passengers).

A flying tour of the Napa Valley offers a truly unique and breathtaking perspective of our enchanted valley. You realize just how much of the surrounding area is still in its natural state. It's also the only way to see how the "other half" live (well, maybe less than half). The hills on both sides of the valley are filled with estates and compounds built by the wealthy. Most of these homes are visible only from the air.

Bubbling Well Pet Memorial Park

2462 Atlas Peak Road, Napa CA 94558
707.255.3456
www.bubbling-well.com

It's not exactly a major wine country tourist attraction, but the pet memorial park is open 365 days a year for visitation. The park is located in the hills behind Napa, two miles beyond Silverado Country Club. Established in 1971, it is now the final resting place for over 10,000 pets. The park was the star of the unique documentary film *Gates of Heaven*.

Buckhorn Grill

1201 Napa Town Center (near Mervyn's)
Napa CA 94559
707.265.9508
American Grill - Entrees $6-$10

Buckhorn was a weekly hit for years at the summertime Chef's Market in Napa. Now it's permanent. It's a place for a tasty and reasonably priced meal, specializing in tri-tip sandwiches, chicken and salmon. Popular with locals and tourists.

Butter Cream Bakery

2297 Jefferson Street Napa CA 94558
707.255.6700

Try their "champagne cake." No, it doesn't have champagne in it. But it deserves to accompany a glass of the bubbly. If you can't handle a whole cake, you can buy it by the slice. Lots of other goodies, too, all with Butter Cream's special touch.

Truly a Napa institution and a popular hangout place for breakfast or lunch. There's usually a line of people waiting to select their favorite goodies from a wide variety of delicious pastries, so don't forget to take a number when you walk in.

Café Society

1000 Main St. Napa, CA 94559
707.256.3232
www.cafesocietystore.com

It's hard to describe this place, which is near the corner of First Street in downtown Napa, right near the Opera House. It displays and sells antique and hand-made new French café furniture,—tables, chairs, stools, and café art and collectibles—old bistro posters and signs, glasses, absinthe spoons, cups and saucers, and much more. Owners Joan and Steve Osburn also offer interior design and feng shui services, and their work looks intelligent, colorful and warmly livable.

But Café Society also has an authentic zinc bar serving wine, beer, aperitifs, espresso, teas, chocolate, sandwiches, salads, gelato and pastries. It holds poetry readings, musical events, and weekly French conversation gatherings. The sales side is aimed at people starting cafés or restaurants, or who want their home to look like one. The coffee bar is open till 7 p.m. weeknights, and 10 p.m. or later on weekends. You can even hook up to the Internet. A very comfortable and friendly place to enjoy a cup of coffee.

And if you really like the table you're sitting at, you can buy it!

Caffe Cicero

1245 First Street
Napa CA 94559
707.257.1802
www.caffecicero.com
American - Entrees $8.99-$13.99

Open for breakfast, lunch and dinner until midnight during the week, and until 1 a.m. on Friday and Saturday evenings. Dinner menu includes soups, salads, pastas, sandwiches and burgers. Beer and wine. One of the very few places in town open late at night after a movie, play, concert or other event. Comfortable décor featuring the old bar from the sadly-departed Carriage House. Acoustic music, book and dramatic readings, and other events.

Celadon

829 Main Street Napa , CA 94559
707.254.9690
www.celadonnapa.com
Wine Country - Entrees $16-$20

An immediate favorite of locals since it opened in 1996, now located at the historic Napa Mill. Owner/chef Greg Cole says his place serves "global comfort food." The 2002 Zagat Survey gave Celadon its Award of Distinction, and the Wine Spectator gave its Award of Excellence. The S.F. Examiner once said Cole was one of the Top 10 Undiscovered Chefs in Northern California. He's not undiscovered any longer.

Chablis Inn

3360 Solano Avenue Napa CA 94558
800.443.3490 707.257.1944
www.chablisinn.com
34 rooms - $90-$235

Located just off Highway 29 at the north end of Napa. All rooms recently renovated and some include whirlpool bath or private spa room.

Chateau Hotel and Conference Center

4195 Solano Avenue Napa CA 94558
707.253.9300
www.napavalleychateauhotel.com
115 rooms - $100-$175

At the north end of Napa just off Highway 29. Nine thousand square feet of meeting space.

Christian Brothers Retreat & Conference Center

4401 Redwood Road Napa CA 94558
707.252.3810
www.christianbrosretreat.com
14 rooms, 2 suites - $115-$170

Surrounded by 500 acres of vineyards and wooded hills. Conference room and dining for up to 100 people. Perfect for individuals, focus groups, budget meetings, seminars, marketing "think tanks," team building, retreats or just a company "getaway."

Cinedome 8

825 Pearl Street Napa CA 94559
707.257.7700
www.centurytheatres.com

There's nothing unique or interesting about this theater. It's part of a large chain and exists solely to show mainstream movies. Despite its promises to the city the last time it was allowed to expand, it seldom shows art or independent films. The web site has current listings, but you'll first have to search for the Napa theater to find them.

Cole's Chop House

1122 Main St Napa, CA 94559 707.224.6328
www.coleschophouse.citysearch.com
Classic Steakhouse - Entrees $16-$38

Greg Cole was so successful with his Celadon restaurant (see above) that he opened his dream restaurant nearby—a classic American steak house. The menu features 21-day dry-aged prime steaks, certified Angus Beef, formula fed veal, New Zealand lamb and fresh seafood. And a large variety of martinis and other classic cocktails.

Sunset Magazine says the "aged prime steaks are incredible." You will, too.

Copia - The American Center For Wine, Food And The Arts

500 First Street Napa CA 94558
707.259.1600 (tickets)
707.265.5900 (admin)
www.copia.org
Adults:$12.50 Seniors/Students: $10.00
Children: $7.50. Annual memberships available

Copia is situated on 12 acres on the banks of the Napa River, a short walk from downtown Napa. The center celebrates America's contributions to wine, food and the arts. It includes a 280-seat theater for films and lectures, a café gift shop, an 80-seat demonstration kitchen, a 500-seat concert terrace, a restaurant—"Julia's Kitchen (see separate listing)—named after honorary trustee Julia Child, and 3.5 acres of landscaped edible organic gardens for hands-on learning about soils, farming and viticulture. It offers films, classes, readings, lectures, demonstrations, tastings and workshops.

Another feature at Copia is the *Wine Spectator Tasting Table* with wines from throughout the world. Visitors can sample from more than 40 wines, changed monthly.

Copia offers a variety of wine education classes with such titles as *The ABCs of Starting a Wine Cellar* and *The Carpenters of Wine: All About Wine Barrels and Cooperage*, as well as Wine Certificate programs in partnership with the Wine and Spirits Education Trust. Over 40 different wine courses are offered, most paired with food. It also offers more than 200 food classes, including both cooking and non-cooking programs.

Visual and performing arts programs include photography, design, music, theater, film, dance, art, performance, literature, history, archaeology and fashion. Copia also offers an artist-in-residence Legacy Program for prominent winemakers, chefs, artists, poets, authors, filmmakers, dancers, nutritionists and scientists.

Copia is the inspiration of winemaker Robert Mondavi and his wife Margrit, and it was he who purchased the land and donated it to the non-profit institution for its new home, along with $20 million to get the project going. Many other individuals and organizations also donated funds. Honorary trustees include chef Alice Waters, good-taste expert Martha Stewart, and wine critic Robert Parker.

Del Dotto Wine Caves and Tasting Room

1055 Atlas Peak Road　Napa, California
707.256.3332
www.deldottovineyards.com

Open daily. Tours and tasting by appointment only. Located near Silverado Country Club in the historic Hedgeside Distillery building, constructed in 1884. Cabernet Sauvignon, Merlot, Cabernet Franc, Sangiovese.

Downtown Joe's

902 Main Street Napa CA 94559
707.258.2337
www.downtownjoes.com
American - Entrees $8.50-$18

Joe's is a popular lunch, dinner and evening spot for locals and those visitors who are lucky enough to find out about it. It has live music almost every night and "open mike" nights on Tuesday. Not the place for a quiet, intimate dinner, but nice outdoor dining where you can sit and look at the river. Great beers too, brewed right on the spot at Joe's own microbrewery.

Downtown Trolley

707.255.7631
www.nctpa.net/trolley

There's now a free trolley service that travels a circuit in Napa, arriving at each stop every 20 minutes. The trolley, a diesel-powered replica of an early 1900s trolley, stops at 14 locations, including the downtown Napa plaza, the Napa Town Center, Napa Premium Outlets, Napa Valley Expo, Copia, the Wine Train, Fuller Park in the heart of Old Town and the public library.

Napa's downtown trolley shuttles visitors—and residents—throughout the downtown area between Copia and the factory outlets just west of Highway 29. Photo courtesy of Napa County Transportation Planning Agency.

The trolley runs every day except Tuesday, from 11 a.m. to 7 p.m., except Friday and Saturday when it runs until 10 p.m. Each trolley holds about 30 seated passengers and two wheelchairs. The trolley also connects to the city/county bus system for travel to other areas.

The fact that it's fun to ride is indicated by the number of local residents who can be found on the trolley. You'll like it too, particularly if you're staying at a hotel or B&B near one of the stops.

Dreamweavers Theatre

1637 Imola Avenue
River Park Shopping Center
Napa CA 94559
707.255.5483
www.dreamweaverstheatre.org

Local non-profit live theater. Small, comfortable theater with a varied line-up of shows. Examples from their 2002 schedule give an idea of the variety of their plays: *Steambath*, David Mamet's *Oleanna*, *Getting Away with Murder*, *Gross Indecency—The Three Trials of Oscar Wilde*, *To Kill a Mockingbird*, *Waiting for Godot*, *The Man Who Came to Dinner*, and *Measure for Measure*.

Embassy Suites

1075 California Boulevard Napa CA 94559
707.253.9540 • 800.433.4600
Fax: 707.253.9202
www.embassynapa.com
205 two-room suites - $144-$294

A large and conveniently located inn just off Highway 29 (take the First Street exit). All 205 units are two-room suites, each with two phone lines with voice mail.

Suites face the indoor, skylighted atrium, the outdoor pool, or the sun-drenched (and swan-inhabited) mill pond. There's also an indoor pool, spa, sauna and steam room. Guests enjoy a complimentary cooked-to-order American breakfast each morning, and an equally complimentary beverage reception each evening—with Napa Valley wine, of course. *Rings Restaurant* in the courtyard serves from an Italian menu, and *Joe's Bar* offers live music and great drinks.

First Presbyterian Church

1333 Third St. Napa CA 94559
707.224.8693
www.fpcnapa.org

A beautiful late-Victorian Gothic church, all of wood, built in 1874. Designated by the state as a historical landmark and on the National Register of Historic Places.

Foothill Café

2766 Old Sonoma Road Napa CA
707.252.6178
Dinner only. Wed-Sun 4:30-9:30 p.m.
California - Entrees: $12.00-$18.00

DIRECTIONS: On Highway 29 at the south end of Napa, take Imola Avenue west, then turn right (north) on Foster Road, and left on Old Sonoma Road. It's in the J&P Shopping Center on the right.

An out-of-the-way place with tremendous food, thanks to the skills of owner/chef Jerry Shaffer. Get grilled anything. Delicious. The San Francisco Chronicle says it's the equal of any restaurant in the Napa Valley. Many of us locals think it's even more than that.

Fujiya Restaurant

921 Factory Stores Drive Napa CA 94559
707.257.0639
Japanese - Entrees: $12-$17

Although Fujiya is located at the Napa factory outlets, it was there before they appeared, and has always been our favorite Japanese restaurant in the valley. The sushi is excellent with a wide range of choices served at the sushi bar or at your table. The rest of the menu offers dishes such as tempura, teriyaki and sukiyaki. All are very good. Add in prompt and friendly service and you'll see why Fujiya is well patronized by locals. The only flaw? The shrill cat meow that takes the place of the normal telephone ring. You might point that out to them if it bothers you.

Fumé Bistro & Bar

4050 Byway East Napa, California 94558
707.257.1999
www.fumebistro.com
American/California - Entrees $14.50-$19.50

DIRECTIONS: In north Napa, turn east off Highway 29 onto Trower, take the first left and the first left again (just past the John Muir Inn). Continue a short distance along the highway frontage road and you'll see Fumé on the right.

A comfortable neighborhood restaurant already discovered by visitors. A mouthwatering list of pizzas and pastas that might include Asparagus Ravioli with fresh sage cream sauce and baby cress salad or Rock Shrimp Pizza with braised leeks, sun dried tomatoes, kalamata olives and herb goat cheese. Entrees such as Roasted Sea Bass and Manila Clams and Oven-Roasted Sonoma Organic Chicken.

Genova Delicatessen

1550 Trancas Street Napa CA 94558
707.253.8686
www.genovadelicatessen.com

A wide selection of cheese, meats and Italian specialties. They'll whip you up a sandwich or an entire picnic basket. If you can't find something here to delight your taste buds, you probably shouldn't have come to the Napa Valley in the first place. Take a number when you walk in, or you may be left watching while everyone else gets their food.

Gillwoods Restaurant

Napa Town Center
(next to the Visitors Center)
707.253.0409
American - Entrees $7.95-$9.75. Breakfast and lunch only.

One of the nicest places in downtown Napa for breakfast or lunch. Excellent comfort food at reasonable prices. Outdoor tables. Lots of people passing by. And it's right next to the Visitors Center.

Gondola Servizio

Hatt Market
500 Main Street
Napa CA 94559
www.gondolaservizio.com/services/napa/

Gondola rides on the Napa River. Authentic Venetian gondolas with a singing gondolier. Half-hour ride for two people is $55. $125 for two includes a one-hour ride and a bottle of vino. Rides not operating during most of the winter, but Venetian glass shop remains open.

Hakusan Sake Gardens

One Executive Way Napa CA 94558
707.258.6160
www.hakusan.com
Complimentary tasting.

DIRECTIONS: South of Napa on Highway 29 at the intersection of Highway 12. Entrance is off North Kelly Road.

Situated on 20 acres amid beautiful Japanese gardens. Constructed in 1989, Hakusan produces 180,000 cases of sake annually, using rice grown in the Sacramento Valley. A unique experience in the Napa Valley.

Hawthorn Inn & Suites

314 Soscol Avenue Napa CA 94559
707.226.1878 800.527.1133
www.napavalleyinns.com
60 rooms - $149-$199

Located on the east side of Soscol Avenue as you enter Napa from the south. Studios and suites. Two phone lines in each room with T-1 Internet connection.

Henry's

823 Main Street Napa CA 94559
707.257.3008

There aren't many stand-alone bars in the Napa Valley, and even fewer that are worth stepping into. Henry's is one that is. It offers honest drinks for honest prices. At an earlier location it had a back door off an alley where lawyers and judges could pop in unobserved for a quick drink and negotiations. At its current location it has only a front, very visible, door across the street from Veterans' Park, so the legal profession is seldom to be seen. As a matter of fact, until a few years ago, even Henry's was seldom to be seen. It didn't have a sign out front, so only the regulars knew it existed. But new owners decided they'd like some new, additional customers, and it's now clearly marked.

Henry's doesn't open until late in the afternoon, so if you're looking for action, wait until late in the evening. The later it gets, the younger the crowd is. Of course, if you're just looking for a good drink, any time it's open is fine.

Hess Collection Winery

4411 Redwood Road Napa CA 94558
707.255.1144
www.hesscollection.com
DIRECTIONS: Off Highway 29 in north Napa, turn west on Redwood Road (to the east this road is called Trancas Street). Stay on Redwood Road approximately 6.5 miles to the winery on the left, being careful to turn left over a bridge at the junction of Mount Veeder Road. Look for the sign on the bridge.

The Hess Collection is both a winery and an art museum. Swiss owner Donald Hess, who now lives in Argentina, has assembled one of the largest modern art collections available for public viewing in California.

The Hess Collection offers one of the finest selections of art in the Napa Valley—and great wine. Photo courtesy of the winery.

This remarkable collection complements a winery that produces superb wines. Plus there's an excellent 12-minute audio-visual presentation on the winery. Highly recommended.

Hilton Garden Inn Napa

3585 Solano Avenue Napa CA 94558
707.252.0444 Fax 707.252.0244
www.hiltongardeninn.com
80 rooms - $109-$379

Located at the north end of Napa just north of Trancas Street. Solano is the frontage road on the west side of Highway 29.

All rooms have two phone lines with voice-mail and high speed Internet access. Includes the *American Grill* restaurant and a wine tasting bar.

Inn at the Vines (Best Western)

100 Soscol Avenue Napa CA 94559
707.257.1930 877.846.3729
www.innatthevines.com
68 rooms $102 - $252

At the south end of Napa on Soscol Avenue near Napa State Hospital and Napa Valley College. Swimming pool, jacuzzi.

In-N-Out Burger

820 Imola Avenue Napa CA 94559
(Just off Soscol Avenue.)
www.in-n-out.com

Okay, so it has nothing to do with the Napa Valley or even wine country. It's just a California hamburger chain. But if it's possible to say "healthy fast food", this is the place. In-N-Out uses 100% pure beef, hand leafs its lettuce, bakes its own buns, slices fresh potatoes right in the store and cooks them in vegetable oil, uses real cheese, and puts only real ice cream in the shakes.

The wait is longer than most fast-food places but that's because they cook your order on the spot. They don't use a microwave, heat lamp or freezer. And their wages and benefits are the best in the industry. An In-N-Out burger may not be wine country cuisine, but it's delicious.

Real fans also know the "secret menu" such as "protein style" (hamburger wrapped in lettuce without the bun), "Animal style" (bun is grilled with mustard, and grilled onions, pickles and extra sauce are added), and "Neapolitan shake" (a mix of chocolate, vanilla and strawberry).

Jarvis Conservatory

1711 Main Street Napa CA 94559
707.255.5445
www.jarvisconservatory.com

An absolutely exquisite theater devoted to an art form little known in this country: Spanish opera, called "zarzuela," something like a Spanish version of Gilbert & Sullivan. Situated in the building that once housed the Joseph Mathews distillery (and later winery), the Conservatory offers classes and public performances of zarzuela and other operatic music. If there's a performance happening while you're in the valley (they're usually in June), give it a try.

On the first Saturday of each month, Jarvis hosts "opera night". Vocalists from around the San Francisco Bay Area come to perform. Tickets are $15 and include complimentary tapas, wine and mineral water at intermission. Tickets are available at the door on the day of the event, opening at 6:30 pm for ticket sales. Doors open at 7:30 and singing starts at 8:00.

Jarvis Vineyards

2970 Monticello Road   Napa CA 94558
800.255.5280
www.jarviswines.com

Tasting tours are daily by appointment only. Cost is $15 per person. Four miles east of Napa on the road toward Lake Berryessa. The entire winery is located within a stunning 45,000 square feet of caves, with cast bronze doors, fiber optic chandeliers, and an underground stream and waterfall. Cabernet Sauvignon, Cabernet Franc, Merlot, Malbec, Chardonnay, Petit Verdot.

John Muir Inn

1998 Trower Avenue Napa CA 94558
707.257.7220 800.522.8999
www.johnmuirnapa.com
60 rooms $95 - $210

At the north end of Napa on the northeast corner of Highway 29 and Trower. Convenient to both downtown Napa and upvalley wineries.

Jonesy's Famous Steak House

Napa Valley Airport 2044 Airport Road
Napa CA 94558
707.255.2003
www.jonesyssteakhouse.com
Steakhouse - Entrees: $9.75 - $18.95

Since 1946. Known by pilots all over the country who fly in just for lunch or dinner. Steak, chicken and seafood. A favorite of old-time Napans.

Julia's Kitchen

500 First Street Napa CA 94558
707.265.5700
www.juliaskitchen.com
California-French - Entrees $18.50-$27.00
Hours vary depending on season and day of
the week. Call for current information.

Located at Copia (see separate listing),
Julia's Kitchen is named after famed chef
and cookbook author Julia Child. Child is
also an honorary trustee of, and adviser to,
Copia. She not only donated her name, she
also donated her collection of copper cookware to the center.

The open kitchen allows 75 guests to
watch the chefs—and visiting chefs and
cooking teachers—at work while they dine
on regional and seasonal foods highlighting
produce and herbs from Copia's own gardens. While at Copia, you can tour the
three and a half acres of organic gardens.

JV Wine & Spirits

426 First Street Napa CA 94559
707.253.2624
www.jvwineandspirits.com

The place where Napans go for good prices
on wine and spirits. It's right next door to
(and over the river from) Copia. The largest
wine selection in the Napa Valley, with over
1200 different wines, including more than
250 Cabernets, 320 Chardonnays, 120
Zinfandels and 140 Merlots. If that's not
enough for you, try one of the more than
115 different micro and imported beers.
Wednesday through Sunday their tasting
bar offers samples from a rotation of 45 different wineries. It's by far the biggest selection in the valley.

Kelley's "No Bad Days" Café

976 Pearl Street   Napa CA 94559
707.258.9666 Fax 707.255.7066
California – Entrees $9.50-$16.50

Just off Main Street towards the Cinedome
Theater. Kelley Novak offers a tasty menu
that includes such dinner entrees as grilled
ribeye steak with Cabernet sauce, grilled

baby back ribs with Hoisin glaze, and
sautéed seasonal vegetables with shallots
and garden herbs. Appetizers include tiger
prawns wrapped in pancetta, beef satay, and
panko sautéed oysters. A comfortable local
place with excellent food.

Kirkland Ranch Winery

1 Kirkland Ranch Road   Napa CA 94559
707.254.9100
www.kirklandranchwinery.com

Open daily for tours and tastings.   On
Highway 12 in Jamieson Canyon between
Interstate 80 and Highway 29. Sangiov ese,
Gewürztraminer, Sauvignon Blanc, Merlot,
Cabernet Sauvignon, Syrah, Chardonnay,
Pinot Grigio, Muscat Canelli.

La Boucane

1778 Second St. Napa CA 94559
707.253.1177
Classic French - Entrees $15.00-$23.00

We hesitated a long time before listing this
restaurant. Most visitors haven't the slight-
est idea that it exists. We prefer it that way
because that means we're usually able to get
a reservation.

But to be fair to visitors—and to
chef/owner Jacques Mokrani—we decided
to mention it. If you dine only in trendy
restaurants and wish your taste buds to
encounter only the very latest in strange but
fashionable food and seasoning combina-
tions, this is not your place. But if you
appreciate the value of food made with
great care, much love, and years of experience, this is the place.

This is French food. Traditional, not
nouvelle. Jacques refuses to allow what he
calls "architectural food" in his place. You
won't find meat draped over a pile of
mashed potatoes. Nor will you puritanical-
ly be given olive oil for your warm and
crusty French bread instead of butter.
Jacques creates classical French cuisine,
with magnificent sauces, incredibly tender
cuts of meat, and desserts that are almost
painfully delicious. Excuse our waxing so

poetically here. We like this place. A lot. Maybe it's because Jacques wants to produce food that makes his diners moan. We moan. Particularly over the raspberry soufflé.

Labyrinth at the Methodist Church

Napa First United Methodist Church
625 Randolph Street at Fifth Street
Napa, CA 94559
707.253.1411
www.napaumc.org

The labyrinth is patterned after the original in France's Chartres Cathedral. Visitors walk along the path, winding back and forth, until they reach the center of the design. Unlike a maze, a labyrinth has a specific path with no confusing choices. No one gets lost in a labyrinth.

Walking the labyrinth is a sacred act, a moving meditation that can have profound effects on the walker.

The church's congregation has designed an outdoor labyrinth with the help of the Veriditas Project at Grace Cathedral in San Francisco. It makes the labyrinth public so that others can enjoy the peaceful, healing and self-understanding effects of working with the labyrinth.

The labyrinth is open for walking Monday through Friday from 11 a.m. to 2 p.m. Groups may arrange for group walks, with or without a facilitator, between 9-11 a.m. and 2-4 p.m. Suggested donation is $3/person. For more information, call the church at the above number.

Laird Family Estate

5055 Solano Avenue
Napa CA 94558
877.297.4902
www.lairdfamilyestate.com

Tours and tastings by appointment. On the west side of Highway 29 at the intersection of Oak Knoll Avenue. The Laird family has been growing grapes since 1970 and eventually opened their own winery. The winery also serves as a "custom crush" facility for a number of other Napa Valley wineries. Chardonnay, Cabernet Sauvignon, Merlot.

Misto Restaurant

916 Franklin Street, Napa,CA 94559
707.252.4080
www.mistorestaurant.com
Italian - Entrees $13-$20
Between First and Second Streets.

Misto endeared itself to us one Valentine's Day when we first discovered it. After a movie at a nearby theater, we wanted to have dinner. It was late, and as was then typical in Napa, everything was closed. But Misto was still open, after obviously having been busy all evening. When we asked if we were too late, they responded "If you'd like to have dinner, we're open." It's been one of our very favorite places ever since.

Dishes range from Shrimp Brandy to Duck Rillette Risotto to Canneloni Naples to Osso Bucco (a fellow diner said it was the best he'd ever had) to free range Veal Tenderloin. Highly recommended.

Monticello Vineyards

4242 Big Ranch Road Napa CA 94558
707.253.2802
www.monticellovineyards.com

The Corley family has been producing limited-edition wines for over 30 years. Try their beautifully soft Corley Proprietary Red, a blend of Cabernet Sauvignon, Cabernet Franc and Merlot. It's available only at the winery. Picnic grove available to visitors.

Murals

Throughout Downtown Napa.

Outdoor murals depicting the history of Napa Valley. (See separate listing later in this book.)

Napa County Historical Society

1219 First Street Napa CA 94559
707.224.1739
www.napahistory.org

Located in the historic Goodman Building in downtown Napa. Books, manuscripts, photographs, newspaper clippings, maps and videos. Operated by volunteers. Call for hours.

Napa Firefighters Museum

1201 Main Street Napa CA 94558
707.259.0609
www.cityofnapa.org/Departments/Fire/WebPag
es/Fire/museum.htm

Free Admission. Open Wednesday through Sunday Call first to make sure they're open.

The Napa Firefighters Museum—classic fire equipment for kids and adults.

Features an 1859 handpumper, a 1904 horse-drawn steamer, a 1913 Model T Ford, and 1926, 1931 and 1948 engines. Also tools, equipment and uniforms, and badges from all over the world. A great place for kids!

Napa General Store

500 Main Street Napa CA 94559
707.259.0762
www.napageneralstore.com

A specialty market and cafe with an outside dining terrace overlooking the Napa River. Part of the Napa Mill complex. Also offers pizza, picnic baskets, and a tasting bar. Visitors can choose from a daily selection of four reds and four whites, which are in turn chosen from a rotation of 25-30 varietals.

Napa Mill

500 Main Street Napa CA 94559
707.252.9372
www.napamill.com

Napa Mill includes the Napa River Inn and the Hatt Market. The project is located on nearly three acres along the Napa River, on the site of the 1884 Hatt Building. The former feed and grain business and flour mill has been redeveloped into a sixty-five room hotel, restaurants, shops and food markets. A weekend farmers' and craft market is also planned. This is one of the key features of the Napa River development plan and a favorite place for locals as well as visitors.

Napa Premium Outlets

Highway 29 at First Street Exit
707.226.9876
Monday - Saturday 10a.m.-8p.m.
Sundays 10a.m.-6p.m.

Includes Esprit, Jones New York, Calvin Klein, J. Crew, Kenneth Cole, Dansk and Mikasa. Are these factory outlets filled with unique wine country gifts? No. Are they popular with tourists? You bet. That's why we've included them. And, if you get hungry, there's a great local Japanese restaurant, *Fujiya*. It also has an excellent sushi bar.

Napa River Adventures

Next to Downtown Joe's restaurant
(902 Main Street) in Napa
707.224.9080
www.napariveradventures.com

Canoe and kayak rental for leisurely boating on the Napa River. $30-$40. If you'd rather not paddle yourself, they also offer guided tours of the river on a comfortable electric-powered boat. It's also available for weddings and other private charters.

Napa Riverfront District

www.napariverfront.com

Organization of shops, restaurants and businesses along Main Street. Website offers news of events and other information.

Napa River Inn

500 Main Street Napa CA 94559
707.251.8500
www.napariverinn.com
66 rooms - $159-$399

New, elegant and a couple of minutes walk from downtown. Rooms right on the Napa River. Restaurants and spa on site as well as shops. In the former Hatt Building, and part of the Napa Mill complex.

Napa State Hospital

2100 Napa-Vallejo Highway
Napa, CA 94558-6293
707.253.5026
www.dmh.cahwnet.gov/Statehospitals/Napa/

It's not a tourist spot, but this hospital for the mentally ill has had an important role in Napa's history and economy, and deserves mention. The 500-bed, four-story Gothic hospital building opened in 1875. It had a perimeter of one mile. Its first two clients were San Franciscans. It began on 192 acres purchased for $11,506 from Don Cayetano Juarez, part of the original Rancho Tulocay Mexican Land Grand that Juarez had received from General Mariano Vallejo. Over the years the property expanded to over 2,000 acres.

The land extended from the Napa River to the eastern edge of what is now Skyline Park, providing room for dairy and poultry ranches, orchards, vegetable gardens and farming. Farming ended in the late 1960's and most of the land is now occupied by Kennedy and Skyline Parks and Napa Valley College. The hospital's highest population was in 1960 with over 5,000 patients. The current population is approximately 1,000.

There are rumors that the hospital will be closed in the next five years.

Napa-Vallejo Flea Market and Auction

303 South Kelly Road   Napa CA 94559
707.226.8862

On the east side of Highway 29 a short ways north of American Canyon and south of Highway 12. Entrance is on South Kelly Road. Sundays from 5 am to 5 pm.

Over 500 vendors, primarily Hispanic, selling new and used items including collectibles, CDs, food, produce, furniture, and clothing.

Napa Valley Coffee Roasting Company

948 Main Street   Napa CA 94559
707.224.2233   800.852.5804

Freshly-roasted coffee in downtown Napa. At corner of First and Main. Small but convenient. They have a larger version in St. Helena.

Napa Valley Conference and Visitors Bureau

1310 Napa Town Center Napa CA 94559
707.226.7459
www.napavalley.org

Hidden in the Napa Town Center deep in the heart of downtown Napa, yet it gets tens of thousands of visitors a year. (Just follow the blue and white "Tourist Information" signs through Napa.) The CVB volunteers are outstanding: helpful, friendly and knowledgeable. Take advantage of their expertise to plan your valley destinations. (Even if you have this book, it can't hurt.)

These people volunteer because they love talking with visitors. And they love the fact that they're wined and dined by the valley's best wineries and restaurants so that they'll have first-hand experience of the area's attractions. Most, but not all, are retired, so they have the time to help you and your fellow visitors enjoy their home.

Napa Valley Emporium

1319 First Street Napa CA 94559
707.253.7177
www.napavalleyemporium.com

A must as you wander through downtown Napa. The most complete selection of Napa Valley-themed gifts and souvenirs in the valley. Art, gifts, clothing, t-shirts. If you don't want something for yourself, bring something back to a loved one.

Napa Valley Exposition

575 Third Street Napa CA 94559
707.253.4900
www.napavalleyexpo.com

Expo is home to the annual *Napa Town & Country Fair*, which is held every August and is the biggest fair in Napa County. It's also the site of a large number of community and visitor events, including the *Mustard Festival Marketplace* in March.

Napa Valley Marriott

3425 Solano Avenue Napa CA 94558
707.253.7433 Fax: 707.258.1320
www.napavalleymarriott.com
272 rooms, five suites - $129-$279

DIRECTIONS: Turn west on Redwood Road, cross the Wine Train tracks and turn right on Solano Avenue. Hotel is on the left.

Two restaurants, and a spa. Heated outdoor pool and water spa. Lighted tennis courts. Fitness center. Summer training home of the Oakland Raiders football team. (They practice at Redwood Middle School just in back of the hotel).

Napa Valley Opera House

1040 Main Street Napa CA 94559
707.226.7372
www.napavalleyoperahouse.org

The theater was built in 1879, and although never actually used for opera, presented everything from readings by Jack London and performances by John Philip

Sousa's band to vaudeville, political rallies and local dance recitals. It closed in 1914 but has now been restored, offering theatrical performances and musical revues since June of 2002.

The Napa Valley Opera House opened in 1879—and reopened in 2002. It's one of the cultural highlights of the valley.

The Café Theatre on the ground floor has cabaret-style seating for 180 people, where patrons can enjoy wine and snacks before and after performances. It offers performances of popular, jazz, blues, Latin, world and chamber music, as well as comedy and shows for the family.

The larger Margrit Biever Mondavi Theatre is located upstairs and seats 380 on the main floor and 120 in the balcony. It offers similar entertainment as well as plays, musical theater, opera and dance.

Napa Valley Redwood Inn

3380 Solano Avenue Napa CA 94558
707.257.6111
www.napavalleybudgetinn.com
58 rooms - $62-$148

Two-story motel. High-speed Internet access in all rooms. Swimming pool.

Napa Valley Traditions

1202 Main Street (corner of Pearl)
Napa CA 94559
707.226.2044 Fax: 707.226.2069
www.napatraditions.com

Traditions is a coffee house that also sells (and offers tasting of) food and wine. It specializes in Napa Valley products, including nuts, wine vinegars, olive oils, wine jellies, mustards and, of course, wines. Their Bayview Cellars offers Chardonnay, Gewürztraminer, Cabernet. Sauvignon and Merlot. Lots of wine paraphernalia too, such as wine racks, coasters, cork pullers and the like.

Traditions is one of the original coffee hangouts in both Napa and California. It's a quiet and cool place to sip coffee or tea, with a play area for your little ones to occupy themselves while you relax. Traditions also happens to be just across the street from the Napa Firefighters Museum which is also a great place to take kids.

Napa Valley Trail Rides

PO Box 5808 Napa CA 94581
707.255.2900
www.napasonomatrailrides.com

Trail rides at Skyline Wilderness Park in Napa from April through November, including special rides for groups. Reservations required.

Napa Valley Travelodge

853 Coombs Street, Napa CA 94559
707.226.1871
www.the.travelodge.com/napa09557
45 rooms - $119-$159

Located in the heart of downtown Napa, a short walk from restaurants, shops and Copia.

Napa Valley Trolley Systems

PO Box 1011 Middletown CA 95461
707.987.9887
www.wecaninc.com
$12.50/person. Children 12 and under are free.
Operates during the summer and other periods of good weather.

Horse-drawn carriage tours of Napa operated by Wagoneers Express Carriages and Nags, Inc. Half-hour tours start at the Napa River Inn and go through Old Town Napa, passing by some of Napa's finest Victorian homes. Jake and Tom, or Jerry and Bill, are the two teams of draft horses that do the heavy work. They're former residents of an Amish community in Indiana.

Napa Valley Wine & Cigar

3780 Bel Aire Plaza Napa CA 94558
707.253.8696
www.napavalleywineandcigar.com

Located in the same local shopping plaza just of Highway 29 (and Trancas Street) where Trader Joe's is located. A small but excellent wine shop focusing on Napa and Sonoma wines but also offering wines from elsewhere in California and around the world. A particularly good selection of ports and a wide range of cigars.

Napa Wine Merchants

1146 First Street Napa CA 94559
707.257.6796
www.napawinemerchant.com

A shared tasting room offering wines from such wineries as Gustave Thrace, Benessere, Bacio Divino, Harrison, Liparita, Rocca, Michael Scott, Young Ridge, Astrale Terra and Hendry.

Napa Valley Wine Train

1275 McKinstry Napa CA 94559
707.253.2111. 800.427.4124
Fax: 707.253.9264
www.winetrain.com

On-Train Restaurant: *Wine Country Cuisine*
$85-$110 prix fixe

A 36-mile, three-hour fixed-price brunch, lunch or dinner excursion that travels year round through the heart of the Napa Valley. Meticulously restored 1917 Pullman dining car, damask linens, bone china, silver flatware, lead crystalware. Lounge and wine tasting cars are resplendent in polished mahogany, brass and etched glass. Wine Emporium stocks over 200 Napa Valley wines for purchase or shipping. Special "Winemaker Dinner" trips. There's also a less expensive "open-air" car—the "Silverado", and a more expensive vista dome car. Basic no-food fare is $40. A la carte lunches $6.95 to $16.95.

The Wine Train carries passengers between Napa and St. Helena. Photo courtesy of the Wine Train.

You can take the brunch, lunch or dinner runs all the way to St. Helena and back to Napa, or you can enjoy the special luncheons that include a tour of Grgich-Hills Winery in Rutherford or Domaine Chandon Winery in Yountville.

You can also take the new *Yountville Shuttle*, which lets you stay in lodging in either Napa or Yountville, but easily visit the attractions in the other town. The shuttle's schedule varies seasonally, travelling between the main Wine Train station in Napa and the new station in Yountville. It connects with Napa's free *Downtown Trolley* (see separate listing in Napa section), which runs between major attractions in that city. Adult fare for the Yountville Shuttle is $7 one way, and $12 round trip. Children 12 and under are $4 and $7.

Shuttle service will probably be much slower coming to St. Helena due to the resistance of many St. Helenans to what they perceive will be hordes of tourists pouring out of the train and invading their town. (Never mind that they've already got a state highway running through the main part of town, and that almost all their shops are now aimed at tourists.)

The Wine Train is fun. If you like trains, great food, great service and/or a great view, take a trip. The whole thing is done with superb flair. If you think you'll be hungry soon, make sure you get the first seating. The second seating doesn't happen until one and half hours later when the train starts its return trip from St. Helena—

although you'll have hors d'oeuvres and beverages on the trip upvalley.

During your trip you may still see a few signs that seem to indicate that some of the locals don't care for the train. This is true. Some don't. The opponents are primarily "upvalley". They complain about the traffic that it allegedly produces, about the environmental damage, the noise, the danger at crossings; some have even alleged that the noise bothers their grapevines.

The Wine Train's opponents, although vocal, are greatly outnumbered by its proponents, and certainly by those who don't care one way or another. It's just a train. It's very pretty. It's a lot of fun to watch it go by—and even more fun to ride. Enjoy your trip.

The Neighborhood

1400 First Street Napa CA 94559
707.259.1900

Located on downtown Napa's main street, The Neighborhood represents sixty different antique dealers from throughout the San Francisco Bay Area. Merchandise includes antique collectibles, new quality reproductions and decorator pieces.

New Technology High School

1746 Yajome Street, Suite A
Napa, CA 94559
707.253.4400
www.newtechhigh.org

A unique high school where there are as many computers as students. Students develop not only computer skills but strong individual research and study skills. All work is *project-based* and much is done as teams. Completed work is turned in, usually as multimedia, on computer. Students can also study at local high schools and the community college.

New Tech High is a true pioneer in digital education, and was created by a joint effort of the local business and education communities. It has received a multi-million dollar grant from the Bill and Melinda

Gates Foundation to replicate itself in other parts of the country. While it isn't open to the public, educators can arrange a tour by appointment.

The author's daughter attended this school and he was particularly impressed by two non-academic features: The students are treated as adults, and the school is spotless; no graffiti, no trash. There just might be a connection.

Off the Preserve!

1142 Main Street Napa CA 94559
707.253.8300
www.dirosapreserve.org

The di Rosa Preserve (see separate listing in the Carneros section) has opened a gallery in downtown Napa. It offers exhibitions, educational programs, artist lectures and performances.

Omega 3 Seafoods

1740 Yajome Street
Napa CA 94559
707.257.3474 (FISH)
www.omega3seafoods.com

DIRECTIONS: Across the street from New Technology High School, two blocks east of Main Street.

Fresh seafood retail store that also offers a delicatessen. Clam chowders, oysters, shrimp or crab cocktails and Louies, sushi, ceviche and more. Outside tables in good weather.

Osprey Seafood Market

1014 Wine Country Avenue
Napa CA 94558
707.252.9120

At the north end of Napa just west of Highway 29. An attractive selection of deliciously fresh seafood. Includes live crab and lobster.

The Oxbow School

530 Third Street, Napa, CA, USA 94559
707.255.6000
www.oxbowschool.org

This school, a short walk from downtown Napa, was founded by Bay Area resident Ann Hatch, who also founded the Capp Street Project in San Francisco. Her goal was to "give young people meaningful access to living artists and a chance to practice [visual] art at a high level." She was joined in the project by Robert and Margrit Mondavi, who at the same time were also launching the nearby *Copia—The American Center for Wine, Food and the Arts*. The school opened in 1999.

The Oxbow School is open to high school juniors and seniors who come from across the country and abroad for a one-semester residential program. There are no public tours, but occasional guest lectures by visiting artists are free and open to the public.

Paint Your World

3367 Solano Avenue, Napa CA 94558
707.226.7484
Open from 11 a.m. Closed Tuesdays.
DIRECTIONS: In North Napa turn west off Highway 29 onto Redwood Road. It's in the shopping center on the left, next to Vallerga's Market.

Paint Your World is one of the few places in the Napa Valley that kids can enjoy. At Paint Your World you buy an unfinished white ceramic plate, cup, bowl, tile, pitcher or other item, then paint it yourself. The cost of the object includes use of paints and an hour of studio time. You can buy additional time if you need it, but most people seem to find an hour sufficient.

If you're unsure of your artistic abilities, the staff can give very supportive tips. Kids love the place, but so do people of any age. And it's a wonderful place for families to interact and work together.

After you've finished painting, you leave your work to be fired, and two days later you can come back and pick it up. It's a real kick seeing your artistic creation in final form. If you're from out of town, they'll ship it to you at an additional charge.

Pasta Prego

3206 Jefferson Street Napa CA 94558
707.224.9011
Italian - Entrees $11.95-$18.95

Excellent food in a neighborhood restaurant in a small, non-descript mall. The locals all know about it, and apparently some of them have passed on news of its existence to visitors as well. The usual palette of pastas—lasagna, ravioli, fettuccini—all with delicious sauces, as well as risotto, pizzas, veal piccatta and fish. On our last visit we had *Gamberi e Finocchio*, sauteed prawns on a bed of leek pancake with fennel, and a sun-dried tomato shrimp and cumin sauce. And that was just for openers.

Pearl

1339 Pearl Street #104 Napa CA 94559
707.224.9161 Fax: 707.255.6825
www.therestaurantpearl.com
California Cuisine - Entrees $9.75 - $18.95

Open for lunch and dinner Tuesday through Saturday. Pearl owners Nickie and Pete Zeller formerly owned the Brown Street Grill in Napa, and Nickie was co-owner of the legendary Diner in Yountville. Pearl is a gem and one of Napa's very best restaurants. The beautiful hex symbol paintings on the walls are all for sale.

Piccolino's Italian Café

1385 Napa Town Center Napa, CA 94559
707.251.0100 Fax: 707.224.1232
Entrance on First Street at Franklin
www.piccolinoscafe.com
Old World Italian - Entrees $10.95-$17.95

A popular Italian restaurant on downtown Napa's main street. Comfortable atmosphere with lots of windows so you can look out on sidewalk and street. Pasta, seafood and meat specials, wine bar with music on Friday and Saturday evenings, Italian night every Wednesday evening with an Italian accordianist. Patio dining available in season. Lunch and dinners seven days a week.

Pilar

807 Main Street   Napa CA 94559
707.253.8203
Mediterranean/Mexican

Pilar Sanchez is the former executive chef of the Wine Spectator restaurant at the Culinary Institute of America at Greystone in St. Helena. She and co-owner Dieder Lender were both previously chefs at Meadowood Resort in St. Helena. Now they have their own place in downtown Napa.

Pizza Azzurro

1400 Second at Franklin Napa CA 94559
707.255.5552
Pizza - Entrees $8.95-$10.95

Chef/owner Michael Gyetvan offers pizzas, pastas, salads and wine at prices that appeal to locals. But it's not your local pizza joint. Gyetvan is a graduate of the Culinary Institute of America in New York and former *chef de cuisine* at *Tra Vigne* in St. Helena. The place is casual and comfortable, and the food, featuring local produce, is delicious and very popular.

Posticino

1408 Clay Street, Napa CA 94559

Located at the former location of Cafe Lucy.

Red Hen Antiques

5091 St. Helena Highway (Highway 29) Napa
CA 94558
707.257.0822
Open daily 10:00am to 5:30pm
Oak Knoll Avenue west of Highway 29 between Napa and Yountville

A unique collective of 70 antique dealers set in a vineyard in the heart of the Napa Valley. You could easily spend all day here.

Red Hen Cantina

4175 Solano Avenue Napa CA 94559
707.224.8464
www.redhencantina.com
Mexican - Entrees $9.75-$15.95

For years the Red Hen was located north of Napa on the west side of Highway 29. It had a great outdoor dining area with a view of vineyards and hills. It's now in Napa at the former location of Pairs Restaurant. It's still got outdoor dining on the deck.

Red Rock Café and Catering

1010 Lincoln Avenue Napa CA 94558
707.226.2633
American Burger - Entrees $4.50-$14.95

Great hamburgers and onion rings. Tri-tip and barbecued ribs too. Consistently voted the best hamburger in Napa.

Restaurant Budo

River Terrace Inn
Randean Way at Soscol Avenue
Napa CA 94558
www.restaurantbudo.com
Asian-fusion

Opening in 2004 by James McDevitt, founder and executive chef of Scottsdale, Arizona's award-winning Restaurant Hapa. (Budo is the Japanese term for martial arts.)

Ristorante Allegria

1026 First Street   Napa CA 94559
707.254.8006
www.ristoranteallegria.com
Northern Italian - Entrees $10.95-$23.95

Northern Italian food with an elegant décor. Located in an historic bank building in Downtown Napa next to the plaza (where the much-despised Clocktower formerly stood). Friends say it has the best tiramisu they've ever tasted.

RiverBend Hotel

McKinstry Street   Napa CA 94558
www.napariverbend.com
160 rooms

Luxury hotel scheduled for a future opening. 10,000 square feet of conference space. Separate restaurant fronting on Soscol Avenue.

River City

505 Lincoln Avenue Napa CA 94558
707.253.1111
American – Entrees $10.50-$19.50

Traditional menu with entrees such as salmon, halibut, chicken, pork chops, lamb and steak. Very pleasant outdoor dining with a view of the Napa River. 3,000 sq. ft. of banquet facilities.

River Terrace Inn

1600 Soscol Avenue
Napa CA 94559
866.627.2386
www.riverterraceinn.com
106 guest rooms including 28 suites - $139-$339

An "upscale boutique hotel"on the Napa River. Complimentary high-speed Internet and Wi-Fi access, wine bar with tapas, pool, and all suites have whirlpool/hot tubs. A stop on the Downtown Trolley route and a close walk to the Wine Train station.

Robert Craig Wine Cellars Tasting Room

880 Vallejo Street Napa CA 94559
707.252.2250
www.robertcraigwine.com
Tasting $5/glass.
Open Thursday, Friday, Saturday and Monday.
DIRECTIONS: From downtown Napa take Main Street north to Vallejo Street. Turn right and continue two blocks east.

Although his wine is made elsewhere and comes from vineyards in such varied locations as Coombsville, Mt. Veeder, Howell Mountain and the Carneros, Robert Craig has opened a convenient tasting room just minutes from downtown Napa. Stop by to try his wines, or phone in advance for a barrel tasting.

Ruffino's

645 First Street Napa CA 94559
707.255.4455
Classical Northern Italian - Entrees $9.50 -
$18.95

The Ruffino family has been running the restaurant since 1942. Traditional dishes, including osso buco, cannaloni, calamari, seafood, steaks and pizza.

Saketini Asian Diner and Lounge

3900 Bel Aire Plaza, Suite B Napa CA 94558
707-255-RICE
Japanese, Chinese, Hawaiian - Entrees $5.95-
$14.95

In the Bel Aire Plaza, located at the north end of Napa at the corner of Highway 29 and Trancas Street.

Delicious and reasonably priced dishes with an Asian flair. A favorite of locals (it's also got a great bar and DJ/live music dancing) and not yet discovered by visitors because of its out-of-the-way location. Our favorites include The Return of Tod's Black 'n' Blue Tuna Tataki with Hot Mustard Sauce, and Ginger Soy Grilled Hibachi Style Salmon with Ponsu Sauce.

Seguin Moreau Napa Cooperage

151 Camino Dorado Napa CA 94558
707.252.3408
www.seguin-moreau.fr
Small charge for tour. Just off Highway 29 south of Napa. Call for directions.

How many places can you actually watch wine barrels being made? A fascinating part of the wine business that most visitors miss. A wonderful educational experience for kids as they watch skilled coopers plying their art in nearly the same fashion as their ancestors have for hundreds of years. Yes, kids, people still do this. And isn't that neat the way they build a fire inside the barrel to "toast" it?

Shackford's Kitchen Store and More

1350 Main Street Napa CA 94559
707.226.2132
Open Monday through Saturday, 9:30 a.m. to 5:30 p.m.

Complete collection of cookware and cutlery, kitchen accessories, baskets and gifts, canning and candymaking tools. This place is absolutely loaded with kitchen stuff. We always walk out with something, generally more than we came in for. It's the kind of place every town used to have. Napa still has one. The staff is friendly and knowledgeable and its prices are competitive with factory outlet stores. What more could you ask?

Skyline Wilderness Park

2210 Imola Avenue Napa CA
707.252.0481
www.skylinepark.org
Hours: Monday-Thursday 9 a.m. to dark Friday-Sunday 8 a.m. to dark

Skyline Park is an 850-acre wilderness area, totally operated by volunteers. It has over 25 miles of trails for hiking, biking and equestrian use. (If you're put off by the occasional horse droppings, keep in mind that it was the horse people that saved the park.)

The two-and-a-half mile main trail leads to Lake Marie at the eastern end. There's also an alternate route along the ridge trail that is a much better workout, but is not for those out of shape. From this trail on a clear day you can see San Francisco Bay, Mr. Tamalpais and Mr. Diablo. Beautiful.

Skyline also offers picnic and barbecue areas, an RV park, and tent camping. Daily visitor's fee is $4.00 per vehicle, RV camping is $14.00, and tent sites are $8.00. The best place to hike in Napa.

TRAILS

Buckeye

Horizontal trail length 2.27 miles, terrain distance 2.29 miles.

From access road, elevation 208 ft, a smooth gradual climb to 631 ft over a terrain distance of .68 miles, average grade 13%.

Continuing, covers a terrain distance of .98 miles and rises to 688 ft with an average grade of 7%.

Trail ends at the junction of Skyline Trail at a distance of .61 miles, rises to 857 ft with several ups and downs with an average grade of 14%.

Skyline and Lower Skyline

Skyline. Horizontal trail length 3.34 miles, terrain distance 3.37 miles.

From access road elevation 239 ft, a brisk climb to 776 ft over a terrain distance .63 miles, average grade 16%.

Continuing to end, rises to 1010 ft, several ups and downs.

Lower Skyline. Horizontal distance .89 miles to junction, terrain distance .9 miles.

From access road, elevation 231 ft, a smooth gradual climb to 781 ft at the junction of Skyline, average grade 13%.

Chaparral

Horizontal trail distance is .46 miles, terrain distance is .47 miles.

From the junction of Skyline at the east end of Lake Marie, elevation of 861 ft., trail drops and rises for .15 miles to an elevation of 893 ft.

Continues for a distance .03 miles, rises to 951 ft, average grade 24%.

Continues for a distance .16 miles, several ups and downs, average grade 19%.

Ends at Marie Creek Trail, a distance .08 miles, gradual drop average grade 15%.

Bay Leaf

Horizontal and terrain distance .61 miles.

From the junction of Skyline to the junction of Lake Marie Road, trail drops 323 ft, average grade 10%. At one point near the top, the grade is severe at 27%.

Lake Marie Road

Road begins at the Kiosk and ends at Lake Marie, distance of 2.32 miles.

Gradual rise from trail head elevation of 138 ft. to the lake, 2 miles, elevation 819 ft, average grade 7%.

Toyon (Hikers Only)

Trail begins at the Bikers Bypass of Manzanita Trail, elevation 465 ft. trail distance .44 miles.

Drops to elevation 389 ft at .2 miles at a 10% grade.

Rises to 449 ft. where it rejoins Manzanita Trail, .38 miles at a 7% grade.

Toyon Creek (Hikers only)

Junction along Toyon Trail, elevation 389 ft. trail distance .23 miles.

Drops to creek .03 miles at 22% grade, travel along creek and rises back to rejoin Toyon elevation 370 ft., .17 miles 7% grade.

Marie Creek (Lower Marie Creek, Hikers only north of Fig Tree)

Horizontal distance 1.65 miles. Begin at Marie Creek Road, elevation 364 ft. Gentle rise to point for 1.13 miles to elevation 587 ft., 6% grade. Continue to peak, .28 miles, smooth rise to elevation 844 ft, 20% grade. Continuing down and up, .2 miles at an average grade of 11%. Flat to end, junction Chaparral.

Hikers Bypass, Marie Creek

Horizontal distance of .31 miles. Begin at elevation 584 ft. steady rise to rejoin Marie Creek, elevation 800 ft. Average grade 14%.

Manzanita

Horizontal distance 1.31 miles, terrain distance 1.32 miles.

Begin at access road near Disc Golf course at an elevation of 201 ft., drops to 162 ft then climbs to 465 ft to Bikers Bypass at a grade of 14%.

Continuing, climbs at 24% grade to peak then down at 20% grade. Continuing, rises at an average of 8% then drops at an average of 10%, to flat.

Bikers Bypass

Horizontal distance of .14 miles.

Rim Rock (Suggest Hikers only)

Horizontal distance 2.29 miles, terrain distance of 2.33 miles. Steady climb 1.67 miles from the junction of Marie Creek and Manzanita trails to an elevation 1630 ft at the top, average grade of 14%. Trail drops to 947 ft in a distance of .65 miles, average grade of 20% to trail end at the junction of Skyline Trail.

Napa Valley Trail Rides offers guided horseback rides on Skyline Park's trails. See their listing above in this Napa section.

Sweet Finale

1146 Main Street, Napa CA 94559
707.224.2444 Fax: 707.224.7124
www.sweetfinale.com

A bakery specializing in cakes and pastries, offering classical European pastries and traditional American desserts. Looking for something really different? How about their pyramid cake with chocolate hieroglyphs? Or maybe their banana-macadamia nut Napoleon with a warm caramelized pineapple and kumquat compote. Take them home or enjoy them with coffee at the shop. Open until 8 p.m. Fridays and Saturdays.

Sweetie Pies

520 Main Street, Napa CA 94559
707.257.8817
www.sweetiepies.com

A bakery located at the Hatt Mill that offers light lunches, coffee, breads and individual

desserts as well as specialty cakes, breakfast pastries and cookies. Also beer and wine.

Taco Trucks

Along Soscol Avenue between First Street and Lincoln Avenue in Napa
Mexican - $1.25 and up

In the afternoon and early evening you'll find trucks with kitchens and serving windows parked along both sides of Soscol Avenue. These independently-owned mobile restaurants cook and sell Mexican food such as tacos, quesadillas and burritos. Customers sit on the grass along the sidewalk, eat in their cars or take their meals home. It's tasty, home-made fast food at a very reasonable price.

Trader Joe's

3654 Bel Aire Plaza, Napa CA 94558
www.traderjoes.com
Located just off Trancas Street at Highway 29. Turn east on Trancas and take the first left into the shopping center.

A chain of nearly 200 stores located throughout the United States. Trader Joe's offers food (fresh and packaged—much of it organic and/or vegetarian) and beverages, including spirits and wines. Their selection includes specialty and imported items, and prices on everything are exceptionally low.

Trader Joe's has built a fanatic following of customers, and the public clamor (including letters to the editor) for a TJ's in the Napa Valley took on near-cargo cult dimensions. The pleas were successful.

Tulocay Cemetery

411 Coombsville Road Napa CA 94558
707.252.4727
www.tulocaycemetery.org
Open 8 a.m. to sundown

Napa's historic cemetery, 50 acres established on land deeded in 1858 by Don Cayetano Juarez from his 8,800-acre Rancho Tulocay. Juarez was himself buried there in 1883. Another inhabitant of the cemetery is Lilburn Williams Boggs, who was born in Kentucky in 1796, married Daniel Boone's granddaughter, and was governor of Missouri from 1836 to 1840. Also interred there are Nathan Coombs, who founded the city of Napa in 1848, and Mary Ellen Pleasant, known as the "mother of the civil rights movement in California" and (to her intense dislike) as "Mammy Pleasant." For more on Pleasant, see the *Napa Valley Trivia* section.

Tuscany

1005 First Street (corner of Main)
Napa CA 94558
707.258.1000
Northern Italian - Entrees $10-$30

A very popular place whose food is exceeded by its ambiance. At the corner of First and Main in downtown Napa. Open windows so you can watch the passers-by.

Uptown Theater

1350 Third St. Napa CA 94559
707.256.0150
www.napauptown.com

The Uptown has been under renovation for several years and its reopening date is not certain. The theater originally opened in 1937. Over the years it was divided into two theaters and eventually into four. In the 1980s and 1990s, several different owners tried to compete with the chain-owned multiplex in town by focusing on independent and art films.

Local businessman Robert Vogt and his wife Teresa worked long and hard on improvements to the theater, founding the non-profit Napa Valley Film Society and gaining wide community support because of the quality of films they presented. Eventually the Vogts, along with fellow investors Tim Herman and Tom Bird, partnered with landlord (for much of downtown Napa) George Altamura and Rutherford resident Francis Ford Coppola to totally restore the art deco theater to its former glory, relying on Coppola's access to outstanding artisans, designers and technicians. Margrit Mondavi, a patron of the newly restored Napa Valley Opera House, and prime mover behind the long-time summer music series at Robert Mondavi Winery, also joined in on the theater's restoration.

The Uptown will now hold 1000 people in one big-screen theater furnished with plush French-made theater seats. Murals on walls and ceiling are being painstakingly restored, and an authentically restored marquee is now in place outside the theater. The goal is to present high quality live entertainment as well as special movies and satellite broadcasts. Other possible events include a Napa Valley film festival and ongoing arts and lecture series.

Uva Trattoria Italiana

1040 Clinton Napa CA 94558
707.255.6646
Northern Italian - Entrees $6-$16.50

A comfortable and tasty northern Italian restaurant. A very short walk from downtown Napa's main street. Half portions of pasta are available, which is a great idea that we'd like to see other restaurants offer.

Vallerga's Market

3385 Solano Avenue Napa CA 94558
707.253.2621
www.vallergas.com

An excellent supermarket. Outstanding gourmet foods and Napa Valley food products, perfect for picnic lunches. Vallerga's is also at two other location in Napa (Silverado Trail at First—just a block from Copia—and Imola Avenue just off Highway 29), but this store just off Highway 29 at Redwood Road is the one you're most likely to be near if you're headed upvalley.

Villa Corona

3614 Bel Aire Plaza   Napa CA 94558
707.257.8685
Mexican – Entrees $3.95-$10.25

Our favorite Mexican restaurant. A small place in a shopping center (the same one where Trader Joe's is located) that's a little hard to find, but worth the effort. They're at the southeast corner, off the alley. A few tables inside, and more outside overlooking the parking. People go there for the food, not the ambiance.

Great Mexican cooking with everything from chile rellenos, burritos and chimichangas to enchiladas, flautas, and the T's—tacos, tamales and tostadas. Beer is available but if you're going to eat outside, tell them and they'll pour it in a paper cup. They don't take checks, but cash and plastic work fine. Closed Mondays. They also have a location in St. Helena.

Villa Romano

1011 Soscol Ferry Road, Napa CA 94558
707.252.4533
www.villaromanorestaurant.com
Northern Italian – Entrees $15-$21

DIRECTIONS: Located near the divide of Highway 29 and Highway 121 south of Napa. At the traffic light at the divide, make an immediate left onto Soscol Ferry Road, which is the southern extension of Soscol Road. See the web site for a map.

The two-story restaurant was built as a stagecoach stop in 1855. It offers an extensive selection of appetizers, salads and pastas, and entrees such as Scallopine, Osso Bucco and Misto Griglio—grilled King Salmon, prawns and Ahi tuna served over linguini. A comfortable place for dining by candlelight and fireplace.

Vineyard Outlet

649 Factory Stores Drive
Napa CA 94559
707.252.4000
www.vineyardoutlet.com

Located at the factory outlets on the west side of Highway 29 off the First Street Exit. Owners Erica Valentine and Michael Mittleman offer "wine without attitude". Discounted wines by the bottle or case, wine accessories, specialty food products, and books and tour information. Wines are from the Napa Valley, California, the U.S. and worldwide, and include hard-to-find wines. Sample some of these wines at their tasting bar.

They also offer "guided" tastings, where you can learn the process of tasting, and how to distinguish various grape varieties and their colors, aromas, tastes and possible defects, as well as other good and bad qualities found in wine. Call for times.

Vintner's Collective

1245 Main Street Napa CA 94559
707.255.7150 Fax: 707.255.7159
www.vintnerscollective.com

A co-op tasting room representing ten Napa Valley boutique wineries. This is the only place in the valley you can sample these excellent wines. Wineries include D Cubed Cellars, Elan Vineyards, Frazier Winery, Judd's Hill, Mason Cellars, Melka Wines, Mi Sueño Cellars, Patz & Hall, Strata Vineyards and Vinoce Vineyards. The Collective also offers additional "guest wineries" on Saturdays.

Wine Plane

PO Box 4074 Napa CA 94558 707.747.5533
888.779.6600
www.wineplane.com
$89-$199

Fly over the wine country and see views, including canyons, lakes and palatial estates, that you'll never see from the roads. Flights every day, by reservation.

Wine Valley Lodge

200 South Coombs Street Napa CA 94558
707.224.7911
www.winevalleylodge.com
55 rooms $99 - $165

One-story motel at the south end of Napa a few minutes' drive from downtown. Frommer's travel guide says: "Dollar for dollar, the Wine Valley Lodge offers the most for your vacation budget in the entire wine country." If Elvis Presley, Marilyn

Monroe and Rock Hudson could stay here, why not you?

Wineries of Napa Valley

1285 Napa Town Center Napa CA 94559
707.253.9451 800.328.7815
www.napavintages.com

Open daily with sales, tasting and concierge services located right next to the Visitors Center in downtown Napa. Wines from Baldacci Family Vineyards, Burgess Cellars, Edgewood Estate Winery, Girard Winery, Goosecross Cellars, Reid Family Vineyards and Zahtila Vineyards.

Zinsvalley Restaurant

3253 Browns Valley Road Napa CA 94558
707.224.0695
www.zinsvalley.com
American/California - Entrees $13.50-$17

DIRECTIONS: From downtown Napa take First Street west over Highway 29, go 1.3 miles and turn left into the Browns Valley Shopping Center.

Lunches served Wednesday, Thursday and Friday, dinners Monday through Saturday.

Out of the way and unknown to most tourists, Zinsvalley is a local favorite. Friendly service, good food, and a relaxing creekside patio for dining. One of the nicest places for outside dining in the valley. (You can dine indoors, too.) No corkage fee.

ZuZu

829 Main Street Napa CA 94559
707.224.8555
www.zuzunapa.com
Spanish Tapas - Plates $3-$8 each.

Located across the street from Veterans' Park and the Napa River, ZuZu has been packing them in since the day it opened. (The *San Francisco Chronicle* gave it the most amazing review we've ever seen in that paper.) They don't take reservations, so be prepared to wait.

ZuZu serves Spanish "tapas," the little mini-dishes that come in both cold (*tapas frias*) and warm (*tapas calientes*). Enjoy

them with a glass of sherry. Our consistent favorites are the Flat-Iron Steak and the Mexican Corn Soup, but there are always new, wonderful surprises. Excellent, friendly service, a lively atmosphere, and wonderfully tasty food. In fact, we get more excited about the food each time we go there. It's delicious.

Yountville

In 1831, George Yount, the first American settler in the Napa Valley, came to the area now called Yountville. He received an 11,000-acre Mexican Land grant and built the first structures in the area, a Kentucky blockhouse and mill. Even more importantly, he planted the first grapevines in the Napa Valley.

In 1855 Yount hired a surveyor to lay out a town site and named it "Sebastopol", ignoring the fact that a town in neighboring Sonoma County already had that same. In 1865, two years after death, the town was renamed in his honor. His grave can be found in Pioneer Cemetery, next to Yountville Park at the north end of town.

When Yountville incorporated, it wanted to be called a "village." The State of California didn't allow for villages, so Yountville had to refer to itself as a town. It still feels like a village, with a population of approximately 3,500, which includes 1,100 residents of the Veterans Home of California.

Yountville is a walking town filled with excellent shops, restaurants, and lodging. Spend some time here. You'll enjoy it. Oh, yes, and it does happen to have a whole bunch of really good restaurants.

Bistro Jeanty

6510 Washington Street
Yountville CA 94599
707.944.0103
www.bistrojeanty.com
French Bistro - Entrees $15-$25

Chef Philippe Jeanty, former long-time chef at Domaine Chandon, has created an authentic French bistro. A very popular place. Open till 10:30 p.m.

Bouchon

6534 Washington Street
Yountville, CA 94599
707.944.8037
French Bistro - Entrees $15-$25

Another traditional French bistro, this one owned by Thomas and Joseph Keller. Thomas owns the renowned *French Laundry* just down the street.

Bouchon Bakery

6528 Washington Street Yountville CA 94599
707.944.2253
www.bouchonbakery.com

Adjacent to Bouchon restaurant and also owned by the Keller brothers. Supplies breads and pastries to both Bouchon and French Laundry restaurants, as well as to the public. One of our favorites (we have many) is their namesake Chocolate Bouchon.

Brix

7377 St. Helena Highway
Yountville, CA 94599
707.944.2749 Fax: 707.944.8320
www.brix.com
Wine Country - Entrees $16-$32

One of the Napa Valley's nicest restaurants, with excellent food and service and a very comfortable atmosphere. Absolutely one of our favorites.

Compadres Bar & Grill

6539 Washington Street
Yountville CA 94599
707.944.2406 Fax: 707.944.8407
California-Mexican - Entrees $10-$19

Located between Vintage 1870 and the Vintage Inn.

Indoor and outdoor seating. Reservations not required. Award-winning Cal-Mex cuisine, with traditional and not-so-traditional favorites complemented by an array of grilled items, including fajitas, carnitas and pollo borracho, as well as fresh fish Vera Cruz style. Very casual, great for families and large parties. Sample from their "Wall of Fire"—over 50 hot sauces, or try one of the 50 tequilas at the bar. No corkage fees, but who cares when the margaritas are so good?

Cosentino Winery

7415 St. Helena Highway Yountville CA 94599
707.944.1220
www.cosentinowinery.com

Open daily for tasting. Located just north of Mustard's Grill. More than 30 wines, including Cabernet Sauvignon, Cabernet Franc, Pinot Noir, Zinfandel, Merlot, Meritage, Port, Sauvignon Blanc, Chardonnay, Viognier, Semillon, Gewürztraminer, Pinot Grigio.

Cucina à la Carte

6525 Washington Street
Yountville CA 94599
707.944.1600
www.cucinaalacarte.com

A "Franco-Italian" delicatessen and bakery. Outdoor tables. On the grounds of Vintage 1870.

Domaine Chandon Winery & Restaurant

1 California Drive Yountville CA 94599
707.944.2280
www.chandon.com
French-inspired California - Entrees $18-$29
Restaurant hours vary depending on season and day of the week. Call for current information.
DIRECTIONS: West side of Highway 29 (at Yountville). Take the Veterans Home exit. Cross railroad track and turn right into Domaine Chandon.

Domaine Chandon is owned by Moët et Chandon, and its sparkling wines are superb. It also offers an excellent tour, giving you a chance to see how sparkling wine is made, which is a quite different process from the "still" wines made in most other Napa Valley wineries (although Chandon is starting to produce some still wines).

Domaine Chandon's restaurant is one of the most outstanding in the valley. The food, presentation, service and views are superb. Unless you're very lucky, you'll need reservations well in advance.

French Laundry Restaurant

6640 Washington Yountville CA 94599
707.944.2380
www.frenchlaundry.com
French Laundryish - $105 prix fixe

Reservations are made 60 days in advance, but once in a while they actually get a cancellation and the vacancy could be yours. Reservations got even harder when Chef Thomas Keller was named the top chef in America by the James Beard Foundation.

Then the *New York Times* called the Laundry the "most exciting restaurant in the United States." In 2002 Keller was named the first-ever World Master of Culinary Arts, competing against top chefs from all over the world. And to top it off, in 2003 Restaurant Magazine in the U.K., after a poll of 300 chefs and food critics around the world, declared the Laundry the "best restaurant in the world."

The French Laundry is a fixed-price restaurant, and that price most recently was $105.

Goosecross Cellars

119 State Lane (off Yountville Cross Road)
Yountville CA 94599
707.944.1986   800.276.9210
www.goosecross.com

Open daily by appointment. Small family-owned winery producing Chardonnay, Sauvignon Blanc, Merlot, Syrah, Zinfandel, Cabernet Sauvignon, Viognier. You can even pick up some of their Chardonnay smoked wild Alaska salmon.

Goosecross also offers an excellent "Wine Crash Course", a 90-minute wine class held every Saturday morning September

through November. In this free class you'll learn about tasting techniques, the structure and components of wine, winemaking styles, wine jargon, serving and storing wine and much more. We took the class and enjoyed it a lot. Contact the winery for reservations.

Gordon's Café and Wine Bar

6770 Washington Street
Yountville, CA 94599
707.944.8246
California - Entrees $6.55-$11.95
Friday night Prix fixe 3-course dinner $45

A local hangout for breakfast and lunch. Delicious, organic, fresh, locally grown foods. Dinners served every Friday evening.

Havens Wine Cellars

2055 Hoffman Lane
Yountville CA 94558
707.945.0921
www.havenswine.com

A small family (actually two families) winery run by a close-knit group of friends who have been producing award-winning wines since 1984. Their Carneros Syrah is exceptional. They're the only winery in the valley to produce an Albariño, grown from that unique white grape originally from Spain and Portugal. Tastings and tours are by appointment, and the winery is open for retail sales throughout the week.

Hurley's Restaurant

6518 Washington Street
Yountville CA 94599
707.944.2345
www.hurleysrestaurant.com
Wine Country - Entrees $12-$23

Bob Hurley is one of Yountville's favorite chefs—and that's saying a lot in a town with so many outstanding restaurants. Formerly at the Napa Valley Grille, he now has his own place across the street from Vintage 1870. Hurley serves fresh seasonal wine country food with a Mediterranean flair. Fun and casual with outdoor dining in the patio.

Mustard's Grill

7399 St. Helena Highway (Highway 29)
Yountville CA 94599
707.944.2424
www.mustardsgrill.com
Wine Country - Entrees $10-$27

One of the most popular restaurants in the Napa Valley and one of the pioneers of California Cuisine. And one of the best. If you try the Mongolian pork chops, you might end up asking for them every time. However, if it's within your price range, try the filet mignon; it's pure manna from heaven and simply melts in your mouth.

Mustard's prides itself on its outrageously comprehensive wine list (nearly 400 wines at last count) and the highly professional staff is well educated and able to advise you on an appropriate wine for your meal. Mustard's is truly a dining experience.

Napa River Ecological Reserve

East of Yountville on the north side of Yountville Cross Road between Highway 29 and the Silverado Trail.

The 73-acre habitat of riparian forest and meadows is a remnant of the riparian habitat that once existed all along the Napa River. The land is managed by the California Department of Fish and Game.

On both sides of the river are large meadows, which are sometimes flooded in winter. The meadows are a favorite place for deer to browse and a home to California quail and many species of finches and sparrows, including Lincoln's sparrow.

The interior forested area is a haven for birds, including breeding, wintering and migrating species. It is the most southerly point in Napa County where yellow-breasted chats breed. Wood ducks nest near the river, and varied thrushes and red-breasted sapsuckers winter here.

Willow flycatchers and s warbler species settle in for t ing on their migration routes. Acorn woodpeckers, scrub jays, white-breasted nuthatches, Anna's hummingbirds, and dozens of other species live here year-round. A total of 146 bird species have been sighted in the reserve, with 67 species known to nest here.

Other birds that can be seen here include cormorants, herons and egrets, Canada geese, golden eagles, falcons, great horned owls, and woodpeckers.

The reserve is also home to at least 40 different species of butterflies, including swallowtails, whites, sulphurs, coppers, hairstreaks, blues, brushfoots and skippers.

(Thanks to the Napa-Solano Audubon Society for the above information.)

Napa Valley Grille

6795 Washington Street (in Washington Square)
Yountville CA 94599
707.944.8686 Fax: 707.944.2870
Banquets: 707.944.8506
www.calcafe.com/napa_valley
Wine Country - Entrees $12.95-$25.95

The Grille, just off Highway 29 and Madison, is one of Yountville's and the valley's favorite places. Seasonal, ingredient-driven wine country cuisine with an emphasis on hard-to-find California wines. Outdoor dining with a great view of vineyards and hills, and a wide variety of seating choices, including a number of private dining rooms. Best of Award of Excellence 1997-2001 from Wine Spectator. Highly recommended.

Napa Valley Lodge

2230 Madison Street Yountville, CA 94599
707.944.2468 800.368.2468
www.napavalleylodge.com
55 rooms - $282-$595

Guest rooms and conference facilities at the north end of Yountville. Just across the street from Yountville Park and a comfortable walk to all shops and restaurants in town.

Napa Valley Museum

55 Presidents Circle (in the Veterans Home)
Yountville CA 94599
707.944.0500
www.napavalleymuseum.org
Open Wednesday - Monday from 10am to 5 pm. Adults $4.50, Students/Seniors $3.50, Ages 7-17 $2.50, Children under 4 Free.

DIRECTIONS: Take Yountville-Veterans Home exit off Highway 29, turn west onto California Drive. Follow the tree-lined drive to the stop sign and turn right.

The museum is devoted to the land, the people, and the art of the Napa Valley. A special permanent interactive exhibit is entitled: *California Wine: The Science of an Art.*

Pacific Blues

6525 Washington Street (Vintage 1870)
Yountville CA 94599
707.944.4455
www.pacificbluescafe.com
American - Entrees $9.00-$15.00

Open daily for breakfast, lunch and dinner. Blues, burgers and barbequed oysters. Great list of local wines and on-tap beers. Dining on the deck or inside. A local favorite.

Pére Jeanty

6772 Washington Street, Yountville CA 94599
707.945.1000
www.perejeanty.com
French Provençal Entrees $10-$25

The latest restaurant of Philippe Jeanty, who also owns Bistro Jeanty down the street in Yountville and Jeanty at Jacks in San Francisco. At the site of the former Frankie, Johnnie and Luigi Too restaurant. (And Mama Nina's, for those whose memories go way back.)

Piatti Ristorante

6480 Washington Yountville CA 94599
707.944.2070
www.piatti.com/yountville.shtml
Italian Country - Entrees $10-$18

A favorite of locals and visitors. A focus on light, moderately priced meals. Comfortable and enjoyable. Outdoor dining, too.

Ranch Market Too!

6498 Washington Street
Yountville CA 94599
707.944.2662.
www.ranchmarketsnapavalley.com

Open 6 a.m. to 10 p.m. daily. Delicatessen closes at 8 p.m.

Yountville's "supermarket." A great place to pick up a deli sandwich or Napa Valley products. Call ahead with your order to save time.

Veranda Club Spa

Washington Square, Yountville CA 94599
707.944.1906 Fax: 707.944.0766
www.verandaclubspa.com

Proprietor Wil Anderson has practiced and taught in Germany and Switzerland, and is a specialist in a variety of massage techniques, including the esoteric and remarkably effective deep body massage called *Chua Ka.*

This mini-day spa has no lodging, but it does offer massage, facials, body treatments and total fitness programs. It's one of those intimate little places that make the Napa Valley so special, and it's very popular with locals who want the personal attention that larger spas can't provide. If you're staying at one of the inns or B&Bs in Yountville, you can walk here in minutes. Spoil yourself. After all, you're on vacation.

Veterans Home of California, Yountville

Yountville CA 94599
707.944.4600
www.cdva.ca.gov/homes/yountville.asp
On California Drive west of Highway 29

The Veterans Home of California, Yountville opened in 1884. It's open to anyone from California who served in the military and currently has over 1400 residents—and a waiting list. The grounds are open to the public; feel free to wander around.

You also might want to visit the museum near the entrance. (The Napa Valley Museum is also located on the Vet's Home grounds.) The Napa Valley Symphony performs in the home's Lincoln Hall, and Fourth of July fireworks are held here every year. In fact, this is probably the most popular place in the valley for fireworks.

Villagio Inn & Spa

6481 Washington Street
Yountville CA 94599
707.944.8877 800.351.1133
www.villagio.com
112 rooms - $210-$950

From the same group that owns Vintage Inn. Nicely designed complex of buildings, vineyards, gardens, fountains and waterways. A very complete spa offering just about every kind of body care you can think of. It doesn't have its own restaurant, but Yountville's many restaurants are just a minute or two away.

Vintage Inn

6541 Washington Street
Yountville CA 94599
707.944.1112
www.vintageinn.com
80 rooms - $210-$485

A beautifully designed (by the same architect who did the spectacular *Ventana Inn* at Big Sur) and landscaped inn in the heart of Yountville. This used to be an old-growth vineyard with gnarly old vines just across

the street from an earlier home of the writer of this book. If the vineyard had to go—and there was no way of preventing it—there could be no better development to replace it than the Vintage Inn. An excellent place to stay and relax.

Vintage 1870

6525 Washington Street
Yountville CA 94599
707.944.2451 Fax: 707.944.2453
www.vintage1870.com
Hours: daily 10 am to 5:30 pm

Listed in the National Registry of Historic Places, Vintage 1870 was built as distillery and winery by Gottlieb Groezinger in 1870. Today it offers more than 30 specialty shops, restaurants and a picnic garden. One of our favorite shops is the *Toy Cellar*, for kids of all ages. Vintage 1870 is probably the most popular place for tourists to shop in the entire Napa Valley.

Vintage 1870 Wine Cellar

6525 Washington Street (in Vintage 1870),
Yountville Ca 94599
707.944.9070 800.946.3487
www.vintagewinecellar.com

A wine shop offering more than 800 wines with a tasting bar offering 12-15 wines each day.

Wine Garden Food and Wine Bar

6476 Washington Street
Yountville CA 94599

As yet unnamed. To be opened on the site of the legendary *Diner*, which has now passed into history.

Yountville Inn

6462 Washington Street Yountville CA 94599
707.944.5600 808.972.2293
www.yountvilleinn.com
41 rooms - $150-$325

A new, nicely appointed inn at the south entrance to Yountville. A short walk to all Yountville shops and restaurants.

Yountville Park

On Washington Street at the north end of Yountville just across the street from the Napa Valley Lodge.

A very popular place for picnics and one of the best parks around for kids, boasting a unique assortment of play equipment. Across the street from the park is Pioneer Cemetery and the grave of George Yount, first settler in the valley and the founder of Yountville. When Yount first saw the valley in 1831, he said: "In such a place I would like to live and die." He did, dying in 1865.

Oakville

An unincorporated area with a great little post office. Famous for its grocery store and surrounding wineries.

Cardinale Winery

7585 St. Helena Highway   Oakville CA 94562
707.944.2807
www.cardinale.com

Tours and tastings by appointment only. Originally the site of Pepi Winery, now owned by Kendall-Jackson and producing wines from their estate vineyards on the valley floor, as well as from the slopes of Mt. Veeder and Howell Mountain.

Far Niente Winery

P.O. Box 327
Oakville CA 94562
707.944.2861
www.farniente.com

Far Niente was founded in 1885 by John Benson, a Gold Rush arrival in California and uncle of the famed painter Winslow Homer. The building was designed by Hamden McIntyre, the architect for Greystone, the former Christian Brothers Winery in St. Helena now occupied by the Culinary Institute of America. Far Niente closed during prohibition, was restored in 1979 by Gil Nickel, and is now on the National Register of Historic Places.

The winery has 13 acres of landscaped gardens and 40,000 square feet of wine caves. It also houses an extensive collection of automobiles and vintage BMW motorcycles, including a 1966 Ferrari 500 Superfast, a 1935 Bentley 3.5 liter Sports Saloon, and a 1951 Ferrari 340 America. The winery produces award-winning Chardonnay and Cabernet Sauvignon. Tours are now available by appointment.

Napa Cellars

7481 St. Helena Highway   Oakville CA 94562
707.944.2565   800.535.6400
www.napacellars.com

Open daily for tasting. Chardonnay, Merlot, Zinfandel, Late Harvest Zinfandel, Syrah, Cabernet Sauvignon.

Napa Wine Company

PO Box 434 7840 St. Helena Highway
Oakville CA 94562
707.944.1710 800.848.9630
www.napawinecompany.com

Tastings by appointment of wines from more than 15 different wineries, all custom crushed at these same facilities. Tastings include Napa Wine Company's own brands, all made from organic grapes, as well wines from Crocker & Starr, Del Bondio, Downing Family Vineyards, Fife, Joel Gott, La Sirena, Lamborn, Larkmead, Larraine, Madrigal, Mason, Marilyn Merlot, Pahlmeyer, Napa Wine Company, Oakford, Pavi, Michael Pozzan, Showket, Tria and Vinum.

Nest

7787 St. Helena Highway (Highway 29)
Oakville CA 94562
707.944.0206 Fax 707.944.1207
Delicatessen - Sandwiches $6-7

Nest is a café, delicatessen and catering service located on the Oakville Grade just off Highway 29. Formerly the site of the very popular Pometta's Delicatessen, Nest is operated by a mother-daughter team, Mardi and Katie Schma (rhymes with "may"). Nest offers breakfasts, lunch entrees, sandwiches, salads, desserts (a large variety of cakes, pies, cookies and other tasty morsels), and a variety of exotic sodas and juices. Enjoy your meal outside where you can look at the the hills, the vineyards, and, if your timing is good, the Wine Train as it rolls by.

Nickel and Nickel

8164 St. Helena Highway
Oakville CA 94562
707.944.0693
www.nickelandnickel.com

Tours and tastings by appointment only. Founded by Gil Nickel, owner of Far Niente Winery, and his nephew Erik. 100% varietal, single-vineyard wines. Chardonnay, Cabernet Sauvignon, Merlot and Zinfandel.

Oakville Grocery

7856 Saint Helena Highway (Highway 29)
Oakville CA 94562
707.944.8802 Fax: 707.9044.1844
www.oakvillegrocery.com

The Grocery's building opened as a general store in 1880 and it's in the National Registry of Historic Places. The Grocery has been featured on national TV shows and in major food and wine publications as one of the best specialty food stores in the country. Grocery, charcuterie, fresh foods, cheese, olives, gift baskets, wines, espresso, baked goods, sandwiches, box lunches, picnics to go and they'll ship anywhere.

The Oakville Grocery—the first gourmet specialty shop in the valley, and still the most popular.

Opus One Winery

7900 St. Helena Highway   Oakville CA 94562
707.944.9442
www.opusonewinery.com

Tours and tastings by appointment only. Tours are free but there is a $25 charge for tasting. Founded in 1979, Opus One is a joint venture between Robert Mondavi and Baroness Philippine de Rothschild.

Robert Mondavi Winery

7801 St. Helena Highway (Highway 29)
Oakville CA 94562
888.766.6328
www.robertmondaviwinery.com
On the west side of Highway 29, just 1/2 mile north of Oakville.

Robert Mondavi Winery in Oakville. Photo courtesy of the winery.

The place that rekindled the Napa Valley wine industry. Opened in 1967, it was only the second winery built in the valley after Prohibition (that weird "experiment" when Americans decided they didn't want to let themselves drink alcohol). Founder Robert Mondavi has a well deserved reputation as a wine-making icon, and his public relations efforts have benefited every winery and person in the valley.

Visitors to Mondavi can find beautiful Spanish-mission style architecture, excellent tours, wonderful wines, frequent art shows and the winery's famous annual *Mondavi Summer Music Festival.*

If you've never before visited the valley, this is a must stop. Even if you're a frequent visitor, you'll want to stop by again and

autiful Beniamino
ncis at the main

St. Francis of Assisi—by sculptor Beniamino
Bufano. On display at Robert Mondavi Winery.
Photo courtesy of the winery.

Silver Oak Cellars

915 Oakville Cross Road Oakville CA 94562
800.273.8809
www.silveroak.com

On the Oakville Cross Road between Highway
29 and the Silverado Trail. Open Monday
through Saturday from 9 a.m. to 4 p.m.; tastings are $10 and include a logo glass. Tours
Monday through Friday at 1:30 p.m., for which
reservations are recommended.

Founded in 1971 and producing only a very
highly regarded Cabernet Sauvignon.

Turnbull Wine Cellars

8210 St. Helena Highway   Oakville CA 94562
800.887.6285
www.turnbullwines.com

Tours and tastings by appointment only.
Focuses on Cabernet Sauvignon, but also
produces Merlot, Sangiovese, Zinfandel,
Syrah and Sauvignon Blanc.

Rutherford

Another unincorporated town best known
for its two major wineries on Highway 29
- Beaulieu and Niebaum-Coppola (formerly Inglenook).

Beaulieu Vineyard

1960 St. Helena Highway (Highway 29)
Rutherford, CA 94573
707.967.5200
www.bv-wine.com

Tours daily. Complimentary wine taste at
entrance.. Charge for others.

Historic redwood tanks at Beaulieu Vineyard.
Photo courtesy of the winery.

For many locals and wine aficionados, Napa
Valley wineries can be divided into two categories: Beaulieu Vineyard, and all the others. BV was winning awards worldwide
when most other current Napa Valley vineyards were still planted with prunes. The
winery was founded in 1900 by Georges de
Latour and survived Prohibition by producing sacramental wines. BV's wines have
been served by every president of the
United States since Franklin Roosevelt.

A beautiful visitor's center offers outstanding complimentary wines and tours by
friendly, very knowledgeable guides. The
redwood vats and aging areas smell like a
winery is supposed to smell—musky,
winey, and absolutely enticing. A must for
your first visit to the valley. And a great

"let's just stop in for a glass or two" for repeat visits.

Cakebread Cellars

8300 St. Helena Highway
Rutherford CA 94573
800.588.0298
www.cakebread.com

Open daily for tasting, tours by appointment.
Sauvignon Blanc, Chardonnay, Pinot Noir,
Merlot, Cabernet Sauvignon.

Frog's Leap Winery

8815 Conn Creek Road Rutherford CA 94573
707.963.4704   800.959.4704
www.frogsleap.com

Tours and tastings by appointment only Monday through Saturday. The Red Barn was originally built in 1884 as Adamson Winery and renovated in 1994 by Frog's Leap. The winery's name comes from its earlier location at what used to be a commercial frog farm, and founder John Williams' connection with Stag's Leap Wine Cellars. The winery's motto is "Time's Fun When You're Having Flies." Organically and biodynamically grown grapes. Sauvignon Blanc, Cabernet Sauvignon, Merlot, Zinfandel, Chardonnay, Syrah, Leapfrögmilch (Riesling/Chardonnay).

Grgich Hills Cellar

1829 St. Helena Highway (Hwy 29)
Rutherford CA 94573
707.963.2784
www.grgich.com

Daily 9:30 a.m. to 4:30 p.m. Tours by appointment

Miljenko "Mike" Grgich made the Chateau Montelena Chardonnay that won the legendary Paris tasting in 1976. His wines have gotten even better since then. Mike's also involved in establishing a winery in his native Croatia.

La Toque

1140 Rutherford Cross Road
Rutherford CA 94573
707.963.9770
www.latoque.com
Wine Country French - $72 Prix-fixe

A fixed-price French restaurant at the Rancho Caymus Inn with a high reputation.

Wine Spectator magazine called it the "quintessential wine country restaurant" and one of the top 20 in the United States. It's a place where you'll spend the entire evening, and love every minute of it.

Napa Valley Grapevine Wreath Company

PO Box 67 Rutherford CA 94573
707.963.8893 Fax: 707.963.3325
Open 10:30 to 5:30 daily except Tuesday.

Every year after harvest, the Wood Family collects pruned cuttings from Cabernet Sauvignon grapevines and weaves them into wreaths, baskets and other useful and decorative shapes. They're a favorite with visitors and can be found at their store on the Rutherford Cross Road just off the Silverado Trail.

Niebaum-Coppola Winery

1991 St. Helena Highway
Rutherford CA 94573
707.963.9099
www.niebaum-coppola.com
Open daily, tours by appointment.

In 1995, owner Francis Ford Coppola (director of *The Godfather* and *Apocalypse Now*) and his wife Eleanor expanded their wine estate with purchase of the former Inglenook Winery, which dates back to 1879. The chateau and grounds include a museum of wine and film. A visit gives you both excellent wine and the opportunity to see Oscars won by Coppola, a Tucker automobile from his movie *Tucker*, the boat from *Apocalypse Now*, photos and other memorabilia.

Oscar-winning movie director Francis Ford Coppola and his wife Eleanor own what is now called Niebaum-Coppola Winery. Photo courtesy of the winery.

Peju Province

8466 St. Helena Highway
Rutherford CA 94573
707.963.3600   800.446.7358
www.peju.com

Open daily for tours and tastings. Chardonnay, Sauvignon Blanc, Cabernet Sauvignon, Cabernet Franc, Merlot, Syrah, Late Harvest Chardonnay.

Provenance Vineyards

PO Box 668 Rutherford CA 94573
707.968.3633
www.provenancevineyards.com

Open daily for tastings. Cabernet Sauvignon and Merlot. Winemaker and general manager Tom Rinaldi was winemaker at Duckhorn Vineyards for 22 years.

Rancho Caymus Inn

1140 Rutherford Cross Road
Rutherford, CA 94573
707.963.1777 800.845.1777
www.ranchocaymus.com
26 rooms - $205-$375

Spanish California-style inn whose owners also own Flora Springs Winery. Rooms feature spacious hand-carved walnut beds, wrought iron lamps and distinctive handmade furnishings. Ceiling beams are 100-year-old oak, while the timbers that make up the room's surroundings are black walnut, fir, and redwood. Each suite offers soft wool rugs, hand dyed and woven by the Salazaca and Otavalon Indians of Ecuador. Sink basins are unique hand-thrown stoneware. The excellent *La Toque* restaurant is located here.

Rutherford Gardens

1796 South St. Helena Highway
St. Helena 94574
877.627.2645
www.longmeadowranch.com

Open Thursday through Sunday from 11 a.m. to 5 p.m. when produce is available.

DIRECTIONS: Located on the east side of Highway 29 across the street from grgich-hill cellar, just north of Rutherford.

The property has been producing vegetables at least since the 1930s. This 5.8-acre property was recently acquired by Long Meadow Ranch, renowned for its organic produce and other foods, including olive oil, wines and Scottish Highland cattle. The roadside stand currently offers a wide variety of heirloom tomatoes, sunflowers, basil, melons, figs and sweet corn. In the fall, visitors can pick a potential jack-o'-lantern from over 2.5 acres of pumpkins.

Rutherford Grill

1180 Rutherford Road Rutherford CA
707.963.1792
American Grill - Entrees $9-$26

A fun, but often very noisy place. Excellent and varied menu suitable for both kids and adults. And with all the noise, nobody's going to care about a little kid noise. Right next to Beaulieu Vineyard, so you can sip great wine before lunch or after. Outdoor dining. No corkage fee.

St. Helena Olive Oil Company

PO Box 389 8576 St. Helena Highway
Rutherford CA 94573
800.939.9880
www.sholiveoil.com

Located at the corner of Highway 29 and
Rutherford Cross Road, the store sells extra
virgin olive oil, vinegars and a variety of
other foods and kitchen/culinary paraphernalia.

Sawyer Cellars

8350 St. Helena Highway
Rutherford CA 94573
707.963.1980
www.sawyercellars.com

Open daily for tours and tasting. Tram
tours of the vineyard May through
November. Cabernet Sauvignon, Sauvignon
Blanc, Merlot and Meritage.

Sequoia Grove Vineyards

8338 South St. Helena Highway
Rutherford CA 94573
707.944.2945 800.851.7841
www.sequoiagrove.com

Open daily for tours and tasting. Cabernet
Sauvignon and Chardonnay, including the
Allen Family Wines available only at the
winery.

St. Supéry Vineyard & Winery

8440 St. Helena Highway Rutherford CA 94573
707.963.4507   800.942.0809
www.stsupery.com
DIRECTIONS: Located on east side of Highway 29
between Oakville and Rutherford

Self-guided tours are available anytime, free
of charge. One-hour guided tours with
wine tasting several times a day, no reservations required.

Tours include the display vineyard, where
you can wander among the vines, taste the
grapes (in season), see how different trellising systems work and take photographs.
Meticulously designed exhibits explain the
making of fine wines from soil to bottle.

The guided tours end with a conducted
tasting of St. Supéry Wines.

A highlight of the tour is *Smella Vision*,
which includes two exhibits, one for
Sauvignon Blanc (a white wine) and one for
Cabernet Sauvignon (a red). Each stand displays four bottles of the specific varietal so
you can see that even within a Sauvignon
Blanc or Cabernet Sauvignon there are
often great variations in color, clarity and
appearance. The "smell" part of the
exhibits comes into play when you push
any one of the four levers at each stand, put
your nose over a long plexiglass "sniffer
tube" and get a whiff of one of the many
aromas that are often used in describing
these wines. At the wine tasting that follows
the tour, you're ready to search for these
aromas in a real glass of wine.

St. Helena

Founded in 1853 and the high-profile
center of the Napa Valley wine industry.
This is still a small town with less than
6,000 people. The main street of St.
Helena is, coincidentally, called Main
Street. (It's also Highway 29 and the St.
Helena Highway." Main Street is loaded
with enough boutiques to sink a boatload
of yuppies. Enjoy yourself. It's small town
America with a designer's touch.

1351 Lounge

1351 Main St. St. Helena CA 94574
707.963.1969
www.1351lounge.com

Live music on the weekends, with funk,
rock, blues and more. Open mike last
Sunday of the month.

Antidote

3010 St. Helena Highway North
St. Helena CA 94574

Opening at the site of the former Brava
Terrace in the Freemark Abbey complex a
few miles north of St. Helena. Owner-chef

is Eric Torralba, former executive chef at Domain Chandon's highly-rated restaurant.

Artisan Wine Tasting

3000 St. Helena Highway (at Lodi Lane)
St. Helena CA 94574
707.967.0666
www.artistanwinetasting.com

Winetasting, sales and delicatessen with outdoor tables overlooking vineyards. Features such Napa Valley wines as Adams Ridge, Domaine Charbay, Destino, Eagle and Rose, Fife, Howell Mountain, Koves-Newlan, Lamborn Family, Livingston, Reverie, Spelletich, and Von Strasser. At the same location as Cafe 29.

Bale Grist Mill
State Historic Park

3369 North Saint Helena Highway (Hwy 29) St. Helena, CA 94574
707.963.2236
www.parks.ca.gov/default.asp?page_id=482
Three miles north of St. Helena
Hours 10 a.m. to 5 p.m.

Open throughout the year. Built in 1846, the mill has been restored to operating condition, complete with its 36-foot wooden waterwheel and big millstones. On weekends, you can watch the mill in action, grinding grain to produce stone ground flour.

You can even buy flour to take home for your own baking. A fun and educational experience for the kids—and parents, too.

Ballentine Vineyards and Winery

2820 North St Helena Highway
St. Helena CA 94574
707.963.7919
www.ballentinevineyards.com

Open Wednesday through Saturday for tasting. The present winery was founded in 1995 but the Ballentine Winery goes back to 1933 and owners Van and Betty Ballentine's grapegrowing roots in the Napa Valley go back to the early 1900s. Zinfandel, Merlot, Syrah.

Beringer Vineyards

1000 Pratt Avenue St. Helena CA 94574
707.963.4812
www.beringer.com

The historic Rhine House at Beringer Vineyards. Photo courtesy of the winery.

Built in 1876, the winery has been operating continuously ever since. It is now owned by Foster's Group, known for Australia's Foster's Beer. The famous "Rhine House" contains the visitors' center. This classic Napa Valley winery is a good place to stop for photographs.

The winery has been offering tours since 1934, so they've got it down right. The $5 tour includes tasting and a trip inside their hand-dug wine caves. The gardens are so beautiful that they're worth the trip on their own.

Café 29

3000 St. Helena Highway (at Lodi Lane)
St. Helena CA 94574
707.963.9919
www.cafe29.com

Breakfast and lunch seven days a week. Private group dinners. Outside covered patio seating with vineyard views. Shares location with Artisan Wine Tasting room.

Cameo Cinema

1340 Main Street St. Helena CA 94574
707.963.9779
www.cameocinema.com

A beautifully renovated single-screen movie theater located in downtown St. Helena.

Currently it's the only place in the valley to see quality new release films.

Cantinetta at Tra Vigne

1050 Charter Oak Avenue
St. Helena, CA 94574
707.963.8888
www.travignerestaurant.com

The Cantinetta Wine Bar offers more than 100 wines by the two or five-ounce taste. Hard-to-find cult wines are available for tasting at considerably higher prices.

Charbay Winery and Distillery

Spring Mountain Road St. Helena CA 94574
800.634.7845
www.charbay.com

Charbay is owned by the Karakasevic family, whose master distillers have been making distilled spirits for thirteen generations. Miles Karakasevic and his son Marko oversee the very limited production at Charbay, while Miles' wife Susan handles marketing and daughter Lara runs the tasting room. Visits are by appointment only, and the tasting charge is $50 per person, which can be applied to purchases.

Charbay produces limited release wines and fortified wines at its Napa Valley facility, and spirits at its other facility in Mendocino County. Charbay spirits include fresh fruit vodkas (Meyer Lemon, Key Lime, Blood Orange and Ruby Red Grapefruit), a clear vodka that will produce a truly memorable martini, a black walnut liqueur, an apple brandy, a pastis and an extremely limited amount of absolutely amazing, and expensive, whiskey.

Wines include a special port (blended from Cabernet and Sirah, and five unique brandies); a white port of Chardonnay, Sauvignon and brandy; their dessert wine; and a number of Cabernet Sauvignons.

If you want to experience the finest beverages available, and are willing to pay an appropriate amount for a handcrafted, unique product of the very highest quality, you owe it to yourself to pay a visit to Charbay. State law prohibits tasting of spirits at the winery, but you can taste and purchase their Cabernets, ports (classical and white) and Charbay dessert wine during your visit.

This is a friendly, dedicated family producing unforgettable products. Needless to say, we highly recommend a visit to the "Still on the Hill".

Charles Krug Winery

2800 St. Helena Highway
St. Helena CA 94574
Daily: 10:30am - 5-30pm
707.967.2201
www.charleskrug.com

Founded in 1861, Krug is the oldest operating winery in the Napa Valley. It's the long-time location of a number of musical and theatrical events. The owners, the Peter Mondavi family (Peter's brother, Bob, founded Robert Mondavi Winery), have over 800 acres of grapes in the Napa Valley.

Cindy's Backstreet Kitchen

1327 Railroad Avenue,St. Helena CA 94574
707.963.1200
www.cindysbackstreetkitchen.com
Classic Home Cooking –Entrees $12.95-$19.95

One block off Main Street between Hunt and Adams in the old Miramonte Hotel, built as a railroad hotel in the late 1800s. Owned by Cindy Pawlcyn, whose restaurants include the extremely popular Mustard's Grill just north of Yountville.

This restaurant offers "Cindy's Cuisine"; fun, rustic variations on classic home cooking. Main entrees include Spring Chicken Vegetable Pie, Sunday Glazed Pork, Wood Oven Duck, and Kitchen Curry Lamb Shank. Wine list focuses on Napa Valley wines while the bar specializes in Kentucky Bourbon, Mexican Tequila and Mezcal.

Corison Winery

987 St. Helena Highway St. Helena CA 94574
707.963.0826
www.corison.com

Tours and tastings by appointment. Cathy Corison produces a limited amount of highly-regarded Cabernet Sauvignon.

The Culinary Institute of America at Greystone

2555 Main Street St. Helena, CA 94574
707.967.1100
www.ciachef.edu/greystone

Greystone is a majestic building that's a favorite for photographers.

Formerly Christian Brothers Winery. Literally filled with kitchens, as well the outstanding *Wine Spectator Restaurant* (see separate listing), demonstration theaters and the Spice Island Marketplace shop. The West Coast branch of the renowned New York State cooking school, referred to by locals as the "CIA."

Cooking demonstrations are open to the public daily. $12.50 charge. For reservations call 707.967.2328.

These are a great bargain and we highly recommend them. We've gone to many of them ourselves and found them very enjoyable and useful.You'll be able to take the recipe they give you, go home and replicate the same dish you saw created at the demonstration.

For a special experience, try Greystone's *A Very Special Afternoon in the Napa Valley*, held Monday through Thursday. The $25 charge includes a cooking demo, glass of wine and *Today's Temptations* (spectacular culinary tastings) in the restaurant. It also includes shopping time and a free Napa Valley food gift in Greystone's food and kitchenware shop which features over 2,000 cookbooks.

Greystone also displays a famous collection of over 1,500 corkscrews gathered over a period of 40 years by former Christian Brothers cellarmaster Brother Timothy.

Dean and Deluca

607 South St. Helena Highway
St. Helena CA 94574
707.967.9980

The famous New York delicatessen is also in the Napa Valley. It's not a coincidence that the owner also lives in the valley. A vast selection of deli foods, kitchenware, and a multitude of jars and cans of exotic foods, sauces, condiments and other goodies. And, of course, wines.

Eagle and Rose Residence Inn

1431 Railroad Avenue
St. Helena CA 94574
707.963.1532
www.eagleandroseinn.com
12 rooms - $149-$209

Victorian style hotel for short term or extended stays. Kitchenettes, private baths and covered parking. Short walking distance to restaurants and shops.

El Bonita Motel

195 Main Street. St. Helena, CA 94574
707.963.3216
www.elbonita.com
41 rooms - $89-$279

El Bonita looks like an art-deco motel, but it's much, much more. It's a charming, comfortable, and reasonably priced place to stay, with 2.5-acres of beautifully landscaped gardens. It's where St. Helena residents suggest that their friends stay when they come to the valley.

Esquisse Winery and Vineyards

1155 Mee Lane
St. Helena CA 94574
707.963.9999
www.esquissewines.com

Open daily for tastings. A collective tasting room serving not only Esquisse's Sauvignon Blanc but also such labels as White Cottage, Allora, and Voss Vineyards.

Flora Springs Tasting Room

677 St. Helena Highway St. Helena CA 94574
707.967.8032
www.florasprings.com

While the actual winery is on nearby Zinfandel Lane, the Komes-Garvey family has a convenient tasting room on Highway 29 at the south end of St. Helena, right next to Dean and Deluca. The wines are excellent and very highly regarded. The tasting room selection includes all current vintages as well as some special wines available only here.

Folie à Deux

3070 North St. Helena Highway
St. Helena CA 94574
707.963.1160 800.473.4454
www.folieadeux.com

Open daily for tasting; tours by appointment. Founded in 1981 by Larry and Evelyn Dizmang, psychiatric medicine professionals whose colleagues suggested the name. It means "two people sharing the same delusional idea". The fantasy, however, was a success. Zinfandel, Cabernet Sauvignon, Sangiovese, Merlot, Chenin Blanc, Sparkling Wrotham Pinot.

Franciscan Oakville Estate

1178 Galleron Road (Highway 29 at Galleron one mile north of Rutherford)
St. Helena, CA 94574
707.963.7111 800.529.9463
www.franciscan.com

Open daily for tasting. Franciscan has been making wine in the valley for over 25 years. Its dramatically renovated visitor center also offers special tastings at an additional charge. They include *Mastering Magnificat - The art of blending* (blend your own Bordeaux-style wine); *Riedel Vinum Glass Tasting*, where you can experience the difference that fine glassware makes in the enjoyment of wine; and *Personality of Pinot*, which lets you sample various clones of Pinot Noir.

Freemark Abbey

3022 St. Helena Highway North
St. Helena CA 94574
800.963.9698
www.freemarkabbey.com

Open daily for tasting; tours by appointment. Freemark Abbey was founded in 1939 by three men, portions of whose names were combined to create the winery name. The winery, and the site, had been home to two previous wineries. From 1898 to the onset of Prohibition in 1919 it had been Lombarda Cellars. Originally it had been Tychson Cellars, founded in 1886 by Josephine Marlin Tychson, the first woman to build and operate a winery in California. Cabernet Sauvignon, Merlot, Viognier, Chardonnay, White Riesling, late harvest Johannisberg Riesling.

Gillwood's Restaurant

1313 Main Street St. Helena CA 94574
707.963.1788
American - Entrees $7.95-$9.75

Popular local hangout with a community table where solo diners can have mealtime company.

Giugni & Son Grocery Company

1227 Main Street St. Helena CA 94574
707.963.3421
Sandwiches - $4.25-$4.75

Cheapest, best, and biggest sandwiches in town. An institution for years.

Green Valley Café

1310 Main Street St. Helena CA 94574
707.963.7088
www.greenvalleycafe.com
Italian - Entrees: $10-$18

A neighborhood Italian restaurant with excellent food and reasonable prices. Great hamburgers, too.

Hall

401 St. Helena Highway South
St. Helena CA 94574
707.967.2620
www.hallwines.com

Open daily for tasting. On the former site of Edgewood Estate and the even earlier St. Helena Co-Op. Owned by Kathryn and Craig Hall of Kathryn Hall Vineyards (www.kathrynhallvineyards.com). Cabernet Sauvignon.

Harvest Inn

1 Main Street St. Helena CA 94574
707.963.9463 800.950.8466
www.harvestinn.com
54 suites, rooms and cottages - $240-$675

An English Tudor-style country inn on eight beautifully landscaped acres. Most of the guestrooms have brick fireplaces and private terraces. Two outdoor pools and whirlpool spas, and adjacent jogging and bike trails.

Heitz Cellars

Winery
500 Taplin Road St. Helena CA 94574
707.963.3542
www.heitzcellar.com

Sales/Tasting Room
436 St. Helena Highway South
St. Helena CA 94574

Although the actual winery is off the Silverado Trail, the sales room is on Highway 29 and open daily for tasting. Tours of the winery are only by appointment. Founded in 1961 by Joe and Alice Heitz, who produced one of the very first "cult" wines—"Martha's Vineyard"—long before the term "cult wine" was every coined. Cabernet Sauvignon, Chardonnay, Grignolino, Zinfandel, Rosé, Port.

Hotel St. Helena

1309 Main St. St. Helena CA 94574
707.963.4388
www.hotelsthelena.com
18 rooms - $165-$375

Historic building built in 1881. Downtown. Antique doll collection.

Inn at Southbridge

1020 Main St. St. Helena CA 94574
707.967.9400
www.innatsouthbridge.com
20 rooms - $275-$535

Vaulted ceilings, fireplaces, health spa. Near restaurants and shops.

Louis M. Martini Winery

254 South St. Helena Highway (Highway 29)
St. Helena CA 94574
707.963.2736 800.321.9463
www.louismartini.com
Open daily for tours and complimentary tasting; charge for reserve wines.

In operation since 1933, it was the oldest family-owned winery in the valley until it was purchased by Gallo in fall of 2002. (Well, Gallo is family-owned too, but it's hardly a warm and fuzzy little wine operation.) Great tour guides. Nice picnic facilities. Cult wineries come and go, but Martini stands out as a fine winery that dependably turns out excellent wines at fair prices. A favorite of ours. Martini produces more than 20 different varietals.

Market Restaurant

1347 Main Street St. Helena CA 94574
707.963.3799
www.marketsthelena.com
American Neighborhood – Entrees $7-$12.50

Something rare in the valley. A restaurant that focuses on locals and offers reasonable prices. Especially remarkable when you consider the owners were previously connected with highly-rated (and expensive) restaurants *Gary Danko* and *Jardinière* in San Francisco.

Some of the tables in the bar area are communal—for those who'd like to dine with friends they haven't met yet—and the restaurant has also taken pains to keep the noise level down without losing a lively energy.

Entrees include fried chicken, pork chop, meat loaf, catfish, chicken pot pie, and pulled slow roasted pork sandwich. If this food doesn't comfort you, nothing will.

Markham Vineyards

2812 North St. Helena Highway
St. Helena CA 94574
707.963.5292
www.markhamvineyards.com

Open daily for tasting. Tours by appointment only for trade and corporate groups. Originally founded in 1874 as Laurent Winery, reborn in 1977 as Markham. Merlot, Cabernet Sauvignon, Sauvignon Blanc, Chardonnay.

Martini House

1245 Spring Street at Oak (Just off Highway 29, also known as Main Street)
St Helena, CA 94574
707.963.2233 Fax: 707.967.9237
www.martinihouse.com
Wine Country - Entrees $17-$28

Pat Kuleto, who designed and owns top restaurants in San Francisco (*Boulevard*, *Farallon*, and *Jardinière*), teamed up with Todd Humphries, formerly at Campton Place in San Francisco and the Wine Spectator restaurant at the Culinary Institute of America in St. Helena, to open Martini House. The comfortable and beautifully decorated restaurant was an immediate hit. A percentage of corkage fees goes to local non-profit organizations, particularly to provide housing for migrant farm-workers.

The restaurant is in the former home of the late Walter Martini, opera singer and bootlegger. Two floors of indoor seating and outdoor garden seating around a 75-year-old fountain and under a vine-covered arbor. Wine selections from the world's great appellations, with an extensive collection of Napa Valley wines.

Merryvale Wineyards

1000 Main St. (Hwy 29)
St. Helena CA 94574
707.963.777   800.326.6069
www.merryvale.com
DIRECTIONS: Winery is south of the bridge leading into the heart of downtown St. Helena and within walking distance from town.

A favorite stop on the Merryvale Vineyards tour is the barrel room, where wines are aged.

Merryvale offers *Saturday Morning Seminars* that focus on wine and its essential components: sugar, alcohol, acid and tannin. Merryvale wines are tasted in conjunction with these basic ingredients to demonstrate how they blend together to create balance in wines. But, more important, you'll have a chance to map your own palate and find out about your likes and dislikes. You'll find this an entertaining and educational experience.

Seminars are held from 10:30 a.m. until noon every Saturday. Reservations are required.

Milat Vineyards

1091 St. Helena Highway
St. Helena CA 94574
707.963.0758   800.54.MILAT
www.milat.com

Open daily for tasting. All wines are estate grown. Guest rooms available on winery property. Zinfandel, Cabernet Sauvignon, Merlot, Chardonnay, Chenin Blanc.

Model Bakery

1357 Main St. St. Helena CA 94574
707.963.8192
www.themodelbakery.com

An excellent bakery offering breakfast pastries, coffee, breads, cookies, sandwiches, wonderful soups, salads and pizza. Did we forget anything? It's all delicious.

NapaStyle

801 Main Street St. Helena CA 94574
707.967.5021
www.napastyle.com

Michael Chiarello, founding chef of Tra Vigne restaurant in St. Helena and star of the PBS food, lifestyle and cooking television series "Michael Chiarello's Napa", has opened a specialty store just across Highway 29 from Tra Vigne. (You'll find parking at the rear of the store.)

Chiarello's shop offers a wide variety of his delicious NapaStyle food products, as well as tableware, handcrafted furniture, and his own cookbooks and Chiarello Family wines. (You can also buy his books at www.napavalleybooks.com.)

Napa Valley Coffee Roasting Company

1400 Oak Avenue St. Helena CA 94574
707.963.4491   800.852.5805
Fax: 707.963.1183

There's one of these in Napa, too, but this one has lots more room and outdoor seating. Great coffee. Great atmosphere. Close to many of the Main Street shops such as Vanderbilt and Company, this is the place to start your morning of shopping in St. Helena.

Napa Valley Olive Oil Manufacturing Company

835 Charter Oak Avenue St. Helena CA 94574
707.963.4173

A favorite of locals and visitors. Quite out of the way, so you're unlikely to stumble on it unless someone gives you a hint. Great cheese and other Italian goodies. And tremendous (and economical) olive oil by the jug, made by the owners.

Napa Valley Wine Hardware

659 Main St. St. Helena CA 94574
707.967.5503 866.611.WINE

The best source in the valley for wine racks, and wine storage equipment. Also lots of wine books and accessories.

Napa Valley Wine Library

St. Helena Public Library
1492 Library Lane, St. Helena, CA 94574
707.963.5145
www.napawinelibrary.org

A vast collection of books, magazines, interviews, clippings and other materials devoted to enology, viticulture and wine lore, with a focus on the Napa Valley.

Pizzeria Tra Vigne

1016 Main Street St. Helena, CA 94574
707.967.9999
Pizza

At the Inn at Southbridge just north of Charter Oak Street. Tasty pizzas at reasonable prices.

Prager Ports and Wines

1281 Lewelling St. Helena CA 94574
707.963.7678
www.pragerport.com
Between Sutter Home Winery and Harvest Inn

A small, family-owned winery whose ports and wines are sold only at the winery. Prager also has a two-suite B & B, one suite over the winery, the other in the vineyards.

Raymond & Company Cheesemongers

Main Stret
St. Helena CA 94574

Cheese expert John Raymond's new shop in downtown St. Helena.

Raymond Vineyard & Cellar

849 Zinfandel Lane   St. Helena CA 94574
800.525.2659
www.raymondwine.com

Open daily for tasting; tours by appointment. Founded in 1971 by the Raymond Family. The father, Roy Sr., had entered the wine industry as a cellar worker at Beringer Brothers Winery in 1933. The woman he eventually married, Martha Jane Beringer, was the granddaughter and grandniece of the founders of that winery. The family is now on its fifth generation as Napa Valley winemakers. Sauvignon Blanc, Chardonnay, Cabernet Sauvignon, Merlot, Zinfandel.

Salvestrin Estate Vineyard & Winery

397 Main Street   St. Helena CA 94574
707.963.5105
www.salvestrinwineco.com

Tours and tastings by appointment. The family has been growing grapes in the Napa Valley for 70 years. Guest rooms available at the family bed and breakfast inn on the property. Cabernet Sauvignon, Sangiovese.

Silverado Brewing Company

3020-A North St. Helena Hwy
St. Helena CA 94574
707.967.9876
www.silveradobrewingcompany.com
Wine Country Brew Pub - Entrees $11-$14

Ales, beer, stout, root beer and cream soda, all made on the premises. Plus a great selection of food, from oysters, mussels and calamari to burgers, steaks, sausage and fish. And live entertainment on the weekends. Casual and popular with great food.

Silverado Museum

PO Box 409 1490 Library Lane
St. Helena CA 94574
707.963.3757 Fax: 707.963.0917
Housed in a wing of the St. Helena Public Library. Open daily except Monday and holidays from noon to 4 p.m. Free admission.

Devoted to Robert Louis Stevenson, the author of such classics as *Treasure Island*, *Dr. Jekyll and Mr. Hyde* and *A Child's Garden of Verses*. In 1880, Stevenson spent his honeymoon in an abandoned bunkhouse at the old Silverado Mine on the slope of Mount St. Helena. *The Silverado Squatters* is his account of his stay there. The museum works at all levels, for eager six-year-olds as well as bibliophiles and scholars. Includes original letters, manuscripts, first and variant editions, paintings, sculptures, photographs and memorabilia.

St. Clement Vineyards

2867 St. Helena Highway
St. Helena CA 94574
707.963.7221   800.331.8266
www.stclement.com

Open daily for tasting; tours by appointment. Tasting room is in a 19th Century Victorian. Owned by Australia's Foster's Brewing Company. Sauvignon Blanc, Merlot, Petite Sirah, Cabernet Sauvignon, Chardonnay.

St. Helena Premier Outlets

Highway 29 North, 2 miles past St. Helena
707.963.7282
Daily 10 am - 6 pm

Includes Donna Karan, Brooks Brothers, and Jones New York.

St. Helena Wine Center

1321 Main Street, St. Helena Ca 94574
707.963.1313 800.331.1311
www.shwc.com

Located in an historic stone building that was formerly a bank (the vault is definitely more interesting now than when it had just money in it). Offers a large selection of Napa Valley and other California wines, as well as imported wines and an outstanding selection of ports and spirits.

St. Helena Wine Merchants

699 S. Helena Highway St. Helena CA 94574
707.963.7888 800.729.9463
www.shwinemerchants.com

DIRECTIONS: Located on the west side of
Highway 29 just south of Dean and Deluca and
St. Helena

Wine shop specializing in hard-to-find,
allocated and small production Napa Valley
wines. Hundreds of wines from California
and elsewhere.

Spirits In Stone

St. Helena Premium Outlets, Suite 2D
3111 Saint Helena Highway
St. Helena CA 94574
707.963.7000   800.974.6629
www.spiritsinstone.com

Contemporary Zimbabwe Shona Sculpture.
Newsweek says, "Perhaps the most important new art form to emerge from Africa in
this century." The gallery's brochure says,
"Sculpting with simple tools, the self-
taught artists carve stones that illumine
with more than 200 color variations. A
diverse body of work with dynamic, spiritual themes." We say, "This stuff is absolutely beautiful." Go see it!

The Spot

587 South St. Helena Highway
St. Helena CA 94574
707.963.2844

Formerly a popular burger, pizza and ice
cream spot for locals and visitors, now just
burgers and sandwiches as current owner
Dean & DeLuca (located right next door)
decides what to do with the place.

Spring Mountain Vineyard

2805 Spring Mountain Road.
St. Helena CA 94574
707.967.4188
www.springmtn.com

Tours (by appointment only and there is a
charge) of the 1885 estate include winery,
vineyards, gardens, caves and tasting in the
Miravalle Victorian, a familiar sight for fans
of the former TV series Falconcrest. The
winery produces Sauvignon Blanc, Syrah,
Cabernet Sauvignon.

Sunshine Foods

1115 Main St. St. Helena CA 94574
707.963.7070

It's hard to find a plain old, down-home
grocery store in the Napa Valley. Sunshine
was once, but no longer. Now it offers a
fantastic selection of foods and deli products. You'll find everything you need for a
picnic. It's located on the west side of Main
Street (Highway 29) at the south end of the
business district.

Sutter Home Winery/Trinchero Family Estates

277 St. Helena Highway South (Hwy 29)
St. Helena CA 94574
707.963.3104
www.sutterhome.com

Complimentary wine tasting.

DIRECTIONS: At south end of St. Helena on west
side of Highway 29 (across from Louis Martini
Winery). Approximately 3.5 miles north of
Rutherford.

The House of White Zin. Originally a small
family winery, their invention of White
Zinfandel made them a fortune. If you've
ever enjoyed a glass of White Zin, you owe
it to yourself to stop by Sutter Home, have
another and thank the Trinchero (it's pronounced with a hard sound—"Trin-ker'-o")
Family for all their work.

Yes, there is a "Red Zin," and has been
for many years In fact, that's what true
Zinfandel is. Zinfandel is not a white grape,
it's red. (Of course red wines actually come
from black grapes and real white wines
come from green grapes, but that's another
story.) White Zinfandel is made by removing the wine from contact with the grape
skins very early in the fermentation process,
so that very little color is extracted. The
result is a whitish wine that's usually served
cold and is definitely very popular.

Tasting on Main

1142 Main Street
St. Helena CA 94574
707.967.1042
www.tastingonmain.com

Open daily. Tasting bar in downtown St. Helena offering tastes from a variety of Napa Valley wineries including Schweiger Vineyards, Kelham Vineyards, Robert Keenan Winery, Saddleback Cellars, Venge Family Reserve, Ehlers Grove, Oakville Ranch, Richard Partridge and Broman Cellars.

Taylor's Refresher

933 Main St. (Hwy 29) St. Helena CA 94574
707.963.3486
www.taylorsrefresher.com
Open 11 am to 9 pm, seven days a week.
American - Burgers/Sandwiches $4-$9

Sure it's just a walk-up hamburger joint. But how many hamburger joints do you know that serve premium Napa Valley wines, or have a corkage fee if you want to bring your own wine? Plus, the hamburgers and shakes are delicious, and they've got great microbrews. Oh, yeah, and a legendary ahi sandwich. A favorite spot for locals—and, yes, you'll probably spot a winemaker or two here at lunchtime. Taylor's also has a branch at the San Francisco Ferry Building.

Terra

1345 Railroad Avenue St. Helena CA 94574
707.963.8931
www.terrarestaurant.com
Wine Country - Entrees $18.50-$29

A Napa Valley institution. Husband-and-wife team Hiro Sone and Lissa Doumani founded Terra restaurant in 1988. A heritage of Japanese, French and California cuisine adds up to an outstanding selection of dishes. Try appetizers such as Fricasse of Miyagi Oysters and Chanterelle in Chardonnay Cream Sauce, or an entree such as Grilled Lamb T-bones with Potato Ricotta Gnocchi.

Tra Vigne Restaurant

1050 Charter Oak Avenue
St. Helena CA 94574
707.963.4444
www.travignerestaurant.com
Wine Country Italian - Entrees $14.50-$32.95

Many consider this one of the best restaurants in the Napa Valley. No one denies that it's right up there among the very finest. It's a great place in which to hang out, munching on the marinated olives they serve at the bar.

Tra Vigne also has its Cantinetta, a gourmet deli with pastries, breads and pastas. (See separate listing.)

V. Sattui Winery

1111 White Lane St. Helena CA 94574
707.963.7774   Fax: 707.963.4324
www.vsattui.com

Open daily. Complimentary tasting

DIRECTIONS: Just 1 1/2 miles south of St. Helena along the east side of Highway 29 across from the Beacon gas station. To avoid a parking ticket, park in the winery parking lot, not on White Lane.

Some wineries used to mumble about Sattui being a retail shop rather than a winery (overlooking how many things they sell in their own retail shops). The reality is that Darryl Sattui does a very good job at both winemaking and retailing. Visitors love it.

The award-winning wine is excellent and complimentary. (And it's not available anywhere but the winery.) The gourmet deli offers over 200 different cheeses. And visitors can enjoy lunch in the two-acre shaded picnic area. Highly recommended.

White Sulphur Springs Retreat & Conference Center

3100 White Sulphur Springs Road
St. Helena CA 94574
707.963.8588 Fax 707.963.2890
www.whitesulphursprings.com
Rooms and cottages - $85-$205
DIRECTIONS: In St. Helena, turn west on Spring St. at the Exxon gas station. Go 3 miles to end of road.

White Sulphur Springs was California's first hot springs resort. Its natural beauty has been retained since the resort was founded in 1852. Nestled in a canyon just west of St. Helena, this 45-acre resort offers seclusion and tranquillity. Hiking trails lead through mature redwoods, madrone and fir trees, over meandering creeks and around cascading waterfalls.

Creekside Cottages provide a private and comfortable setting. The Inn has rooms with rustic charm. The Carriage House offers cozy rooms with shared baths and an inviting hospitality lounge. Sulphur soaking pool, sauna, whirlpool bath.

Whitehall Lane Winery

1563 St. Helena Highway
St Helena CA 94574
707.963.9454   800.963.9454
www.whitehalllane.com

Open daily for tasting. Founded in 1979, owned today by the Leonardini family. Cabernet Sauvignon, Merlot, Sauvignon Blanc, Chardonnay.

Wine Spectator Greystone Restaurant

2555 Main Street, St. Helena, CA 94574 (located at the Culinary Institute of America)
707.967.1010 Fax: 707.967.2375
www.ciachef.edu/greystone/spectator
Wine Country Mediterranean -
Entrees $16-$26

Open for lunch and dinner. Greystone's terraced gardens of herbs, vegetables, and flowers provide the perfect introduction to the vibrant colors, enticing aromas and bustling activity of the Wine Spectator Greystone Restaurant. Local, seasonal ingredients are the inspiration for the cuisine, which features California's bounty from the land and sea.

Calistoga

Calistoga was developed in the 1860s and its name is reputed to have been accidentally coined by town founder Sam Brannan. Brannan apparently intended to refer to it as the "Saratoga of California", the *Saratoga* referring to the well-known spa area in New York State. Brannan, having had a few drinks, instead came out with the "Calistoga of Sarafornia". Calistoga it stayed.

Brannan's fortunes didn't get any better. He had to sell most of the resort in 1875 and he died penniless in 1889. A sad end for California's first millionaire.

Calistoga is the place for spas, and it's the only town in the Napa Valley with any real nightlife—despite the fact that it has only one-tenth the population of the city of Napa. People walk along the sidewalks; wander in and out of bars, restaurants and shops; smile at each other; and, in general, have a great time. After all, after lying in mud, soaking in bubbling mineral water and getting massaged throughout the day, you'd be pretty mellow, too.

Alex's Restaurant

1437 Lincoln Avenue
Calistoga CA 94515
707.942.6868
American – Entrees $7-$19.95

Family-owned restaurant founded in 1958. Home-style food at very reasonable prices. Prime rib, steak, meatloaf, fried chicken, burgers and salads. Fish and pasta specials. The prime rib and the cheesecake are legendary. Very popular with Calistogans. Open for breakfast, lunch and dinner.

All Seasons Bistro, Wine Bar and Wine Shop

1400 Lincoln Avenue Calistoga CA 94515
Restaurant: 707.942.9111
Wine Shop: 707.942.6828 800.804.9463
www.allseasonswineshop.com
California Bistro - Entrees $18-$35

Legendary, with a killer wine list. Established in 1983, it was one of the first great restaurants in the valley. Great vegetarian fare and desserts. A favorite with locals as well as visitors. Wine bar offers wines of the world with a focus on Napa Valley and Northern California, and a daily selection of 10-20 wines.

American Indian Trading Company

1407 Lincoln Avenue Calistoga CA 94515
707.942.9330 877.735.7755
www.spiritfeather.com

An outstanding selection of authentic Native American art, including jewelry, beadwork, drums, pipes, knives, pottery, dolls, bows, quivers, tomahawks, lances, rattles, prayer staff wands, chokers, kachinas, dolls, and more. Tribes represented include Sioux, Navajo, Choctaw, Cherokee, Lakota, Yavapai, Hopi, Zuni, and Navajo.

Bosko's Trattoria

1364 Lincoln Avenue
Calistoga CA 94515
707.942.9088
www.boskos.com
Pasta - $8.95-$14.50

Located in a building constructed in 1883 from rock quarried in the valley. Pizza, too.

Bothé-Napa Valley State Park

3801 North Saint Helena Highway (Hwy 29)
Calistoga CA 94515
707.942.4575
www.napanet.net/~bothe

Over 10 miles of excellent trails (see Hiking section later in this book.) Picnic grounds and and 50 campsites. Includes one campsite for hikers/bikers and another designed for disabled visitors. Outdoor swimming pool. A wonderful place for all ages. Open year round. We consider it the loveliest public place to hike in the entire valley. For reservations, call 1.800.444.PARK.

Brannan's

1374 Lincoln Avenue
Calistoga CA 94515
707.942.2233
www.brannansgrill.com
New American - Entrees $16-$28

Located in a renovated 1906 building in the heart of downtown Calistoga. Menu includes Lamb Shank, Roasted Sonoma Chicken, and Pistachio Crusted Mahi-Mahi. Offers seating by the window so you can watch fellow visitors stroll the sidewalks.

Calistoga Depot

1458 Lincoln Avenue
Calistoga CA 94515

Built in 1868, it's the second oldest railroad depot in California. Train service is long gone, but the depot offers six renovated rail cars with shops and historical exhibits, including a restaurant and the Calistoga Chamber of Commerce.

Calistoga Inn

1250 Lincoln Avenue Calistoga, CA 94515
707.942.4101 Fax: 707.942.4914
www.calistogainn.com
19 rooms - $75-$100

Turn-of-the-century inn with comfortable rooms and no minimum nightly stay. European-style shared bath accommodations. Each room has sink and mirror; down the hall are shared men's and women's facilities with restrooms and showers. Continental breakfast included. Recommended by *The New York Times* and *Wine Spectator*.

Calistoga Inn Restaurant

1250 Lincoln Avenue
Calistoga, CA 94515
707.942.4101
www.calistogainn.com
California Cuisine - Entrees $14.50-$21.50

Another long-time favorite of locals and visitors. Great English-style pub. Live, local musicians on the weekends and dynamite buffalo wings. It also has its own excellent microbrewery, the Napa Valley Brewing Company. Large and attractive patio dining along the Napa River. One of our very favorite outdoor dining places in the valley. Corkage $10.

Calistoga Mineral Water Company

865 Silverado Trail North
Calistoga CA 94515
707.942.6295
www.calistogawater.com

One of the country's most famous bottled water companies, it has been owned by Perrier for years. Visitors are very welcome. During your visit you'll enjoy a water tasting with lots of different flavors. Due to government regulations the company can't advertise its water as healthful, but the reality is they've got lots of testimonials and people have been drinking (and bathing in) Calistoga's water for more than a hundred years as a health tonic.

Calistoga Pack Goats

4762 Petrified Forest Road
Calistoga, CA 94515
707.942.5504
Email: Goatwalk@aol.com

Two-hour hikes on Napa Valley trails. Goats carry your food and water. You get to stroll along unencumbered.

Calistoga Ranch

www.calistogaranch.com
$400 - $650

Auberge Resorts, which also owns Auberge du Soleil in Rutherford, is building a new "private residential resort" on a former RV park 157 acres east of the Silverado Trail and south of Calistoga. It will include 27 "owner lodges" and 47 guest lodges, for a total of 200 rooms. It will also offer spa services, and a restaurant and lounge.

Calistoga Roastery

1426 Lincoln Avenue
Calistoga CA 94515
707.942.5757
www.calistogaroastery.com

The "Coffee Guys" run a friendly local hangout with pastries and great coffee. Mail order coffee available.

Calistoga Village Inn & Spa

1880 Lincoln Avenue, Calistoga, CA 94515
707.942.0991
www.greatspa.com
$69 - $159

Rooms, some with whirlpool tubs, and a full spa located on Calistoga's main street. Three mineral-water pools for spa and overnight guests.

Calistoga Wine Stop

1458 Lincoln Avenue #2
Calistoga CA 94515
800.648.4521
calistogawinestp@aol.com

Located in an old railroad car in the middle of the Calistoga Depot. A wide selection of wines, specializing in California labels with a focus on Napa and Sonoma counties.

Checkers

1414 Lincoln Avenue Calistoga CA 94515
707.942.9300
Pizza – $8.95 and up

Thin-crust pizza, calzones, pasta ($7-$14), sandwiches ($7.95-$8.95) and salads ($6.50-$11). Popular place with the same owners as Brannan's and the Flat Iron Grill.

Clos Pegase Winery

1060 Dunaweal Lane Calistoga CA 904515
707.942.4981
www.clospegase.com

Open daily, guided tours twice a day. Reservations appreciated.

DIRECTIONS: 7 miles north of St. Helena to Dunaweal Lane and turn right. 1/2 mile to winery on the left

Clos Pegase is named after Pegasus, the winged horse of Greek mythology. According to legend, the birth of both wine and art occurred when Pegasus' hooves unleashed the sacred Spring of the Muses.

After an international competition, the winery was designed by renowned architect Michael Graves, who was commissioned to build a "temple to wine." The architecture is absolutely stunning. It's a rather amazing place for a picnic, which you can do in the company of a 300-year-old oak tree and adjacent Merlot vineyard.

On the third Saturday of each month (except December and January), owner Jan Shrem's slide presentation, *Wine Seen Through 4,000 Years of Health, Literature, History and Art*, is presented free to the public.

Crush 29

1457 Lincoln Avenue (At Washington Avenue in the Mount View Hotel)
Calistoga CA 94515
www.crush29.com
French-inspired Wine Country - Entrees $15-$28

Over 300 wines from Napa Valley winemakers as well as 30 wines by the glass. Also offers a charcuterie and cheese bar, and the 30-seat Bar Café, with the same menu as the main restaurant. Live piano music on weekends.

Enoteca Wine Shop

1348-B Lincoln Avenue
Calistoga CA 94515
707.942.1117

A wide selection of wines from all over the world, ranging from under $10 to over $2,000 in price. Owner Margaux Singleton has assembled cult wines, foreign favorites, reasonably-priced U.S., South African and Australian wines, as well as ports, sherries, sparkling and dessert wines. The interior of the shop has been painted in tromp l'oeil style by Carlo Marchiori, Calistoga resident

and owner of Villa Ca'Toga, to look like the interior of an underground wine cellar.

Flat Iron Grill

1440 Lincoln Avenue Calistoga CA 94515
707.942.1220
www.flatirongrill.com
American Grill - Entrees $11-$20

Very comfortable and beautifully decorated, right on Calistoga's main street. A very basic and delicious menu designed for the meateater. Steaks, salmon, chicken, ribs and pasta. Their New York Steak special is just $150.95 and includes a bottle of 1998 Opus One. (You can skip the wine and pay only $19.95.)

Golden Haven Spa Hot Springs Resort

1713 Lake Street Calistoga CA 94515
707.942.6793
www.goldenhaven.com
29 rooms - $65-$175

Off the beaten path, this inexpensive motel is located three blocks from Calistoga's main street. Open to the public 9 a.m. to 9 p.m A favorite for mud baths, whirlpools, blanket wraps, mineral baths, massage, foot reflexology, swimming pool and hot mineral pool. It's not as fancy as the others, but the prices are reasonable, and it's one of the few places in Calistoga where a couple can enjoy a mud bath together. We like it a lot.

Graeser Winery

255 Petrified Forest Road Calistoga CA 94515
707.942.4437
www.graeserwinery.com

Open daily for tasting. Cabernet Sauvignon, Cabernet Franc, Merlot. All from vineyards on Diamond Mountain. A beautiful setting one mile above Calistoga.

Hans Fahden Vineyards

5300 Mountain Home Ranch Road
Calistoga CA 94515
707.942.6760
www.hansfahden.com

Open daily for tasting. Driving from Calistoga, the winery is located shortly before the Petrified Forest. It's at 1200 feet elevation. This beautiful property has been in the Fahden family since 1912. Hiking, picnicking among the water gardens. Fly-fishing and wine cave events by appointment. Estate-grown Cabernet Sauvignon. Also produces vinegar (intentionally).

Hurd Beeswax Candles

1255 Lincoln Avenue Calistoga CA 94515
707.963.7211   800.977.7211
www.hurdbeeswaxcandles.com

This was a little ways north of St. Helena for 37 years, now it's in downtown Calistoga. A wonderful place for gifts for friends, family and even yourself. Candles in all sizes, styles, colors and shapes. Custom candles, too. Handmade pure beeswax candles made weekdays. Don't miss the demonstration beehive. (Don't worry—it's behind glass.)

Hydro Bar and Grill

1403 Lincoln Avenue Calistoga CA 94515
707.942.9777
American Grill - Entrees $7.95-$19.95

Burgers, steaks, ribs and chicken. Great bar and large selection of draft beers. Traditional jazz and swing Wednesday and Sunday evenings. Definitely one of the liveliest places in the valley and a good place to meet people.

Indian Springs Resort

1712 Lincoln Avenue Calistoga CA 94515
707.942.4913
www.indianspringscalistoga.com
16 bungalows and 2 houses - $215-$500

The oldest continuously operating thermal pool and spa facility in California. Situated on three thermal geysers and 16 acres of ancient volcanic ash. The 1913 bath house has been restored to pristine condition. Ceiling fans circulate the air, thermal geysers warm the volcanic ash in the mud baths and sterilize the mud after each use, gentle music is piped throughout the treatment rooms, and mineral water fragrant with fresh citrus and cucumber is provided by the well trained and solicitous staff throughout the treatment.

Mud baths, mineral baths, massages, Remy Laure facial and body polish treatments. Large mineral pool. Lodging available in bungalows.

Mayacamas Ranch Conference Center, Group Retreat and Resort

3975 Mountain Home Ranch Road
Calistoga, CA 94515
707.942.5127
www.mayacamasranch.com
26 rooms - $150-$240

On 80 acres in the beautiful Mayacamas Mountains, five miles from Calistoga and 1.25 hours from San Francisco. Mayacamas Ranch is an ideal setting for groups that want to get away from the city to a rustic, yet sophisticated, facility. Groups with 50 or more people can rent the ranch for their exclusive use for overnight visits, meetings, workshops, conferences and other events. Or several smaller groups may occupy separate sections of the ranch at the same time, accessing their own conference room and lodging.

Decorated throughout in a colorful hacienda style, the ranch has one 2,000-sq. ft conference room and two mid-size conference rooms, as well as many outdoor venues for activities. The ranch is a full-service facility complete with gourmet chef and professional kitchen, indoor and outdoor dining rooms and AV systems.

Recreational facilities include horseback riding, hilltop pool and spa, massage/spa treatments, hiking trails, a small lake with canoes and fishing, and gardens. The ranch also has a large, grassy meadow area with awesome mountain views perfect for group activities, weddings, parties and picnics.

Mount View Hotel & Spa

1457 Lincoln Avenue Calistoga CA 94515
707.942.5789. 800.772.8838
Fax: 707.942.9165
www.mountviewspa.com
20 rooms, 9 suites, 3 cottages - $145 - $225

An inviting health spa featuring a pool, natural mineral water, whirlpool tub, poolside dining, Swedish massage, sports massage, shiatsu massage, reflexology, whirlpool baths, body wraps (herbal, mud, seaweed, and valerian) and facials.

Mountain Home Ranch

3400 Mountain Home Ranch Road Calistoga, CA 94515
707.942.6616 Fax: 707.942.9091
www.mountainhomeranch.com
23 rooms - $45-$132

A family resort ten minutes from Calistoga run by the same family since the turn of the century. 350 acres with two swimming pools, horseshoes, ping-pong, pool table, tennis court, volleyball, basketball, hiking trails, a lake for fishing and swimming, stream, picnic area, barbeque pit, and natural warm mineral springs. No phones or televisions in the rooms, but plenty of books and board games. Quiet and secluded, but only ten minutes from the spas. All prices include full breakfast.

Lodge rooms; cabins with kitchen, fireplace and bathroom; and rustic cabins with beds, toilet, basin and shared showers

Nance's Hot Springs

1614 Lincoln Avenue
Calistoga CA 94515
707.942.6211 . 800.201.6211
www.nanceshotsprings.com
24 motel-style rooms - $65-$125

Founded in 1922 and family-owned ever since. Full spa treatments, including mud

bath. Lodging includes unlimited use of indoor hot mineral pool.

Napa Valley Ovens

1355 Lincoln Ave. Calistoga CA 94515
707.942.0777

A local bakery with real bread, hearty and crusty. Pastries as well. Open 7 a.m. to 3 p.m.

Napa Valley Trolley Systems

PO Box 1011   Middletown CA 95461
707.987.9887
www.wecaninc.com
$12.50/person. Children 12 and under are free. Operates during the summer and other periods of good weather.

Horse-drawn trolley and carriage tours of Calistoga operated by Wagoneers Express Carriages and Nags, Inc. Historical tours of Calistoga last 30 minutes, tours to nearby wineries take one-and-a-half hours. The 18-passenger trolley weighs 2,500 pounds, which isn't a lot more than the Belgian and Percheron horses that pull it. Jake and Tom, or Jerry and Bill, are the two teams of draft horses that do the heavy work. They're former residents of an Amish community in Indiana.

Nicola's Delicatessen & Pizzeria

1359 Lincoln Avenue Calistoga CA 94515
707.942.6272
Delicatessen - Sandwiches $3.70-$6.50, Pizza - $5.95 and up

Also burgers, salads and breakfasts. All soups, sauces, salads, cookies, cinnamon rolls and muffins are homemade. Ten beers on tap. A popular place that's been there for years.

Oat Hill Mine Trail

The trail is an old wagon road that originally went to mercury mines. The trailhead is at the intersection of Highway 29 and Silverado Trail, about one-half mile north of Calistoga. Park alongside either road or on Lake Street, but not in the small dirt lot at the trailhead. The trail begins at the metal gate.

The trail is a strenuous hike, rising 1,900 feet over nearly five miles. Best time to visit is spring. Make sure you bring water.

Old Faithful Geyser Of California

1299 Tubbs Lane Calistoga CA 94515
707.942.6463 Fax: 707.942.6898
www.oldfaithfulgeyser.com
Open daily at 9 a.m. Charge for admission

Calistoga's Old Faithful Geyser erupts approximately every 40 minutes. Photo courtesy of Old Faithful Geyser.

One of only three "Old Faithful" geysers in the world, erupting approximately every 40 minutes and shooting water 60 feet into the air.

Geothermal exhibit hall, gift shop, picnic area and self-guided geothermal tour. Private moonlight parties for 20 or more by reservation only.

Palisades Market

1506 Lincoln Ave. Calistoga CA 94515
707.942.9549

Upscale market/deli that's an excellent source of picnic goodies. Owned by the same people who own Taylor's Refresher in St. Helena.

Petrified Forest

4100 Petrified Forest Road
Calistoga CA 94515
707.942.6667
www.petrifiedforest.org
Open daily 10a.m.- 6p.m .(Winter: 10 a.m.- 5 p.m.) Six miles west of Calistoga. Charge for admission

A fascinating and educational example of the powers of nature and the vastness of time. Huge petrified trees scattered throughout the grounds as well as a museum and gift shop. Excellent for older kids.

Robert Louis Stevenson State Park

3801 North St. Helena Highway
Calistoga CA 94515
707.942.4575
www.parks.ca.gov/default.asp?page_id=472

DIRECTIONS: Drive north from Calistoga on Highway 29 almost eight miles until you see signs for the park. Park in lots on either side of the road. The trailhead is on the west side.

Open during daylight hours. Five mile hiking trail to the top of Mount St. Helena. It's a strenuous hike with an elevation gain of 2,100 feet. The park itself is some 5,000 acres, all undeveloped.

Bring your own drinking water for the long, sometimes very hot, climb up the mountain. Best time to visit is spring or fall, when it's not too hot or not too wet. View from the summit includes the nearby geyser country and, weather permitting, distant mountains such as Lassen, Shasta and the Sierra Nevada. No restrooms.

Famous writer Stevenson, who wrote such classics as *Treasure Island* and *A Child's Garden of Verses*, honeymooned here in an abandoned bunkhouse in 1880. His story *The Silverado Squatters* describes his stay. (See *Robert Louis Stevenson Museum* in St. Helena.)

Schat's Bakkerij

1353 Lincoln Avenue
Calistoga CA 94515
707.942.0777   Fax 707.942.1120
www.schats-bakery.com

Breads, bagels, pastries, cakes, crepes, soups and sandwiches. Closed Tuesdays.

Schramsberg Vineyards

1400 Schramsberg Road
Calistoga CA 94515
707.942.6668   800.877.3623
www.schramsberg.com

Tours and tastings by appointment only. $20 per person. Designated a California historical landmark. Founded in 1862 by Jacob Schram with caves dug by Chinese laborers at the turn of the century. Robert Louis Stevenson visited the winery in 1880 and devoted a chapter of his book "Silverado Squatters" to Schramsberg and its wines. Schram's original gardens were restored by Jack and Jamie Davies, who purchased the then-abandoned winery in 1965.

Schramsberg wines have been served at state occasions by every president since Richard Nixon. Jack Davies was a pioneer in preserving agricultural land in the Napa Valley and the winery's *Querencia Brut Rosé* was created to honor his efforts and generate funds to continue preserving the valley. Sparkling wines from Chardonnay, Pinot Noir and Pinot Meunier, made using the Méthod Champenoise.

Sharpsteen Museum

1311 Washington Street
Calistoga CA 94515
707.942.5911
www.sharpsteen-museum.org

DIRECTIONS: One block west of Lincoln Ave. on Washington St.

Hours: 10 a.m. - 4 p.m., April - October, and Noon - 4 p.m., November - March. Free admission.

Sweeping dioramas, fascinating artifacts and unusual exhibits in a museum created by Ben Sharpsteen, Walt Disney Studio animator and Oscar-winning producer.

Exhibits include a 32-foot-long diorama depicting 1860s life at the opulent resort that gave Calistoga—"the Saratoga of the Pacific"—its name. An elaborately furnished "Sam Brannan" cottage from the lavish Victorian spa resort. A restored stagecoach that encountered many a bandit on its mountain journeys. A working model of an 1871 train. Vintage car memorabilia. A Native American exhibit. A Robert Louis Stevenson exhibit and bronze sculpture.

Sterling Vineyards

1111 Dunaweal Lane Calistoga CA 94515
707.942.3344
www.sterlingvyds.com
Open daily.
North of St. Helena turn east on Dunaweal Lane. Sky tram charge includes tasting (for adults).

Sterling Vineyard's airtram is a popular visitor attraction because of its spectacular views—and the wine in the tasting room up top.

A beautiful Mykonos-style winery, sparkling white on top of a hill just south of Calistoga. Travel the Sky Tram to the winery where you can take a leisurely self-paced tour. Gorgeous views of the valley below.

Treasures of Tibet

1458 Lincoln Avenue Suite 4
Calistoga CA 94515
707.942.8287

Books, clothing, music and other items from Tibet and India.

Triple S Ranch

4600 Mountain Home Ranch Road Calistoga
CA 94515
707.942.6730
www.triplesranch.com
Cabins - $50-$70

Located in the mountains above Calistoga. A family-run, inexpensive way to stay in the wine country. Swimming pool, bocce ball, horseshoes.

TRIPLE S RESTAURANT

American Ranch - Entrees $13.50-$23.00

Steaks, chicken, ribs, seafood, pasta.

Villa Ca'toga

3061 Myrtledale Road, Calistoga CA 94515
707.942.3900
www.catoga.com
One tour weekly, every Saturday at 11 a.m. from May through October. Charge for tour.

A Palladian villa, created by artist Carlo Marchiori, that serves as his residence and workshop. A large salon and six other rooms are completely decorated in *trompe l'oeil* frescoes. The garden and grounds include pools, statues, fountains, Roman ruins and 18th century follies. The Gallery D'arte sells Marchiori's art and other works, and is open daily.

Ca'toga Galleria d'Arte

1206 Cedar Street, Calistoga CA 94515
707.942.3900

The Ca'toga Galleria D'Arte in downtown Calistoga sells Marchiori's art and other works, and is open daily except Tuesday and Wednesday.

Villa Ca'toga's rooms are filled with fascinating art by Carlo Marchiori. Photo courtesy of Villa Ca'toga.

Von Strasser Winery

1510 Diamond Mountain Road
Calistoga CA 94515
707.942.0930
www.vonstrasser.com

Tours and tastings by appointment only. Only wines from the Diamond Mountain appellation. Cabernet Sauvignon, Zinfandel, Chardonnay.

Wappo Bar & Bistro

1226 Washington St, Calistoga, CA 94515
707.942.4712 fax 707.942.4741
www.wappobar.com
Globally inspired - Entrees $12-22

A unique and sophisticated blend of regional cuisines of the world. Warm copper topped tables and wine bar with a redwood interior, this neighborhood bistro with its relaxed and casual ambience is a favorite among locals, winemakers and food enthusiasts. In the warmer months, a table under the grapevine-covered arbor next to the fountain is a must. There's also a private dining room for large parties and special events.

Dr. Wilkinson's Hot Springs

1507 Lincoln Avenue Calistoga CA 94515
707.942.4102
www.drwilkinson.com
Rooms and cottages - $109-$189

DIRECTIONS: Located at the corner of Lincoln
and Fairway in the heart of Calistoga.

Mud baths, message, mineral baths, facelifts, salt glow scrubs, Terra-Thalasso body treatment and cerofango treatments (a unique application of mud, clay, botanicals and paraffin to the hands and feet). Indoor and outdoor pools, comfortable lodging.

For nearly 50 years, Dr. Wilkinson has offered visitors the soothing, invigorating magic of his mud treatments. Some people say just mentioning Doc's name can relieve stress and relax the soul. Lodging available.

Wine Garage

1020 Foothill Boulevard #C
Calistoga CA 94515
707.942.5332
www.winegarage.net

A very personalized wine shop. Owner Todd Miller drives and tastes his way throughout the wine regions of California, seeking great buys from small wineries with limited distribution. No wine is more than $25 and many are less than $10.

Angwin

Nestled at the top of Howell Mountain, overlooking the Napa Valley, is the quiet college community of Angwin.

Right across from the college is a shopping center with a post office and a vegetarian grocery store with a huge selection of bulk, natural foods. Both are closed Saturdays (but open Sundays).

Angwin Airport

One Angwin Avenue
Angwin CA 94508
707.965.6219   Fax 707.965.6685
www.puc.edu/angwinairport

Angwin Airport (Virgil O. Parrett Field) is owned by Pacific Union College. The college operates the airport, and a small fleet of aircraft, to train new pilots for missionary work in isolated parts of the globe. The runway length is 3,200 feet. Tie down, gasoline, oil and mechanical services are available.

Angwin (203) 1848' 1E. 38º 34.71'N 122º 26.12'W.

Att 8 am-5pm Sun-Fri; other on req 707.815.6868. Deer. Noise Abate. Keep E. Avoid flight over town. TRCV for night use only. PCL 123.0 – Rwy, TRCV (tx)

Largest aircraft permitted: King Air or Citation

TPA MSL:2698   CTAF U-123.0
FSS: Oakland   122.35

VOR	FREQ	RAD	NM
STS	113.0	061º	18
SGD	112.1	336º	24

Burgess Cellars

1108 Deer Park Road   PO Box 282
St. Helena CA 94574
800.752.9463 Fax 707.963.8774
www.burgesscellars.com

Open daily by appointment only, Burgess is located just a few minutes down the hill from Angwin. You'll see the sign on the left side of the road as you drive up Deer Park Road from the Silverado Trail.

The winery and adjacent vineyards were originally started in the 1880's, and owner Tom Burgess has been operating here for 30 years. He makes excellent wines, and the view from the winery is spectacular. Bring your camera.

Elmshaven

125 Glass Mountain Lane
St. Helena CA 94574
707.963.9039
www.elmshaven.org

Elmshaven is a Victorian home built in 1885, and now registered as a National

Historic Landmark. From 1900 to 1915 it was the home of Ellen G. White, author and spiritual leader of the Seventh-Day Adventists. It is open for visitors Sunday through Thursday 10 a.m. to 5 p.m., Friday from 10 a.m. to 1 p.m., and Saturday from 2 p.m. to 6 p.m. Closed Thanksgiving and Christmas.

Pacific Union College

Angwin CA 94508
800.862.7080   Fax: 707.965.6390
www.puc.edu

With a student body of 1,500 and a student-teacher ratio of 13:1, this Seventh Day Adventist college is rated one of the top liberal arts colleges in the West. Example: It's one of the top 10 schools in the nation whose graduates are accepted into medical school. PUC's 200-acre campus is surrounded by 1,800 acres of agricultural and forested land—a great hiking area.

Pope Valley

A gorgeous area that 95% of our visitors don't even know exists, let alone take time to visit it. Yet it offers beautiful drives and a number of excellent wineries and other attractions. Since visits to most of the wineries in this area are by appointment only, we recommend that you call first.

Aetna Springs Cellars

7227 Pope Valley Road
Pope Valley CA 94574
707.965.2675
www.aetnaspringscellars.com

A family-owned winery producing small amounts of ultra-premium Cabernet Sauvignon, Merlot and Chardonnay. By appointment.

Aetna Springs Golf Course

1600 Aetna Springs Road
Pope Valley CA 94574
707.965.2115
www.aetnasprings.com

A nine-hole public course built in the late 1800s. For more information, see our Golf section.

Eagle and Rose Winery

1844 Pope Canyon Road
Pope Valley, CA 94567
707.965.9463
www.eagleandrose.com

Family owned winery producing Syrah, Merlot, Cabernet Sauvignon, Sangiovese and Sauvignon Blanc. By appointment. Winery grounds include a 3,700-foot paved lighted private airstrip. Call in advance for landing permission.

Litto's Hubcap Ranch

6654 Pope Valley Road
Pope Valley CA 94574

One of California's exceptional twentieth century folk art environments. Over a period of 30 years, Emanuele "Litto" Damonte (1892-1985), with the help of his neighbors, collected more than 2,000 hubcaps. All around Hubcap Ranch are constructions and arrangements of hubcaps, bottles and pulltops that proclaim that "Litto, the Pope Valley Hubcap King," was here.

Pope Valley Winery

6613 Pope Valley Road
Pope Valley CA 94574
707.965.1246
www.popevalleywinery.com

Originally built 100 years ago. Historic blacksmith shop. Picnicking. Merlot, Zinfandel, Chardonnay, Sangiovese, Chenin Blanc, Late Harvest Chenin Blanc.

Chiles Valley

The Chiles Valley District is a separate wine appellation, located in the hills east of Napa Valley at an average of 1,000 feet above sea level.

Brown Estate Vineyards

707.963.2435
www.brownestate.com

Family-owned winery producing Zinfandel, Chardonnay, Cabernet Sauvignon. Tasting by appointment only.

Catacula Lake Winery

4105 Chiles Pope Valley Road
St. Helena CA 94574
707.965.1104
www.cataculalake.com

Owned by the Keith family. Tours and tasting by appointment. Produces Sauvignon Blanc, Zinfandel, Petite Sirah and Cabernet Sauvignon. Over 1,000 acres, all deeded to the Napa Valley Land Trust.

Nichelini Winery

2950 Sage Canyon Road
St. Helena CA 94574
707.963.0717
www.nicheliniwinery.com

The Nichelini family has been growing grapes since the 1890's, and their winery in Sage Canyon is the oldest family-owned continuously operating winery in the county. They produce Zinfandel, Cabernet Sauvignon, Merlot, Sauvignon Vert and Petite Sirah. Open daily for sales and complimentary tasting. Picnic area and bocci ball court.

RustRidge Winery

2910 Lower Chiles Valley Road
St. Helena CA 94574
707.965.9353
www.rustridge.com

Family-owned winery on 450 acres, also offering a bed and breakfast inn. By appointment. Chardonnay, Sauvignon Blanc, Zinfandel, Cabernet Sauvignon, Late Harvest Riesling, Late Harvest Zinfandel.

Volker Eisele Family Estate

3080 Lower Chiles Valley Road
St. Helena CA 94574
707.965.2260
www.volkereiselevineyard.com

Family-owned winery producing highly-acclaimed Cabernet Sauvignon and Merlot, all made from organically grown grapes. By appointment.

Lake Berryessa

Bureau of Reclamation
Lake Berryessa Field Office

5520 Knoxville Road Napa, CA 94558
707.966.2111
www.recreation.gov (then search for "Lake Berryessa")

Lake Berryessa is less than 45 minutes from the Napa Valley in the eastern part of Napa County.

Prior to 1957, the lake was Monticello Valley and the town of Monticello. When Monticello Dam was completed, the lake started filling. Today it is one of the largest man-made lakes in California, 25 miles long, 3 miles wide and 275 feet deep at its deepest point, with 168 miles of shoreline.

The lake has rainbow trout, brown trout, bluegill, crappie and catfish. Campgrounds and picnic areas are abundant.

Lake Berryessa
Marina Resort

5800 Knoxville Road Napa CA 94558
707.966.2161 Fax: 707.966.0761
www.lakeberryessa.com
15 cabins $75 - $150

All lake-view cabins (non-housekeeping), 45 RV sites, 70 primitive tent camping sites. Convenience store with food, clothing and camping supplies.

A variety of facilities and services including four-lane launch ramp, tackle shop, volleyball, restaurant, picnic areas with BBQ and tables, convenience store, fuel dock and courtesy dock. Houseboat rentals, along with other water craft including jetskis, ski boats, runabouts, pontoon boats and fishing boats.

Markley Cove Boat Rentals

PO Box 987 Winters CA 95694
707.966.2134 800.242.6287

Houseboat and fishing boat rentals. Annual berth rental. Rental houseboats include dinette, gas oven and range, bathroom with tub/shower, bunks, refrigerator, gas BBQ, air conditioner, 110-volt generator, microwave, and 140 hp I/O engine. More deluxe models include such things as wet bars, second full bath, second refrigerator and/or trash compactor.

Oak Shores Park

Knoxville Road Napa CA 94558
707.966.2111

A recreation development operated by the U.S. Bureau of Reclamation. Eight different areas with a total of 100 picnic sites with tables and barbecue grills, swimming beaches, cartop boat facility for non-powered boats, and shore fishing. $4.00 per car fee for day use.

Putah Creek Resort

7600 Knoxville Road Napa CA 94558
707.966.2116

Full marina, tackle shop, 200 campsites, 55 RV sites, 26 air-conditioned motel kitchenettes, grocery, delicatessen, snack bar, restaurant with cocktail lounge and dancing to live music.

Quail Ridge Reserve

530.758.1387
www.quailridge.org

Overlooks Lake Berryessa. Operated by the non-profit Quail Ridge Conservancy, it is 2000 acres of black oak, blue oak, interior live oak, oracle oak, scrub oak and valley oak in one of the few nearly untouched nat-

ural areas remaining in the California Coast Ranges. The reserve is home to a wide variety of native plants and animals including as many as 15 different native California grasses.

Quail Ridge is primarily a research site. However, with advance reservations the public can participate in monthly interpretive walks as well as four-hour and day-long boat ecotours. The boat tours offer bird watching and information on the history, plants and animals of the area.

Spanish Flat Resort

4290 Knoxville Road Napa CA 94558
707.966.7700 Fax: 707.966.7704
www.spanishflatresort.com
12 cabins $75 - $100

An RV/campground on Lake Berryessa. Camping is $22 per night and RV camping is $26.

Complete marina facilities. Power boats, boat ramp, jet ski rental, open and covered berths, secure boat garages, gas, fishing boats and supplies. Less than one mile from grocery store, deli, sporting goods, beautiful shops, post office, service station, restaurant and bar.

Steele Park Resort

1605 Steele Canyon Road Napa CA 94558
707.966.2123 800.522.2123
www.steelepark.com

Motel rooms and cottages with swimming pool and championship tennis courts, restaurant, bar, store, full service marina, launch ramp, campsites and RV park.

Silverado Trail

The Silverado Trail runs along the east side of the valley from Calistoga at the northern end to Napa at the southern end. Even though these attractions do have town mailing addresses, we've listed them here for convenience because they're all located on the Trail. Keep in mind that there are more wineries along the trail than the ones we've listed here.

Auberge du Soleil

180 Rutherford Hill Rd.
Rutherford CA 94573
707.963.1211 800.348.5406
Fax: 707.963.8764
www.aubergedusoleil.com
50 rooms and suites - $525-$2250

Auberge du Soleil Restaurant

800.348.5406 Fax: 707.967.3818
French Mediterranean - Entrees $34-$37

A Relais & Chateaux Property. A renowned restaurant and 50-room inn. Even if you don't stay here, you can enjoy a breakfast with a spectacular view as the morning fog gradually burns off revealing the vineyards on the valley below. Or order one of the excellent burgers and salads from their "deck menu" for lunch.

As close to heaven as you can get, with beautiful views of the Napa Valley, wonderful food and the largest restaurant/wine selection in the Napa Valley; 1,280 selections and 14,000 bottles. A truly romantic place on a moonlit evening.

Chappellet Vineyard

1581 Sage Canyon Road St. Helena CA 94574
707.963.7136
www.chappellet.com

Tours and tastings by appointment. Chardonnay, Chenin Blanc, Cabernet Sauvignon, Merlot, Sangiovese, Zinfandel. Molly Chappellet's highly-regarded books on gardening and cooking are available at the winery.

Chimney Rock Winery

5350 Silverado Trail Napa CA 94558
800.257.2641
www.chimneyrock.com

Open daily for tasting, tours by appointment. A Cape-Dutch style winery whose vineyards include the site of a former 18-hole golf course, gone in a links-to-vines

sacrifice. Cabernet Sauvignon, Cabernet Franc, Fumé Blanc, Rosé of Cabernet Franc.

Clos Du Val Wine Company

5330 Silverado. Trail   Napa CA 94558
707.259.2220 800.993.9463
www.closduval.com

Open daily for tasting, tours by appointment. Co-founder Bernard Portet established the winery in the Stag's Leap area after a two-year worldwide search for the ideal château location. Pétanque (French bocce ball) courts and picnic tables available to winery visitors. Cabernet Sauvignon, Merlot, Chardonnay.

Conn Creek Winery

8711 Silverado Trail   St. Helena CA 94574
707.963.9100
www.conncreek.com

Open daily for tasting. Cabernet Sauvignon, Merlot, Cabernet Franc.

Cuvaison Winery

4550 Silverado Trail Calistoga 94515
707.942.6266
www.cuvaison.com

Open daily. Tasting fee of $5 includes logo glass. Free tours of wine caves. Picnic grove with 350-year-old oaks.

Outstanding wines with a focus on Carneros Chardonnay, since Cuvaison was farsighted enough to buy Carneros land back when few people realized what an excellent winegrowing region it was.

Darioush Winery

4240 Silverado Trail   Napa CA 94558
707.257.2345
www.darioush.com

Open daily for tasting. A new winery facility whose style was inspired by the Persepolis, the ancient Persian city founded by Darius, the first king of Persia. Cabernet Sauvignon, Merlot, Shiraz, Chardonnay, Viognier. They also produce an olive oil.

Duckhorn Vineyards

1000 Lodi Lane St. Helena CA 94574
888.354.8885
www.duckhornvineyards.com

At the corner of Lodi Lane and the Silverado Trail. Open daily for tasting; tours by appointment. Founded in 1978 by Dan and Margaret Duckhorn. Gardens, waterfowl art collection. Sauvignon Blanc, Merlot, Cabernet Sauvignon, and a dry Vermouth.

Dutch Henry Winery

4300 Silverado Trail Calistoga CA 94515
707.942.5771 888.224.5879
www.dutchhenry.com

Tours and tastings by appointment only during spring and summer. Cabernet Sauvignon, Merlot, Meritage, Zinfandel, Chardonnay, Syrah.

Hagafen Cellars

4160 Silverado Trail Napa CA 94558
707.252.0781 Fax: 707.252.4562
www.hagafen.com

Established in 1979, Hagafen (meaning "the vine") Cellars is the only kosher winery in the Napa Valley. Winemaker Ernie Weir turns out award-winning wines, which have frequently been served at state occasions at the White House. Tours are by appointment only. Chardonnay, Pinot Noir, Syrah, Sauvignon Blanc, Merlot, Cabernet Sauvignon, White Riesling and a sparkling Brut Cuvee.

Miner Family Vineyards

7850 Silverado Trail Oakville CA 94562
800.366.9463
www.minerwines.com

Open daily for tasting and tours by appointment. Cabernet Sauvignon, Merlot, Chardonnay, Petite Sirah, Sauvignon Blanc, Zinfandel. A beautiful view of the valley from the winery.

Meadowood Resort

900 Meadowood Lane St. Helena CA 94754
707.963.3646 800.458.8080
www.meadowood.com
85 cottages, suites and lodges - $375-$3585

A Relais & Chateaux Property. Croquet anyone? Meadowood, one of Napa Valley's most exquisite resorts, has the only professional croquet court in the Napa Valley and is the site of many tournaments. You can take lessons from the croquet pro, or enjoy any of the other activities at this luxurious 250-acre resort in a wooded park-like setting. Choose from tennis, golf, biking, swimming, hiking, sleeping or reading in the sun, or revitalizing yourself in the health spa.

In the quiet of the early morning, you may see deer wandering across the nine-hole golf course. Sumptuous breakfasts await early risers seven days a week. Meadowood's superb restaurants attract both locals and visitors from afar.

The resort's wine school offers unique wine and food courses. Not surprising considering that Meadowood each June hosts the prestigious Napa Valley Wine Auction - one of the most famous events of its kind in the world.

Meadowood is elegant, luxurious, comfortable, and convenient to many of the Napa Valley's most renowned wineries. It's *the* place to stay upvalley.

Mumm Napa Valley

8455 Silverado Trail Rutherford CA 94573
707.942.3434 Fax: 707.942.3470
www.mummnapavalley.com

On the west side of Silverado Trail, approximately two miles north of Oakville Cross Road.

The Wine Spectator has called Mumm Napa Valley "perhaps the best sparkling wine producer in California." Very friendly staff and a beautiful view of the valley, particularly at sunset. Mumm is owned by Allied-Domecq, headquartered in England.

Joseph Phelps Vineyards

200 Taplin Road St. Helena CA 94574
707.963.2745
www.jpvwines.com

Tours and tastings by appointment only. Taplin Road runs east off the Silverado Trail, 1/4 mile north of Zinfandel Lane. Founded in 1972 by Joseph Phelps, who currently has160 acres of vines on a 600-acre ranch. Phelps donated some of his land on the valley floor to be used for farmworker housing. Cabernet Sauvignon, Sauvignon Blanc, Chardonnay, Merlot, and dessert wines.

Pine Ridge Winery

5901 Silverado Trail. Napa CA 94558
800.575.9777
www.pineridgewinery.com

Open daily for tasting; tours by appointment. Tours include wine caves. Cabernet Sauvignon, Merlot, Chardonnay, Chenin Blanc-Viognier.

Quintessa

1601 Silverado Trail St. Helena CA 94574
707.967.1601
www.quintessa.com

Tours and tastings by appointment only. Founded by Agustin and Valeria Huneeus. Agustin was formerly CEO of Chile's largest winery, and head of Franciscan Estates. Valeria is an advocate of biodynamics and uses those agricultural techniques on their vineyards. Cabernet Sauvignon, Merlot, Cabernet Franc.

Regusci Winery

5584 Silverado Trail Napa CA 94558
707.254.0403
www.regusciwinery.com

The Regusci family has been farming in the Napa Valley since 1932. Their Stags Leap District winery is located in a "ghost winery," built in 1878, and crafted from lava stone with two-foot thick walls. Their focus is on reds—Cabernet Sauvignon, Merlot and Zinfandel. All are delicious.

Reynolds Family Winery

3266 Silverado Trail Napa CA 94558
707.258.2558
www.reynoldsfamilywinery.com

Open daily for tasting. Small family winery. Cabernet Sauvignon, Pinot Noir. The winery also operates *Napa Valley Off-Road Tastings* that carry visitors through vineyards and other areas in a comfortable Pinzgauer all-terrain vehicle.

Robert Sinskey Vineyards

6320 Silverado Trail Yountville CA 94599
707.944.9090   800.869.2030
www.robertsinskey.com

Open daily for tastings; tours by appointment. Sinskey is farming its vineyards organically, and also using the even stricter methods of biodynamics. Pinot Noir, Chardonnay, Merlot, Cabernet Sauvignon, Cabernet Franc.

Rombauer Vineyards

3522 Silverado Trail St. Helena CA 94574
707.967.5120 800.622.2206
www.rombauervineyards.com

Tours and tastings by appointment only. Founded in 1982. Over one mile of caves. Chardonnay, Zinfandel, Merlot, Cabernet Sauvignon.

Rutherford Hill Winery

200 Rutherford Hill Road
Rutherford CA 94573
707.963.1871
www.rutherfordhill.com

Rutherford Hill opened in 1976 producing Merlot, and still focuses on that varietal, although it makes others .

The winery makes picnic areas available to visitors, and its $10 winery tour includes a walkthrough of its extensive system of wine caves, perhaps the largest in North America.

The winery also offers *Blending in the Caves*, which allows participants to create their own blend of Rutherford Hill Merlot. After a tour, your wine instructor will assist you by informing you about vineyard locations, varietal characteristics, flavor, taste and a few basic principle of blending. Then, sampling three varietal wines taken directly form the barrel, you'll create your own blend that you will bottle and take home to enjoy. For a special experience, your group can enter team blends into a "Merlot Blend-Off" competition. Reservations required.

Shafer Vineyards

6145 Silverado Trail. Napa CA 94558
707.944.2877
www.shafervineyards.com

Tours and tasting by appointment only. Vineyards were originally planted in 1922. Fifty years later John Shafer founded this winery, one of the first in the Stag's Leap area. Cabernet Sauvignon, Chardonnay, Merlot.

Silverado Country Club and Resort

1600 Atlas Peak Road Napa CA 94558
707.257.0200 800.523.0500
Fax: 707.257.5400
www.silveradoresort.com
280 cottage suites - $280-$1415

1,200 acres whose cornerstone is a mansion built in the 1870s. Two hundred and eighty deluxe cottage suites complete with living room, wood burning fireplace, full kitchen, master bedroom and bath, and private patio or terrace. Health spa. Nine swimming pools. Two championship 18-hole golf courses designed by Robert Trent Jones, Jr. Twenty-three tennis courts. Three excellent restaurants. Live music in the bar. It's *the* place to stay in Napa.

Silverado Vineyards

6121 Silverado Trail Napa CA 94558
707.257.1770
www.silveradovineyards.com

Jack Stuart, acknowledged to be one of the finest winemakers in the Napa Valley, has been producing outstanding wines for years at this winery founded by the family of Walt Disney. Beautiful views from the tasting room area.

Soda Canyon Store

4006 Silverado Trail Napa CA 94558
707.252.0285
www.sodacanyonstore.com

Delicatessen, picnic lunches, espresso, groceries. Picnic tables. Wine tasting bar, where you can taste three local wines. The tasting bar focuses on vineyards in Soda Canyon (such as Atlas Peak Vineyards) as well as wineries along the Silverado Trail. It's the only store on the Trail between Napa and Calistoga.

Stag's Leap Wine Cellars

5766 Silverado Trail Napa CA 94558
707.944.2020
www.stagsleapwinecellars.com

Stag's Leap staggered the international wine community—and particularly the French part of it—when its 1973 Cabernet Sauvignon took first place in a blind wine tasting in Paris in 1976. The renowned (and very French) wine tasters were horrified that an upstart California winery would best France's finest wines. Some even tried to get their tasting notes back.

Stag's Leap Wine Cellars' place in history was secure. Other Napa Valley wineries have since won many awards in France and other international competitions, but owners Warren and Barbara Winiarski have never rested on their laurels, and continue to produce superb wines, including their celebrated Cask 23. It well deserves your visit.

ZD Wines

8383 Silverado Trail Napa CA 94558
800.487.7757
www.zdwines.com

Open daily for tastings. Founded in 1969 in Sonoma County, and moved to the Napa Valley in 1979. Chardonnay, Pinot Noir, Merlot, Cabernet Sauvignon.

Scenic Drives

HIGHWAY 29

Every road in the Napa Valley is scenic. Some are just more scenic than others. Highway 29, the main road up the (west-ish) center of the valley, takes you through all the valley towns and right by some of the area's most famous wineries and restaurants. From Napa to St. Helena it parallels the route of the Napa Valley Wine train. Wave at the engineer and passengers. That's half the fun for everybody.

California State Route 29—the road that runs through the heart of the Napa Valley.

Passing through St. Helena, Highway 29 is called Main Street. Along most other stretches it's referred to as the Saint Helena Highway. In reality, it's all Highway 29—a divided highway from Napa to Yountville, and a two-lane highway (with frequent left-turn lanes) all the way from Yountville to Calistoga.

Caltrans, the State of California's transportation department, would love to make "29" a divided highway the whole length of the valley, but the natives have fought valiantly and successfully to prevent this from happening. Even most of those who commute up or down the valley are willing to put up with the inconvenience of a two-lane road in order to preserve the beauty of the drive.

SILVERADO TRAIL

The Silverado Trail runs along the east side of the valley. It goes outside most of the towns, and there are fewer wineries and much less traffic. Yet it still offers beautiful views, many wineries and quicker driving if you're in a hurry. Don't be in too much of a hurry, however. The view is too lovely and this road can be dangerous, because people drive much faster than on Highway 29 and seem to get more impatient, passing on stretches where it is unsafe to pass. Use caution and you'll enjoy "the Trail" immensely. We do.

The name "Silverado" comes from the road's history carrying quicksilver (mercury) wagons from the mines in northern Napa County. The quicksilver was eventually transported to the gold fields of California where it was used to separate gold from the ore or sand in which it was found. The Trail also led to the Silverado Silver Mine on Mt. St. Helena, where years later Robert Louis Stevenson gathered the notes for his story *The Silverado Squatters*.

CROSS ROADS

Crossing the valley from west to east, connecting Highway 29 with the Silverado Trail, are three major crossroads. Each road crosses the valley at the town that it's named after. They are: Yountville Cross Road, Oakville Cross Road, and Rutherford Cross Road. (Several other roads make this connection, too, but they don't quite have the flair that the crossroads do.) Each road passes wineries and beautiful homes, and all offer gorgeous views. Try any one of these to get off the beaten path.

CUTTINGS WHARF ROAD

Don't be too disappointed if after turning off Highway 121/12 south of Napa, you follow the "Napa River Resorts" signs to Cuttings Wharf and have trouble finding the "resorts." Perhaps once there were resorts in this area, although there appears to be no historical record that this was ever the case. Still, it's a pleasant drive, taking you through some of Napa County's section of the Carneros wine district, famous for its Chardonnays and Pinot Noirs.

SOLANO AVENUE & WASHINGTON STREET

Between Yountville and Napa is an 8-mile stretch of divided highway. The highway provides beautiful views, but for more leisurely sightseeing we offer two tips. Northbound from Napa, turn right (east) at the Washington Street turnoff, then turn immediately left to go north again. Follow the frontage road to Yountville, enjoy the view of the vineyards by the side of the road, and take pictures of the beautiful views toward the mountains to the east.

Coming back at the end of the day, skip the divided highway again. Instead go west off Highway 29 at the Veterans Home turnoff, cross the tracks and turn left on the frontage road (Solano Avenue) to go south toward Napa. This will give you beautiful views of homes, vineyards and wineries to the west toward the Mayacamas Mountains. If this is at sunset, it's even more beautiful. Follow Solano into Napa and then, when you reach the business/residential areas, turn back onto the highway again and continue your journey on the main highway.

YOUNT MILL ROAD

A beautiful drive that will take you from Yount Street in Yountville to Highway 29 north of town. You'll pass the site of the original mill built by town founder George Yount in 1836.

OTHER SCENIC DRIVES

See also *California Motorcycle Roads* for Napa-Sonoma-Solano.
www.pashnit.com/motoroads.htm

Just Outside the Napa Valley

They're not in the Napa Valley but they're close by and might interest you. Most of these destinations are a 20-30 minute drive from the valley.

Anheuser-Busch Brewery

3101 Busch Drive
Fairfield CA 94533
707.429.7595
www.budweisertours.com

Open September-May Tuesday through Saturday from 9 a.m. to 4 p,m. June-August open Monday through Saturday. Free 45-minute tours depart on the hour.

The world's largest brewer. Enjoy samples of fine beers and snacks. Visit the production floor to see packaging lines that fill thousands of cans and bottles every minute.

Calpine Geothermal Visitor Center

15500 Central Park Road
Middletown CA 95461
866-GEYSERS
www.geysers.com

The Geysers is the world's largest geothermal energy source, and is operated by Calpine. Wells drill deep into the earth to tap the natural steam, which is used to power turbines, generating energy for customers in Northern California. The energy efficient visitor center is heated and cooled by geothermal energy, and features interactive exhibits, a gift shop and picnic area, and free bus tours to an operating geothermal power plant. Advance registration is required for the bus tours. Free. Open Thursday through Monday.

Crazy Creek Soaring

18896 Grange Road
Middletown CA 95461
707.987.9112
www.crazycreekgliders.com

DIRECTIONS: Take Highway 29 through the town of Calistoga and on north to Middletown.

Crazy Creek isn't close, but unfortunately the Calistoga Gliderport closed down some years ago. So if you'd like to go for a glider ride, this is the nearest place to do it.

Reservations are recommended, particularly if you're going to drive that far. Flights can range from 15 minutes to 40 minutes, and cost from $110 to $245. For a 15-20 minute flight for two people, the charge is $150.

Jelly Belly

Herman Goelitz Candy Company
2400 North Watney Way
Fairfield CA
800.9JELLYB
www.jellybelly.com

DIRECTIONS: Take Interstate 80 north toward Sacramento. At Fairfield, exit freeway at Highway 12/Chadbourne Road, and exit at Chadbourne. Turn right at stop sign onto Chadbourne, then left onto Courage Drive. Turn left onto North Watney Way. Tours Monday through Friday from 9 a.m. to 2 p.m. Closed holidays, April 1, and the last week of June through the first week of July.

The makers of Ronald Reagan's favorite snack—the first jelly beans in outer space—and another long-time favorite, Candy Corn. The factory makes up to 40,000,000 jelly beans a day and sells enough each year to circle the earth's equator 2.5 times. It's the only place in the world where you can buy Belly Flops, beans that don't meet Goelitz's high standards for size or color, but they're still delicious. A fun tour and great for kids.

Safari West

3115 Porter Creek Road
Santa Rosa CA
707.579.2551 800.616.2695
www.safariwest.com

DIRECTIONS: From the Napa Valley, go north on Highway 128/29. Do not turn right into Calistoga. Continue to Petrified Forest Road. Turn left, pass the Petrified Forest and turn right on Porter Creek Road. Go 2.5 miles, cross the bridge, and immediately turn right onto Franz Valley Road. Turn into the very first driveway.

Daily tours by appointment. Tours last 2 1/2 hours and cost $58 for adults, $28 for children 12 and under.

A private wildlife preserve of 400 acres that is home to 350 exotic mammals and birds. Includes antelope, cheetah, eland, gazelle, zebra, giraffe and many more. Bring your cameras.

Six Flags Marine World

Marine World Parkway
Vallejo CA 94589
707.643.6722
www.sixflags.com/marineworld

Open all year, Wednesday through Sunday from 9:30 a.m. to 5 p.m., and every day during the summer from 9:30 a.m. to 6:30 p.m. (Memorial day to Labor Day). Kids under 48 inches $27, general admission $43.

Whales, tigers, elephants, sharks, kangaroos, water-skiing shows, trained seals, giraffes, butterflies and scads of other animals and performances. Plus lots of thrill rides, including five roller coasters. It's probably the premier place in the entire San Francisco Bay Area for a family outing.

Smith's Mount St. Helena Trout Farm

Ida Clayton Road
Calistoga CA 94515
707.987.3651

DIRECTIONS: Take Highway 128 from Calistoga toward Healdsburg/Geyserville, turn right on Ida Clayton Road. Also accessible from Middletown in Lake County, and from Santa Rosa via Mark West Springs Road and Franz Valley Road.

Fishing for the entire family for rainbow trout raised in cold mountain water. No license. No limit. Bait and poles available. Open Saturday, Sunday and observed holidays, February through October. Hours 10 a.m.-6 p.m.

Traintown

20264 Broadway - Highway 12
Sonoma, CA 95476
707.938.3912
www.traintown.com

Open daily 10 a.m. to 5 p.m .June 1-Labor Day. Friday, Saturday and Sunday September 1-May. $3.75 adults, $3.25 children.

There's not much for young kids to do in the Napa Valley. Fortunately Traintown is only twenty minutes away from Napa. It's located in the town of Sonoma on 10 acres, with one and a quarter miles of railroad track.

During the twenty-minute trip on the small-scale train, you'll travel over five bridges and trestles and through two tunnels, one of them 140 feet long. Admission includes a petting zoo and three full-size cabooses to explore. Extra charge for ferris wheel and carousel.

Twin Pine Casino

Highway 29 at Rancheria Road
Middletown, CA 95461
707.987.0197 Fax 707.987.9786
www.twinpine.com

A casino owned by the Middletown Rancheria band of Pomo Indians. Open 24 hours a day, seven days a week. Nearly 500 slot machines, blackjack, pai-gow poker, keno, electronic bingo, video poker and accessible from Middletown in Lake County, and from Santa Rosa via Mark West Springs Road and Franz Valley Road.

Lodging and Spas

Lodging Reservations

The Napa Valley is filled with bed and breakfast inns, hotels, resorts, and spas. The easiest way for you to find a place to spend the night is through one of the reservation services. They'll know which places have rooms available, and can recommend accommodations suitable for your needs. Plus there's no extra charge for their services.

Wine Country Bed & Breakfast Reservations

PO.Box 5059 Napa CA 94581
707.257.7757

Napa Valley Reservations Unlimited

1819 Tanen Street Napa CA 94559
707.252.1985 800.251.6272
www.napavalleyreservations.com

Bed & Breakfast Inns of the Napa Valley

PO Box 2937 Yountville CA 94599
707.944.4444

Hotel Hotline

707.963.8466 800.499.8466 (California)

B&B Style

707.942.2888 800.995.8884

Hotels, Motels, Inns, Resorts, Retreats and Ranches

We've listed only the *names* of facilities in these categories of lodging. For specific information, see their listings in their respective town sections.

Hotels/Motels/Inns

AMERICAN CANYON

Comfort Inn

CALISTOGA

Calistoga Inn
Calistoga Village Inn & Spa
Mount View Hotel
Carneros
Carneros Inn

NAPA

Chablis Inn
Chateau Hotel
Embassy Suites Napa Valley
Hawthorn Inn & Suites
Inn at the Vines (Best Western)
John Muir Inn
Napa River Inn
Napa Valley Budget Inn
Napa Valley Marriott
River Terrace Inn
Wine Valley Lodge

RUTHERFORD

Rancho Caymus Inn

ST. HELENA

Harvest Inn
The Inn at Southbridge

YOUNTVILLE

Napa Valley Lodge
Villagio Inn & Spa
Vintage Inn
Yountville Inn

Resorts

(Listed in Silverado Trail section)

Auberge du Soleil (Rutherford)
Calistoga Ranch

Meadowood Resort (St. Helena)
Silverado Country Club (Napa)

Retreats

Christian Brothers Retreat & Conference Center (see listing in Napa section)

Mayacamas Ranch Conference Center, Group Retreat and Resort (see listing in Calistoga section)

Mountain Home Ranch (see listing in Calistoga section)

White Sulphur Springs Resort and Spa (see listing in St. Helena section)

Ranches

Mountain Home Ranch (see listing in Calistoga section)

Triple S Ranch (see listing in Calistoga section)

Bed and Breakfast Inns

Note: Rates may have increased since publication of this book. Most rates given do not include tax.

ANGWIN

Forest Manor

415 Cold Springs Road Angwin, CA 94508
800.788.0364 Fax 707.965.1962
www.forestmanor.com
6 suites - $210-$395

Located in the hills above St. Helena on 20 acres, just minutes from wineries, shops, restaurants and attractions. Six spacious suites, a gourmet breakfast each morning, an outdoor pool and jacuzzi.

CALISTOGA

Angels Are Inn

1018 Myrtle Street Calistoga, CA 94515
800.386.1939 (California) 707.949.4424
Fax 707.942.1524
www.angelsareinn.com
3 units - $175-$195

Rooms have cushy down featherbeds, beautiful antiques, stereos with CD players, mini-fridges and coffee makers. Continental breakfast buffet is served daily, and afternoons feature selected wine and cheese tasting. Relax in the whirlpool tub in the grapevine and jasmine-filled garden under the stars, dawdle on the wrap-around veranda, and stroll to Calistoga's famous healing volcanic mudbaths, gourmet dining and world-class wineries.

Bear Flag Inn

2653 Foothill Boulevard Calistoga 94515
800.670.2860

Brambles, The

1322 Berry St. Calistoga 94515
707.942.4781 707.942.5919

Brannan Cottage Inn

109 Wappo Avenue, PO Box 81
Calistoga 94515
707.942.4200
www.brannancottageinn.com
6 rooms - $125-$160

A Victorian country cottage built in the 1860s and listed on the National Register of Historic Places. All rooms have private entrances and garden views.

Calistoga Country Lodge

2883 Foothill Blvd. Calistoga, CA 94515
707.942.5555 Fax: 707.942.5864
www.countrylodge.com
6 rooms - $120-$195

Secluded inn nestled in the western foothills of Calistoga. Beautifully decorated with American antiques, bleached pine and contemporary art. Outside is a heated pool and spa, inside is a large living room with a fieldstone fireplace. Prices include a glass of local wine with cheese in the evening and a buffet breakfast for two in the morning. Located five minutes from the spas, restaurants and shops of downtown Calisotoga.

Calistoga Wayside Inn

1523 Foothill Boulevard Calistoga 94515
707.942.0645 707.942.4169
www.calistogawaysideinn.com
3 rooms

Carlin Cottages

1623 Lake Street Calistoga 94515
800.734.4624 707.942.9102
www.carlincottages.com
15 cottages - $110-$205

Spring-fed mineral baths and pool. Shaker-style furniture, Irish country motif.

Casa Lana

1316 South Oak Street Calistoga 94515
707.942.0615 707.942.0204
www.casalana.com
2 rooms - $175-$225

A river setting just a short walk from downtown Calistoga. Also offers culinary tours, and gourmet weekends and cooking classes in the B&B's professional kitchen.

Chateau de Vie

3250 Highway 128 Calistoga 94515
707.942.6446 877.558.2513
www.chtaeaudv.com
3 units - $189-$279

Right in the vineyards with a spectacular view of Mount St. Helena.

Chien Blanc Lodging, a Vacation Rental

1441 Second Street Calistoga, CA 94515
800.676.4205 Fax 707.942.8682
www.chienblanc.com
3 suites with private gardens - $125-$175

Three bungalows with private entrance, living room, bedroom (queen), bath with standard tub-shower arrangement and very

functional kitchen. Each unit has a small garden. TV, telephones, and all the comforts of home, including washer and dryer. An easy walk to the spas, restaurants and shops. Wineries are located throughout the area.

Christopher's Inn

1010 Foothill Boulevard Calistoga 94515
707.942.5755
www.christophersinn.com
22 units - $175-$425

All rooms with private baths, most with fireplaces, many with patio gardens, several with whirlpool tubs.

Cottage Grove Inn

1711 Lincoln Avenue 800.799.2284
707.942.8400
www.cottagegrove.com
16 cottages $235 - $295

Private cottages with king-size beds, 2-person deep whirlpool tubs and wood burning fireplaces. Listen to a favorite CD or watch your favorite movie as you relax. Located within walking distance to town, on a beautifully landscaped property.

Culver Mansion

1805 Foothill Boulevard Calistoga 94515
877.281.3671 707.942.4535 707.942.4557
www.culvermansion.com
6 rooms - $170-$190

A three-level Victorian built in 1867. The bedrooms are decorated in period styles such as Victorian, Edwardian, Art Deco, Art Nouveau and Early Twentieth Century. Great view of Mount St. Helena, the Palisades and the valley. A short walk from downtown.

Czech Inn

1102 Pine St. Calistoga 94515
707.942.9341

Elms, The

1300 Cedar Street Calistoga 94515
800.235.4316 707.942.9476
www.theelms.com
7 rooms - $145-$245

A French Victorian built in 1871 in downtown Calistoga. The four gigantic elm trees on the property were planted the same year the house was built and are said to be the tallest and oldest elms in the Napa Valley.

The house is the last of the "great eight" Victorians that once graced the town of Calistoga, and within walking distance to all spas, restaurants and shops. All rooms have private bathrooms and include afternoon wine and cheese, and full gourmet breakfast. Property available for family reunions and weddings.

Fanny's

1206 Spring Street Calistoga 94515
707.942.9491

Foothill House

3037 Foothill Boulevard Calistoga 94515
800.942.6933 707.942.6933
www.foothillhouse.com
1 room, 2 cottages, 2 suites - $175-$325

In the foothills just north of Calistoga.

Garnett Creek Inn

1139 Lincoln Avenue Calistoga 94515
707.942.9797 707.942.5288
www.garnettcreekinn.com
5 rooms $155 - $295

On Calistoga's main street.

Hacienda Guest House

707.942.5259
www.napavalleybnb.com
1 house - $350-$425

A Mexican-style hacienda vacation rental just minutes from Calistoga.

Hillcrest Country Inn

3225 Lake County Hwy. (Highway 29)
Calistoga CA 94515
707.942.6334
www.bnbweb.com/hillcrest
6 rooms $69 - $193

Small lake for fishing. Hiking, barbeque area.

Holiday House

3514 Highway 128 Calistoga 94515
707.942.6174

Hotel d'Amici

1436 Lincoln Avenue Calistoga 94515
707.942.1007 707.963.3150
www.rutherfordgrove.com/hotel.html
4 suites - $150-$225

La Chaumiere

1301 Cedar Street Calistoga 94515
800.474.6800 707.942.5139
www.lachaumiere.com
2 rooms, 1 cottage - $165-$250

One half-block from downtown. Patio gardens.

Larkmead Country Inn

1103 Larkmead Lane Calistoga 94515
707.942.5360
www.larkmeadinn.com
3 rooms - $150

Built in the early 1900s. Vineyard setting.

Meadowlark Country House

601 Petrified Road Calistoga 94515
800.942.5651 707.942.5651
www.meadowlarkinn.com
7 rooms - $165-$265

Secluded 20-acre estate, magnificent views, privacy, naturist pool, deck, sauna and hot tub, massage, fireplace, AC, gourmet breakfast, gay friendly, dogs welcome, one mile to shops and dining.

Mora Lane

2087 Mora Avenue Calistoga 94515
707.942.1395

Oakwood

1503 Lake Street Calistoga 94515
707.942.5381

Pink Mansion, The

1415 Foothill Boulevard Calistoga 94515
800.238.7465 707.942.0558
www.pinkmansion.com
6 rooms - $155-$295

Built in 1875 by William Fisher, who founded Calistoga Water. It was purchased by the Semic family in the 1930s, who painted it pink and added the indoor heated pool. Most suites have fireplaces, king beds and whirlpool tubs. The Pink Mansion is two blocks north of Lincoln Avenue and within walking distance to most of the spas and restaurants.

Quail Mountain

4455 North St. Helena Highway
Calistoga 94515
707.942.0316 707.942.0315

Scarlett's Country Inn

2918 Silverado Trail, N. Calistoga 94515
707.942.6669
members.aol.com/scarletts
1 room, 2 suites

1890 country house in a private canyon.

Scott Courtyard

1443 Second Street Calistoga 94515
800.942.1515 707.942.094890
www.scottcourtyard.com
3 suites - $160-$180

Stevenson Manor Inn (Best Western)

1830 Lincoln Avenue Calistoga 94515
707.942.1112 707.942.0381
34 rooms - $134-$234

Trailside Inn

4201 Silverado Trail Calistoga 94515
707.942.4106 707.942.4702
www.trailsideinn.com
3 suites - $165-$185

A 1930s farmhouse. Pool, hot tub, neighboring vineyards and two acres of flower-filled lawns.

Washington Street Lodging

1605 Washington Street Calistoga 94515
707.942.6968
www.napalinks.com/wsl
5 cottages - $90-$135

Large oaks, lovely garden, close to downtown and overlooking the Napa River.

Wine Way Inn

1019 Foothill Boulevard Calistoga 94515
800.572.0679 707.942.0680 707.942.4656
www.napavalley.com/wineway
6 rooms - $115-$175

NAPA

The 1801 Inn

1801 First Street, Napa, CA 94559
707.224.3739
www.the1801inn.com
8 cottages and suites - $165-$325

An intimate urban retreat located in the heart of downtown Napa, strolling distance to fine restaurants, quaint shops and historic sites. The beautifully restored Queen Anne Victorian now offers resort style accommodations and contemporary amenities, catering to savvy travelers who demand excellence. Features include romantic fireplaces and gracious sitting areas; large, private baths with two-person tubs or whirlpool tubs; gourmet breakfast; evening wine and hors d' oeuvres; and a 24-hour complimentary minibar. Guests can linger on the sun porch with a cup of custom-blend 1801 Inn coffee, or enjoy the evening breeze and a glass of wine on the delightful patio and shade garden.

Arbor Guest House

1436 G St. Napa, CA. 94559
707.252.8144 866.627.2262 (Toll free)
5 rooms - $175-$250

Located on a quiet residential street just 10 minutes walking distance from downtown Napa and a short four blocks from Highway 29. The beautiful gardens, where three- to four-course gourmet breakfasts are usually served, have many areas where you can relax and listen to the birds, read or enjoy a bottle of wine.

Beazley House

1910 First Street Napa CA 94559
800.559.1649
www.beazleyhouse.com
11 rooms - $125-$295

Napa's oldest B&B. A 1902 mansion. Gardens and private whirlpool tubs.

Blackbird Inn

1755 First Street Napa CA 94559
707.226.2450   888.567.9811
www.foursisters.com/inns/blackbirdinn.html
8 rooms - $135-$275

Beautifully handcrafted restoration in the early 20th Century Craftsman style. A short drive to downtown Napa.

Blue Violet Mansion

443 Brown Street Napa CA 94559
707.253.2583 800.959.2583
www.bluevioletmansion.com
17 rooms - $199-$359

An 1886 Queen Anne Victorian mansion in Old Town Napa. Each room is painted in *trompe l'oeil* fashion. Surrounded by an acre of manicured gardens, including a rose garden centered by a period gezebo with swing, expansive porches and swimming pool. A short walk to downtown Napa.

Candlelight Inn

1045 Easum Drive Napa CA 94558
707.257.3717 800.624.0395
www.candlelightinn.com
10 rooms - $135-$295

A lovely English Tudor built in 1929 on a quiet park-like one-acre garden setting. Nestled among redwood groves and trees along Napa Creek. Beautiful landscaping and large swimming pool.

Cedar Gables Inn

486 Coombs Street Napa CA 94559
707.224.7969 Fax 707.224.4838
www.cedargablesinn.com
9 rooms - $189-$ 329

Styled after a 16th century English country manor, this dark brown shingled mansion is located just four blocks from downtown Napa. Winding staircases lead to antique appointed rooms. Full breakfast, wine and cheese hour, whirlpool tubs, fireplaces, queen size beds, comfy robes. Luxurious surroundings and warm hospitality.

Churchill Manor

485 Brown Street Napa CA 94559
707.253.7733
www.churchillmanor.com
10 rooms - $155-$255

A three-story, 10,000-square foot mansion built in 1889 by one of Napa's founders and listed on the National Register of Historic Places.

Daughters Inn

1938 First Street Napa CA 94559
866.253.1331
www.thedaughtersinn.com
10 rooms - $235 - $325

All rooms have fireplaces and whirlpool tubs. English country garden setting.

Frog Hollow House

472 Seminary St Napa, CA 94559
925.831.4989
www.froghollowhouse.com
2 bdrm 1 bath home - $225-$275

Vacation rental. A charming and beautifully decorated 18th-century Victorian home located in historic downtown Napa. The bedrooms are decorated with antique iron beds, down comforters and pillows and lovely furniture. A lovely backyard and front yard for sipping wine and outdoor cooking. Full kitchen and all the amenities of home. Shops, restaurants, antiques and Copia are all within walking distance.

Hennessey House

1727 Main Street Napa CA 94559
707.226.3774
www.hennesseyhouse.com
10 rooms - $145-$295

A Queen Anne Victorian built in 1889. Just minutes from the downtown Napa's restaurants, shops and Copia.

Hillview Country Inn

1205 Hillview Lane Napa CA 94558
707.224.5004 707.224.6422
www.hillviewinnnapa.com

Inn of Imagination

470 Randolph Street Napa, CA 94559
707.224.7772 Fax 707.257.9827
www.innofimagination.com
3 rooms - $240.00-$280.00

Rooms capturing the lives and works of Lewis Carroll, Dr. Seuss and Jimmy Buffett. Features many murals, period furniture, expansive grounds, sculpture gardens, rain forest library, private baths and a whimsical feel. A classic example of Spanish Revival architecture, the inn is on the National Registry of Historic Places, and is located in the historic Arroyo Grande section of Old Town Napa.

Inn on Randolph

411 Randolph Street Napa, CA 94559
707.257.2886 800.670.6886
www.visitsoon.com
5 rooms - $119-$229

A Gothic Revival Victorian built in 1860.

La Belle Epoque

1386 Calistoga Avenue Napa CA 94559
707.257.2161 800.283.8070
www.labelleepoque.com
7 rooms, 2 suites - $160-$325

Built in 1893. In the center of Old Town Napa.

McClelland - Priest B&B Inn, The

569 Randolph Street Napa CA 94559
707.224.6875 800.290.6881
www.historicinnstravel.com
5 suites

In Old Town Napa. Built in 1879.

Milliken Creek Inn

1815 Silverado Trail Napa CA 94558
888.622.5775
www.millikencreekinn.com
10 rooms - $295-$525

A luxury inn on the Napa River. Three acres of gardens, fountains and trails. River and garden views. Concierge services, massage and spa treatments, live jazz piano, breakfast in bed, even private yoga classes. *Travel & Leisure Magazine* said it's one of the top 30 inns in the country, and *Travel Holiday* called it Napa Valley's finest inn.

Napa Inn, The

1137 Warren St. Napa CA 94559
707.257.1444 800.435.1144
www.napainn.com
14 rooms/suites - $120-$300

Oak Knoll Inn

2200 E. Oak Knoll Avenue Napa CA 94558
707.255.2200
www.oakknollinn.com
4 rooms - $250-$450

Surrounded by 600 acres of vineyards just minutes north of Napa. Swimming pool and whirlpool tubs.

Old World Inn

1301 Jefferson St. Napa CA 94559
707.257.0112 800.966.6624
www.oldworldinn.com
10 rooms - $150-$265

All room rates include a full gourmet breakfast, afternoon tea, a wine and cheese social hour, and their evening chocolate lover's desserts.

Stahlecker House

1042 Eastum Drive Napa CA 94558
707.257.1588 800.799.1588
www.stahleckerhouse.com
3 rooms, 1 suite - $160-$268

Located on one and a half acres of manicured lawns and flowering gardens.

Tall Timbers Chalet

1012 Darms Lane Napa 94558 707.252.7810
707.252.1055
www.talltimberscottages.com

POPE VALLEY AND CHILES VALLEY

RustRidge Bed & Breakfast Inn

2910 Lower Chiles Valley Road
St. Helena 94574
800.788.0263 707.965.9353   707.965.9263
www.rustridge.com
3 rooms - $165-$225

Tennis, hiking. On the grounds of RustRidge Ranch & Winery

ST. HELENA

Adagio Inn

1417 Kearney Street St. Helena, CA 94574
707.963.2238 888-8ADAGIO
Fax 707.963.5598
www.adagioinn.com
3 rooms - $220-$315

Located in a quiet area, this luxuriously decorated Edwardian residence is two blocks from world-class restaurants and unique shops. A lavish breakfast is served in the sunroom or on the veranda. Afternoon refreshments are served in the parlor with its baby grand piano. Extra large rooms/suites all have a European elegance along with king-sized beds, air conditioning and cable TV.

Ambrose Bierce B&B

1515 Main St. St. Helena CA 94574
707.963.3003
www.ambrosebiercehouse.com
3 rooms - $199-$269

Former residence of the 19th century author of short stories and "The Devil's Dictionary"

Bartels Ranch & Country Inn

1200 Conn Valley Road St. Helena CA 94574
707.963.4001
www.bartelsranch.com
4 rooms - $235-$455

60 acres, hiking/biking trails, lake, pool, whirlpool tub.

Bylund House

2000 Howell Mountain Road St. Helena CA 94574 707.963.9073
www.bylundhouse.com
2 rooms $95 - $200

A northern Italian Villa tucked into a "Tuscan" valley just two miles outside of downtown St. Helena. A separate tower, with a private entrance into a parlor with a fireplace, houses two rooms with private baths, balconies and sweeping views. Complimentary wine and hors d'oeuvres at poolside or starlight in the spa. Gourmet continental breakfast.

Cinnamon Bear

1407 Kearney St. St. Helena CA 94574
707.963.4653
$115-$185

Historic home. Walk to town.

Eagle & Rose Inn

1189 Lodi Lane St. Helena CA 94574
707.967.0466
www.eagleandroseinn.com
5 rooms - $110-$165

Erika's Hillside B&B

285 Fawn Park Drive St. Helena CA 94574
707.963.2887

Vineyard views, hillside retreat, whirlpool tub.

Glass Mountain Inn

3100 Silverado Trail St. Helena CA 94574
707.968.9400 877.968.9400 (toll free)
www.glassmountaininn.com
3 suites, 1 cottage

Victorian home, century-old wine cave, gazebo, private decks. On the mountainside east of St. Helena.

Hilltop House B&B

9550 St. Helena Road St. Helena CA 94574
707.944.0880
www.napanet.net/hospitality/hilltop-house
3 rooms - $135-$195

On the mountain. Hiking, spa.

Ink House, The

1575 St. Helena Highway St. Helena CA 94574
707.963.3890
www.inkhouse.com
7 rooms - $110-$215

Historic home with observatory with 360-degree view. Built in 1884, and listed on the National Registry of Historic Places.

La Fleur

1475 Inglewood Avenue St. Helena 94574
707.963.0233
www.lafleurinn.com
$150-$195

Napa Valley Spanish Villa Inn

474 Glass Mountain Road
St. Helena CA 94574
707.963.7483
www.napavalleyspanishvilla.com
3 rooms - $155-$275. Entire home available at reduced rate.

Country villa, two-mile drive from town.

Oliver House

2970 Silverado Trail St. Helena CA 94574
800.682.7888 707.963.4089
www.oliverhouse.com
4 rooms, 1 cottage - $165-$295

European-style chalet located on the historic Silverado Trail. Nestled on a hillside above St. Helena and within walking distance of five major wineries. Relax on private balconies or in beautiful common areas, or enjoy the views of the valley from the extensive grounds. Vibrant colors, unique custom painting and beautiful antiques throughout the guestrooms and living areas. All rooms and suites include private baths, down comforters, luxurious 100% cotton linens, and individual heat and air conditioning controls. A full gourmet breakfast is served every morning.

Prager Winery B & B

1281 Lewelling Lane St. Helena CA 94574
707.963.3720
www.pragerport.com
Next to Prager Winery and Port Works.
Two 3-room suites - $225

Shady Oaks Country Inn

399 Zinfandel Lane St. Helena CA 94574
707.963.1190
www.shadyoaksinn.com
4 rooms - $189-$239

Sunny Acres

397 Main Street St. Helena CA 94574
707.963.2826
www.sunnyacresbandb.com
2 rooms - $195

Restored building originally constructed in 1879. In the middle of a 20-acre vineyard. All rooms have private bath.

Vineyard Country Inn

201 Main St. St. Helena CA 94574
707.963.1000
www.vineyardcountryinn.com
21 suites - $160-$240

Vineyard setting, woodburning fireplaces, wet bars. Pool, whirlpool tub. Close to wineries and restaurants.

Wine Country Inn

1152 Lodi Lane St. Helena CA 94574
707.963.7077
www.winecountryinn.com
24 rooms - $185-$430

Wine Country Victorian & Cottages

400 Meadowood Lane St. Helena CA 94574
707.963.0852
1 suite, 2 cottages - $205-$255

Turn-of-the-century Victorian and cottage, vineyard and woodland setting.

Zinfandel Inn

800 Zinfandel Lane St. Helena CA 94574
707.963.3512
www.zinfandelinn.com
3 rooms - $175-$330

English Tudor on two beautifully land-scaped acres. Fireplaces, whirlpool tub, gazebo and aviary.

YOUNTVILLE

Bordeaux House

6600 Washington Street Yountville 94599
707.944.2855
www.bordeauxhouse.com
5 rooms - $135-$165

A very short walk to all Yountville shops and restaurants.

Burgundy House

6711 Washington Street Yountville 94599
707.944.0889
www.burgundyhouse.com
6 rooms - $125-$175

A French country stone building from the early 1890s. Just a short walk to Yountville shops and restaurants.

Castle in the Clouds

7400 St. Helena Highway
Yountville CA 94599
707. 944.2785
www.castleintheclouds.com
4 rooms - $235-$325

Perched high atop a hill on eight acres in the heart of Napa Valley. Looks down upon world famous wineries and vineyards, and provides easy access to fine dining and wine tasting. Decorated with museum quality antiques, the B&B offers luxurious comforts including king or queen beds with down comforters, plush robes, private baths and air conditioning.

The large parlor has a 52-inch digital satellite TV, fireplace, guest refrigerator with complimentary beverages and snacks, coffee/tea bar and a variety of board games. A hot tub carved into the side of the mountain, patio with gardens and fountains, a picnic area, a balcony and rooftop sitting area offer many ways to enjoy the best views in Napa Valley.

Oleander House

7433 St. Helena Highway, Yountville, CA 94599
707 944-8315   800 788-0357
www.oleander.com
5 rooms - $145-$195

Oleander House is just north of Yountville, set amongst the vineyards and countryside. Guest rooms are spacious and antique filled, with Laura Ashley wallcoverings. Within five minutes of world-class restaurants, wineries and shopping.

Petit Logis

6527 Yount Street Yountville 94599
707.944.2332
www.petitlogis.com
5 rooms - $105-$200

In the very heart of Yountville. Each room has a fireplace and large bathroom with double whirlpool tub.

Horse Camping

Skyline Wilderness Park

2201 Imola Avenue, Napa CA 94559
707.252.0481
www.ncfaa.com/skyline/horse_camping.htm

10 spacious horse camping sites, each accommodating two horse and two rigs, with water and picnic table. Bathrooms with showers within a short walking dis-

tance. Fifteen miles of trails through wooded forest, valleys and hilltops.

Recreational Vehicle (RV) Camping

Rancho Monticello Resort

6590 Knoxville Road, Napa CA 94558
707.966.2188
www.ranchomonticelloresort.com

Located on Lake Berryessa, the resort offers picnicking, boat launching, fishing from shore or boats, and fifty campsites for tents or RVs. All campsites have picnic tables and barbecues, with water faucet access, restrooms and showers nearby. Trailer sites have full hookup with electrical, water and sewer. Long-term sites based on annual leases are also available for mobile homes, travel trailers and RVs.

Skyline Wilderness Park

2201 Imola Avenue, Napa CA 94559
707.252.0481
www.ncfaa.com/skyline/rvcamp.htm

Thirty-nine spaces available in the park, 19 with full hookups at $27 per night, and 20 with water and electricity only at $25 per night.

RV camping is also available at the locations. See their respective Town sections for detailed information.

Calistoga

Napa County Fairgrounds

Lake Berryessa

Most Lake Berryessa resorts

Napa

Napa Valley Exposition

Spas

The first thing people think of when they hear "Napa Valley" is *wine*. But the second thing some people think of is *mud*.

Why? Because the Napa Valley—particularly the town of Calistoga at the north end of the valley—is famous for its spas and mud baths.

Calistoga is on top of an active geothermal zone, meaning the area is filled with hot springs and hot pools of water that can be tapped.

Ever since Sam Brannan founded the town in the 1860s, Calistoga has been famous for mud baths and mineral baths. Today the town is filled with spas, and other valley towns offer spa facilities. You'll find some of the spas in the Towns section of this book ,and a complete listing of all of them following this section.

What happens in a spa? Why would someone pay to get slimed? Ah, but it's far more than that.

Your Typical Spa Experience

What follows is typical, but each spa has its own physical layout, amenities and treatment order.

If you planned ahead, you already made an appointment before you left home for the Napa Valley. If not, try to do it as soon as you arrive in the valley. If that's not possible, just show up and hope they have an opening.

When you arrive at the front desk, you'll choose your various treatments from an extensive menu of options: baths, wraps, facials, scrubs, massages. Wraps, facials and scrubs can involve many different herbs and scents, all designed to make your skin cleaner and healthier; remove toxins and dead cells from your body; and invigorate your skin, your body and your psyche. Each spa has its own particular formulas.

Mud baths are always optional, and not every spa has them, but if they're available we recommend that you try one.

Once you've picked your choices, you'll be assigned to a room, usually a private one. A few spas are set up so that you and your partner can take mud baths and mineral baths together.

You will disrobe, wrap yourself in a towel, and then be led into another room. There you'll shower and walk over to a mud bath. There are separate rooms for men and women.

A mud bath for two in Calistoga. Photo courtesy of Golden Haven Spa.

Mud Bath

The bath is (usually) a rectangular cement tub filled with dark mud. It's not your average mud, but a mixture of clay or local volcanic ash, imported peat moss and local hot springs water. The purpose of the mud is to remove toxins from your body, relax your muscles and joints, and cleanse and invigorate your skin.

You sit on the edge of the tub, swing your legs into the tub, and then kind of scoot the rest of you over until you're all in. Lie down on your back in the mud, wiggle down as much as possible, then use your hands and arms to pile mud on top of yourself, until as much of you as possible is covered. If you can't get it all, don't worry. The bath attendant will cover the rest of you until only your head is uncovered.

You'll then lie there for 10-12 minutes and soak. Nothing else is expected of you. From time to time an attendant will come

by, wipe the sweat off your forehead with a cool washcloth, and give you a glass of cold water to drink (through a straw.)

When the time is up, your attendant will tell you to get out. Do it slowly. Actually, you have no choice. You can't do it quickly anyhow. Hold onto the sides of the tub with your hands, then use the strength of your hands and arms to lift your rear up and swing it over to the side of the tub. Then shove, scrape and wipe as much of the mud off your body as you can back into the tub.

When you're done (don't worry, everyone still has lots of mud on them) go back into the shower and wash off the rest of the stuff. Yes, it does stick into all those cracks and crevices, so do a pretty thorough job.

Once you've showered, it's time for the mineral bath.

Whirlpool Mineral Bath

This bath often takes place in the same room as the mud bath. If not, you'll be led to the right location. There you'll remove your towel, get into the tub and relax for 10-15 minutes while whirlpool jets blow streams of air and bubbles in the warm water, and you soak peacefully. One spa we like even has a rubber ducky for you to play with. If you have the energy for it, you can always take a sip from the ever-present glass of cold water.

Whirl away your tension in a mineral water whirlpool. Photo courtesy of Golden Haven Spa.

Blanket Wrap

Your attendant will reappear and tell you that it is time for the blanket wrap. You'll get out of the mineral bath, dry off a little, then head to the wrap room. Here you'll lie down on a comfortable bed on your back, be wrapped in blankets, and again have your forehead wiped and another glass of cold water.

Once again, your only job is to lie there, rest, and slowly cool off from the heat acquired in the mud and mineral baths. It's a good place for a short nap.

After another 10 to 15 minutes, you're once again beckoned from your reverie and led off, most likely to yet another room.

Massage

At most spas, you can choose between a half-hour or full-hour massage, or sometimes even one lasting an hour and a half. A shorter massage will cover your back, neck and shoulders. A long massage will very thoroughly cover everything from nose to toes.

Styles of massage vary, and you can request the kind you like. They range from gentle Esalen-type massage—which is pure, gentle pleasure—up to the much more vigorous Swedish massage, which frequently feels a lot better after you've gotten it than it does during.

During your massage only the area of your body that is being worked on will be exposed. The rest will be discreetly covered with a sheet. If you want to specify a male or female massage therapist, make sure you do it when you book the appointment.

At the end of your massage, you'll be allowed to lie there (many people fall asleep after or even during the massage) until you're ready to get up. You'll probably have carried your belongings along with you, so eventually you can get dressed and go back out into the world, a very different person than when you entered the spa.

Spas with Lodging

Calistoga Oasis Spa

1300 Washington St. Calistoga, CA 94515
707.942.2122 800.404.4772
www.oasisspa.com
Located on the grounds of the Roman Spa Resort Hotel
www.romanspahotsprings.com
60 rooms - $82-$230

Calistoga Spa Hot Springs

1006 Washington Street
Calistoga, CA 94515
707.942.6269
www.calistogaspa.com

Calistoga Village Inn & Spa

1880 Lincoln Avenue Calistoga, CA 94515
707.942.0991
www.greatspa.com
$69-$159

Dr. Wilkinson's Hot Springs

1507 Lincoln Ave. Calistoga, CA 94515
707.942.4102
www.drwilkinson.com
Rooms and cottages - $109-$189

Golden Haven Spa and Resort

1713 Lake Street Calistoga CA 94515
707.942.6793
www.goldenhaven.com
Rooms - $65-$175

Mount View Spa

1457 Lincoln Avenue Calistoga CA 94515
707.942.5789
www.mountviewspa.com
20 rooms, 9 suites, 3 cottages - $145-$225+

Nance's Hot Springs

1614 Lincoln Avenue Calistoga CA 94515
707.942.6211 800.201.6211
www.nanceshotsprings.com
24 rooms, all include kitchenettes and private baths - $65-$125

Family-owned since it was founded in 1922. Mud baths, indoor mineral pool.

Roman Spa Hot Springs

1300 Washington St. Calistoga, CA 94515
800.404.4772
www.romanspahotsprings.com
60 rooms - $82-$230

Silver Rose Inn

351 Rosedale Rd. Calistoga,
California 94515
707.942.9581 800.995.9381
www.silverrose.com
20 rooms - $165-$300

White Sulphur Springs Resort and Spa

3100 White Sulphur Springs Road
St. Helena, CA 94574
707.963.8588 800.593.8873
www.whitesulphursprings.com
Rooms and cottages - $85-$205

Spas without Lodging

Cedar Street Spa

1107 Cedar St. Calistoga CA 94515
707.942.2947
www.cedarstreetspa.com

Health Spa Napa Valley

1030 Main St. St. Helena CA 94574
707.967.8800
www.napavalleyspa.com

Lavender Hill Spa

1015 Foothill Boulevard
Calistoga, CA. 94515
707.942.4495 800.528.4772
www.lavenderhillspa.com

Lincoln Avenue Spa

1339 Lincoln Avenue Calistoga CA 94515
707.942.5296
www.lincolnavenuespa.com

Veranda Club Spa

6795 Washington Street
Yountville, CA 94599
707.944.1906
www.verandaclubspa.com

Corporate & Personal Tour Planning

If you're bringing a corporate group to the valley, or just want to organize things before you arrive, here are some companies that will assist you in making your visit both productive and enjoyable.

Alliance Wine Tours

838 School Road Napa CA 94559
707.257.1737. Fax 707.257.2001

Alliance can plan or assist with wine country tours, meetings, and events. Services also include programs for spouses, corporate gifts, and transportation.

Destination: Napa Valley Tours

295 West Lane Angwin CA 94508
707.965.1808
www.tournapavalley.com

Personalized tours for individuals, couples, groups and business events.

Wine Country Concierge

PO Box 789 Napa CA 94559
707.252.4472
www.winecountryconcierge.com

Wine Country Concierge can arrange lodging, restaurants, spas, tours, and small events, including getting you in to visit wineries not normally open to the public.

Wine & Dine Tours

P.O. Box 513 345 La Fata Suite E
St. Helena CA 94574
707.963.8930   800.WINETOUR
www.wineanddinetour.com

Designs, organizes, and conducts winery tours and events for groups as small as two and as large as 25,000. Focuses on such things as wine and food pairing meals, off-the-beaten-path wineries, educational seminars, enology lectures, meet the winemaker special events, and cooking demonstrations.

Meeting and Conference Facilities

For specifics on each location, see Town section listing.

Calistoga

Calistoga Village Inn & Spa - Conference space for 70

Silver Rose Inn - Conference space for 50

Napa

Chateau Hotel - 10,000 square feet of meeting space

Christian Brothers Retreat & Conference Center - Meeting space for up to 150

Embassy Suites - Up to 8 meeting rooms and more than 6,900 square feet of meeting space

Marriott Napa Valley - 11 meeting rooms, 11,000 square feet

Napa River Inn - 2 meeting rooms for a total of 124 people and 2,200 square feet

Napa Valley Exposition - 4 meeting halls, each holding from 250 - 350 people with tables and chairs

River Terrace Inn – 2,500 sq. ft. of meeting space, including one board room, one breakout room, and one 900 square foot conference room.

Silverado Resort - 25,000 square foot executive conference center (See listing in Napa section)

Rutherford

Rancho Caymus Inn - Meeting space for up to 75

Silverado Trail

Auberge Du Soleil - Meeting space for up to 150 (Rutherford)

Meadowood - Over 3,300 square feet of meeting space in four buildings (St. Helena)

St. Helena

Harvest Inn - 8 meeting and special event spaces (over 6,000 square feet)

Yountville

Napa Valley Lodge - Meeting space for up to 60

Villagio - Up to 7 meeting rooms with more than 3,700 square feet

Vintage Inn - Meeting space for up to 150

Yountville Inn - Meeting space for up to 60

NOTES

Things to Do

Napa Valley Cuisine

For information on specific Napa Valley restaurants, see the Town sections earlier in this book.

For a complete listing of Napa Valley restaurant web pages, we recommend you go to www.westsong.com/restaurants.

What is Napa Valley Cuisine?

It's fresh, it's artistic, and it's often a blend of cultures.

Most produce is locally grown, if not in the Napa Valley, then in Northern California. It's also frequently organic and often grown right at the restaurant.

Entrees can include anything from beef to fish to vegetarian. Most chefs tend toward the light side, without heavy sauces and large amounts of meat. However, there is currently a noticeable trend in many restaurants toward the heavier "comfort food."

Meals are customarily prepared to complement local wines, although with the variety of wines offered in the Napa Valley, it's likely you can find a bottle to go with any kind of food.

California cuisine is generally regarded to have started with Chez Panisse in Berkeley, although the Napa Valley was quick to join in. The legendary, and now departed, Diner in Yountville was the first in the valley to serve the lighter and fresher food now known as "California cuisine" or, more recently, "wine country cuisine." The still-famous *Mustard's Grill* was another early pioneer.

"Fusion" is a popular style where ingredients and seasonings from two or more countries are blended into a unique dish. "Pan-Pacific" is a popular subset of fusion in which chefs blend dishes and ingredients

from various locations around the Pacific Rim, including Japan, China, the Philippines, Hawaii, Australia and South America.

Despite its strong ties with Spain and Mexico, the Napa Valley seems to have turned into "Tuscany West", although to be fair it *was* largely the Italians that established the modern wine industry in the valley. Tuscan-style wineries, homes and restaurants abound, and you'll have no problem finding Italian and Cal-Italia cooking in the style you like.

Prices are not low. While you can find "fair" prices, you'll have a hard time finding inexpensive ones. You'll be lucky if two of you can leave a restaurant—after having had an entrée, an appetizer or a dessert, and a glass of wine—for less than eighty dollars. One hundred dollars and up is more common. But you'll more than likely have enjoyed an excellent meal with fine service and attractive surroundings.

We discuss restaurants in the various town sections of this book. We don't list them all, but we have tried to present the best known, most typical or unique. Not all aspire to be Yountville's *French Laundry*—considered by many to be the top restaurant in the United States—but almost all have highly trained chefs deeply committed to their art.

Don't hesitate to ask the locals for their restaurant recommendations. You'll find the staff of winery tasting rooms particularly helpful. They like to eat as much as they like to drink.

VEGETARIAN RESTAURANTS

Currently there are no vegetarian-only restaurants in the Napa Valley, but there is such a focus on fresh fruit and vegetables at most valley restaurants, that it really doesn't matter. You should have no trouble ordering vegetarian dishes from the menu at almost any restaurant you visit. If you have any doubt, just ask your waiter.

Cooking Classes

CasaLana
1316 South Oak Street
Calistoga 94515
707.942.0615 877.968.2665
www.casalana.com

A bed and breakfast inn that also offers hands-on cooking classes in a professionally equipped kitchen. Classes range from essential skills to advanced techniques. Personalized courses for groups are also available.

Copia - American Center for Wine, Food and the Arts (Napa)
www.copia.org

Culinary Institute of America at Greystone (St. Helena)
www.ciachef.edu/greystone/

Professional cooking classes. Also one-hour demonstrations and short classes for home chefs.

Napa Valley Cooking School (St. Helena)
www.napacommunityed.org/cookingschool/

Camp Napa Culinary
PO Box 114 Oakville CA 94562
707.944.9112 888.999.4844
www.hughcarpenter.com

Chef/cooking teacher Hugh Carpenter has written over a dozen popular cookbooks. His articles have appeared in numerous newspapers and magazines, including *Cook's Illustrated* and *Bon Appetit*. Carpenter and his photographer wife Teri Sandison conduct six-day tours that include cooking classes and visits to wineries and private estates throughout the valley.

Farmers Markets

CALISTOGA
Farmers Market
1546 Lincoln Avenue (at the former Gliderport)
707.942.4343
Saturdays June-September,
8:30 a.m.-12:30 p.m.

NAPA
Chef's Market
Downtown Napa
707.257.0322
Fridays, Late May - August. 2 p.m.-6 p.m.,
Music and food till 9 p.m.

Farmer's Market
500 First Street in Copia's south parking lot.
707.252.7142
Tuesdays, May-October, 7:30 a.m. to noon.

ST. HELENA
Farmer's Market
Crane Park
707.252.2105
www.sthelenafarmersmkt.org
Fridays, May-October. 7:30 a.m.- Noon
DIRECTIONS: At St. Helena High School turn west off of Highway 29 onto Grayson, left on Crane.

YOUNTVILLE
Farmer's Market
Parking lot of Compadre's Restaurant
6539 Washington Street
707.944.0904
Wednesdays, June-September, 4-8 p.m.

Foods and Food Products

BAKING MIXES
Napa Valley Pantry
www.napavalleypantry.com

BEER

People don't drink just wine here, particularly in the summer. In fact, everyone will admit that the beverage of choice for people working during the harvest is beer.

The Napa Valley currently has three microbreweries. You'll find more information in their entries in their respective town sections.

Microbreweries

Downtown Joe's (see Napa listing)

Napa Valley Brewing Company (see Calistoga listing for Calistoga Inn)

Silverado Brewing Company (see St. Helena listing)

BEEF

Napa Valley Free-Range Beef
866.661.9111
www.napagrassfedbeef.com

100% free-range, grass-fed, Argentine-style Black Angus Beef from the Gamble Ranch in Lake Berryessa Valley. Also available at farmers' markets in the valley.

CHEESE

Goat's Leap Cheese
3321 St. Helena Highway
St. Helena CA 94574
707.963.2337
www.goatsleap.com

Currently produces four varieties of goat cheese, available at fine cheese shops throughout the Napa Valley and the San Francisco Bay Area. Not open to the public.

Skyhill Napa Valley Farms
2431 Partrick Road
Napa CA 94558
707.255.4800

Produces goat cheese and yogurt at its farm in the Carneros hills. Retail outlets include Trader Joe's and Costco. Not open to the public.

CHOCOLATE

Anette's Chocolate Factory
www.anettes.com
(also see Napa listing in Towns section)

FAMILY FARMS

Some of this information is courtesy of the University of California, Small Farm Center. The Center publishes *Napa Yolano Harvest Trails*, a map and directory of farms, wineries, parks, trails, bed and breakfast inns and other attractions in Napa, Yolo and Solano Counties.
www.sfc.ucdavis.edu

Forni Brown Gardens
Foothill Boulevard
Calistoga CA 94515
707.942.6123

Forni Brown provides produce to some of the country's finest restaurants. Not open to the public, except for their annual Spring Plant Sale every April, but you can phone in advance for special orders throughout the year.

Hoffman Farm
2125 Silverado Trail
Napa CA 94558
707.226.8938
Open daily August-November.
DIRECTIONS: On the west side of the Silverado Trail, 1/4 mile north of Trancas Street.

Pears, walnuts, prunes and persimmons.

Omi's Farm
4185 Silverado Trail
Napa CA 94558
707.224.0954
kniesar@napanet.net

Located on the Silverado Trail 3.5 miles north of Trancas Street. Open year-round, by appointment only. Sustainable family farm offering seasonal produce, eggs, walnuts and berries. Also sells sheep and Australian cattle dogs.

Rancho Gordo

PO Box 3228   Napa CA 94558
707.363.0993
www.ranchogordo.com

Specialty produce organically grown (but not yet organically licensed) to support "rancho" cooking, a blend of Mexican, Native American and California cooking. Tomatoes, chile peppers, beans and corn, tomatillos, squash and cucumbers, amaranth, Persian cress, culantro, quelite, cilantro, chard and other Mexican herbs, greens and grains. Available at farmers markets in the area.

Stewart's Farm

Silverado Trail at Deer Park Road
St. Helena CA 94574
707.967.8360
Open daily May-November

A roadside stand that sells produce grown on adjacent property and from nearby farms. Depending on the season, you'll find green beans, apricots, cherries, pumpkins, squash, zucchini, tomatoes and corn.

FOOD PRODUCTS (ASSORTED)

NapaStyle
www.napastyle.com
(also see St. Helena listing in Towns section)

Napa Valley Naturals
www.napavalleytrading.com

Napa Valley Traditions
www.napatraditions.com
(also see Napa listing in Towns section)

Tulocay's Made in Napa Valley
www.madeinnapavalley.com

Wine Country Kitchens
www.winecountrykitchens.com

GRAPESEED OIL

Salute Santé Grapeseed Oil
Food & Vine Inc.
68 Coombs Street Suite I-2
Napa CA 94559
707.251.3900
www.salutesante.com

HONEY

Marshall's Farm Honey
www.marshallshoney.com

(also see American Canyon listing in Towns section)

"IT'S-IT" ICE CREAM

It's not from the Napa Valley, but who cares? It's very San Francisco—and delicious. The It's-It is an ice cream sandwich consisting of vanilla ice cream between two oatmeal cookies covered with chocolate and then frozen. (They come in additional flavors now as well—chocolate, strawberry or mint.) The It's-It was invented in 1928 by George Whitney, owner of the now sadly-departed—it closed in 1972—Playland at the Beach amusement park in San Francisco. Fortunately the It's-It survived. You can find them at various grocery stores around the Napa Valley.

JELLIES

Napa Valley Wine Jelly
www.winejelly.com

LAMB

Napa Valley Lamb Company
4320 B. Old Toll Road Calistoga CA 94515
707.942.6957 Fax 707.942.8852

The company provides succulent lamb to local restaurants. In addition to becoming the entrée at your restaurant table, the flock also doubles as agricultural consultants. They're hired by local vineyards to remove weeds, keep crop cover down, and fertilize.

NUTS

NapaNuts
www.napanuts.com

OLIVE OIL

A large number of new olive oils have appeared on the California market in the last few years. Olives are becoming an important, although still small, crop in the Napa Valley. For a complete list of U.S. olive oil producers, see www.oliveoil-source.com.

Extra virgin olive oil means the oil has less than one percent free fatty acids, a standard set by the International Olive Oil Council. No chemicals or heat can be used in the extraction process.

An olive tree can produce 2/3 to 4 1/2 gallons of oil per tree. The entire fruit is crushed, including the pit. Oil should be stored in a dark, cool area and used within one to two years of pressing.

According to the Council, a certified olive oil will have the following positive attributes, and will have no negative attributes.

Positive Attributes

Fruity - perceived directly or through the back of the nose

Bitter - perceived on the back of the tongue.

Pungent - perceived in the throat

Negative Attributes

Fusty - results from olives stored in piles, which have undergone anaerobic fermentation.

Musty - moldy flavor resulting from fungi and yeast

Winey-Vinegary - resulting from aerobic fermentation

Rancid - oil has oxidized

Other negative attributes include heated/burnt, hay/wood, greasy, briny, metallic and cucumber.

Olive Oil Producers

You'll find olive oils at stores and wineries throughout the Napa Valley, including these olive oil producers:

Araujo Estate
www.araujoestatewines.com

Big Paw Grub
www.bigpawgrub.com

Organic olive oils and vinegars infused with wild herbs and mushrooms hand-foraged from the wilds of the Napa Valley. Really.

Cakebread Cellars
www.cakebread.com

Dutch Henry Winery
www.dutchhenry.com

Long Meadow Ranch (St. Helena)
www.longmeadowranch.com

Napa Valley Olive Oil Manufactory (St. Helena)

Regusci Winery (Silverado Trail)
www.regusciwinery.com

Silver Oak Cellars (Oakville)
www.silveroak.com

St. Helena Olive Oil Company (Rutherford)
www.sholiveoil.com

Vine Village
www.vinevillage.org

PUREES

Perfect Purée of Napa Valley
Hayward Enterprises
2700 Napa Valley Corporate Drive, Suite L
Napa CA 94558
707.261.5100   800.556.3707
Fax 707.261.5111
www.perfectpuree.com

Natural fruit purées to be used as a base for soups, sauces, soufflés, sorbets, marinades, glazes and mixed drinks. Nearly 40 flavors, including Berry Strawberry, More Mango, Passion Fruit Concentrate, Red Raspberry and Prickly Pear Cactus Fruit, Positively Pomegranate, and Roast Sweet Yellow Pepper. Most are certified kosher.

ROTO

ROTO Beverage

945 Main Street St. Helena CA 94574
707.967.0707 Fax: 707.942.1121
www.drinkroto.com

Roto is a beverage developed by Napa Valley winemaker Cary Gott, who decided to create an adult soft drink. Roto is made from natural extracts and flavors in a mixture of citruses, fruits and spices in sparkling water. It's fresh, zippy, non-alcoholic, has just a touch of sweetness, is great over ice and is available at stores throughout the valley. We like it. Particularly as an aperitif.

SAUSAGE

Gerhard's Napa Valley Sausage

www.gerhardsausage.com

No artificial flavors and preservatives. They started at Vintage 1870 in Yountville, now they're everywhere.

SLOW FOOD

Napa Valley Convivium

www.slowfoodusa.org (for nationwide information)

Slow Food began in Italy in 1986 as a reaction to (and protest against) the primarily American fast food industry, which has contributed not only to fast, mass-produced meals but a fast, mass-produced society in most developed countries. Slow Food's manifesto states that it is a "movement for the protection of the right to taste."

Slow Food supports and encourages quality foods and beverages, and supports local growers, chefs, winemakers and others who share their goals. Slow Food USA's mission is to "rediscover pleasure and quality in everyday life precisely by slowing down and learning to appreciate the convivial traditions of the table." It does this through local chapters called "convivia" that organize educational, cultural and, most important, gastronomic events.

There is an active Slow Food group in the Napa Valley. It has monthly events focusing on small food producers and the chefs who use their products. For more information, email:
Christopher.Carpenter@lokoya.com.

VINEGAR

You'll also find vinegar at some of the Olive Oil producers.

Sparrow Lane

1455 Summit Lake Drive Angwin CA 94508
707.815.1813
www.sparrowlane.com

Premium varietal vinegars include Cabernet Sauvignon, Champagne, Balsamic, Zinfandel, Golden Balsamic.

Shopping

The Napa Valley is filled with unique shops, offering all sorts of things ranging from clothing to furniture to art to books to, of course, wine.

Main shopping areas are the First Street area and the Premium Outlet Stores in Napa, Washington Street and Vintage 1870 in Yountville, Main Street in St. Helena, and Lincoln Avenue in Calistoga

ALPACAS

Alpacas of Napa Valley

3233 Dry Creek Road Napa CA 94558
866.431.8978 707.257.2226
www.alpacasofnapavalley.com

Open seven days a week by appointment only. Alpaca wool products including sweaters, shawls, baby blankets, fiber and yarn, and even an entire Alpaca (or more) if you'd like to breed them.

ANTIQUES

Antique Fair

6512 Washington Street
Yountville CA 94599
707.944.8440
www.antiquefair.com

French furnishings and art, European art.

Red Hen Antiques

5091 St. Helena Highway Napa CA 94558
707.257.0822
Open daily 10 a.m. - 5:30 p.m.
Take Oak Knoll Avenue west off Highway 29 between Napa and Yountville.

A collective of nearly 100 antique dealers in a vineyard setting.

The Neighborhood

1400 First Street   Napa CA 94559
707.259.1900
Open daily 10 a.m.-6 p.m., Sunday 10 a.m.-5p.m.
DIRECTIONS: Located in downtown Napa one block from the Napa Valley Conference and Visitors Bureau.

Over 50 antique dealers in a 20,000 square foot showroom.

ART GALLERIES

The Artful Eye

1333 Lincoln Ave. Calistoga CA 94515
707.942.4743

Eclectic jewelry, wearable art, blown glass, ceramics, paintings, metal, art furniture and unique gifts.

Art on Main

1359 Main Street, St. Helena CA 94574
707.963.3350

Original art, some by Napa Valley artists.

Blue Heron Gallery

Vintage 1870, 6525 Washington St. Yountville CA 94599
707.944.2044

The artwork of a dozen local artists. Welded sculpture, watercolor, oil, acrylic, pastel and prints. A focus on painted Napa Valley landscapes and florals. Also includes a wide variety of artwork from pounded metal masks and small wire sculpture to handmade dolls and jewelry.

Calistoga Pottery

1001 Foothill Boulevard Calistoga CA 94515
707.942.0216
www.calistogapottery.com

Handcrafted dinner and serving pieces.

Ca'Toga Galleria d'Arte

1206 Cedar Street Calistoga CA 94515
707.942.3900
www.catoga.com

Unique works of art from Carlo Marchiori, including ceiling murals, porcelain, ceramics, watercolor, paintings, tiles, stone plaques, sculpture, furniture, accessories, book, cards and posters.

Chajo Fine Art Furnishings

929 Main St. (across from Tra Vigne)
St. Helena CA 94574
707.257.3676
www.chajo.com

One of a kind furniture from Cook & Edie. Also the work of Robert Gouthier, turned wood artist; Dan Cox, wildlife photographer; and David Coddaire, functional metal sculptor.

di Rosa Art & Nature Preserve

5200 Carneros Hwy (Hwy 121)
Napa CA 94559
707.226.5991
www.dirosapreserve.org

A unique museum of San Francisco Bay Area art located in the Carneros Region. Gift shop.

Glass Gallery

815 Main Street Napa CA 94559
707.253.7763
www.ggallery.net

Across the street from the river, near Third Street. Beautiful handcrafted works of glass.

Henry Joseph Gallery

2475 Solano Ave. Napa CA 94558
707.224.4356

"California style watercolors" by artists such as Vernon Nye, Justin Faivre, Charles Surendorf and Crandell Norton. Also Napa Valley artists such as Roger Blum, Jay Golik, Joanna Matthews and Kristi Rene.

Imani Gallery

1144 Main St. Napa CA 94559 707.224.7886
www.imanigallery.com

Contemporary painting, limited edition prints and original photographs.

I. Wolk Gallery

1354 Main St. St. Helena CA 94574
707.963.8800
www.iwolkgallery.com

Contemporary paintings, works on paper, photography and sculpture. Emphasis is on representational imagery including landscapes, still life and figurative subjects.

Jessel Gallery

1019 Atlas Peak Road Napa CA 94558
707.257.2350
www.jesselgallery.com

Unique gifts, crafts, books, tools and decorations. Works by Clark Mitchell, Alan Sanborn, Brigitte McReynolds, Mei Yulo and gallery founder Jessel Miller.

Lee Youngman Galleries

1316 Lincoln Avenue Calistoga CA 94515
707.942.0585
www.leeyoungmangalleries.com

North Light Gallery

1272 Hayes Street, Suite D Napa CA 94558
707.226.8885
www.northlightgalleryonline.com

Large selection of artwork including fine etchings by Carol Collette, Stephen Whittle and Alice Scott. Co-owner Robin Stein does beautiful framing work.

Raku Ceramics

6540 Washington Street   Yountville CA 94599
707.944.9424
www.rasgalleries.com

Ceramics by Greg Milne, Tom Neugebaur, Ed Risak, Kerry Gonsales and George Witten.

Raspberry's Art Glass

6540 Washington Street   Yountville CA 94599
707.944.9211
www.rasgalleries.com

One-of-a-kind works in glass by Jerry Cebe, Richard Silver, John Lotton and others in a collection of vases, perfume vials and sculpture.

Spirits in Stone

St. Helena Premium Outlets
Two miles north of St. Helena
3111 N. St. Helena Highway
St. Helena CA 94574
800.95SHONA9
www.spiritsinstone.com

Beautiful contemporary sculpture from the Shona of Zimbabwe

BOOKSTORES

We encourage you to patronize our (and your) local independent bookstores. However, if that's not convenient, or you can't find a particular book that you're seeking, visit www.napavalleybooks.com for the largest selection on the Web of books on the Napa Valley, and by Napa Valley authors.

Bookends Book Store

1014 Coombs (at First Street)
Napa CA 94559
707.224.1077
www.bookends-napa.com

General, children's. Napa Valley books and authors. Napa's oldest bookstore

Calistoga Bookstore

1343 Lincoln Avenue Calistoga CA 94515
707.942.4123

General, regional West, health and bodywork, self-help. Home of Sara the Cat.

Copperfield's Annex

1303 First Street Napa CA 94559
707.252.8002
www.copperfields.net

Used, antiquarian, new and bargain books.

Copperfield's Books

1330 Lincoln Avenue Calistoga CA 94515
707.942.1616
www.copperfields.net

General, children's, children's Spanish, literature, cooking, story hour, used, rare, new and bargain books.

Main Street Books

1315 Main Street St. Helena CA 94574
707.963.1338

New, used and special order. Liza and her bookstore have a special place in the hearts of St. Helena bibliophiles of all ages.

Napa Book Tree

1405 Second Street Napa CA 94559
707.259.5400
www.napabooktree.com

General, literature, local interests and authors, children's.

Pacific Union College Bookstore

Angwin Plaza Angwin CA
707.965.6271

Textbooks, paperbacks, children's books. Closed Saturdays.

CHRISTMAS TREE FARMS

The Napa Valley once had a large number of Christmas tree farms. Now most of those have been replaced by grapes, or in a few cases, by houses. But there are two left.

Napa Valley Christmas Tree Farm

2130 Big Ranch Road Napa CA 94558
707.252.1000

DIRECTIONS: Take Highway 29 north through Napa to Trancas Street. Turn east on Trancas to Big Ranch Road. Turn left (north) and go 1/2 mile north. Farm is on the right. Open: Friday after Thanksgiving until a few days before Christmas. Hours Noon to 4:30 pm, but call first to confirm.

Five acres under night lighting. Douglas Fir. Cut Silvertip, Noble Fir, Fraser Fir and Douglas Fir. Special order trees. Commercial tree service. Certified flame retarding. Flocking available. Picnic area. Free garlands/boughs. School tours available by reservation.

Peterson Family Christmas Tree Farm

1120 Darms Lane Napa CA 94558
707.259.1712

DIRECTIONS: Go north on Highway 29 through Napa. North of Napa, turn left at the signal lights at Oak Knoll Avenue. Immediately turn right on Solano Avenue, which is the fontage road. Continue almost one mile on Solano to Darms Lane and turn left. The farm is a short distance down Darms Lane on the righthand side.

Open: Friday after Thanksgiving to approximately December 21st. 1-5 pm weekdays, 9 am - 5 pm Saturday and Sunday. Closed Mondays.

3.5 acres of Douglas and White Fir. Also walnuts and other assorted goodies.

LAVENDER

Harms Vineyard and Lavender Fields

3185 Dry Creek Road
Napa CA 94558
707.257.2683
damery@napanet.net

Tours by appointment. Certified organic lavender (actually their lavender is not only organic, but *biodynamic*, which is even more stringently controlled.)

Napa Valley Lavender Company

PO Box 2509
Yountville CA 94599
707.257.8920
www.napa-lavender.com

Products from eight different types of lavender plants. Sachets, pillows, clothing, candles, bath salts, soaps and lotions.

LINEN

Napa Valley Linen Company

PO Box 482   Calistoga CA 94515
707.942.6339
www.napavalleylinen.com

Hand-painted table linens. If you live in the valley, you can host a linen party and paint your own linens.

ORCHIDS

Napa Valley Orchids

707.255.8266
www.napavalleyorchids.com

Species, hybrids and orchid supplies. Also sold at local farmers' markets and through "orchid parties".

SOAP

Napa Valley Soap Company

1644 Yajome Street
Napa CA 94559
707.257.1151
www.napavalleysoapcompany.com

Handcrafted soaps, lotions, bath gels and shampoos. Call for hours.

Arts and Entertainment

The following is a list of key arts and entertainment sites and events. You'll find detailed information under their listings in other sections.

DRAMA

Dreamweavers Theatre (*Napa*)
Napa Valley College Theater (*Events*)
Napa Valley Repertory Theatre (*Events*)
Napa Valley Shakespeare Festival (*Events*)
White Barn (*Events*)

FINE ARTS

Arts Council of Napa Valley

68 Coombs St. D4 Napa CA 94559
707.257.2117
www.artscouncilnapavalley.org

The Arts Council's mission is to support and provide programs for the literary, visual and performing arts of Napa County. It promotes and supports the artistic community, provides arts education in the schools and holds the annual *Open Studios* event in the fall, where hundreds of local artists welcome visitors to their studios.

Clos Pegase (*Calistoga*)
Di Rosa Preserve (*Carneros*)
Hess Collection (*Napa*)
Galleries (*Shopping*)

MUSEUMS

Copia (Napa)
Napa Firefighters Museum (*Napa*)
Napa Valley Museum (*Yountville*)
Sharpsteen Museum (*Calistoga*)
Silverado Museum (*St. Helena*)

MUSIC

Chamber Music in the Napa Valley (*Events*)
Jarvis Conservatory (*Napa*)
Mondavi Summer Music Festival (*Events*)
Music in the Caves (*Events*)
Music in the Vineyards (*Events*)
Napa Valley Jazz Festival (*Events*)
Napa Valley Music Festival (*Events*)
Napa Valley Opera House (*Napa*)
Napa Valley Symphony (*Events*)
White Barn (*Events*)

MUSICIANS

North Bay Entertainment

1040 Main Street Suite 110
Napa CA 94559
707.224.0241
www.northbayentertainment.com

Booking agency for private and corporate entertainment with a varied list of singers, musicians, bands and other acts.

MOVIES

Cameo Cinema (*St. Helena*)
Napa Cinedome 8 (*Napa*)

Napa Valley Film
(www.napavalleyfilm.com) – Online guide to current movies and events
Uptown Theater (*Napa*)
Wine Country Film Festival (*Events*)

PUPPETRY

Magical Moonshine Theater (*Events*)

MURALS

The Napa Chamber of Commerce has an ongoing mural project, creating large hand-painted murals on the sides of buildings in downtown Napa. The murals depict various scenes and times in Napa's history. The project was initiated by Leadership Napa Valley and intends to produce at least one dozen murals.

Mural #1 - 19th Century Napa River

LOCATION: First and Main Streets
Artists: Steve Della Maggiora & Susan Clifford

The scene selected for this mural is the Napa River circa 1900. The view is from the Third Street Bridge looking south. The two artists, Steve Della Maggiora of Napa and Susan Clifford of St. Helena, have used a realistic style with true colors and hues with a warm summer sky casting glistening shadows onto the river. The colorful history of Napa is exemplified with the many

The bustling port of Napa circa 1900 can be seen in this mural on Main Street at First Street in downtown Napa.

wharfs, mills, wineries, schooners and steamships. It is important to note that no 19th century structure directly related to Napa's maritime commerce still exists.

The schooner "Emma," piloted by Captain George Pinkham, and the sternwheeler "Zinfandel," piloted by Captain N.H. Wulff, are both depicted in the mural. Both men lived in Napa and their original homes still stand and have been designated City Landmarks by the Cultural Heritage Commission.

"Emma" (on the left) began serving Napa in the 1870s and could carry up to 70,000 square feet of lumber, 25 tons of flour, 80 tons of wheat, or 60 tons of sand. The "Zinfandel" (in the center) was brought to Napa in June 1889. She could carry 250 tons of cargo, had facilities for 36 passengers, and made three weekly round trips (down one day, back the next) between Napa and San Francisco.

Mural #2 - Famous Napa Valley Residents and Buildings (circa 1907)

LOCATION: First and Randolph Streets
Artist: Mikulas Kravjansky

Credit the 1908 "Napa City and County Portfolio and Directory" and extensive research by the artist for this remarkable reflection of Napa in the year 1907. Prominently featured are Sheriff David Dunlap (with hat), Napa Mayor David Sterling Kyser (moustache and sideburns), Superior Court Judge Henry C. Gesford (with beard), and Justice of the Peace (and later State Senator) Nathan Coombs. Shown on the newspaper page is Lena A. Jackson, school superintendent.

The mural also includes noteworthy buildings of the day, including (left to right) the Goodman Library, Napa County Courthouse, Migliavacca Mansion, and Central School. Prominent industries and styles of the time are also featured.

Napa resident Mikulas (Miky) Kravjansky devoted months of effort to this work of art. The Czechoslovakian-born artist has gained an international following, with his works featured around the world.

Mural #3 - Independence Day in Napa

LOCATION: Pacific Bell Building (East side on Randolph Street, across from the Napa Valley Conference and Visitors Bureau in the Napa Town Center)
Artist: David Huddleston

A scene depicting the July 4, 1908 Independence Day parade. "Miss Liberty" (Mazie Behrens) rides in a vehicle invented by fellow Napan Lyman Chapman.

Huddleston is an artist and teacher of art whose primary medium is watercolor. He has taught in France, Mexico, Hong Kong and China as well as the United States.

Mural #4 - Napa Valley Wine Industry Pioneers

LOCATION: East wall of "The Neighborhood" at First and Franklin Streets.
Artist: Cor Greive

Pictured are Charles Krug (Charles Krug Winery), Captain Gustave Niebaum (Inglenook [now Niebaum Coppola] Winery), Frederick and Jacob Beringer (Beringer Vineyards), Jacob Schram (Schramsberg Vineyards) and Georges de Latour (Beaulieu Vineyard).

Greive, a native of the Netherlands, is a past president of the Napa Valley Art Association and the Artists of the Bay Area. He teaches for the Napa Valley College Adult Education division. He works in a variety of mediums including oils, acrylics, watercolors and pastels.

Mural #5 - Hispanic Americans in Napa County

LOCATION: 1127 First Street (across from the plaza in front of Mervyn's)
Artists: Cor Greive and Jose Charles

This mural honors Hispanic Americans in Napa County, including historic (General Mariano Vallejo, who once owned what is now Napa Valley) and contemporary (including Hope Lugo and Tala De Wynter, both local Hispanic community leaders).

The mural also includes Mexican-American labor activist Cesar Chavez and Mexican painters Diego Rivera and Frida Kahlo. It's interesting to note that although the farmworkers who tend the vines and pick the grapes are the backbone of the Napa Valley's economy, not one is pictured working in this mural.

Events

A wide variety of events occur year-round, many of them fundraisers for local schools and non-profit organizations, others just for the sheer enjoyment of the participants. We've listed those that occur on an annual or regular basis.

April in Carneros

800.825.9457
www.carneroswineries.org

Annual open house and festival sponsored by wineries in the Carneros District.

Carols in the Caves

707.224.4222
www.carolsinthecaves.com

Weekends during November and December in the wine caves of various wineries.

David Auerbach, who should be declared a Napa Valley treasure, plays sacred music on rare and unusual instruments. As David says, "If you've heard of it, I probably don't play it." A rare treat.

Chamber Music in the Napa Valley

707.252.7122
www.chambermusicnapa.org

Outstanding performances usually held in the beautiful and acoustically excellent First Methodist Church in Napa. Call for schedule.

Clos Pegase Wine/Art Culture

Calistoga
707.942.4981
www.clospegase.com

Clos Pegase' winery founder Jan Shrem gives a free monthly talk on "4,000 years of Wine in Art" at the winery just south of Calistoga. Call for date and time of next lecture.

Domaine Chandon Bastille Day Celebration

Domaine Chandon, Yountville
707.944.2280
Held every July 14.

Festival Of Lights

Town of Yountville
707.944.0904
December

Beautiful Christmas display, music, entertainment.

Harvest (Crush)

The grape harvest takes place every year in the fall. Depending on the weather, it can start in early August for sparkling wine grapes, which are picked at lower sugar levels. It picks up steam in late August and is in full swing during most of September and October. This is the time to actually see how wine is made. The stemmer-crushers are operating throughout the day, the fermentation tanks are full and bubbling with carbon dioxide, and gondolas overflowing with grapes are travelling along every countryside road in the valley.

Home Winemakers Classic

Held at St. Supery Winery
www.homewine.com

The Home Winemakers Classic is an annual tasting and judging of award-winning home wines by Napa Valley enologists and viticulturists, with music, silent auction of vintage wines, raffle and food. Held every July, it is an extremely popular event for residents and the local wine community.

Land Trust Hikes

Napa County Land Trust 1040 Main Street
Napa CA 94559
707.252.3270
www.napalandtrust.org

Hikes held throughout the year, usually at locations that are normally closed to the public.

Magical Moonshine Puppet Theater

PO Box 2296 Yountville CA 94599
707.257.8007
www.magicalmoonshine.com

This is another Napa Valley treasure. Unfortunately, performances are only held sporadically. Fortunately for locals, they're frequent enough to be a favorite, and held at locations throughout the valley. A wonderful experience for kids, no matter what their age.

Mountain Men (Skyline Park)

Skyline Park, Napa
707.252.0481

Mountain men in furs and deerskin with muzzle-loading rifles. An annual event, open to the public. Call the park to find out when this takes place.

Napa Valley Classic

PO Box 586
Calistoga CA 94515
707.942.4222
www.napavalleyclassic.com

Equestrian show jumping held in July at the Napa County Fairgrounds in Calistoga.

Napa Valley College Theatre

2277 Napa-Vallejo Highway
Napa CA 94558
707.253.3200
DIRECTIONS: South of Napa on Soscol just south of Imola

The *Napa Valley College Division of Fine and Performing Arts* sponsors approximately 100 events each year: plays, musicals and concerts (choral, jazz, and instrumental), including events for young audiences.

Tickets at the NVC Cashier, Blumer's Music Center in Napa and Main Street Books in St. Helena. Or use Visa/MasterCard and phone the college for tickets. Free parking; wheelchair access.

Napa County Iris Gardens

9087 Steele Canyon Road
Napa CA 94558
707.255.7880
www.napairis.com

DIRECTIONS: Near Lake Berryessa. From Highway 29 in north Napa take Trancas Street east. Past the Silverado Trail, Trancas becomes Monticello Road and Highway 121. Continue on 121 to Highway 128. Turn left on Highway 128 and then right on Steele Canyon. The gardens are 1.5 miles on the right.

A commercial one-acre garden of tall bearded irises. Mail order for bare-root iris. The garden is open to the public for five weeks every spring in April and May. No charge. Picnic tables available.

Napa County Fair

Napa County Fairgrounds
1435 Oak Street Calistoga CA 94515
707.942.5111
www.napacountyfairgrounds.com

The annual county fair with a parade, exhibits, carnival rides, food, music and lots of other events, always held over the 4th of July holiday.

Napa Town & Country Fair

Napa Valley Exposition, Napa
707.253.4900
www.napavalleyexpo.com

The really big fair in Napa County. Held in early August.

Napa Valley Academy Awards Benefit

707.257.8686
www.napavalleyacademyawards.com

Held every year the night of the Academy Awards. Includes more than two dozen wine and food pairings from Napa Valley's finest wineries and restaurants. Dancing, silent auction and big-screen simulcast of the Academy Awards. A very popular event that benefits local AIDS projects.

Napa Valley Jazz Festival

707.944.1373
www.napavalleyjazzfestival.org

Jazz performances at various locations benefiting music programs for local public high schools.

Napa Valley Marathon

PO Box 4307 Napa CA 94558
www.napa-marathon.com

Held every spring and sponsored by the Silverado Trail Wineries Association. Route goes from Calistoga south on Silverado Trail to Napa.

Napa Valley Model Railroad Club

Napa Valley Exposition Third Street Gate Napa CA 94559
707.253.8428
www.napavalleyexpo.com/f-railroad.html

Open Friday evenings from 7:30 p.m. on and during major fairground events.

This elaborate model railroad occupies a 3,600 square foot room at the Napa Valley Exposition.

The "Napa Valley Northern" runs from Napa north through Lake County with northbound connections to Portland, and southbound connections to Stockton. The layout has more than 1,500 feet of track and the time period is from 1940 to present. Great for kids and railroad fans of any age.

Napa Valley Mustard Festival

707.942.9762
www.mustardfestival.org

Held in February and March at locations throughout the valley.

Napa Valley Repertory Theatre

PO Box 5716 Napa CA 94581
707.815.6878
www.naparep.com

Napa Rep consists of theatre veterans who have acted and directed elsewhere, and are now creating the first professional troupe in the Napa Valley. Still looking for a permanent home, they currently perform in various locations throughout the valley. Their offerings so far have tended toward the sophisticated and offbeat.

Napa Valley Shakespeare Festival

Riverbend Plaza, Napa Mill
500 Main Street
Napa CA 94559
707.251.WILL (Information)
800.965.4827 (Tickets)
www.napashakespeare.org

The festival, which for some years was located upvalley, is now at the Riverbend Plaza at the newly-restored Napa Mill in downtown Napa.

Performances take place outdoors and are presented for six weeks in July and August. Patrons can reserve box dinners in advance through the festival, or enjoy a meal catered by Celadon restaurant. Naturally, this being

the Napa Valley, wine is sold at all plays. All food and wine must be purchased at the site. Performances are held Friday, Saturday and Sunday evenings. Gates open at 6:15 p.m. and performances begin at 7 p.m.

We recommend you purchase tickets in advance due to the limited seating. General admission is $18-$24. Seniors, students and children are $14-$18. Tickets also available on www.ticketweb.com or at Copperfield's Books on First Street, the Napa General Store at the Napa Mill, or Main Street Books in St. Helena.

If you're in the valley at the right time, we highly recommend the festival. The acting is excellent, the sets are colorful, and the environment—a starlit summer evening in the Napa Valley— is magnificent.

Napa Valley Symphony

2407 California Boulevard Napa CA 94558
707.226.6872
www.napavalleysymphony.org

The Napa Valley has developed an outstanding group of musicians. Most concerts are held in the Lincoln Theater at the Veterans Home in Yountville. There's also an annual free concert by the river at Veterans Park in downtown Napa. Call the Symphony for a schedule of all performances.

Napa Valley Wine Auction

1091 Larkmead Lane Calistoga CA 94515
707.963.5246
www.napavinters.com

The Napa Valley Wine Auction has been held every year since 1981. It is the world's largest wine charity event, with all of the auction's proceeds staying within Napa County.

During that time, the auction's sponsor, the Napa Valley Vintners Association, has donated more than $42 million to Napa County hospitals, clinics, youth and housing organizations. In 2002, the vintners contributed $5.8 million to local non-profit organizations, and was the primary donor to the Napa Valley Vintners Community Health Center in Napa. The center offers a variety of medical, dental and counseling services for low income, medically uninsured or underinsured county residents.

Highlight of the annual auction is the Friday night dinner, which seats nearly 2,000 people in huge tents on the grounds of Meadowood Resort in St. Helena.

The auction takes place the following day. Auction goers are well-primed with Napa Valley wines as they vie to outbid each other for some of the finest wines in the world—and some of the most unusual auction packages.

The auction is very elegant and very expensive. Admission by prior registration only.

To give you an idea of the wine auction, here's the menu from one of the auctions.

Vintner's Gala
Meadowood, Napa Valley

Caviar on Ice
Sparkling Wine

Seaforms
Chilled Lobster and Wasabi Tobiko
Sauvignon Blanc, Viognier and Pinot Grigio

Wild Mushroom Chandelier
Layers of Wild Mushrooms and Basil
Lasagna with Golden Beets
Chardonnay and Pinot Noir

Spring Lamb Kaleidoscope
Pinwheels with Vegetable Art Forms
Cabernet Sauvignon, Merlot, Zinfandel and Meritage, presented in 3-Liter Bottles

LaBelle Oh La La
Meyer Lemon Mousse Grapes with Cassis on Chihuly Sugared Persians
Moscato, Late Harvest and Botrysized Dessert Wines
Accompanied by a performance by diva Patti LaBelle

Napa Valley Wine Festival

Napa Valley Exposition

This is a major annual event, held every November and sponsored by the Napa Valley Unified Education Foundation as a benefit for Napa public schools. Over 50 wineries participate, so it's a unique opportunity to try a wide variety of Napa Valley wines.

Napa Valley Wine Library Tasting

PO Box 328, St. Helena CA 94574
707.963.5145
www.napawinelibrary.org

Every August more than 100 Napa Valley wineries pour a particular wine at this special wine tasting benefitting the wine library. Held each year at Silverado Country Club in Napa. Open to members only, but membership is available at the door for $40.

Open Studios

Arts Council of Napa Valley
68 Coombs St. D4 Napa CA 94559
707.257.2117
www.artscouncilnapavalley.org

Open house at several hundred artists' studios, held every September and October on two weekends. The first weekend is upvalley, the second in Napa.

Robert Mondavi Summer Festival

Robert Mondavi Winery Oakville CA
707.226.1395
www.robertmondaviwinery.com

Margrit Biever Mondavi, vice president of cultural affairs at the Robert Mondavi Winery and wife of the founder, has made this her pet project since 1969. Concerts are open-air, held on the winery's main lawn, and take place in June, July and August. Most concerts begin at 7 p.m., with gates open for picnicking.

This past entertainment lineup gives an idea of the outstanding quality of the perforners: New Orleans' Preservation Hall Jazz Band, Cesaria Evora, Buena Vista Social Club, Dan Fogelberg, and Dave Koz.

Wine and cheese tasting are offered at intermission. 2001 tickets ranged from $42-$75, depending on the performer. While children are allowed, we've seldom seen any there.

It's an elegantly casual affair, with most attending in jeans and shorts but some finely dressed. Picnic baskets brought by guests range from French bread and cheese to elegantly prepared meals served with fine china and crystal. It's great fun and outstanding entertainment. Tickets, which go on sale the end of April, go fast. They're available at the winery and all BASS outlets. A sign at the front of the winery, easily visible from Highway 29, shows the season's schedule and ticket availability.

Society for Creative Anachronism

Skyline Wilderness Park, Napa
707.252.0481
www.vinhold.org

The Society for Creative Anachronism (SCA) meets annually at Skyline Park in Napa for a day of jousting, swordsmanship, wenching, dining, and general rollicking fun. Open to the public for a small donation. Call Skyline Park to find the date of the SCA's next visit.

Symphony on the River Festival

Downtown Napa at the Third Street Bridge.
Sponsored by Friends of the Napa River
707.254.8520
www.friendsofthenapariver.org.

A free event held every September. The Napa Valley Symphony performs early in the evening and is followed by fireworks at dark. Activities include local entertainment, food and drink, and a boat parade on the river.

Valley Men Who Cook

Upvalley location
707.255.5911

Held on Father's Day each year. Amateur but well-known chefs from around the valley compete in a wide variety of food categories. A very popular and fun event.

Veterans Home Fourth Of July Fireworks

Veterans Home, Yountville
707.944.4600

The biggest fireworks display in the valley.

Victorian Holiday Candlelight Tour

707.255.1836

Annual tour in December of some of Napa's most beautifully restored Victorian homes by Napa County Landmarks.

White Barn

2727 Sulphur Springs Avenue
St. Helena CA 94574
707.963.7002

Theatrical and musical performances held throughout the year in an 85-seat theater that was originally a carriage house. All proceeds go to charity. A labor of love for founder Nancy Garden and her family.

Wine and Crafts Faire

Downtown Napa
707.257.0322

Wine tasting, crafts, food, entertaining. Held in September, it's the big street fair of the year.

Wine Country Film Festival

www.winecountryfilmfest.com

707.935.3456 for program information, advance tickets to al fresco screening, and passes. Tickets are available at BASS outlets.

Founded in 1986, the Wine Country Film Festival stretches over four weekends in July and August. It has a true, casual, wine country feeling. Many of the films are screened outdoors, at wineries in the Napa and Sonoma Valleys. Tickets can be purchased at show time and range from $6-$20. A Weekend Pass gives reserved seating for all films and events on a given weekend. Silver Passes, which are $100, ensure reserved seating for every film in the month-long festival.

The program always includes new features from major studios and the latest in independently produced features, documentaries and shorts from around the world. It has premiered such films as *A Fish Called Wanda*; *Honeymoon in Vegas*; *sex, lies and videotape*; and *Married to the Mob*, and held tributes to such stars as Anthony Quinn and Gregory Peck.

Recreation and Outdoors

Napa River

(INFORMATION COURTESY OF *Friends of the Napa River*, www.friendsofthenapariver.org).

The Napa River is one of the largest Central Coast Range Rivers draining 426 sq. miles on its 50 mile journey from Mt. St. Helena to the San Pablo Bay. The last 17 miles of this journey, from Trancas St. in Napa to Vallejo, are an estuary system. In summer, the salinity at Trancas may be 10%, in winter, it is freshwater.

The Napa River and its 47 tributaries serve as a linear wilderness running through the heart of an intensely farmed and partially urbanized valley. At one time, a dense canopy of riparian habitat dominated by cottonwoods and willows lined the river's upper reaches. For the most part, the gallery forest bordering the riparian zone is gone and the remaining vegetation exists only in the channel. Friends of the Napa River is working to restore the riparian habitat.

Health of the River

Pollution is caused by the run-off of fertilizers. During summer, algae bloom decreases the oxygen available to aquatic life.

Water diversion from the streams is decreasing the fresh water flow, affecting the fish habitat.

Stream bank erosion and removal of plant life due to development causes sedimentation.

70 to 200 thousand tons of sediments enter the Napa Valley watershed every year due to roads, development and hillside vineyards.

Sediment deposits in stream channels, gravel and ponds, impair anadromous fish spawning thereby reducing habitat diversity and the food supply for fish.

Wildlife along the River

The endangered Chinook Salmon and steelheads spawn in the Napa River and in its many tributaries. The steelhead run has been reduced from historical levels of 6000 adults to a few hundred fish. Nonetheless, the river still supports an active recreational fishery. We find bluegill, black bass in the upper river; and striped bass, sturgeon and many non-game species such as the endangered splittail, yellowfin globy and silversides in the lower river.

Bird species dependent on the river include mallards, green-winged teals. mergansers, wood ducks, herons, egrets, kingfishers, rails and grebes as well as the endangered Clapper Rail.

Mink muskrat, raccoons, deer, gray fox and bobcat also live in the riparian habitat.

River Trails

1. Kennedy Park features a trail on the river.

2. West of Lincoln Bridge near Soscol go through the RV Park and hit a trail on the west bank going north to Trancas.

3. North-west of Soscol at Trancas go in at Towpath to connect with a river path (west bank).

4. A Californian Dept. of Fish and Game eco-reserve at the Yountville Cross Rd. bridge is a beautiful spot to see the river.

Boating

1. Small boats, kayaks and canoes can be put in the river at China Point at First and Soscol streets in downtown Napa.

2. There is a boat launch at John F. Kennedy Park, just south of Napa Valley College.

3. Canoes and kayaks can be rented from *Napa River Adventures* at the 4th Street city dock in Napa. (see separate listing).

4. A gondola can be hired from *Gondola Servizio* at the 4th Street city dock or at their office at the Napa Mill. (see separate listing).

Napa River Watershed

The area that drains into the Napa River contains 250 miles of streams and covers over 270,000 acres at the north end of the San Francisco/San Pablo Bay. It runs approximately 40 miles north to south and 15 miles east to west at its widest point. About forty thousand acres are vineyards, and 102,000 acres are range and grazing lands. Only 3% of the area is urbanized. Between 1992 and 1997 vineyard land in the watershed expanded approximately 2.1% annually. An additional 17,000 acres had to be replanted in the 1990's due to phylloxera.

Planning officials expect Pope Valley, the hillside areas of American Canyon, Jameson Canyon, and the western side of the Napa Valley to be the primary vineyard expansion areas in the future. They anticipate that over 4,000 acres will be planted in the next 10 years, primarily on hillsides, since there is very little acreage left unplanted on the valley floor.

There are currently 134,500 acres of Napa River watershed land in protected status in public or quasi-public ownership. This includes over 50,000 acres protected through fee title or conservation easement by the Napa County Land Trust. There are nearly 20,000 acres of the watershed under hardened pavement or rooftops, and over 6,500 acres of valley floor wetlands have been drained and filled since the 1800's.

The result is that Steelhead Trout runs that once surpassed 6000 adults have been reduced to several hundred. A Silver Salmon run that once numbered up to 2,000 adults is now extinct. Stream channel and floodplain modification has resulted in the discharge of more water at high velocities, producing increased bank erosion, sedimentation and downstream flooding.

In 1987 the Napa River was listed as "impaired" by the State Water Quality Control Board under the authority of the federal Clean Water Act. As we mentioned early, *Friends of the Napa River* and other agencies are working hard to restore the river to full health.

Archery

Silverado Archery Club
www.ncfaa.com/skyline/archery.htm
Silverado Archers
www.ncfaa.com/silverado.html

Silverado Archery Club is located on 25 acres within the boundary of Skyline Wilderness Park in Napa. The club is NFAA charted with 3 separate NFAA marked yardage ranges, each range having 14 permanent targets as well as an area for 14 unmarked distance targets utilizing McKenzie 3-D's.

The club hosts a number of tournaments each year for target archers and hunters, including a 16 week un-marked distance series (open to the public) on Thursday evenings from April through July for hunters in preparation for the hunting season. Their facilities are open to the public on the second Sunday of each month.

Bicycling

Bicyclists can be found throughout the Napa Valley. Highway 29 is a popular stretch. There is a bike lane on the frontage road (Solano Avenue) that runs along the west side of Highway 29 from Napa to Yountville. North of Yountville you're on your own. If you're going to continue north, watch out for the railroad tracks crossing Highway 29 at Whitehall Lane south of St. Helena. Many inattentive cyclists have hit the asphalt here.

Silverado Trail has bike lanes all the way from Napa to Calistoga. The main caution here is the drivers, who travel much faster on this road than on Highway 29.

South of Napa, in the Carneros District that overlaps both Napa and Sonoma counties, you'll find the least traffic—and cooler temperatures. There are low, rolling hills covered with vineyards, lots of wineries and far fewer tourists.

To give you an idea how bicyclists feel about the Napa Valley, it was proposed that the Napa Valley host the bicycling events if San Francisco was awarded the 2012 Summer Olympics. (It wasn't.) It's not known if San Francisco Olympic organizers were aware that the Olympics occur at the same time as Crush, and what effect tens of thousands of visitors would have had on a successful harvest.

Bicycle Shops

Bicycle Madness (Napa)
707.253.2453

Bicycle Trax (Napa)
707.258.8729

Bicycle Works (Napa)
707.253.7000

Bike Tours of Napa Valley (Napa)
707.255.3380

Palisades Mountain Sport (Calistoga)
707.942.9687
www.bikeroute.com/Palisades/

Pedals Past (Calistoga)
707.942.9469

St. Helena Cyclery (St. Helena)
707.963.7736
www.sthelenacyclery.com

Bicycle Rentals

Bicycle Trax (Napa)
707.258.8729

Getaway Wine Country Bicycle Tours and Rentals
707.942.0332 800.499.2453

Napa Valley Bike Tours and Rentals (Napa)
707.255.3377 800.707.BIKE
www.napavalleybiketours.com

Palisades Mountain Sport (Calistoga)
707.942.9687

Pedals Past (Calistoga)
707.942.9469

St. Helena Cyclery (St. Helena)
707.963.7736

Other Bicycle Contacts

Napa Valley BMX
707.224.8269

Bicycle Events Information 707.226.7066

CalTrans Highway Information
800.427.7623

California Highway Patrol 707.253.4906

Napa Police Department
707.257.9550

Napa Valley Transit
707.255.7631

Napa Valley Transit buses are equipped with front-mounted bike racks that can accommodate up to two bikes very quickly and easily. If the racks are occupied, additional bikes can board the bus on a space-available basis.

Boating

Boating is available at Lake Berryessa and on the Napa River.

Lake Berryessa

Lake Berryessa Resorts
(see Lake Berryessa in Towns section)

Offer rentals of fishing boats, ski boats, patio boats, houseboats, and jet skis.

Napa River

Gondola Servizio
(see Napa listing in Towns section)
Gondola rides in downtown Napa.

Napa River Adventures
(see Napa listing in Towns section)
Kayak and Canoe rental in downtown Napa. Also rides on a slow-paced electric-powered boat.

Disc Golf

Disc Golf Course

Skyline Wilderness Park
707.252.0481
www.ncfaa.com/skyline/disc_golf.htm

A short but technical course. 18 holes with dirt tees and disc-catcher baskets. Framed signs at the tee show alternate pin placements. Can be easily played in two hours. Discs are available at the kiosk as you enter Skyline Park. Entrance to the park is $4 per vehicle.

Fishing

Napa County offers fishing at Lake Berryessa and its surrounding streams, and on the Napa River. Here's the place to find all the information you need, including what's biting, where, and what on.

Sweeney's Sport Store

River Park Shopping Center
1537 Imola Avenue West
Napa CA 94559
707.255.5544
www.sweeneyssports.com

Open 7 days a week. Sweeney's is the place for fishing tackle and information. Free flycasting classes every Saturday morning at 9 a.m.

Lake Berryessa Resorts
(see Lake Berryessa in Towns section)

Offer everything you need from lodging to boats to tackle, and the very latest information on fishing the lake.

Spanish Flat Resort provides a current Berryessa fishing report at: www.spanishflatresort.com/fishing.php

State of California Department of Fish and Game

7329 Silverado Trail
Yountville CA 94599
707.944.5500

Napa Valley Fly Fishermen

PO Box 2373
Napa CA 94558

Geocaching

Geocaching (pronounced "GEO-cashing") combines the high-technology of Global Positioning System (GPS) satellites and the low-technology of walking around on the ground. Geocachers hide a "cache" somewhere in a publicly-accessible area (perhaps a park, forest, beach area) and then use an electronic GPS unit to determine the precise location of the cache in latitude and longitude. That location is posted on the Web, and others can then hunt for the cache, using the provided coordinates. The cache may contain some sort of object, but will always contain a logbook, in which the finder will note his or her discovery of the cache.

Geocachers have, naturally, discovered the Napa Valley and there are caches hidden throughout the area. Use the following web site to get their coordinates.

Geocaching
www.geocaching.com

The primary web site for geocachers. It gives information about the hobby of geocaching, provides discussion forums, and lists cache locations all over (currently more than 180 countries) the world.

Golf

Aetna Springs Golf Course - 9 holes (Pope Valley)
1600 Aetna Springs Road
Pope Valley, CA 94567
707.965.2115
www.aetnasprings.com

9-hole, par 70. Beautiful setting. Reputedly the oldest golf course west of the Mississippi.

Chardonnay Golf Club - 36 holes (Napa)
2555 Jamieson Canyon Road (Highway 12 between Highway 29 and Highway I-80) Napa CA 94558
707.257.1900
www.chardonnaygolfclub.com

Vineyards Course 18-hole, par 72. Open to the public. 5,200/6,816 yards - five sets of tees including two ladies'.

The Club Shakespeare Course 18-hole, par 72. 5,448/7,001 yards - four sets of tees . Open to members, their guests, and members of other private country clubs (reciprocal).

Meadowood Resort - 9 holes (St. Helena)
900 Meadowood Lane St. Helena CA 94574
707.963.3646 800.458.8080
www.meadowood.com

9-hole, par 31. 2,014 yards. A walking course.

Napa Golf Course - 18 holes (Napa)
2295 Streblow Drive Napa CA 94558
707.255.4333
www.playnapa.com

18-hole, par 72. 6,730 yards Public golf course located in Kennedy Park off Highway 221 at the south end of Napa. Reasonable fees, uncrowded. Discounts for residents of Napa city and county.

Silverado Country Club - 36 holes (Napa)
1600 Atlas Peak Road Napa CA 94558
707.257.5460
www.silveradoresort.com

South Course - 6,500 yards par 72. North Course - 6,700 yards par 72. Designed by Robert Trent Jones, Jr. Home of the Senior PGA "Transamerica" tournament.

Vintner's Golf Club - 9 holes (Yountville)
7901 Solano Avenue Yountville, CA 94599
707.944.1992
www.vintnersgolfclub.com

9-hole, par 34. 4,258/5,573 yards. Three sets of tees. Located just off Highway 29 at the Veterans Home.

Mt. St. Helena Golf Course - 9 holes (Calistoga)
P.O. Box 344 Calistoga CA 94515
707.942.9966
www.napacountyfairgrounds.com

9-holes, par 34. Men - 2,759 yards. Women - par 35 - 2,650 yards. Public course.

Napa Valley Country Club - 18 holes (Napa)
3385 Hagen Road, Napa,CA 94558
Golf Shop 707.252.1114.
Business Office 707.252.1111.
www.napavalleycc.com

Private course. Members and guests only. Reciprocal with other private clubs. Guest

Fees - $90, includes cart. 18-holes. 5,285/6,148 yards - par 72. Three tees.

Hiking

There is some beautiful country in the Napa Valley, but most of it is privately owned. There are only a few places where members of the public can hike whenever they wish.

However, there are several organizations that schedule hikes throughout the year on private lands. Anyone can go on these hikes, as long as they reserve a space.

Because Napa is one of the San Francisco Bay Area counties, it is also part of two Bay Area-wide hiking projects: the Ridge Trail and the Wetlands Trail.

Bay Area Ridge Trail

415.561.2595
www.ridgetrail.org

The Ridge Trail is a 400-mile multiple-use trail connecting parks and preserved open spaces along the ridgelines surrounding California's San Francisco Bay.

In Napa County it currently passes through Skyline Wilderness Park heading east to Solano County. The trail segment west to Sonoma County is not yet in place.

Ridge Trail — Napa County Segment

Length is about 4.4 miles with an elevation change of about +900 feet.

Leave the picnic area near the Skyline Wilderness Park entrance and take gravelled Lake Marie Road, which crosses a causeway between two ponds, Lake Louise and Lake Camille. Lake Marie Road bends left (east), and in about 600 feet you turn right (southeast) off it onto Skyline Trail. In a few yards you pass the junction with Buckeye Trail.

Skyline Trail zigzags up a steep hill and soon enters oak and buckeye woods where the trail straightens, levels off a bit, and heads south. Pass the junction with Bayleaf Trail by staying right on Skyline Trail. Soon, pass the spur road which goes to the right through Passini Gate. Just beyond, you begin climbing to high grasslands. Traverse a steep hillside, pass the skeleton of a house in a small clearing, and continue to follow Skyline Trail on an old, rocky roadbed through oaks and firs. Pass the junction with Chaparral Trail on the left, following a creek on Skyline Trail. Cross to the south side of Marie Creek, draining into Lake Marie below. Soon you reach the locked boundary gate near the southeast corner of the park.

San Francisco Bay Trail

baytrail.abag.ca.gov/

The Bay Trail is a planned recreational corridor that, when complete, will encircle San Francisco and San Pablo Bays with a continuous 400-mile network of bicycling and hiking trails. It will connect the shoreline of all nine Bay Area counties, link 47 cities, and cross the major toll bridges in the region.

To date, approximately 210 miles of the alignment—or slightly more than half the Bay Trail's ultimate length—has been completed. The Trail is frequently referred to as the "Wetlands Trail" since, unlike the Ridge Trail which travels along the mountain ridges encircling the bay, this trail passes through the shoreline/wetland areas.

When completed, the trail will enter Napa County from the west through the Carneros Region, go to the southern edge of the city of Napa at John F. Kennedy Park, and then proceed south to American Canyon and onto Vallejo.

Napa River Trail

www.cityofnapa.org/commres/river/river.htm

The City of Napa is also creating its own trail, running along the banks of the Napa River from Trancas Street at the northern end of town to John F. Kennedy Park at the southern end.

Currently, the segment from Trancas Street to Lincoln Avenue is in place, as is the area at Kennedy Park. The downtown restoration/flood control project will result in the completion of the other segments.

Scheduled Hikes

The Napa County Land Trust and the Sierra Club offer scheduled hikes.

Land Trust of Napa County

707.252.3270
www.napalandtrust.org

Offers scheduled hikes during the year throughout the valley. An opportunity to see creeks, waterfalls and views on private property.

Napa Sierra Club

www.redwood.sierraclub.org/napa

Offers scheduled hikes during the year throughout the valley.

Napa County Hiking Trails

For detailed information on trails, see separate listings in the Town sections and in Parks and Camping for the following.

Bale Grist Mill State Historic Park (St. Helena)

Bothé-Napa Valley State Park (Calistoga)

Robert Louis Stevenson State Park (Calistoga)

Skyline Wilderness Park (Napa)

White Sulphur Springs Resort (St. Helena)

Horseback Riding

Diamond Mountain Stables

1296 Diamond Mountain Road
Calistoga CA 94515
707.942.0719
www.diamondmountainstables.com

Lessons, show training, children's day camp during the summer. Horses for sale.

Napa Valley Trail Rides

PO Box 5808   Napa CA 94581
707.255.2900
www.napasonomatrailrides.com

Trail rides at Skyline Wilderness Park in Napa from April through November, including special rides for groups. Reservations required.

Horse Camping

Skyline Wilderness Park

707.252.0481
www.ncfaa.com/skyline/horse_camping.htm

10 spacious horse camping sites, each accommodating two horse and two rigs, with water and picnic table. Bathrooms with showers within a short walking distance. Fifteen miles of trails through wooded forest, valleys and hilltops.

Hot Air Balloons

Hot air ballooning is something you have to experience to truly appreciate. Drifting almost soundlessly over the hills and vineyards of the valley, you'll come to experience the breathtaking beauty of this famous part of the world.

Most balloons launch from the Yountville area early in the morning. The first "shift" rides in the balloon gondola while the second shift pursues the balloon in the "chase"

Hot air ballooning is one of the most popular, and spectacular, pastimes in the Napa Valley.

vehicle. Then, after the balloon sets down at the end of its voyage, the two crews switch for the second flight. Almost every morning's flight ends in a champagne brunch. You can even get married in a balloon. Cost, including brunch, ranges from $150-$175 per person for a one-hour flight.

Adventures Aloft

707.944.4408 800.944.4408
www.nvaloft.com

Above the West Ballooning

707.944.8638
www.nvaloft.com

Balloons Above the Valley

800.464.6824
www.balloonrides.com

Balloon Aviation of Napa Valley

707.944.4400 800.367.6272
www.nvaloft.com

Bonaventura Balloon Company

707.944.2822 800.359.6272
www.bonaventuraballoons.com

Napa Valley Balloons.

707.944.0228 800.253.2224
www.napavalleyballoons.com

Napa Valley Drifters

707.252.7210 877.463.7438
www.napavalleydrifters.com

Kayaking and Canoeing

(see Boating)

Paintball

Paintball Jungle
Eucalyptus Drive
American Canyon CA 94503
707.552.2426
www.paintballjungle.com

For more information, see listing in American Canyon.

Water Skiing

Lake Berryessa Resorts

(see Lake Berryessa in Towns section)

Lake Berryessa is one of the most popular places in Northern California for water skiing. All resorts provide boats and other equipment.

Willi's Water Ski Center

1434 Grayson Avenue
St. Helena CA 94574
707.963.4409
www.williwaterski.com/

Willi Ellermeier operates a water ski school at Lake Berryessa with instruction for students ranging from beginner to tournament level.

Parks and Camping

Most of the land in the Napa Valley is privately owned, so parks, hiking and camping are limited. Although there is no county park system, cities have a variety of neighborhood and community parks.

The State of California operates two state parks, Bothé-Napa Valley and Robert Louis Stevenson, and one state historical park, Bale Grist Mill. There is also a large equestrian, hiking and limited camping park run by a private, non-profit organization, Skyline Wilderness Park. In the northeastern part of the county, the U.S. Bureau of Reclamation oversees Lake Berryessa.

Calistoga

Parks and Recreation
707.942.2838
www.ci.calistoga.ca

Pioneer Park

1308 Cedar Street

Small park located one black from downtown Calistoga. Gazebo, Picnic tables, BBQ pits. Great spot for weddings, group picnics and concerts. Rental available.

Napa

Parks and Recreation
707.257.9529
www.cityofnapa.org/commres/

Alston Park

On Dry Creek Road on the northeastern edge of town.
707.257.9529

Alston Park is a Napa City "open space" park. Parking for the 157-acre park is at the north and south ends of the park off Dry Creek Road. At each lot there are hiker

entrances and bicycle and horse gates to allow access to three miles of trail.

Three small picnic areas within the park allow for views of the Napa Valley. Portable restrooms are available at the south park entrance.

Fuller Park

Jefferson Street at Oak Street
707.257.9529

Fuller Park is a Napa City park located at the edge of Napa's Old Town. This 10 acre park is a favorite spot for picnics (25 tables and three reservable group sites) and birthday parties.

Located throughout the park are various monuments and plaques commemorating important events. Perhaps the most prominent monument is a watering fountain for horses and small animals. Moved to the park in 1965, the fountain was originally created to stand in the center of the intersection of Polk and Franklin Streets in downtown Napa.

Kennedy Park

On Highway 221 just south of Napa Valley College
707.257.9529
Golf Course: 707.255.4333

J.F. Kennedy Park is a Napa City park that runs along the Napa River. The 350-acre park includes five reservable picnic areas. The park also offers softball, soccer, volleyball, boat launching, hiking, a children's playground, and the 18-hole Napa Golf Course. The Pelusi Recreation building can be reserved for meetings, weddings or private parties.

Skyline Wilderness Park

2201 Imola Avenue
707.252.0481
www.skylinepark.org

Monday - Thursday 9 a.m. to dark Friday - Sunday 8 a.m .to dark.

Daily visitor's fee is $4 per vehicle, RV camping $14, and tent sites $8.

Skyline Park is an 850-acre wilderness area at the southeast corner of Napa. It's managed by a non-profit organization formed to protect the area. You'll find lots of wildlife, including deer and wild turkey.

Skyline has over 25 miles of trails for hiking, biking and equestrian use. The 2.5 mile main trail leads to Lake Marie at the eastern end. There's also an alternate route along the ridge trail that is a much better workout, but is not for those out of shape. From this trail on a clear day, you can see San Francisco Bay, Mt. Tamalpais and Mt. Diablo. Beautiful.

Skyline also offers picnic and barbecue areas, an RV park, and tent camping. The best place to hike in Napa.

Westwood Hills Park

On Browns Valley Road, about one mile west of Highway 29
707.257.9529

Westwood Hills Park is a heavily-wooded Napa City park. The park provides three miles of trails through beautiful groves of oak trees and grassy meadows, and affords expansive views of the city. The park includes benches and picnic tables near the parking lot and along the trails.

The non-profit *Napa Valley Naturalists* operate the Carolyn Parr Nature Museum near the parking lot at the park. The Center's exhibits depict the plants and animals found in Napa County's five different habitats. There's also a children's nature library, "hands-on" corner of skins, nests and bones, and an extensive nature reference library. The Center is open year-round on Saturdays and Sundays from 1-4 pm. During the summer it is open Tuesday-Sunday at the same hours.

St. Helena

Parks and Recreation
707.963.5706
www.ci.st-helena.ca.us

Crane Park

On Crane Ave. 500 ft south of the intersection of Crane Ave. and Grayson Ave.

Ten acres with six lighted tennis courts, four lighted bocce ball courts, two Little League baseball fields, horse shoe pits, children's play ground and individual and group picnic areas and two restrooms. Group picnic areas must be reserved during peak use months of April through October. Crane Park is the home of the St. Helena Farmers Market which is open from 7:30 a.m. to 11:30 a.m. every Friday May through October.

Lyman Park

1300 block of Main St. between Pine and Adams Streets.

A one-acre park with individual picnic tables, grassy areas, a children's play area and historic gazebo. The gazebo may be rented for events such as weddings and birthday parties. Lyman Park is host to the Summer Band Concerts on Thursday evenings during July and August. This is a passive park and no active game playing is allowed. One restroom.

Yountville

Parks and Recreation
707.944.8712

Yountville Park

On Washington Street at the north end of town, just across the street from the Napa Valley Lodge
707.944.8851

Yountville Park is a very popular place for picnics (and post-hot air balloon flight champagne brunches) and one of the best parks around for kids, boasting a unique assortment of play equipment.

Across the street from the park is Pioneer Cemetery and the grave of George Yount, first settler in the valley and the founder of Yountville (although he called it

"Sebastopol", overlooking the fact that Sonoma County already had a town of that name).

State Parks

Bale Grist Mill State Historic Park

3369 North Saint Helena Highway (Hwy 29)
St. Helena CA 94574
707.942.4575
www.parks.ca.gov/default.asp?page_id=482
Three miles north of St. Helena Hours 10 a.m. to 5 p.m.

Open daily throughout the year except New Year's Day, Thanksgiving and Christmas. Built in 1846 by Edward Bale, the mill has been restored to operating condition complete with its 36-foot wooden waterwheel and big millstones. On weekends, you can watch the mill in action, grinding grain to produce stone ground flour. Schedule your visit in October for *Old Mill Days* or December for *Pioneer Christmas*.

The "Bears" who were involved in the Bear Flag Revolt at Sonoma (when Yankees living in California caused it to split off from Mexico and join the United States) gathered here beforehand. A fun and educational experience for the kids and parents, too. Limited picnic facilities.

In addition to scheduled tours and demonstrations at the mill on weekends at 11:30 a.m., 1:00 and 2:30 p.m., groups may schedule visits for Tuesdays or Wednesdays by calling the park at least 30 days in advance.

Bothé-Napa Valley State Park

3801 North Saint Helena Highway (Hwy 29)
Calistoga CA 94515
707.942.4575
www.napanet.net/~bothe/

Bothé is just north of Bale Grist Mill, and the two parks are connected by a one-mile trail.

The nearly 2,000-acre park has excellent trails along Ritchey Creek and through beautiful redwood groves. It offers 50 camping areas either near redwoods along the creekside, or among the oaks and manzanita on sunny slopes above the creek. Campsites are also available for groups, hikers and bicyclists, and one site is fully wheelchair accessible. Picnic areas and an outdoor swimming pool are available.

The Native American Garden, is located next to the Visitor Center. Many of these plants are still used today by the Wappo People.

Day use fees are $5.00 per car. Camping is $16 on the weekends, $15 during the week. It's a wonderful place for all ages and the loveliest public place to hike in the entire valley.

Hiking at Bothé-Napa Valley State Park

1. Ritchey Canyon Trail takes you through the heart of the park on historic routes and paths that parallel a year-round stream shaded by redwoods, firs and other plants that prefer cool, moist environments. The trail becomes steeper after a half mile, but offers solitude and a pleasant picnic spot at the homestead site.

2. Redwood Trail skirts the south side of Ritchey Creek. Along its upper section, the path is heavily shaded by redwoods and mixed-evergreen forest. You will enjoy a peaceful walk along the creek bank among the ferns, Solomon's seal, and other shade-loving plants. Early in the spring, trillium and redwood orchids bloom at the base of the young redwoods that have sprouted from the roots of trees that were felled during settlement of the valley in the 1850s.

3. Coyote Peak Trail climbs out of the canyon bottom offering views of the upper canyon and Napa Valley. Combining this

trail with the Ritchey Canyon, Redwood and South Fork Trails makes a popular loop of 4.4 miles and reveals the variety of plant communities found in the park.

4. South Fork Trail goes up a canyon following a skid road used by early pioneers to haul out redwoods. After 0.4 miles the trail leaves the skid road and continues at an easier grade, passing a spur trail to a good overlook of Ritchey Canyon before rejoining the Spring Trail.

5. History Trail leads from the picnic area to the historic Bale Grist Mill. Near its beginning the trail passes through a pioneer cemetery and the site of the first church of Napa County, built in 1853. It was named after the Reverend Asa White, who gave sermons in a grove of trees on this site. A steep section of the trail climbs from the cemetery onto a ridge paralleling Highway 29.

The trail ends at the mill after passing the remains of the pond and ditches that brought water from Mill Creek to power the mill's overshot water wheel.

Robert Louis Stevenson State Park

3801 North St. Helena Highway
Calistoga CA 94515
707.942.4575
www.parks.ca.gov/default.asp?page_id=472

This undeveloped 5,000-acre park is seven miles north of Calistoga, and open during daylight hours only. There's a hiking trail to the top of Mount St. Helena, exhibits, a picnic area, and an historic landmark monument to Stevenson.

Bring your own drinking water for the long, sometimes very hot, climb up the mountain. Best time to visit is spring or fall. The view from the summit includes the nearby geyser country and, weather permitting, distant mountains such as Lassen, Shasta and the Sierra Nevada. Not only is there no water, there are no restrooms either. And only limited parking. Which

probably explains why there's no entrance fee.

The park contains the old townsite of Silverado, and the tent site where Robert Louis Stevenson, author of *Kidnapped* and *Treasure Island* spent six weeks in the summer of 1880. Stevenson and his bride stayed in an abandoned mining building near the Silverado Mine. The building is long gone and a monument marks the site. While at the site, Stevenson kept a journal which he later used to write *The Silverado Squatters*.

Picnicking

Parks and wineries offer picnic locations throughout the valley. Unless you see an obvious picnic table in a vineyard near a winery's visitor area, avoid the vineyards. Growers don't take kindly to people tromping down the soil or "sampling" grapes.

Fortunately, a number of wineries provide picnic tables. As a courtesy to the winery that provides you with picnic facilities, and for your own enjoyment, we encourage you to purchase a bottle of wine from the winery to go with your lunch. Some of the wineries with picnic areas are:

Casa Nuestra

Silverado Trail between Lodi and Bale Lanes St. Helena
707.963.5783

Chateau Potelle

3875 Mt. Veeder Road Napa
707.255.9440

A mountain setting on Mt. Veeder

Clos du Val

Silverado Trail between Oak Knoll and Yountville Cross Road
707.259.2200

Clos Pegase Winery

North side of Dunaweal Lane between Highway 29 and Silverado Trail Calistoga
707.942.4981

Picnic tables under a 300-year-old oak tree. Bring your own lunch or purchase cheese and other items at the winery.

Cuvaison Winery

Silverado Trail south of Dunaweal Lane Calistoga
707.942.6266

Edgewood Estate

Highway 29 between Zinfandel Lane and downtown St. Helena
707.963.7293

Folie a Deux Winery

Highway 29 north of Lodi Lane, north of St. Helena
707.963.1160

Louis M. Martini Winery

Highway 29 south of downtown St. Helena
707.963.2736

Monticello Vineyards

Big Ranch Road south of Oak Knoll Crossroad Napa
707.253.2802

Beautiful location with a Thomas Jefferson-style building.

Madonna Estate (Mont St. John)

5400 Old Sonoma Road, at intersection with Highway 29 in the Carneros
707.255.8864

Napa Cellars

Highway 29, north of Yountville just past Mustard's Grill
707.944.2565

Nichelini Winery

2950 Sage Canyon Road St. Helena
707.963.0717

In a canyon in the hills east of the Napa Valley.

Niebaum-Coppola Winery

1991 St. Helena Highway Rutherford
707.963.9099

On the grounds of movie director Francis Ford Coppola's winery.

Pine Ridge Winery

West side of Silverado Trail between Oak Knoll and Yountville Cross Road
707.253.7500

Picnic tables and barbecue grills

RustRidge Winery

Pope Valley
707.965.2871

Off the beaten path in Pope Valley east of the Napa Valley.

Rutherford Hill Winery

Silverado Trail north of Highway 128, Rutherford
707.963.7194

St. Clement Vineyards

2867 St. Helena Highway St. Helena
707.967.3033

V. Sattui Winery

1111 White Lane at Highway 29 St. Helena
707.963.7774

Extensive delicatessen selection.

Sterling Vineyards

1111 Dunaweal Lane Calistoga
707.942.3344

OTHER GREAT PICNIC SPOTS

Old Faithful Geyser (Calistoga)

Admission charge

Yountville Park

north end of Washington Street in Yountville across from Napa Valley Lodge

Lyman Park

1300 Main St. in Downtown St. Helena at North end of business district

Vintage 1870

center of Yountville

St. Helena Factory Outlets

Back of parking outlets at rear

Romantic Tips

More than half of the people who visit the Napa Valley arrive in pairs. With good reason: the Napa Valley is a romantic place. The views are gorgeous, the wine is both soothing and stimulating, the dining can be intimate and is always superb, the lodging is luxurious, and the mud baths, whirlpools and massages bring your body to full tingling alert.

Is there something special a couple should do in the Napa Valley? Actually a visit to the valley is almost foolproof for romance. But we can provide a few pointers.

1. Arrive in the valley in time for lunch, buy some goodies at one of the excellent delicatessens listed in this book, and picnic somewhere lovely and private. Or, as an alternative, you could have lunch on the Wine Train.

2. Visit one or two wineries in the afternoon, but no more.

3. Spend a couple of hours at a Calistoga spa, preferably one that allows the two of you to take a mud bath, mineral bath and massage in the same private room.

4. Have a light dinner with just enough wine to feel very relaxed.

5. Stroll the sidewalks of Calistoga for a little fresh air and to work off the dessert you might have had after dinner.

6. Return to your room at one of the many hotels, B&Bs and resorts that offer rooms with their own whirlpool baths.

7. Pop open a bottle of champagne, pour two glasses and, while soaking in your bubbling bath, toast each other for your good sense in coming to the Napa Valley.

8. The rest is up to you.

Kids' Favorites

Here are some sights and activities of special interest to children. (Watching parents taste wine can get boring pretty quickly.) See the *Town* sections for specific information on each of the these listings.

Bothé-Napa Valley State Park (Calistoga)
Mt. St. Helena Trout Farm (Calistoga)
Napa Firefighters Museum (Napa)
Napa Valley Museum (Yountville)
Napa Valley Wine Train (Napa)
Old Faithful Geyser (Calistoga)
Bale Grist Mill (St. Helena)
Rutherford Grill (Rutherford)
Seguin Vineyards Cooperage (Napa)
Sterling Vineyards and airtram (Calistoga)
Swimming Pools at Spas (Calistoga)
Yountville Park (Yountville)

Outside Napa Valley

Jelly Belly (Fairfield)
Six Flags Marine World (Vallejo)

Gay Information

North Bay Unity League

PO Box 711
Napa CA 94559
707.963.0182
www.unityleague.org

An organization providing events, information and support for lesbian, gay, bisexual and transgendered residents and their families, friends and allies.

Night Life

There's still not a lot. But it's better than it used to be.

Calistoga

Calistoga Inn & Brewery

1250 Lincoln Avenue Calistoga CA 94515
707.942.4101
www.calistogainn.com

Open mike on Wednesday evenings from 8:30-11:00 p.m. Friday and Saturday evenings live acoustic music at the same hours. Some Sundays there's afternoon music in the beer garden.

Hydro Bar and Grill

1403 Lincoln Ave Calistoga CA 94515
707.942.9777

Swing band Wednesday and Sunday evenings. Blues and R&B Friday and Saturday evenings.

Napa

Downtown Joe's

902 Main St. Napa CA 94559
707.258.2337
www.downtownjoes.com

Open mike on Tuesdays. Live music Thursday through Saturday evenings. Cover charge Friday and Saturday.

Piccolino's Italian Cafe

1385 Napa Town Center (on First Street)
Napa CA 94559
707.251.0100
www.piccolinoscafe.com

Live keyboard/vocalist Friday and Saturday evenings. Contemporary/jazz.

River City

505 Lincoln Avenue Napa CA 94558
707.253.1111

Live music Wednesday and Sundays from 5:30-8:30 p.m with dancing on the deck. Summer only.

Saketini

3900 Bel Aire Plaza Napa CA 94558
707.255.7423
www.sake-tini.com

DJ and live band dance music with a lively young crowd. Friday and Saturday evenings till 2 a.m.

Silverado Country Club

1600 Atlas Peak Road Napa CA 94558
707.257.0200
www.silveradoresort.com

Music and dancing Friday and Saturday evenings, and you don't have to be staying at Silverado to enjoy it. One of the few places in the valley where you'll want to dress up a little.

Uva Trattoria Italiana

2040 Clinton Street Napa CA 94559
707.255.6646

Jazz in the dining room Wednesday and Thursday evenings, but you can enjoy it from the bar as well.

St. Helena

1351 Lounge

1351 Main St. St. Helena CA 94574
707.963.1969
www.1351lounge.com

Live blues Thursday, Friday and Saturday nights from 9:30 p.m. to 1:30 a.m. $5 cover Friday and Saturday. Open mike on the last Sunday of the month.

Ana's Cantina

1205 Main Street St. Helena CA 94574
707.963.4921

Karaoke Thursday evenings, live bands Friday and Saturday evenings.

Silverado Brewing Company

3020 N. St. Helena Highway
St. Helena CA 94574
707.967.9876
www.silveradobrewingcompany.com

Live music Friday and Saturday evenings. No cover charge.

Downtown Napa Walking Tour

Approximate duration 45 minutes

Historic Buildings and Points of Interest

Indicates the structure is individually listed on the National Register of Historic Places.

DWIGHT MURRAY PLAZA

First Street (North side between Main and Coombs Streets

Formerly called "Clocktower Plaza" until the long-maligned (by most people in Napa) clocktower on the site was torn down. At the southeastern corner of the plaza is a monument to Napa's contribution to the invention of the Magnavox loudspeaker.

The plaza is a controversial testament to the City of Napa's redevelopment plan begun in the 1970s. Numerous historic buildings were demolished to make way for a downtown shopping center. This prompted a group of concerned citizens to form Napa County Landmarks. Thanks in part to their efforts, the City's redevelopment program now emphasizes building *on* Napa's past, not simply over it.

FIRST NATIONAL BANK* (1916-1917)

1026 First Street On the east side of the plaza

Napa County Landmarks revived this handsome Neo-Classical building in 1994 after it stood vacant for five years. Now known as the John Whitridge III Community Preservation Center, after Landmarks' founder and longtime president, it serves as a gathering place for civic activities. The style reflects the appearance of strength and stability long favored by American banks.

In 2002, it was converted to an Italian restaurant.

WATERFRONT MURAL

On Main Street on the northwest corner of Main and First Street

Numerous local groups collaborated to start Napa's downtown mural project. This first mural, dedicated in 1994, depicts the Napa River waterfront (circa 1900) with its wharfs, mills, wineries, schooners and steamships.

OPERA HOUSE* (1879)

1018 Main Street Across the street and slightly north of the mural

Painstakingly restored by local preservationists, the Opera House never really presented classical opera; instead, it offered such notables as John Phillip Sousa and Jack London along with travelling vaudeville shows. Due to the unpredictable nature of the entertainment business, the ground level was devoted to commercial uses in order to provide a steady source of income. The symmetrical façade, large brackets under the eaves, and tall rectangular, pedimented windows are all indicative of the Italianate style. The Opera House reopened in 2002 for the first time since 1914. The upstairs theater is now known as the *Margrit Biever Mondavi Theatre* at the Napa Valley Opera House. Downstairs is the *Café Theatre*.

Underneath Main Street, as it crosses over the Napa Creek, are the remnants of a stone bridge dating from the 1860s. Some long-gone businesses were built over the creek and had trap doors that allowed the merchants to do a little fishing on the job.

KYSER-WILLIAMS BUILDINGS (C. 1886)

1124-1142 Main Street

Designed by Wright and Saunders of San Francisco for the Williams Brothers, this native stone structure was the first multi-tenant building north of Napa Creek. The building was covered by a false front of metal, stucco and mission tiles for almost 50 years before restoration in 1999. David Sterling Kyser (mayor in 1907) purchased the building some time after 1900 for his furniture and undertaking business.

NAPA FIREFIGHTERS' MUSEUM

1201 Main Street

The museum features an outstanding collection of vintage equipment and accessories.

PFEIFFER BUILDING (1875)

1245 Main Street

This is Napa's first stone building (feel the texture of the native sandstone) and oldest surviving commercial structure. Bavarian immigrant Phillip Pfeiffer built it as a brewery. In the 1880s it became the Stone Saloon. Pioneer Chinese businessman Sam Kee later converted it to a laundry. The false front, customarily made of wood, was a common practice in early western towns to give the impression of a larger building.

For those with extra time and interest, two treasures lie several blocks further north: the Lisbon Winery (1880), now the Jarvis Conservatory, a jewel-box theater devoted to the performance of Zarzuela Opera and Baroque Ballet, at 1711 Main Street; and the Hennessey House (1889), 1727 Main Street. Otherwise, retrace your steps back down Main Street to the intersection of First Street.

SEMORILE BUILDING* (1888)

975 First Street

Napa's foremost architect, Luther Turton, designed this building for Italian immigrant grocer Bartolemeo Semorile. It is Napa's finest brick structure, beautifully blending in features such as the cast iron balcony railing, balustrade, and Corinthian columns. Look through the front windows to see the old style of seismic retrofitting.

WINSHIP BUILDING* (1888)

948 Main Street

The Winship Building, a beautiful Italianate building constructed in 1888.

Financier E.H. Winship hired Luther Turton to design this Italianate style building, which was once the tallest on Main Street until the tower that crowned its bay window was removed in 1910. (It was restored in 2003.) Many such towers were removed after the 1906 earthquake for protection. The building had a variety of tenants over the years—including a drug store, dentists, and a pawn shop—before it was restored in the 1980s. The sunburst in the arched pediment along the Main Street façade was a feature repeated in many of Napa's finer homes.

OBERON BUILDING (1934)

902-912 Main Street

The colorful tiles, some of which create stylized Ionic columns, make this the best example of Art Deco architecture in Napa. The various establishments on this site have been serving drinks for well over a century, which is only fitting given that the first commercial building in Napa, the Empire Saloon, was located just a block south.

BANK OF NAPA* (1923)

903 Main Street

Inspired by the Ecole des Beaux Arts in Paris, this Classical Revival building has six colossal Doric columns framing the windows along Main Street. Don't miss the chandeliers, marble wainscoting and plaster ceiling in the lobby.

VETERANS' MEMORIAL PARK

On the east side of Main Street between Downtown Joe's restaurant and the Third Street bridge.

This site was once full of turn-of-the-century commercial buildings that were razed in the 1970s to create the park. The Third Street Bridge (since replaced) once served as a crossing for electric rail cars, much to the dismay of other travellers who were occasionally jolted by the electric lines.

CHINATOWN SITE

Located near the first street bridge where Napa Creek meets the Napa River

Arriving as early as 1851, the Chinese were instrumental in many early trades and industries and built many of the wine caves and stone walls found throughout Napa Valley. Their settlement along the bend in the Napa River once numbered more than 500 residents. The site was razed in 1930 to make way for a yacht harbor that never materialized.

FAGIANI'S BAR (1908)

813 Main Street

One of the few remaining commercial buildings built with native stone, the less visible side walls are brick. The ground-level façade was covered in Art Moderne tiling in the 1940s. The bar has been closed since the 1970s when one of the owners was found murdered inside. The case remains unsolved.

CENTER BUILDING (1904)

816 Brown Street

William Corlett, who along with Luther Turton created many of Napa's finest buildings, designed this fine example of native stone architecture that features the use of contrasting colored stone radiating from the window heads.

COURTHOUSE* (1878)

825 Brown Street

Built on land donated by Napa founder Nathan Coombs, the courthouse is a large-scale version of the popular Italianate style. Rich in 19th century charm, the building has been used as a set for several Hollywood films. There is an excellent photo exhibit of historic Napa County on the first floor. Look for the picture of the courthouse when it had a towering cupola evoking Russian and Gothic styles. The onion-shaped dome was removed in 1931.

The Hall of Records on the west end of Courthouse Square was restored in 1996 after Napa County Landmarks led an effort to save it from the wrecking ball. On the east end of the square is a flag pole (1892) modeled after the Eiffel Tower and a grinding rock used by the Wappo Indians. There were perhaps several thousand Wappo living in the area when the city was established. Through disease and violence their numbers were drastically reduced within a generation of the arrival of the first pioneer settlers. In 1897, California's last public hanging took place here. It was an invitation-only event!

FIRST PRESBYTERIAN CHURCH* (1874)

1333 Third street

This California State Landmark church, constructed entirely of wood, is an exceptional example of the late Victorian Gothic architecture.

UNITED STATES POST OFFICE (1933)

1351 Second Street

Designed by William Corlett during the Great Depression, this is a fine example of a restrained Art Deco style which came to be known as WPA Moderne after the federal government program that put unemployed Americans back to work. Don't miss the glazed terra cotta work, including the rams' heads, along the roof line. Take a look inside.

GOODMAN LIBRARY* (C.1901)

1219 First Street

George Goodman, the co-owner of Napa's first bank, built this native stone structure for $15,000. The building was designed with the rough and heavy feeling of the Romanesque style by Luther Turton. It served not only as a public library, but also as a tea room and social gathering spot. It is now the home of the Napa County Historical Society.

NAPA REGISTER BUILDING (1905)

1202 First Street

The *Napa Register (*now called the *Napa Valley Register)*, the city's oldest newspaper, occupied this Italianate building until 1965 when the paper moved to a more spacious production facility several blocks away.

GORDON BUILDING* (C.1929)

1146, 1142 and 1130 First Street

The glazed terra cotta tiles of the commercial façade exemplify the Spanish Colonial Revival influence that was an attempt to recreate the romantic look of the days of California's ranchos.

Acknowledgment

The above tour is reprinted courtesy of the *Napa Downtown Association* and *Napa County Landmarks*.

This is just one of five walking tours (including Napa's famous Victorians). For a brochure with all five tours, contact:

Napa County Landmarks

1026 First St. Napa CA 94559
707.255.1836 888.255.1836
www.napacountylandmarks.org

Brochures can also be purchased at the Napa Valley Conference and Visitors Bureau in downtown Napa, and in local bookstores and other shops. Napa County Landmarks offers scheduled walking tours of valley towns throughout the year.

For a free map of the historic Napa downtown area, send a self addressed stamped envelope (SASE) to:

Napa Downtown Association

Downtown Map Request
1556 First Street, Ste. 102,
Napa, CA 94559 USA
www.napadowntown.com
707.257.032

Hill and Mountain Biking

BICYCLING THE HILLS OF NAPA VALLEY

Ranking from Toughest to Not-So-Tough

By Bruce DeBell

Thanks to Bruce DeBell and the Eagle Cycling Club (www.eaglecyclingclub.org) for this information.

Hills provide a challenge, a chance to get into condition, a good look at varied scenery, and the only access to those great descents.

The following is a listing and ranking of most of the hills in Napa. I used an Avocet 50 computer for altitude gain and distance. The greater the incline, the more feet climbed per mile.

The Napa hills range from 650 ft/mi. (which in some circles computes to an 18% grade, but not according to my trigonometry book) to 174 ft/mi.

They are also ranked from *most difficult* to *easiest* , which can be somewhat subjective. I base how hard they are usually on how steep ,but sometimes that's not the whole story. If two hills are practically the same pitch but one has no breaks, it will be ranked harder.

1. Oakville Grade (from Hwy 29)—650 ft/mi. Without a doubt the toughest climb in Napa. It's not that far, but it starts out tough and gets a lot tougher. You climb 650 feet in exactly one mile. No breaks, no shade, no fun. The first half isn't so bad, and I can manage it sitting in the saddle using my 39/28. The last half increases in pitch, and it's standing and grunting all the way at a 3.5 mph pace.

2. Spring Mountain (starting from St Helena) - 526 ft/mi. I rank this second even though there are two other climbs that are steeper, but this one is longer and there are

essentially no breaks. Total distance (from the Y in the road to the county line) is 4.5 miles, and the total elevation gain is 1,560 feet. The major pitch however, is 1.9 miles long and 1,000 ft with virtually no breaks. It is covered in shade that helps, but I've only attempted this twice in 7 years, just to give you an idea of how much I enjoy this one.

3. Soda Canyon Road - 633 ft/mi. This is a dead end off of the Silverado Trail. A very pretty ride that takes about 4 miles of not so difficult climbing to get to the real climb. The total distance from Silverado Trail to the peak is 6.1 miles, and the elevation gain is 1,340 feet. The major pitch starts at the fire station 4 miles in and is 1.2 miles with 760 feet of climbing. There are only a couple of short breaks once you start the major climb. No shade, no fun.

4. Wild Horse Valley Road - 600 ft/mi. This is also a dead end that is a continuation of Coombsville Rd. Total distance (from the small bridge to the peak) is 2.4 miles with 1,210 feet of climbing. The major pitch starts at the Y and is 1.6 miles with 960 feet of elevation gain. This one is actually fun, with some great views and some breaks. I break it down into three sections: the first third is toughest, the middle third is flatter and has some breaks, and the last third gets tougher again but still has some breaks.

5. Howell Mountain (from the Pope Valley side) - 504 ft/mi. This is the alternative to Ink Grade and most people don't take it. The total distance is 2.2 miles, with 1,110 feet of climbing. Lots of shade, nice scenery, not a lot of breaks, but I still have fun on this one.

6. Trinity Road (from the Sonoma Hwy 12 side) - 480 ft/mi. I start the climb about a mile in from Hwy 12 just at a sharp right hairpin turn. From there to the fire station at the top it's 2.5 miles with 1,200 feet of climb. The first and last third are the

toughest, with the middle third easiest with more breaks. No shade but still fun.

7. Trinity Road (from the Napa side) - 474 ft/mi. Along with Mt. Veeder, this is one of my favorites. Lots of shade, great descent, great views. The total distance from the first right hand turn to the first vineyard beyond the county line is 1.9 miles with 900 feet of climbing.

8. Cavedale Road - 410 ft/mi. The total distance is 7.0 miles from Hwy 12 on the Sonoma side to the fire station on Trinity and it has 1,850 feet of climb. The major pitch is 4.0 miles with 1,640 feet. This is a very poorly maintained road with lots of potholes and bumps, so it breaks your concentration. There's very little shade and some tough pitches toward the end. Although I rank Trinity harder, I prefer to climb it rather than this brain rattler. Do not take this road on your descent unless you like building wheels.

9. Partrick Road - 380 ft/mi. This one is a dead end off of Browns Valley Rd. It has a very tough little pitch toward the start, some shade but mostly open, and a great descent, but watch for the cattle guards (2). Total distance is about 4 miles from Browns Valley Rd. to where it breaks into a Y of driveways. I don't know the total elevation gain, but I suspect it's around 1,300 feet. However, the major pitch is 2.0 miles and 760 feet. At the beginning there's a 0.5 mile climb of 300 feet gain which is a 600 ft/mi. pitch. That one little pitch is why it's ranked 9th instead of lower.

10. Mount Veeder (from Dry Creek side) - 486 ft/mi. Total distance is 4.0 miles to the last peak (there are several), with 720 ft of elevation gain. This elevation gain is the elevation at the end minus elevation at the beginning, not the total amount of climbing you do. In order to get that figure, I have to remember to zero out my computer at the beginning, which I haven't done yet.
Anyway this is a beautiful mountain and a gorgeous ride. The major pitch is 0.7

miles and 340 feet. Continuing on, you go 1.8 miles with 650 feet of climb. Lots of flats and rollers and gentler climbs to the final peak. One heck of a great downhill after that. Plenty of shade. Part of our 100 miler on the Tour of the Napa Valley.

11. Mount Veeder (from the Redwood Road/Browns Valley side) - 458 ft/mi. Starting at Browns Valley Road/Redwood,you have a gentle climb for 6.0 miles with 600 feet of climbing. Lots of shade, pretty scenery with a babbling brook on your right. After that the major pitch is 1.2 miles and 550 feet of climb. About 3/4 of the way there's a nice flat break of 100 yards or so to the last pitch to the top. One of my favorites.

12. Atlas Peak - 350 ft/mi. This is another dead end but quite beautiful, especially in the spring with a chance for a waterfall. The total distance from Westgate Dr. to the end is 8.3 miles with 1,830 feet elevation gain. There are several peaks, and the first and last are the most difficult. The first peak is 2.6 miles with 910 feet of climbing (watch for the waterfall to your right), then a flat section, rollers and a not so difficult climb to the second peak. After that you go downhill for 1/2 mile or so, and then the road narrows for the last third with a few tough pitches. The ride back down is both scenic and a blast.

13. Mount George (going east on 121) - 333 ft/mi. Total distance is 3.3 miles with 1,100 feet of climbing. Kind of boring, fairly open and a fairly steady climb, though not very difficult. Very nice coming back down, though.

14. Howell Mountain (Napa Valley side off of Silverado Trail) - 271 ft/mi. Total distance from the split with Conn Valley Rd to the top of the hill before Angwin (take right on Deer Park) is 4.1 miles and 1,110 ft of climbing. Very pretty ride on a narrow road with great views, little traffic and plenty of shade.

15. Ink Grade - 247 ft/mi. Total distance from Pope Valley Rd. to White Cottage is 4.5 miles with 1,110 foot of climbing. Very nice ride with plenty of shade and lots of breaks, especially at the start. One of the longer climbs in Napa, but not as difficult as most. Also part of our righteous Tour of the Napa Valley.

16. Oakville Grade (Dry Creek side) - 254 ft/mi. Might be steeper than Ink Grade, but doesn't feel like it and it's much shorter. Total distance is 1.3 miles with 330 feet of elevation gain. Watch out for that descent on the other side though—it's a screamer.

17. Redwood Road - 174 ft/mi. This is a little dead end side road off of Mt. Veeder and the turnoff for Hess Winery (a stop worth making for a look at their art collection). This is probably the prettiest road in Napa with a babbling brook, waterfalls in spring, redwoods, a narrow winding road, and vineyards. Total distance is 3.4 miles with 590 feet of climbing. Most of the climbs are at 267 ft/mi. difficulty, but there are lots of flats and breaks with probably less than 2 miles of actual climbing. The last 0.2 miles are the most difficult.

MOUNTAIN BIKING

Courtesy of Eric Apgar (www.apgar.net)

Skyline Wilderness Park

Napa 707.252.0481 www.skylinepark.org

DIRECTIONS: from the south, take the first Napa exit off Highway 29 which is Highway 221/Soscol Road. Take a right on Imola and drive to the end. The park is on your right.

A group of volunteers runs the park and your entrance fees help pay to maintain the trails. The park is generally open from 8 a.m. until one hour before sunset (they open at 9 a.m. on weekdays). During the long summer days, it is only open until 8 p.m. They will lock the gate with your car inside, so be out on time.

The trails are appropriate for intermediate to advanced riders. There are no easy trails in Skyline Park. The road up to Lake Marie is a steady, easy grade, but rocky and rutted. The single track is fantastic - watch for hikers and equestrians (stop if you see a horse coming in the opposite direction unless the horse rider gives you the okay to proceed). There are some trails for hikers only. You can get a map at the kiosk. The cross-country Grundig-UCI World Cup Open was held at Skyline park in 1997, 1998 and 1999.

Kennedy Park (Napa)

Kennedy Park is behind Napa Valley College and has about one mile of trail that you can mountain bike on. It is an alternative staging area to get to Skyline Park via the River to Ridge Trail and to downtown Napa once the River Trail is complete.

River to Ridge Trail (Napa)

This trail connects Kennedy Park to Skyline Park through a corridor of property between the State Hospital and the Syar quarries.

River Trail (Napa)

The River trail will eventually go along the Napa River from the industrial park in south Napa to Trancas Ave. in north Napa. Currently the only sections open are Kennedy Park and the stretch from Lincoln Ave. to Trancas Ave. This section will eventually be paved. Right now it is hard pack dirt (or mud during the winter rains).

Alston Park (Napa)

Alston Park has perhaps three miles of trails to bike. It's very busy with walkers and dog-walkers (watch out for dogs off leash). It's on Dry Creek Road on the western city of the city of Napa.

Bothé-Napa Valley State Park (Calistoga)

Bothé has several miles of trail (mostly fire roads), camping, and a pool. Lots of nice redwoods. There's a day use fee. Four miles north of St. Helena on Highway 29/128. 707.942.4575.

Oat Hill Mine Road (Calistoga)

NOTE: The new Palisades Trail between Table Rock and the top of the Oat Hill Mine Road is not open to bikes. If you are caught, there is a large fine.

Intermediate to Experts only. This trail climbs from 400 to 2,200 feet on an old county roadbed. It is very rocky and rutted. Stay on the trail; the surrounding property is private. Take lots of water on a hot day. The wildflowers are great in the spring. On the way up, notice the ruts worn into the rock bed from the mining wagons.

To find the trail, follow Highway 29 through Calistoga to the east side of town, and you will come to the intersection with the Silverado Trail. The trail starts just to the left of the trailhead store (currently closed).

Mount St. Helena (Calistoga)

Mount St. Helena is the big peak (4,343 feet) just north of Calistoga. There have been plans to develop the state park there for years, but not much has happened. There are two rides on the mountain that I know. The first is up the fire road. At the top you can choose the South or North peak. Both peaks have various man-made structures. The North peak is a little further and higher.

On a clear day you can see Bodega Head (the ocean), San Francisco, Mount Diablo, the Sierra Nevada mountains, Mount Lassen and Mount Shasta. One of the best views in the world.

The trailhead is at about 2,000 feet. Take lots of water; there is none on the mountain. To get to the hiking trailhead, follow Highway 29 east out of Calistoga and up a very windy road with many switchbacks. People drive like maniacs here. Right at the saddle are the parking lot and hiking trailheads. Keep going about 1/2 mile and you will see where the fire road intersects with Highway 29. There are several pull-outs where you can park. Bikes are not allowed on the hiking trail from the main parking lot. The hiking trail joins up with the fire road.

The other ride follows a paved road out to the former site of the Silverado Mine boomtown. Not much is left except for a few foundations. It's a fairly flat ride. When I last walked it, there were several trees down on the road. I have only walked this road, so I'm not sure of the best way to get to it on bike.

The road does hook up with Highway 29 just before getting to the main parking lot near a red house. I'm not sure if anyone lives there. One way to walk to the road is to take the hiking trail from the parking lot up to the Robert Louis Stevenson monument. Just to the left of the monument is the entrance to the former Silverado Mine and just to the left and below this entrance is an old road bed that is still fairly open. Follow this and it takes you right to the backyard of the red house where the paved road starts.

Wine

"I cook with wine. Sometimes I even add it to the food"—W. C. Fields

"Wine is the most civilized thing in the world."—Ernest Hemingway

"Wine cheers the sad, revives the old, inspires the young, makes weariness forget his toil."—Lord Byron

"Wine brings to light the hidden secrets of the soul, gives being to our hopes, bids the coward flight, drives dull care away, and teaches new means for the accomplishment of our wishes."—Horace

"A bottle of wine begs to be shared. I have never met a miserly wine lover."—Clifton Fadiman

"If food is the body of good living, wine is its soul."—Clifton Fadiman

"Wine is sunlight, held together by water."—Louis Pasteur

"In water one sees one's own face; but in wine, one beholds the heart of another."—Old French Proverb

"Penicillin cures, but wine makes people happy."—Alexander Fleming

"Beer is made by men; wine by God."—Martin Luther

The Paris Tasting

Napa Valley makes only four percent of the wine produced throughout California, but the quality of that wine has made California wines famous throughout the world. The Napa Valley itself is only one-eighth the size of France's Bordeaux region, but that hasn't kept its wines from besting the finest of France in prestigious wine tastings.

The most famous was the event that truly put the Napa Valley on the map. On May 24, 1976, in celebration of the American Bicentennial, a well-known British wine merchant named Stephen Spurrier conducted a blind tasting to see how well American wines held up against the most famous of the French wines. The tasting was held in Paris and was judged by a panel of nine highly respected French wine experts. The French wines included several Grand Cru Bordeaux and first-rate white Burgundies.

Although the bottles were covered, the judges knew they were tasting both American and French wines and, indeed some made comments during the tasting about how obvious it was which wines were American and how inferior they were.

When the results of the tasting were announced, many of the judges were horrified at what they had done. A few judges even tried to retrieve their tasting notes. The top red wine, surpassing the finest of French wine estates, was a 1973 Cabernet Sauvignon from Napa Valley winemaker Warren Winiarski and his Stag's Leap Wine Cellars. Winiarski's Cabernet edged out such highly-regarded entries as a 1970 Mouton Rothschild and a 1970 Chateau Haut Brion.

The top white wine, in an equally horrifying result for the French judges, was also from the Napa Valley. It was a 1973 Chardonnay from Chateau Montelena, made by winemaker Miljenko (Mike) Grgich (now co-owner of Grgich-Hills Cellars). In fact, six of the eleven highest rated wines were from California.

The wine world was stunned, the French were despondent, the Californians ecstatic. Napa Valley wines had truly arrived on the world scene. And things only got better after that.

The Napa Valley's climate and soil have made it one of the world's great winegrowing regions. It has long been famous for its ability to grow Bordeaux grapes such as Cabernet Sauvignon and Sauvignon Blanc. Later it was discovered that the southern part of the valley, particularly the Carneros region next to San Francisco Bay, was ideal for growing the grapes of Burgundy, including Chardonnay and Pinot Noir.

Other popular wines include Merlot, Zinfandel, Riesling, Petite Sirah, Gamay Beaujolais and Chenin Blanc, and some wineries are producing Semillon, Cabernet Franc and Muscat, Recently there has been a return to the old Italian grapes that were once grown in the valley, and wineries are beginning to produce such wines as Pinot Grigio, Sangiovese, Grignolino and Dolcetto.

There are also a number of wineries that produce sparkling wines, and a few produce *only* "sparklers."

WINE VARIETAL BASICS

By: Jon V. Sèvigny

Thanks to Jon Sèvigny, Sommelier, J.V. Wine & Spirits (www.jvwineandspirits.com) in Napa for permission to use the following excellent information on wine varietals produced in the Napa Valley.

Learning about wine is a lot like work and you are never done learning. Part of what I love is knowing that there is always something new out there that I have never tried before. And, part of what I hate is having a snooty winery representative correct my pronunciation of an Italian grape or French village and realizing that I have been pronouncing it wrong for 10 years. So, if you have ever gone into a wine store and asked for Viognier as (ve-gin-ear) instead of (vee-oh-nay), here is a reference that should help. I have compiled 22 of the most common grape varieties used to make wine along with pronunciation, a brief description, food pairing suggestions and serving temperatures.

WHITE WINES

Chardonnay

Chardonnay is the most popular of all white wine grapes and produces a medium to full-bodied wine. Its flavors are often described as being appley, buttery or nutty, with nuances of melon or tropical fruit.

Many of the finest full bodied Chardonnay wines are produced from grapes grown in California or Australia. In France, the clean and crisp White Burgundy and Chablis are made exclusively from Chardonnay.

Enjoy with seafood, poultry, pork, salads, brie and other semi-soft cheeses. The amount of time spent in oak determines the style of the Chardonnay. The less oak, the lighter and crisper it is. The oakier the wine, the richer the food with which you need to pair it.

Serve chilled—but not too cold. Chardonnay shows best at 52 to 55 degrees; so pull it out of the refrigerator and let it warm up before serving.

Chenin Blanc

Is used for making anything from dry to sweet wines. This grape produces Vouvray and other fine white wines in the Loire Valley of France. They are known for their high acidity and high viscosity. Look for good California examples from Chappellet and Pine Ridge.

Another good aperitif wine, good with grilled fish, shellfish, shrimp, scallops, lighter poultry dishes and other light fare.

Like Chardonnay, serve it chilled—but not too cold. It shows best at 52 to 55 degrees; so pull it out of the refrigerator and let it warm up before serving.

Gewürztraminer

Produces a floral, refreshing, spicy wine that can vary from dry to sweet. The best Gewürztraminer is produced in the Alsace region of France. When harvested late, it can produce a rich and complex desert wine.

Enjoy with spicy foods, smoked meats and other pungent dishes. Like Riesling, it complements Thai food or spicy Chinese or Middle Eastern dishes.

Serve this wine well-chilled at 44 to 48 degrees, just above refrigerator temperature

Pinot Blanc

Produces wine similar in body and taste to Chardonnay. Much of the wine produced by these grapes is used for blending or in sparkling wines but many California wineries are now producing excellent pure Pinot Blanc wines.

Excellent sipping wine or enjoy with fish, shrimp, chicken, lobster, dinner salads and other light fare.

Serve this wine well chilled at 44 to 48 degrees, just above refrigerator temperature

Pinot Gris

The Pinot Gris grape lends itself to a variety of styles, from a light aperitif to a rich dessert wine. It produces dry wines of character in the Alsace region of France called Tokay de Alsace. It is known in Italy as Pinot Grigio, a light-bodied, dry white wine. Look for excellent Pinot Gris from Oregon and Washington States.

Riesling

The Riesling grape produces a light to medium-bodied white wine with a great deal of honeyed fruit flavors. Styles of Riesling can vary from off dry to very sweet. When harvested late, it can produce a rich and complex desert wine. Good Rieslings are exceptional wines that improve with age. Wine Guy Note: Not all Rieslings are sticky sweet. Dry Riesling makes great food wine—try the Boony Doon Pacific Rim from California or the Giesen from New Zealand!

Enjoy with spicy foods, smoked meats and other pungent dishes. Try a dry Riesling with Thai food or spicy Chinese or Middle Eastern dishes.

Serve this wine well-chilled at 45 to 48 degrees, just above refrigerator temperature.

Sauvignon Blanc

Sauvignon Blanc grapes produce a crisp, refreshing wine with a variety of fruit flavors. Sometimes known as Fumé Blanc in North America, this wine is produced in France, New Zealand, California and Australia. This is a food-friendly wine that loves garlic.

Wonderful summer sipping wine or enjoy with fish, shrimp, chicken, lobster, dinner salads and other light fare. Raw oysters or shrimp cocktail might be a perfect match.

Serve this wine well chilled at 42 to 48 degrees, just above refrigerator temperature.

Semillon

A white wine grape grown primarily in France, California and Australia's Hunter Valley. It produces a full-bodied wine and is often used to blend with Sauvignon Blanc or Chardonnay.

Excellent sipping wine or enjoy with fish, shrimp, chicken, lobster, dinner salads and other light fare.

Like Chardonnay, serve it chilled—but not too cold. It shows best at 52 to 55 degrees; so pull it out of the refrigerator and let it warm up before serving.

Viognier

Produces a dry wine with a bouquet of pears, peaches and flower blossoms. It is grown to perfection in the Rhone Valley in France, and successfully in Australia and California.

An excellent aperitif wine, good with shellfish, shrimp, scallops, light poultry dishes or a summer salad.

Serve this wine well-chilled at 42 to 48 degrees, just above refrigerator temperature.

RED WINES

Barbera

A red wine grape from the Piedmont region of Italy that produces Barbera d' Asti and Barbera d' Alba. It is also cultivated in California. Barbera produces a red wine with deep color, a light to medium-body, high acidity, light tannins and good fruit flavor.

Enjoy this wine with lamb, pork, chicken or almost any pasta dish.

Try this at cellar temperature, 58 to 63 degrees. If you don't have a cellar, put it in the refrigerator for 20 to 25 minutes before serving.

Cabernet Franc

Produces a full bodied wine with raspberry flavor and an herbal bouquet that, while softer, can be as full-bodied and intense as Merlot or Cabernet Sauvignon. Although used primarily for blending, especially in Bordeaux, it also stands well on its own and is the primary grape in the Chinon wines of the Loire Valley in France.

Pair it with any food you would normally serve with Merlot or Cabernet Sauvignon. Serve it just above cellar temperature, at 62 to 67 degrees. If you don't have a cellar, put it in the refrigerator for 10 minutes before serving.

Cabernet Sauvignon

Cabernet Sauvignon is the most famous of all red wine grapes. It produces medium to full-bodied, dry, deeply colored red wine, possessing flavors of black fruits and aromas of cedar. Cabernet is the basis for the great red wines of the Bordeaux region of France as well as the Cabernet and Cabernet blends from California and Australia.

Enjoy with beef, game, duck and hearty pasta dishes—big wine for big food.

Cabernet shows best at just above cellar temperature, at 62 to 67 degrees. If you don't have a cellar, put it in the refrigerator for 10 minutes before serving.

Gamay

Used to produce the famous wines of Beaujolais. Gamay produces a light, brightly-colored red wine with abundant fruit flavors. It is best drunk very young.

Gamay pairs with all the same foods as Pinot Noir. Think of it as an alternative when the food says white and your head says red.

Gamay is best served at or slightly below cellar temperature, 56 to 62 degrees. Put it in the refrigerator for 25 to 30 minutes before serving.

Grenache

Produces a red wine which is rich in spicy fruit flavors, full-bodied, lightly-colored and low in tannin. Grenache is most often thought of as a blending grape and is a major component of most wines in the southern Rhone Valley of France. It also can produce a short-lived, but very pleasant pure varietal.

Enjoy this wine with lamb, pork, chicken, cassoulet or almost any French country fare.

Try this at cellar temperature, 58 to 63 degrees. If you don't have a cellar, put it in the refrigerator for 20 to 25 minutes before serving

Merlot

The Merlot grape produces a luscious medium-bodied red wine with a soft texture and rich fruity flavors that are approachable at a much younger age than Cabernet Sauvignon. Merlot grapes are often blended with Cabernet Sauvignon to soften the wine and make it more drinkable at an earlier age.

Merlot styles vary based upon ripeness and the use of oak. California Merlots tend to be bigger-bodied and higher alcohol (13.5% to 15%) that makes for easy, stand alone sipping. Look for lower alcohol (12.5% to 13.5%) contents and medium-body to pair with food. Enjoy with red meats, game dishes, pork or rabbit.

Merlot shows best at just above cellar temperature, at 62 to 67 degrees. If you don't have a cellar, put it in the refrigerator for 10 minutes before serving.

Mourvedere

Produces a wine with flavors of plum and black currants, with a spicy herbal taste. It is a principle component of the wines of Bandol in France, is used as a blending grape in the Rhone valley and is also grown in California and Australia.

Like Grenache, enjoy this wine with lamb, pork, chicken, cassoulet or almost any French country fare.

Try this at cellar temperature, 58 to 63 degrees. If you don't have a cellar put it in the refrigerator for 20 to 25 minutes before serving.

Nebbolio

The great black grape from Northern Italy. Nebbolio is used to produce the long lived Barolo and Barbaresco wines in Piedmont. Known for its flavors of chocolate and licorice, along with a floral bouquet, this grape produces some of Italy's best red wines. It is also now being cultivated in California.

This is excellent food wine; enjoy it with beef, pork, veal, chicken or pasta.

Barolos and Barbarescos are best served just slightly above cellar temperature, 62 to 66 degrees. If you don't have a cellar, put it in the refrigerator for 10 to 15 minutes before serving.

Petite Sirah

Produces a dark, fruity, full bodied red wine. This grape is grown primarily in warm weather regions, particularly in California. Full-bodied with firm tannins, Petite Sirah can be a very long lived wine.

Hearty wine for hearty food, serve it with beef, pork, duck, game, pizza or with any spicy cuisines like Thai or Indian.

Serve just-above cellar temperature, at 62 to 67 degrees. If you don't have a cellar, put it in the refrigerator for 10 minutes before serving.

Pinot Noir

Pinot Noir is one of the world's great varieties of grapes. In France, Pinot Noir is used to produce what the world knows as Burgundy. It produces a delicious soft to medium-bodied dry red wine, filled with complex flavors of fruit and spice. A cooler weather grape, Pinot Noir is the most difficult of all grapes to cultivate and produce wine with. The best domestic Pinot Noirs are made in Oregon. A Wine Guy caution: When it's good, it's very good and when it's bad—yuk! It may taste like cross between battery acid and asparagus. Be careful choosing California Pinot Noirs...

Enjoy with lamb, turkey, pork and pasta with cream sauces. I think of it as the best alternative when the food says white and your head says red. Try it with grilled salmon!

Pinot Noir is best served at cellar temperature, 58 to 63 degrees. If you don't have a cellar, put it in the refrigerator for 20 to 25 minutes before serving.

Sangiovese

Sangiovese is the most widely planted red grape of Tuscany in Italy, and the primary component of Chianti. Sangiovese is now being successfully grown in California and produces a versatile, fruity, medium-bodied, dry red wine. Italian Chianti and Sangiovese tend to be higher in acidity, making them good food wines but a little astringent for just sipping. California Sangiovese tends to be riper and less acidic.

This is the ultimate food wine; enjoy it with beef, pork, veal, chicken, pasta or anything Italian!

Sangiovese is best served just above cellar temperature, 65 to 68 degrees. If you don't have a cellar, put it in the refrigerator for 20 to 25 minutes before serving.

Syrah / Shiraz

Syrah is the great black grape of the Rhone region of France where it is a primary component in the blended wines of Rhone valley. Syrah produces a rich, deeply fruity, full-bodied, dry red wine of great complexity. It is known as Syrah in California and Shiraz in Australia.

Because of its full-body soft tannins, Shiraz makes a great stand-alone wine or enjoy it with hearty dishes, beef, pork, duck, game, pizza or BBQ! Also makes good accompaniment for spicy cuisines like Thai or Indian.

Shiraz is best at just-above cellar temperature, at 62 to 67 degrees. If you don't have a cellar, put it in the refrigerator for 10 minutes before serving.

Zinfandel

Zinfandel is used to produce the only wine considered truly American. While probably of obscure European origin, Zinfandel produces a big, jammy, spicy and complex red wine, with a full body and soft finish. Zinfandel can produce anything from a dry, claret-style to dense, chewy, high-alcohol reds. It is also used to produce a "blush" wine, usually marketed as White Zinfandel, a fruity, light pink wine.

A nice stand-alone "glass on the deck" kind of red. Big wine for big food or enjoy with pizza, red meats, BBQ or pasta with red sauce.

Zinfandel is best at just above cellar temperature, at 62 to 67 degrees. If you don't have a cellar, put it in the refrigerator for 10 minutes before serving.

Agricultural Crop Production—Napa County 2002

How important are wine and winegrapes to the Napa Valley? The total value of 2002 agricultural production in Napa County was $387,863,000. Winegrapes accounted for $379,930,000 of that total. The other

approximately $8,000,000 came from grapevine rootstock, vegetables, olives, livestock, hay, walnuts, ornamental grapevines, cut flowers and Christmas trees.

Year 2002 Wine Harvest Statistics

Total value of the winegrape crop was $379,930,000.

Total tonnage of grapes was 130,098, of which 91,278 were black and 38,820 were white.

Total acreage of producing vineyards at the time of the 2002 harvest was 37,072 acres, of which 26,853 were black and 10,219 were white.

Average price per ton for all grapes was $2,942, with an average of $3,250 for black varieties and $2,075 for whites.

Highest average price per ton was $4,865 for Petite Verdot. Cabernet Sauvignon was $4,020 per ton, Cabernet Franc was $3,665, and Merlot was $2,817. Chardonnay brought in an average of $2,316 per ton, followed by Pinot Noir at $2,188, Viognier at $2,144, White Riesling at $2,010, Zinfandel at $1,900 and Sauvignon Blanc at $1,608.

Appellations and American Viticultural Areas (AVAs)

VITICULTURAL AREAS

The Bureau of Alcohol, Tobacco and Firearms (ATF) started establishing viticultural areas in 1978, and their regulation became mandatory in 1983.

All American viticultural areas were established by ATF until 2003, and are now determined by the Tax and Trade Bureau (TTB) of the U.S. Treasury Department. If a wine is labeled with a viticultural area, at least 85% of the grapes used to produce that wine must have come from within the viticultural area.

APPELLATION VS. VITICULTURAL AREA

They're not the same. A viticultural area is a subset of appellation. It's just one kind of appellation. An appellation can also be the name of a country, a state or a county (such as Napa County).

A viticultural area can be very small (such as Mendocino County's Cole Ranch AVA, 150 acres) or very large (such as the Ohio River Valley AVA which includes all of Indiana, Kentucky, Ohio and West Virginia.) In Napa County they range from the largest (Napa Valley, 225,280 acres) to the smallest (Stags Leap District, 2,700 acres)

Napa Valley AVAs

American Viticultural Area (AVA)
   Size in total acres

Atlas Peak	11,400
Chiles Valley District	6,000
Diamond Mountain	5,000
Howell Mountain	14,080
Los Carneros (located in both Napa and Sonoma Counties)	36,900
Mount Veeder	15,000
Napa Valley	225,280
Oakville	5,760
Rutherford	6,650
Saint Helena	9,060
Spring Mountain District	8,600
Stags Leap District	2,700
Wild Horse Valley (located in both Napa and Solano Counties)	3,300
Yountville	8,260

Napa Valley contains, or is in, 15 viticultural areas.
Map courtesy of Napa Valley Vintners Association.

The Wine Bottle "Package"

A wine bottle consists of the glass bottle, front and back labels, a stopper (cork, synthetic or screw top) to close the bottle, and a capsule or foil to cover that stopper.

BOTTLE SIZES

Most wine bottles are 750 milliliters in size. They were originally called "fifths" because they contained a *fifth* of a gallon. Now wineries all use the metric system.

Split (half-bottle)—375 ml
Bottle—750 ml
Magnum (two bottles)—1.5 liters
Jeroboam (double magnum—four bottles)—3 liters (sometimes 4.5 or even 5 liters)
Rehoboam (six bottles)—4.5 liters
Methuselah (Imperial—eight bottles)—6 liters
Salmanazar (twelve bottles)—9 liters

Balthazar (sixteen bottles)—12 liters
Nebuchadnezzar (twenty bottles)—15 liters

FOIL

The covering on the top (the neck) of a wine bottle is called a *foil* or *capsule*. Its purpose is to further seal the bottle opening and prevent leakage of wine or entry of air into the bottle. Originally the foil was made of metal, usually lead. The industry stopped using lead in 1993 to avoid the possibility of traces of lead ending up in the wine glass, and of contamination of landfills.

Today the capsule is made of tin, plastic or even paper. Should you encounter an older bottle of wine that has a lead foil, after removing the foil, carefully wipe the top of the bottle to remove any possible traces of lead before opening and pouring the wine.

CORKS

For centuries, corks have been used to plug the opening of a wine bottle. Corks come from the bark of cork trees, usually from Portugal or Spain. Corks trees are around 35 years old before their bark can be used to make corks. It then takes another 7 to 10 years before the bark can be stripped again.

A cork prevents wine from spilling out of the bottle and most air from entering into the bottle.

However, corks vary in quality and can deteriorate over time. Eventually they can shrink enough to allow excessive air to enter the bottle, which negatively affects the taste of the wine. Corks can also develop mold. Wine with the taste of a moldy cork (or "wet newspaper") is said to be "corked."

Today more and more wineries, even ultra-premium wineries, are switching to corks made of plastic or a composite material, and even to screw tops.. While some purists still deride the change, the reality is that these solutions can prevent all of the

problems associated with natural corks, with no apparent negative effects on the wine itself.

Inspecting the Cork

When the waiter at a restaurant opens a bottle of wine at your table and gives you the cork to inspect, you may, if you wish, sniff the cork to see if it smells okay. (In some restaurants the wait staff will snicker from a distance if you do it.) But it makes a lot more sense to simply try the sample of wine the waiter has just poured you, since you paid for the wine and not the cork.

The actual reason you're given the cork is historical rather than functional. There was a time in Europe when restaurants would attempt to pass off cheap wine as premium wine. To counter this, wineries started imprinting their name on the corks so that the customer could inspect the cork and see that it really did come from the winery whose wine he had requested.

Keeping the Cork Moist

When storing a bottle of wine, keep the bottle on its side, with the top a little lower than the bottom. This will keep the cork moist, and prevent it from drying out and allowing air to enter the bottle. (If your bottle has a synthetic cork, or screw top, this isn't necessary. The stopper won't dry out.)

PUNT

The *punt* is the concave "dent" in the bottom of the wine bottle. There are a number of explanations as to why the punt is used. One, is that in centuries past, it was created to provide more strength to bottles under pressure—champagne bottles. It then began to be used by all wine bottles.

Another explanation for its current use is to trap sediment along its edges as it sinks to the bottom, although most U.S. wine today is well filtered and has little, if any, sediment.

Another possible explanation is that in the days of hand-blown glass, leaving a concave dent in the bottom of the bottle minimized the possibility that the glass blower would end up making the bottom of the bottle *concave*, and thus unable to stand upright on the table.

FRONT LABEL

Due to bizarre U.S. laws going back to Prohibition, the production of wine fell under the U.S. Bureau of Alcohol, Tobacco and Firearms (ATF). ATF (not so affectionately called "Drink, Smoke and Shoot" by some people) established the standards for what must, or could, appear on wine labels, and approved each and every wine label before it could be used. ATF could even prevent a winery's use of a particular piece of art on the label if ATF found the art to be "inappropriate", i.e. risque. It did this a number of times, even forbidding well-known European works of art. That function moved to the U.S. Treasury Department's Tax and Trade Bureau in 2003.

Required/Permitted Label Information

Wines produced in the United States must have the following on their labels:

Brand Name—The name determined by the bottler. It may, or may not, be the actual name of the winery.

Type of Wine—Such as the variety (Sauvignon Blanc), generic (White Table Wine) or proprietary name (Ryan's Red).

Geographical Origin—Country or state, vineyard or viticultural area. If a Viticultural Area, at least 85% of the grapes used in the wine must be from that area.

Bottle Size/Volume—A standard bottle is 750 milliliters (750 ml)

Alcohol Strength by Volume—Usually 11-15%. If 7-14%, it is not necessary to state the percentage. If it exceeds 14% alcohol, it must state the percentage.

Vintage Year—The year the grapes for the wine were harvested. At least 95% of the wine must be from the designated vintage year. If it isn't, the year is omitted.

Bottling Information—Where the wine was bottled. If 100% of the grapes were grown in vineyards owned or controlled by the winery, the label can say "Estate Bottled."

Vineyard—If the label indicates a Vineyard Designation (such as Martha's Vineyard, or Winery Lake Vineyard), at least 95% of the wine grapes used to produce that wine must be from that vineyard. This is not an appellation but simply the winery's own term.

Name of the Wine—Usually the variety of grape. Can also be the region where it was made or a name created by the producer (Mosaic) or by a group of producers (Meritage). If a varietal name such as Cabernet Sauvignon or Chardonnay is used, at least 75% of the wine must be from that variety of wine grape.

Health Warnings (Required by U.S. government)

"*GOVERNMENT WARNING:* (1) According to the Surgeon General, women should not drink alcoholic beverages during pregnancy because of the risk of birth defects. (2) Consumption of alcoholic beverages impairs your ability to drive a car or operate machinery and may cause health problems."

"*Contains Sulfites*"—For those who may be hyperallergic to sulfites, which are a natural part of the grape, and which are also frequently used on grapes in the vineyard to prevent mildew, or at fermentation to prevent oxidation.

A Note about Sulfites

Some people (approximately .25 of 1%) are allergic to sulfites. Sulfites are an approved material used in the winemaking process. (Sulfur, which is different, is a pure, elemental form that is frequently sprayed in the vineyards to prevent mildew.) In the winery, sulfur dioxide can be added to the wine to prevent oxidation and to enhance the color and extend the shelf life of the wine.

Sulfites are also a natural component of the wine itself, produced in very small amounts during fermentation. They can sometimes be strong enough to cause an allergic reaction in some people.

If a wine contains 10 parts per million (ppm) of sulfites or more, it must state "Contains Sulfites" on the label. Federal regulations consider up to 350 parts per million as safe for non-hypersensitive wine drinkers. Wine yeasts naturally produce at least 10 to 20 parts per million, so almost every wine produced must carry the sulfite warning on its label.

These levels are far less than those frequently found in fresh and dried fruits and fruit juices, which can be as high as 150-330 parts per million.

Legally Meaningless Terms

The front label might also have terms such as *Private Reserve*, *Founder's Estate*, *Cask No. xx*, *Special Select*, *Vintner's Reserve*, and a variety of other phrases intended to give the impression that this wine is not just any ordinary wine. However, these words have no legal meaning, and their usefulness as an indicator of quality is directly proportional to the integrity of the winery.

BACK LABEL

The label on the back of the wine bottle usually contains information about the vineyard, the vintage year, the winemaking process for that particular wine, recommended foods which it will complement, and anything else the winery feels will help sell the wine.

Other Statements

Produced By or *Made By*—Means that the named winery fermented no less than 75% of the wine. This might not be where the grapes are actually from.

Cellared, *Vinted* or *Prepared*—Means that the winery "subjected the wine to cellar treatment." There is no requirement that the wine/grapes actually come from the area where the winery is located.

Bottled For/Packed For—Name and address of the entity for whom the wine was bottled or packed. Says absolutely nothing about where the wine came from.

Barrels

Barrels are used to store and age wine. The wine is "topped up" (the barrel is filled to the top) so that no air remains in the barrel to cause oxygenation of the wine. However, the porous nature of wood does allow a certain "breathing" to occur, which provides a slight exchange of air into the barrel and wine out of the barrel. You'll notice a very pleasant smell of wine in a winery's barrel room, so it's very obvious that a barrel isn't 100% tight.

Barrels are usually made of oak, either French or American. The oak imparts a desirable taste to the wine, particularly in heavier red wines that will age in the barrel for some years. Oak barrels are usually "toasted" on the inside. The current cost of a 55- to 60-gallon oak barrel is around $300-$450 for American oak and $600-$750 for French oak.

An oak barrel can be used for 3-5 years. After that, the barrel is no longer able to impart much of an oak taste to the wine.

In order to enhance the oak taste and add a "caramelized" taste to some wines, most wineries have their barrels "toasted." This slight burning of the inner side of the staves will give the wine tastes of vanillin, caramel, butterscotch and other flavors.

The cooperage will place an unfinished barrel over a hot fire so that the inside of the barrel is slightly burned. Levels of toast include light, medium, medium plus (currently the most popular) and heavy.

Wineries will frequently use a combination of barrels so that, for example, 1/3 might be brand-new, 1/3 three years old, and another 1/3 five years old. This gives a range of flavors of various wines, and also allows for blending wines with various levels of oakiness.

In order to save on the cost of new barrels, some wineries will "shave" the inside of used barrels, removing about 1/4 inch of the wood, revealing fresh wood, which will then impart the oak taste to the next wine that is put into it. They will likely also re-toast the barrel. This shaving can only be done once as the wood staves then become too thin to shave a second time.

In the Vineyard

GRAPEVINES

Grapes are not planted from seed, but from shoots grafted onto roots (rootstock), usually obtained from a nursery that specializes in wine grapes.

Planting grapevines is expensive. In the Napa Valley, an acre of undeveloped vineyard property now goes for over $72,000. It costs more than $50,000 to turn that acre into vineyard. Then you have to wait five years for the vines to be in full production.

Because of the high cost of planting, and the fact that grapevines can last and produce for many decades, planting is done only when existing vines absolutely need to be replaced, or a new area is prepared for a vineyard.

Vines will be replaced for three reasons:

1. Old age. The vines are no longer producing sufficient yield

2. Disease. The vines have one or more disease which cannot be successfully treated

3. New varietal. The grower decides to switch over to a different variety of grape.

Planting is usually done in the spring but can continue on into summer.

Growing grapes is a slow process, and requires a lot of patience. It takes three years for a vine to begin producing, and up to five years for it to reach full production. Add on additional years for the actual making and aging of wine before it's ready to sell, and you can see that no one goes into the wine business for quick profits.

ORGANIC VINEYARDS

More and more organic winegrapes are being grown in the Napa Valley. Currently over 1,200 acres are organic, and other vineyards are being farmed organically but have not yet received certification.

Organic simply means that no chemicals can be used in the vineyard—no chemical fertilizers, weed killers or insecticides. The only substance that can be used is elemental sulfur, which is organic itself and is used to prevent powdery mildew in the fields.

California Certified Organic Farmers (CCOF)

The following Napa County farms have been certified organic by California Certified Organic Farmers (CCOF), the main organic certification organization in California. (www.ccof.org)

Chavez & Leeds Vineyards
Emilio's Terrace Vineyard
Frog Farm (Frogs Leap Winery)
Johnston Vineyards
Juliana Vineyards
Lisa's Vineyard
Madonna Vineyards
Moore Vineyards
Mt. Saint John Organic Farm
Napa Wine Company
Navone Vineyards
Niebaum-Coppola Estate
O'Malley Vineyard
Primativo Vineyards

Pringle Family Vineyards, Inc.
Spottswoode Vineyard
Terra Vin, Inc.
Volker Eisele Vineyard
Yolo Moon Herb Farm
Yount Mill Vineyards
ZD Wines

ORGANIC WINES

Organic wine is wine that is made from organically grown grapes, and that is also free from chemicals during the actual wine-making process.

Current federal law states that an organic wine cannot be subjected to sulfur dioxide during its fermentation process. It is, however, legal to use elemental sulfur in the vineyard.

Because sulfur dioxide is a necessary component during winemaking to prevent oxidation of the wine (which can cause discoloration and off-odors), no Napa Valley winery currently produces organic wine.

However, if you look for a phrase such as "Wine made from organically grown grapes" on the back label, you'll know that the grapes used in the wine were organic.

SUSTAINABLE WINEGROWING

Sustainable winegrowing is following practices that are economically viable, socially responsible and environmentally sound.

Its goals are to

1. Optimize the ecological stability of the vineyard and its productivity and quality

2. Reduce the use of pesticides

3. Promote soil health

4. Enhance financial returns by promoting the quality of wine from sustainable vineyards and by increasing the longevity of vineyards.

The *Napa Sustainable Winegrowing Group* (www.nswg.org) was formed by members of the local wine industry to support the increasing number of grape growers who are moving towards totally sustainable vineyards.

If you approve of this form of agriculture, you might want to let those practicing it know that you support them.

Current members of the Napa Sustainable Winegrowing Group include:

Long Meadow Ranch Winery
Madonna Estate (Mont St. John)
Napa Wine Company
Robert Mondavi
Robert Sinskey Vineyards
Staglin Family Vineyard
Viader Vineyards
Volker Eisele Family Estate
ZD Wines

KOSHER WINES

Kosher wine is a wine that has received special treatment and meets certain cleanliness and production standards so that it can be considered appropriate for use in Jewish religious practices. Its entire production has been supervised by a rabbi or a designated assistant. For the highest of the three levels of kosher wine, the wine must be pasteurized.

Kosher wine will have had no contact with animal byproducts (some wineries, for example, use gelatin to clarify the wine—a kosher wine would use a different clarification agent). It will also be made using special yeast and enzymes.

Currently only one winery in the Napa Valley makes kosher wine. All of the wines produced by Hagafen Cellars in Napa are kosher.

It should be noted, for those of you whose experience with kosher wines has been limited to Mogen David or other sweet East Coast wines, that Hagafen's wines are first and foremost Napa Valley wines. That is, they are delicious, premium wines. And they are *also* kosher.

PIERCE'S DISEASE/GLASSY-WINGED SHARPSHOOTER

Pierce's Disease is a common bacteria-caused disease in the Napa Valley that has plagued grapegrowers for many years. Traditionally it has been spread by the *blue-green sharpshooter*, a small bug with a limited range whose habitat is along streams and creeks.

Growers have learned to live with Pierce's Disease (PD), and because the blue-green sharpshooter's range is so limited, PD usually affects only those sections of vineyards very close to water.

The *glassy-winged sharpshooter* (GWSS) has changed all this. Originally from Mexico, it moved into the southeastern part of the United States, and has now arrived in California—most notably Riverside County and other counties in Southern California, but in a number of other counties throughout the state as well.

The glassy-winged sharpshooter is about one-half inch long, more than twice the size of its blue-green cousin. It can fly much farther than the blue-green sharpshooter, so that almost all vineyards in the Napa Valley would be within its reach. And it passes the bacterium (Xylella fastidiosa) that causes Pierce's Disease deeper into the system of the plant than does the blue-green sharpshooter. The bacteria multiply and block the water system of the plant, leading to its decline and death.

Sharpshooters also damage grapevines (and many other plants including almonds, citrus and alfalfa) by extracting fluids from the plant, eventually weakening the plant and leading to its death. An adult sharpshooter can extract fluids equal to 200 to 300 times its body weight in a single day. This is the equivalent of an adult human drinking about 4,300 gallons of water per day.

If the glassy-winged sharpshooter takes hold in the Napa Valley, it has the potential to wipe out our grape and wine industries.

In the 1880s, the Los Angeles Basin had a thriving, and highly respected, wine industry. It was destroyed by Pierce's Disease, referred to at the time as *Anaheim Disease.*

State and local authorities are taking all possible steps to prevent the GWSS from spreading throughout California. Because the bug often "hitchhikes" on ornamental plants, all shipments from nurseries into Napa County are inspected. Residents and visitors are urged not to bring any plants into the Napa Valley from infected areas.

Scientists are conducting research and experiments to find biological, genetic and chemical ways of dealing with Pierce's Disease and the GWSS. Others are experimenting with various organic methods of dealing with the threat.

Traps have been placed throughout the county and special inspectors have been hired to monitor the traps as well as incoming shipments of grapes and plants.

Egg masses have been found on plants coming into the valley, but so far no live glassy-winged sharpshooters have been found.

For up-to-the-minute information on preventive efforts in Napa County, see www.bugspot.org.

ROSES IN THE VINEYARDS

In the Napa Valley, as throughout the wine regions of France, you'll frequently see roses planted along the edge of vineyards. Traditionally they've served as an early warning system to protect the grapevines—the equivalent of a miner's canary.

Roses and grapevines are both susceptible to a fungus called powdery mildew. In fact, roses are more sensitive than grapevines.

Sulfur won't cure powdery mildew, but it can prevent it. So, if a grapegrower noticed that one day his roses had powdery mildew, he knew it was immediately time to spray sulfur on his grapes to prevent them from getting the same disease.

Roses also warn of other diseases and growing problems before they affect the grapevines, and they serve as a habitat for some beneficial insects that eat other undesirable insects.

And they're beautiful.

Seasons of the Vineyard

As with any agricultural crop, growing grapes is very seasonal. Here's an outline of the year.

Winter

Ground cover, such as mustard or clover, is seeded in the vineyard to keep down weeds and provide nutrients to the soil. The vines are dormant. Old branches are pruned, leaving only the basic trunk of the vine and whichever canes are desired. The smoke you may see coming from the vineyards is simply the controlled burning of old grapevines.

Spring

New vines are planted. You may see them wrapped in growing tubes that look like, and sometimes are, milk cartons. The tubes help train the vines and protect against rabbits and other hungry residents of the area.

Powdered sulfur, an organic fungicide, is sprayed on vines to prevent a fungus called powdery mildew. *Budbreak* takes place as the first small shoots burst forth out of the buds.

This is a time when frost can damage the new shoots, so growers prepare smudge pots (euphemistically called "orchard heaters" by some growers), wind machines and overhead sprinklers to protect against the frost.

Summer

New shoots appear. Vines begin to flower. Some shoots are pruned so that growth energy is focused on the remaining shoots. Shoots that are too long are trimmed, so that fewer, but higher quality, grapes will result. Some leaves are removed to increase the grapes' exposure to the sun and increase

air circulation. This is done because moisture can lead to "bunch rot" or to mildew. Berries appear and begin to grow and swell. In the heat of the summer sun, sugar levels in the grapes begin to rise, and the amount of acid begins to decrease. The grapes soften and approach full maturity.

Fall

Harvest (called "Crush"). The grapes are picked, brought to the winery and crushed, and the juice is fermented into wine.

After picking, the remaining leaves in the vineyards begin to change color. Yellow is normal, red leaves early in the season indicate a problem (disease or lack of appropriate nutrition.)

In the Napa Valley, Crush usually starts in August and goes through most of October. Sparkling wine producers pick first, as they use grapes with lower sugar levels and higher acids. Still wine producers usually start several weeks later. Thinner-skinned grapes ripen first, such as Chardonnay and Sauvignon Blanc. Thicker-skinned reds such as Cabernet Sauvignon are the last to ripen and be picked.

Crush and the Making of Wine

Grape pickers use a special knife to remove a cluster of grapes from the vine.

Most grapes are picked by hand with a special knife, one or more clusters at a time, and put into crates or bins, then dumped into open containers called *gondolas,* which are then taken to the winery.

Mechanical harvesters are used in some areas to harvest the grapes.

Some vineyards now use mechanical harvesters. The harvester is particularly useful in large vineyards in flat areas, although smaller versions can be used on rather steep hills.

The harvester gently shakes the trunk or cordon of the vine, causing the grapes to fall from the vine into a catcher, which then moves them into a waiting gondola or other container.

However the grapes are picked, once they arrive at the winery, they are put into a destemmer/crusher, which removes the leaves and stems and crushes the grapes. Crushing doesn't mean pulverizing; it's done as gently as possible. Just enough to break the skins and allow the juice to come out.

The destemmer is a perforated, rotating drum. The juice and skins drop through the holes in the drum, while the leaves and stems are too big to fit through the holes so they continue on out of the crusher and into waiting trucks to be returned to the vineyard as compost.

The crushed grapes and juice, called *must,* are pumped into the winery.

Some winemakers may skip the crushing and destemming and move the grapes directly to a press for *whole berry* or *whole cluster* pressing. Or they may do *carbonic maceration* in which the weight of the grapes themselves gently crushes the grapes, releasing the juice.

FERMENTATION

Red Wine

The juice, skins and seeds from most red grapes (actually called "black" grapes by growers) go into large stainless steel fermentation tanks for primary fermentation, where yeast is added that breaks down the natural grape sugars into ethyl alcohol and carbon dioxide (CO_2). Fermentation is done at a temperature of approximately $85°$ Fahrenheit for four to six days.

After fermentation, red wines are pressed, and the grape skins and seeds are then separated from the wine. The skins, seeds and dead yeast cells are called "pomace", and can be used as compost.

White Wine

White grapes (which are actually green in color) are not immediately fermented but go first to a "press". A wine press is a stainless steel cylinder containing an inflatable rubber bladder. The must is poured into the cylinder and the bladder is inflated with air. The bladder gently squeezes the skins against the sides of the cylinder, forcing the juice out. The *press juice* then goes to fermentation tanks. White wine is frequently fermented at around $60°$ for 12 to 18 days, although fermentation temperatures can range from $5°$ to $75°$ white wine takes longer because fermentation is slower at lower temperatures.

Sometimes white wines such as Chardonnay are fermented in oak barrels rather than stainless steel tanks. This is referred to as *barrel fermentation*.

POST-FERMENTATION

Settling and Aging

After fermentation, most red and white wines go into large stainless steel tanks, where *settling* takes place. After the skins, seeds, yeast and other particles settle to the bottom of the tank (creating the *lees*), the clearer wine is pumped out and put into small (55-60 gallon) oak barrels for *barrel aging*.

Most reds are barrel-aged to impart the oaky taste that many people find desirable. Many wineries also barrel-ferment Chardonnay. Lighter white wines, such as Sauvignon Blanc or Johannisberg Riesling are seldom, if ever, barrel-aged. An exception is Fumé Blanc, which is a barrel-fermented Sauvignon Blanc. Barrel aging can last from three to ten months for white wine, and anywhere from six months to three years for red wine.

Some red wines are subjected to *malolactic fermentation*. The winemaker adds a specific bacterium to the wine that breaks down the malic acid in the wine into lactic acid. This *secondary fermentation* can give the wine a creamy, buttery taste and texture. It is frequently done for red wines, and often for Chardonnay.

Clarification

During barrel aging, most wines "throw" sediments so that the wine must be "fined" and/or "filtered" to give it the clarity desired by most American wine drinkers. Filtration can also stabilize the wine, making sure that it does not continue to ferment in the bottle, by removing all yeast from the wine.

Several methods of fining are used. Traditionally in Europe, oxblood was poured on top of the vat and allowed to settle down to the bottom. As it settled, it attracted the sediment (yeast, seeds, and

bits of skin) in the wine and pulled it down to the bottom of the vat.

Since blood passing through their wine is not something that appeals to most Americans—even though it didn't remain in the wine after the treatment—this method was long ago discontinued.

These days gelatin and egg whites, also traditional methods, are frequently used to fine the wine. Also, if the wine is run through a filtration machine, diatomaceous earth or filter pads are used in the filter to help remove very fine sediment.

Some winemakers prefer not to clarify their wines, subjecting the wines to as little physical treatment as possible.

After clarification, the wine is then bottled, corked and labeled. Some wines are then ready to drink; others, particularly heavier red wines, may undergoing aging in the bottle for as long as three years before being made available to consumers. Once sold to the customer, most wines are ready to drink, but some will still improve with age if the customer has the space and patience (and money) to store them.

Sparkling Wine

Sparkling wine (not referred to as *Champagne*, because that type of sparkling wine comes only from the Champagne district of France) is primarily made from Chardonnay and Pinot Noir grapes.

Grapes for sparkling wine (*sparklers*) are picked earlier in the season when sugar content is lower, usually starting in late July. Fermentation almost always takes place in stainless steel tanks over a period of two to three weeks.

After five months or so, selected wines are blended to form the *cuvee* that will be the basis for the final wine. After blending, the wine goes into its permanent bottle, and the *tirage* is added, which is a blend of sugar, wine and live yeast that will begin the wine's second fermentation. The bottle is then sealed with a temporary cap like that on a soft drink bottle.

Secondary fermentation takes place in the bottle. Because it is sealed, the carbon dioxide bubbles produced by fermentation remain in the bottle. This continues for at least a year.

During aging, the bottles are *riddled.* Riddling is the process of separating the clear wine from the sediment (primarily dead yeast cells) that forms in the bottle. The bottles are very gently shaken and twisted to allow the sediment to gradually settle at the top of the bottle. Riddling was historically done by hand, but today in most large sparkling wineries it is done by a machine that gently mimics the hand process.

When ready, the tops of the bottles are dipped into a solution to freeze the liquid and sediment in the bottle neck, but not in the rest of the bottle. The temporary bottle cap is removed and the pressure of the carbon dioxide forces out the frozen sediment. This is referred to as *disgorgement.*

The resulting empty space in the bottle is filled with a blend of wine and sugar called *dosage.* The bottle is then recorked, and the traditional cage and foil are placed over the top. Once sealed, the sparkling wine rests for additional months before it's made available for sale.

Wine Caves

The use of caves for storing and aging wine goes back, at least, to the Romans. In the 1800s, Chinese laborers using picks and shovels built the first Napa Valley wine caves. Jacob Schram constructed tunnels (at today's Schramsberg Vineyards) beginning in 1870 and the Beringer brothers began to do the same at their winery (now Beringer Vineyards) soon afterwards.

Today nearly 100 Napa Valley wineries have caves, and more are being created all the time—although the picks and shovels have been replaced by heavy-duty construc-

tion equipment. Originally built for the storage of wine barrels, some caves now contain a winery's entire operations.

Digging a cave is less expensive than constructing a building for similar purposes. Caves reduce energy costs by providing constant humidity (80-90%) and temperature (55°- 60° F), reduce evaporation of wine, and require less governmental approval. Plus they have less visual impact on the landscape, and offer a great—and often magnificent—location for tastings, dinners and musical events.

Caves can be humble tunnels for barrel aging, or...well, for example, take Villa Amarosa in St. Helena. Currently under construction by V. Sattui Winery owner Darryl Sattui, the cave will sit below an 89,000 square foot "14th century" castle with three floors of wine cellars, more than 60 rooms, and a 1,000 square foot well-equipped medieval torture chamber (presumably for viewing only).

Also under construction is Palmaz Winery in Napa, owned by the co-inventor of the cardiovascular stent. The 50,000 square foot winery will be completely underground, and will include a 50-foot high, 75-foot wide dome reminiscent of the interior of a mosque. Wine storage will take place 11 stories underground.

For detailed information on wine cave construction, we recommend this website: www.winecaves.com.

Here are some of the wine caves that can currently be visited.

S. Anderson Vineyard

1473 Yountville Cross Road
Yountville CA 94599
707.944.8020
www.4bubbly.com
Twice daily tours. 7,500 square feet of champagne caves with 18-foot cathedral ceilings.

Beringer Vineyards

2000 Main Street
St. Helena CA 94574
707.963.7115
www.beringervineyards.com
Daily tours. Hand-dug tunnels from the 1800s.

Clos Pegase Winery

1060 Dunaweal Lane
Calistoga CA 94515|
707.942.4981
www.clospegase.com
Daily tours of cave theater and dining room in 20,000 square feet of tunnels.

Cuvaison Winery

4550 Silverado Trail
Calistoga CA 94515
707.942.6266
www.cuvaison.com
Daily tours. 22,000 square foot cave.

Eagle and Rose Estate

1844 Pope Valley Road
Pope Valley CA 94567
707.965.9463
www.eagleandrose.com
Tours by appointment. 7,000 square feet of caves.

Folie a Deux

370 North St. Helena Highway
St. Helena CA 94574
800.473.4454
www.folieadeux.com
Tours by appointment.

Jarvis Winery

2970 Monticello Road
Napa CA 94558
707.255.5250
www.jarviswines.com
Tours by appointment. Underground stream and waterfall.

Pine Ridge Winery

5901 Silverado Trail
Napa CA 94558
707.857.9777
www.pineridgewinery.com
Tours by appointment.

Robert Sinskey Vineyards

6320 Silverado Trail
Napa Ca 94558
707.944.9090
www.robertsinskey.com
Tours by appointment. 18,000 square feet of caves.

Rutherford Hill Winery

200 Rutherford Hill Road PO Box 427
Rutherford CA 94573
707.963.1871
www.rutherfordhill.com
Tours daily. One mile of wine caves.

Schramsberg Winery

1400 Schramsberg Road
Calistoga CA 94515
707.942.4558
www.schramsberg.com
Tours by appointment. Century-old wine caves have been extended to two miles of tunnels.

Shafer Vineyards

6154 Silverado Trail
Napa CA 94558
707.944.2877
www.shafervineyards.com
Tours by appointment. 8,000 square feet of caves with fresh underground springs.

Storybook Mountain Vineyards

3835 Highway 128
Calistoga CA 94515
707.942.5310
www.storybookwines.com
Tours by appointment. Century-old wine caves.

Vine Cliff Winery

7400 Silverado Trail
Napa CA 94558
707.944.2388
www.vinecliff.com
Tours by appointment. 15,000 square feet of caves.

Von Strasser

1510 Diamond Mountain Road
Calistoga CA 94515
707.942.0930
www.vonstrasser.com
Tours by appointment. 6,800 square foot cave.

Wine Tasting

Ordering and drinking wine shouldn't be intimidating. But for many it is, largely because of all the hype and mystique that wine has endured in this country.

The simple method of wine tasting is:

1. Pour a glass of wine.

2. Drink it.

3. Did you like it or not?

That's really sufficient. However, by adding a few more steps, you can make the process of wine tasting much more interesting. And you can learn to determine which kind of wines you like, so that in the future you know what to look for in a store or restaurant.

Here are our suggestions on how to go about tasting a wine.

Look

1. Hold your glass by the stem so that your hand doesn't warm the bowl.

2. Hold the glass in front of your eyes, preferably against a white background, and look at the color and clarity of the wine.

Clarity—Wine should be clear and brilliant, unless the winemaker intentionally kept it unfiltered.

Color—With reds, the darker the color, the more intense the flavors and aromas are likely to be. Color can be red, ruby, purple, or brick red. Brown indicates oxidation. An older wine can be brick-brown. Too brown and it's probably over the hill. If a young wine is brown, it's likely oxidized. (If that is the case, let it sit in the glass for a while anyway. It's possible both taste and aroma will improve, possibly dramatically.)

With whites, the color can vary from almost clear to green to slightly yellow to straw colored to gold. Whites, too, should not be brown.

Blush wines, such as White Zinfandel or a Rose, are pink.

Swirl

1. Swirl the wine. Try to do it suavely without spilling, but if it flies out of the glass, you won't be the first. (If you pour a full glass for your dinner guests at home, they won't be able to enjoy swirling. Try not to fill the glass more than 1/3 to 1/2 full.)

2. Notice if the wine has "legs"—little streams of wine that cling to the inside of the glass and slowly drip back down. "Good legs" indicate good body.

3. Swirl it again. Swirling doesn't just look cool. If you do it right it also "volatizes the esters" releasing aroma molecules into the air, which are somewhat contained in the bowl by the lip of the wine glass.

Sniff

1. Put your nose down into the bowl (where the aroma molecules are lingering) and take a good sniff.

2. See if you can match the various smells with smells from your past. Think of fruits, spices, herbs, and various plants.

Aroma—The smells that come from the characteristics of the grape itself, especially in a younger wine.

Bouquet—The smells that result over time, primarily from the winemaking process and aging.

Common off smells include:

Bitterness—Too heavy on tannins

Burning—Sulfur or excessive alcohol (alcohol is felt further back in the nose)

Nail polish/acetone—Excessive acetic acid

Rotten eggs—Excessive sulfur

You might also notice that you salivate, which indicates excessive acid.

Taste

1. Take a medium-sized sip, sucking air in through your teeth.

2. Swish the wine around in your mouth, "chew" it if you want, hold it in your mouth, and then swallow.

Flavors—Since the sense of taste is largely a result of the sense of smell, the nose of the wine will greatly affect the flavors you can taste.

Palate—Your tongue can notice sweetness, acid, alcohol, bitterness and astringency (tannin). They're sensed on different parts of the tongue and in the following order:

Sweetness—Tip of the tongue
Acid—Sides of the tongue
Vinegary—Acetic acid
Lemon/lime—Citric acid
Apple—Malic acid
Cream/yogurt—Lactic acid

Tannins—Puckery sensation at the back of the mouth and throat. Same as drinking black tea.

Bitterness—Very back of the tongue.

Alcohol—Can register as sweetness, viscosity of the wine, or warmth. Excessive alcohol results in a hot burning in the throat.

Feel

Pay attention to how it feels in your mouth.

Body—How is the "mouthfeel"? Is it light, medium or full? This is largely a function of alcohol content and any residual sugar, but there are other more subtle factors.

Finish—How long does the taste linger in your mouth after swallowing? What is the last taste you can sense? Fruit? Acid? Tannins?

Overall

Is it balanced? Do all the components—fruit, acid, alcohol, tannins and so on—work in harmony together?

Most importantly, did you like it? And why or why not?

The Triangular Test

Wine writer Dan Berger (www.vintageexperiences.com) suggests the *triangular test* as a simple, but effective, way to see if you can tell the difference between two different bottles of wine.

Take three identical glasses and label them A, B and C (Okay, use 1, 2 and 3 if you prefer numbers to letters) in a way that the people taking the test can't see the labels. Pour from one bottle of wine into A and B, and from a different bottle into C. Mix up the glasses and then sample each of the three glasses. All you have to do is determine which two glasses contain the identical wine.

Easy, right? Well, maybe. But the more similar the two wines are, the more difficult it will be. Differentiating between a Cabernet Sauvignon and a Sirah might be easy. Tasting a light, fruity Chardonnay from one winery and comparing it to a heavily-oaked Chardonnay from another might still be relatively easy. But how about two Chardonnays from the same winery that differ only in the year in which they were picked, or the vineyards from which their grapes came?

It's a simple, enjoyable and very educational experiment. Try it. Over time you'll sharpen your ability to pick up those subtle nuances of flavors and aromas that might have escaped you before.

WINE TASTING TOOLS

Aroma Wheel

There is help for understanding the many possible flavors of wines. Wine scientists at the University of California, Davis—considered the top enology school in the country—designed the "aroma wheel." This is a simple device that categorizes 94 different descriptive terms for the smells of wine.

You'll find it a big help in learning to identify wine aromas.

To purchase a full-color, laminated plastic version of the Wine Aroma Wheel or the Sparkling Wine Aroma Wheel, make out a check or money order (drawn on a U.S. bank) for $6.00 ($7.00 international).

Price includes sales tax, handling, and postage. Make checks payable to A.C. Noble.

Send to: A C Noble, Dept. Viticulture and Enology, University of California Davis, CA 95616

For more information, see the Aroma Wheel website at http://wineserver.ucdavis.edu/Acnoble/waw.html.

We highly recommend you consider purchasing an Aroma Wheel. If you're serious about wine tasting, you'll find it invaluable.

Essential Wine Tasting Guide

www.essentialwinetastingguide.com

This guide is another useful tool for wine tasting. It contains a huge amount of information and cleverly folds up into the size of a credit card.

The guide provides over 1000 descriptive terms for white, red, sparkling, dessert and fortified wines; a wine color guide; characteristics of major grape varieties; a wine scoring system; a comprehensive list of specific wine defects; and suggested wine serving temperatures.

Wine Prism

PO Box 2771 Napa CA 94558
800.322.8878
www.wineprism.com

The Wine Prism is a fascinating wine-sipping gadget that enhances wine tasting, letting you more fully experience components of wine such as fruit, tannins, acidity, fermentation and barrel influence.

Varietal Pronunciations

Varietal—Phonetic Pronunciation

Barbera—Bar-BEAR-ah
Cabernet Franc—KA-burr-NAY fronk
Cabernet Sauvignon—KA-burr-NAY SEW-veen-yown
Chardonnay—SHAR-dough-NAY
Chenin Blanc—SHEN-in-BLONK
French Colombard—KOLL-om-BAR
Gewurtztraminer—Guh-VERTZ-tra-MEEN-er
Merlot—MARE-low
Muscat—MUSS-cat
Pinot Grigio—PEE-no GREE-joe
Pinot Noir—PEE-no NWAHR
Riesling—REEZ-ling (Notice it is not RYEZE-ling)
Sangiovese—San-joe-VAY-zee
Sauvignon Blanc—SEW-veen-yown BLONK
Semillon—SEMM-e-yown
Sirah (Syrah)—Si-RAH (as in "Que sera, sera")
Viognier—V-OWN-yay
Zinfandel—ZIN-fan-dell

Glossary of Wine Terms

ACID—A natural component of the grape, primarily tartaric acid. Acid adds flavor and crispness, and its tartness provides "backbone" to the wine.

AGING—Leaving the wine alone in a barrel or bottle for a period of weeks, months or years. This allows the wine to mature, and the flavors and other components to blend and harmonize.

ALAMBIC—The pot, traditionally copper, which is used for distilling spirits such as brandy.

ALCOHOL—Ethyl alcohol. During fermentation, yeast breaks down the sugars in grapes and turns it into alcohol. Before fermentation, it's grape juice. Afterwards, it's wine. Napa Valley wine generally has anywhere from 10 to 14 percent alcohol. (Once a fermenting wine gets up to around 16 percent, which is possible if it started with very high sugar levels, the yeast dies and fermentation stops.)

APERITIF—A wine served before a meal.

APPELLATION—A particular wine-growing region that has been designated by the Bureau of Alcohol, Tobacco and Firearms as having shared characteristics of climate, soil or other conditions.

AROMA—The smell of a wine, particularly from the natural characteristics of the grape itself.

ASTRINGENT—Producing a puckering sensation in your mouth, such as you would experience when drinking tea. Comes primarily from tannins in the wine, which are found in grape skins, seeds and stems. Oak barrels also add tannins to the wine.

AVA—An "American Viticultural Area"; a more specific area than an "Appellation". Wines that have an AVA on the label must have at least 75 percent of the wine from that area.

BACKBONE—The acid in a wine. A wine that has insufficient acidity "lacks backbone".

BALANCE—When a wine is well-balanced, all its components—fruit, acid, alcohol, tannins, body—are in harmony, with no one component dominating the others.

BARREL—A wooden barrel, holding 55—60 gallons, used for aging, and sometimes fermenting, wine. Usually made of French or American oak.

BARREL AGING—Many wines are aged for a period of time in oak barrels, which allows a blending of the flavors in the wine as it matures, and also imparts the flavor of the toasted wood to the wine.

BARREL FERMENTATION—Converting grape juice to wine in a barrel rather than in a stainless steel fermentation tank. This imparts flavors and aromas to the wine from the oak wood. Often used for Chardonnay.

BLACK GRAPES—The grapes used to make red wine are actually almost black in color. Examples are Cabernet Sauvignon and Merlot.

BLEND—To mix together several lots of wine (perhaps from different vineyards and/or years, or even different varietals) in order to produce a desired wine.

BODY—The "weight" of the wine, usually light, medium or full. A wine with a higher alcohol content and heavy tannins is felt to be full-bodied. Usually a fuller-bodied wine also has bigger "legs". Body is also a result of viscosity, which can be increased with higher residual sugar.

BOTRYTIS—A fungus that can form on the skins of late harvested grapes, producing "bunch rot". It can ruin a crop or, under just right conditions, it can produce smaller grapes with intense flavors and high sugar content. Known then as the "noble rot", it results in highly-prized dessert wines.

BOTTLE AGING—Allowing wine to lie undisturbed in the bottle for a period of weeks, months or years. This allows the tannins in the wine to soften and the wine's components to further harmonize after barrel aging.

BOTTLE SICKNESS/BOTTLE SHOCK—Moving wine within the winery, bottling it, or transporting it to a different location can have a temporary negative effect on the flavor. After a period of time—a few days or weeks—it will be back to normal.

BOUQUET—The smells from older wines, primarily resulting from the winemaking process and from aging.

BRIX—A measurement of dissolved compounds in grape juice that approximately indicates the sugar content of unharvested grapes. Most grapes are picked between 21 and 25 degrees Brix. These will produce wines with an alcohol content between 12 to 15 percent.

BRUT—French for "dry". A style of sparkling wine that has little, or no, residual sugar.

BUD BREAK—The time in early spring when new shoots emerge from the buds on a vine.

BUNG—The stopper that goes in the "bung hole" in a wine barrel.

BUTTERY—A taste associated with Chardonnay after it has gone through Malolactic Fermentation. In extreme cases, it can taste like movie theater popcorn butter.

CANE—Older shoots on the vine that have become large and woody.

CANOPY—The leaves and shoots of a grapevine.

CAP—When red wine ferments, carbon dioxide is produced which rises to the top of the tank. As it does, it pushes up the skins and seeds to the top, forming a "cap".

CAPSULE—The "wrapper" placed over the cork to help seal and protect it. Also called Foil. Originally of lead, now made of plastic, tin or paper.

CARBONIC MACERATION—Fermentation of whole grapes without crushing them.

CASK—A wooden barrel. Frequently used to refer to very large barrels.

CHAMPAGNE—Sparkling wine made in the Champagne region of France.

CLARIFICATION—Making the wine clear by removing sediment.

CLUSTER—A single "bunch" of grapes.

COLD STABILIZATION—Lowering the temperature of a wine to 32° F causes the tartrates and other solids in the wine to precipitate and sink to the bottom of the tank, leaving a clearer (clarified) wine. This prevents the formation of tartaric crystals, sometimes called Wine Diamonds, in the bottle after the customer has purchased it.

COOPER—A person who makes or repairs barrels.

CORDON—A method of pruning leaving one cane (cordon) on each side of the trunk.

CORK—A wine bottle stopper made from the bark of oak trees, usually from Spain or Portugal.

CORKAGE—Fee charged by a restaurant for providing glasses to, and opening a bottle for, a customer who brings his own wine. Fees in the Napa Valley range from $5 - $20, although some restaurants have discontinued the charge.

CORKED—A wine that has been tainted by a bad cork that has a mold that produces a chemical compound called TCA (Trichloroanisole). This "dirty sock" or "wet newspaper" smell results in a wine that is said to be "corked" or "corky".

CREAMY—Wines that have undergone Malolactic Fermentation can have a rich, smooth feel that is referred to as "creamy".

CRISP—A young, fresh wine with good acid.

CRUSH—Harvest. When the grapes are picked and crushed. In the Napa Valley, this starts in late August (when grapes with low sugar levels are picked for sparkling wines) and usually goes through most of October, when thicker-skinned grapes finally mature.

DECANT—Wine that was not filtered by the winemaker is often carefully poured into another container—usually a decanter—leaving the sediment at the bottom of the first container. Decanting can also aerate a wine, "opening up" its flavors and aromas.

(DE)STEMMER CRUSHER—The machine, used by most wineries, which removes the stems from, and gently crushes the skins of, grapes that have just been harvested.

DOSAGE—A small amount of sweet wine added to the top of a bottle-fermented sparkling wine, to replace the yeast sediment that is removed just before final corking.

DRY—The absence of sugar in a wine. A wine with no residual sugar is totally dry. It is possible to have a slight amount of residual sugar, and still taste dry to most people.

EARLY HARVEST—Wine made from grapes that are picked early in the harvest, when their acids are high and their sugar content is low.

ENOLOGIST—One who practices Enology.

ENOLOGY—The science and study of winemaking. Also spelled Oenology.

ESTATE BOTTLED—One hundred percent of the wine must be made from grapes grown in vineyards owned or controlled by the winery in the same appellation as the winery.

ESTERS—Chemical compounds responsible for much of the bouquet and aroma of wines. Swirling wine before tasting "volatizes the esters", enhancing the nose of the wine.

FAT—Rich and full-bodied wine.

FERMENTATION—The chemical process of converting grape juice to alcohol. This is done by yeast, which converts the natural sugar in the juice into alcohol—and also produces carbon dioxide, which is released out the top of the tanks. (In sparkling wine, the carbon dioxide is retained).

FILTERING—Removing particles (yeast, pieces of skin) from wine by passing it through physical filters. This makes the wine clearer and prevents any further fermentation.

FINING—A technique for clarifying wine. Europeans used to use ox blood. Today common fining agents are egg whites, gelatin, bentonite or diatomaceous earth. The fining agent combines with particles in the wine, causing them to settle to the bottom of the tank.

FINISH—The taste that lingers in your mouth after you've swallowed the wine. It includes both the type of taste and its length, i.e. a wine can have a "long finish".

FLABBY—A wine that is too soft, lacks sufficient acidity, has no "structure".

FOIL—Same as Capsule.

FORTIFIED WINE—A wine to which alcohol has been added, such as Port.

FOXY—The distinctive character of wine made from *vinifera labrusca*, the native American grapes of which Concord grapes are an example.

FREE RUN—The juice released after the grapes are crushed. It is usually a higher quality than "press juice", which is obtained by squeezing the grapes.

FRUIT—How grape growers usually refer to grapes.

FRUITY—The natural taste of the grape, more obvious in younger wines. A dry wine can taste sweet due to its intense fruitiness.

GLASSY-WINGED SHARPSHOOTER—An insect which spreads Pierce's Disease.

GLYCERINE—An alcohol, formed during fermentation from grape sugar, that contributes to the body of a wine.

GRAFTING—Splicing a vine of one type onto a rootstock of another type.

HARVEST—The time of the year when the grapes are picked. Same as Crush.

HOT—A wine with overdominant alcohol.

INOCULATION—Adding yeast to juice to start fermentation.

LATE HARVEST—Wine, usually dessert wine, produced from grapes picked late in the harvest, when their sugar content is high and their acids are low.

LEES—The sediment that accumulates in the bottom of a container during fermentation. Some wine is aged "on the lees" ("sur lie").

LEGS—Also called "tears" (as in crying). The streaks of wine that form and slide down the inside of a glass after you've swirled the wine. An indication of "body". If the legs are wide and thick and move slowly down the glass, the wine can be said to have "nice legs".

MACERATION—The extraction, during fermentation, of color, tannin and aromas from the skins and seeds to the juice. Wine juice itself has little color. The color comes primarily from the skins.

MAGNUM—A double-sized bottle holding 1500 milliliters of wine.

MALIC ACID—The "apple" acid found naturally in grapes which can be converted to lactic acid during Malolactic Fermentation.

MALOLACTIC FERMENTATION—Also known as "ML" or "Secondary Fermentation". A process by which the malic acid (as in apples) in wine is converted to lactic acid (as in the acid found in dairy products). This softens the acid, making the wine smoother and creamier.

MATURE—A wine is mature when it is ready to drink. This can be a short time after fermentation for a light, fruity white wine, or many years later for a heavy red wine.

MERCAPTANS—A smell resulting from too much sulfur. Smells like garlic or rubber.

MERITAGE—A marketing name that the California wine industry invented for a Bordeaux-style wine that blends such varieties as Cabernet Sauvignon, Merlot, Cabernet France, Malbec and Petite Verdot.

METHODE CHAMPENOISE—The classic Champagne method of making sparkling wine. Secondary fermentation takes place in the bottle, and the carbon dioxide produced is captured as bubbles.

MICROCLIMATE—A small area with unique climatic conditions. These conditions can be quite different from a neighboring area. They include temperature, sunlight, rain and fog.

MINISCUS—The top line of liquid in a container. The miniscus in a wine glass should appear clear. (Note: This is a good "bar bet" item. You'll find very few wine drinkers who know what a miniscus is.)

MUST—The skin, seeds and juice after the grapes have been crushed. Red wines are fermented as must. For white wines, the must is pressed and only the resulting juice is fermented.

NOSE—The smell of a wine, including both Aroma and Bouquet.

OAKY—A strong taste of tannins in the wine due to its contact with oak.

OXIDIZED—Just as a slice of apple turns brown, so can wine be affected by oxygen. A little is good, too much isn't. A wine that has been exposed to too much oxygen is "oxidized". It tastes flat, tired and old.

PALATE—One's ability to taste the subtleties and complexities of a wine. One is said to have a "good palate".

PHYLLOXERA—A tiny louse that damages the roots of vines. During the 1990s, many thousands of acres of grapevines were replaced in the Napa Valley, and throughout California, due to phylloxera.

PIERCE'S DISEASE—A plant disease caused by a bacterium that attacks the vine's water-conducting system. Spread by the Blue Green and Glassy-Winged Sharpshooters.

POMACE—Grape skins, seeds, stems and pulp that remain after the grapes have been pressed. Often used as compost.

PRESS—The machine that gently presses the grapes to squeeze out their juice. Usually an inflatable rubber "bladder" press.

PRESS JUICE—The juice obtained after grapes are pressed.

PUMP OVER—The process of pumping fermenting wine over the Cap. (This used to be done by hand and was called "punching the cap". It is still done this way in some wineries.) Pumping over gives the wine more contact with the cap, extracting more color, flavor and tannins from the skins and seeds in the cap.

PUNT—The concave indentation in the bottom of a bottle.

RACKING—Moving wine from one container to another. This is done to clarify wine, to aerate it, or to move it into another container for a different stage in the process, i.e from fermentation to barrel aging. Racking can be done by gravity or with a pump.

RESERVE—A wine designated as special by the winery that produces it. There are no quality standards or regulations that apply to the use of "Reserve" or "Private Reserve" or "Vintner's Reserve".

RESIDUAL SUGAR—The amount of sugar remaining in a wine after fermentation. For most dry wines, the residual sugar is so low that it is below the threshhold of most people's ability to taste.

RIDDLING—In sparkling wine, the turning (traditionally by hand) of the bottle one-eighth of a turn every day. Over time this causes the yeast in the wine to end up in the neck of the bottle, from where it is eventually removed.

ROOM TEMPERATURE—The ideal temperature for serving red wine. This is probably not your room temperature. This is basicallgthe room temperature of a European castle without central heating. Should be 55°-65°F.

ROOTSTOCK—The roots of a vine.

ROSÉ—A wine with very little red color and usually some slight carbonation. The light color results from minimal contact between the juice and the skins.

RUTHERFORD DUST—The legendary reason why Cabernet Sauvignon grapes grown in the soil of the Rutherford area produce such excellent wines.

SECOND LABEL—A wine sold by a winery that has a different brand than that of the winery's main wines. It is usually less expensive and, although not always, of lesser quality.

SECOND PICK—Home winemakers and others will often be given the opportunity to have "Second Pick". They go through an already harvested vineyard and pick grapes that were missed or that matured after the first picking.

SECONDARY FERMENTATION—(See Malolactic Fermentation)

SEDIMENT—Pieces of dead yeast cells, skin and other materials that can sink to the bottom of an unfiltered red wine.

SOMMELIER (som-MAL-ee-ay)- The knowledgeable person at better restaurants who can give you advice and answer questions about wine. Often wears the traditional tastevin cup attached to a chain around his neck.

SPARKLING WINE—Bubbling wine made usually from Pinot Noir and Chardonnay grapes. When made in the Champagne region of France, it's called Champagne. Napa Valley vintners respect the French rights to that term, and call theirs "sparkling wine".

STEMS/STEMMY—A tannic taste of stems in a red wine.

STILL WINE—A wine with no carbonation—no bubbles.

STRUCTURE—All the components of a wine and how well they work together.

SULFUR/SULFITES—Elemental sulfur is used in the vineyards to prevent a fungus called powdery mildew. Sulfur dioxide (SO_2) is used during fermentation to prevent oxidation, to inhibit wild yeast, and as a preservative. (Too much sulfur can give a wine a "rotten egg" smell.) Sulfur is also used to clean barrels. Some people are allergic to sulfites in wine, which occur naturally at low levels. For this reason, the label must say "Contains sulfites".

SUR LIE (Sir-lee)—French for "on the lees". Some white wines are barrel-aged in contact with dead yeast cells to produce a richer, yeastier-tasting wine.

SWEET—The impression of a sugary taste. It can come from residual sugar, or from the fruity flavor of the grape.

TANNIN—Causes the astringent, mouth-puckering sensation. Much more predominant in red wines. Comes from skins, seeds, stems and oak. Helps preserve the wine and give it aging potential. With proper aging, tannins can soften to produce a velvety wine.

TART—A wine that is too high in acid.

TARTRATES—See Wine Diamonds

TASTE—The sensation in the mouth of bitter, sweet or sour.

TERROIR—French term for the growing conditions of a vineyard, including soil, elevation, climate, slope, and a variety of other factors.

THIEF/WINE THIEF—A glass tube used to sample wine directly from a barrel.

THIN—Lacking in body.

TIGHT—A closedness and underdeveloped quality of a wine where its flavors and aromas are not yet revealed.

TOAST—To heat the inside of an oak barrel. This "caramelizes" its flavors.

TOP UP—During barrel aging, wine can evaporate. Cellar workers "top up" the barrel by adding wine to replace the evaporated wine. This removes air from the barrel and prevents oxidation.

TRELLISING—Training a vine to grow on wires and stakes for better support and exposure to sunlight.

UNFILTERED—Wine that has not gone through filtration. Many consumers and winemakers prefer wines that have had as little treatment as possible.

ULLAGE (UL-ij)—The space in a bottle between the wine and the cork. Also called "headspace". If there is too much, the bottle has obviously leaked.

VARIETAL—A wine made from one type of grape, such as Chardonnay.

VARIETAL CHARACTER—The unique character of a specific variety of grape. For example, Sauvignon Blanc is known for its "new-mown hay" or "grassy" character. Cabernet Sauvignon is associated with black currant, green olive, herb and bell pepper.

VARIETY—A particular type of grape, such as Cabernet Sauvignon or Chardonnay.

VERAISON (Vay-ray-ZON)—The stage in the growing process when grapes begin to acquire their color. Takes place in the summer.

VINIFICATION—The process of making wine from grape juice.

VINTAGE—The year in which a wine's grapes were harvested.

VINTNER—Technically, the person who blends wine. Generally used these days for the person who owns the winery. In a small winery, this person might also be the winemaker.

VITICULTURAL AREA—See AVA.

VITICULTURE—The study and practice of growing grapes.

VITIS LABRUSCA—Native American grapes such as Concord grapes, that are considered of much lower quality for wine than Vitis Vinifera.

VITIS VINIFERA—European grape species to which most wine grapes belong.

WHITE GRAPES—Used to make white wines. Actually green in color.

WILD YEAST—Yeast which naturally occurs on grape skins.

WINE DIAMONDS—A romantic name for the crystals of tartaric acid (sodium bitartrate—the ingredient of Cream of Tartar) that can form in the bottle or on the cork. Although harmless, not everyone likes to see them, so many winemakers put their wine through Cold Stabilization to prevent this from happening.

WINEMAKER—The person who is in charge of the process of actually making the wine.

YEAST—Single-celled organisms that produce enzymes that convert sugar to alcohol and carbon dioxide. There is natural yeast on the grape skins, but most winemakers neutralize this "wild yeast" and use a commercial yeast of their choice.

YIELD—The production of a vineyard in tons per acre. A lower yield is said to produce grapes of greater quality and intensity. Sometimes it's just a lower yield.

Questions/Answers

We've listed some of the most common questions about wine and the Napa Valley.

How do I open a bottle of wine?

Use whatever tool you like best. There is a wide variety of corkscrews and other cork pullers out there. Some have one handle, some have two. Ask for suggestions at a wine shop, and experiment till you find one you really like. And you might want more than one type. Sometimes a dry cork needs one type of opener rather than another.

1. Take the blade of the opener or other type of foil cutter, cut the foil all the way around the neck, and remove the top portion of the foil.

2. Pull the cork with whichever device you settled on.

3. Pour the wine into a glass, no more than half full.

How should I store my wine?

If you don't have a wine cellar, and not many people do, try to keep it in a place that's cool and dark, and has a relatively constant temperature. The best place in most homes is in a closet in an interior room. Store it on its side so that the cork stays moist. This will prevent the cork from drying out, which could allow air to enter the bottle and spoil the wine. (This is not a problem with synthetic corks or screw tops.)

At what temperature should my wines be served ?

"Room temperature" or "cellar temperature" is often given as an answer to this question. It's probably true, if you live in a European castle with no central heating. Your own room temperature is probably too warm. And not too many people have a temperature-controlled wine cellar.

Red wines should be served between around 65° Fahrenheit. If too cold, you won't be able to enjoy the full flavors and aromas. If too warm, the alcohol is more pronounced and the acids less noticeable.

White wines should be served between 55° and 60° Fahrenheit. If too cold, the fruitiness of the wine will be hidden. If too warm, it will seem less crisp and "dull".

But, as always, serve the wines the way you like them, even if it is not necessarily how the winemaker might prefer.

Should I let the wine breathe before drinking it?

Only if it needs it. Wines vary. Most wines are ready to drink when you pour them, or shortly thereafter. Some will improve after five or ten minutes, or even longer. And others will even go downhill over that period of time.

If the wine is "tight" or "closed", i.e. the flavors and aromas seem to be held in, let it breathe for a while—in the glass. The concept of letting the wine breathe in the bottle makes little sense. Not much air can contact the wine through the small opening in the bottle.

How many servings can I get from a bottle?

A 750 ml bottle is about 26 ounces, so you can pour about five 5-ounce servings, which is a generous serving. Six 4-ounce servings is probably a better idea. If you're doing a tasting, you could pour a dozen 2-ounce tastes.

Is wine really healthy?

A glass of wine a day is reported to reduce the risk of heart attack or stroke. All wines contain reservatrol, which can act as an effective preventative against coronary heart disease. It also increases levels of HDL, the "good" cholesterol that helps prevent clog-ging of the arteries. Wine also reduces the risk of certain types of cancer.

How do they make white wine from red grapes?

"Blush" wines such as White Zinfandel are made by separating the juice from the skins shortly after the grapes are crushed. Since the juice is clear, and the color comes primarily from pigments in the skins, this brief contact with the skins leaves the juice with only a slight pink color. The wine is then processed as a regular white wine would be.

Why are white wines fermented at cooler temperatures than red wines?

To retain the fruity flavors and aromas of the white grapes.

What kind of champagne glass should I use?

There are two styles to choose from. One is the open, flatter style that legend says was based on the shape of Marie Antoinette's breast. The narrower flute style is considered the best, however, because it does a better job of retaining the carbon dioxide and aromas of the champagne.

How long can I keep a bottle of wine after opening it?

It depends how many minutes it takes you to drink it. However, if you really don't want to finish a bottle in one sitting, recork it and put it in the refrigerator, although we recommend this more with white wine than with red. (Red is probably better just left on the counter and drunk the next day).

White wine in the refrigerator should last two or three days. If you have any empty half bottles, pour the wine in one of them. That way there will be less air in the bottle, reducing oxidation and helping the leftover wine to last longer.

One new product that is highly recommended by Napa Valley wineries is "Private Preserve". It's a mixture of inert gases that protects open bottles of wine (and fine spirits) against oxidation for weeks and even months. You can find it at wine shops and winery sales rooms throughout the valley or at www.privatepreserve.com.

Why do I get headaches from wine?

Assuming it isn't from drinking too much wine, it's most likely because of the histamines that are naturally present in wine. (And in cheese and other foods).

Red wine is much higher in histamines, so you might try switching to white wine. If that doesn't work, consider taking an antihistamine. Just make sure the package doesn't say to avoid alcohol when using it.

What are the big fans in the vineyards? Are they to cool off the grapes in the summer?

Actually, no. They're to keep the grapes warm in the spring, when there is danger of frost which can damage the young shoots. When the temperature gets down to around 34° Fahrenheit, smudge pots (diesel heaters) are started to heat up the air. The fans then blow the warm air through the vineyard.

Another method of frost protection is the overhead sprinklers that you might have seen. The sprinklers spray the vines, covering the shoots with water, which then freezes. Interestingly, this insulated ice jacket protects the shoots, keeping them just warm enough to avoid freezing themselves.

Who made the Grapecrusher statue at the south end of the Napa Valley?

It was designed by sculptor Gino Miles, and is actually a public relations coup for the industrial park developer whose logo it is.

Do the birds eat the grapes?

Not really. Interestingly enough, the large flocks of starlings that do eat grapes usually don't show up in the Napa Valley until after crush. They take the leftovers. And they create beautiful patterns as large flocks of them weave in and out in the skies over the vineyards.

Those birds that are around before harvest are kept away with owls—fake and real, mylar strips that are tied to vineyard trellisses and flash in the sunlight, and machines that fire off blank cartridges that sound like shotgun blasts.

How long does a vine last?

After 30 or 40 years, a vine's yield starts to decrease, although its quality may still be excellent.

How long should I store wine before drinking it?

The average time that most Americans "lay down" wine is probably about half an hour. That's okay, because most wine, particularly white wine, is ready to drink when it is sold. But some wines, particularly red wines that are heavy on tannins such as a good Cabernet Sauvignon, will improve with age; often as much as ten or fifteen years—or more. Ask the winery and they'll tell you about a particular wine's aging potential.

The Grapecrusher—A corporate logo that became a symbol of the Napa Valley.

Is it a good idea to buy wine at the winery?

You should know right off that you probably won't buy wine cheaper at a winery than at home. Most wineries sell at full retail and you probably have a discount house in your area. Does that mean you shouldn't buy wine at Napa Valley wineries? Absolutely not.

Ten Reasons Why You Should Buy Wine at the Winery.

1. You can find wines that are hard, if not impossible, to find in other parts of the country. With over 250 Napa Valley wineries, it's highly unlikely your local supermarket, or even specialty wine shop, is going to carry all the wines of all the wineries.

2. You can find wines that have a limited production and are sold only at the winery.

3. After tasting the wines, you can buy a bottle of wine that you know you like.

4. You'll get a great-tasting souvenir.

5. When you get home, you can pour the wine for friends and be able to tell them about the winery, how the wine was made, and, if it came from a small winery, possibly even that you met the winemaker.

6. Sometimes wines are on sale at the winery, and you can get an excellent price on an unusual or hard-to-find wine.

7. You can take the wine outside and have it with your picnic lunch.

8. You can take the wine to a Napa Valley restaurant, pay the corkage fee, and enjoy exactly the wine you want with your dinner.

9. If you're lucky enough to live in one of the right (wine-friendly) states, you don't even have to carry it home. The winery will ship it for you.

10. You're helping keep the winery in business, something that's particularly important for small, family wineries. The reason the Napa Valley isn't filled with houses—as is most of the San Francisco Bay Area—is that most of the valley has remained in agriculture. And it has remained in agriculture because that agricultural crop is wine-grapes. (We had far fewer visitors when our main crop was prunes.)

When did Robert Louis Stevenson say that Napa Valley wine was "bottled poetry"?

Actually, he didn't. He said that "wine" was bottled poetry. And he was referring to French wine when he wrote in his book *The Silverado Squatters*..."and the wine is bottled poetry."

But he wrote the book while he and his bride were staying on Mount St. Helena, so the Napa Valley claims him as one of its own. And he'd presumably say it about Napa Valley wine if he were around today.

What's a "wine brick"?

During Prohibition, most wineries closed. A few survived by making medicinal or sacramental wine. (Yes, there did appear to be an increase in the number of sick and deeply religious people during this time.)

In order to survive financially, some wineries also produced "wine bricks". These were bricks of compressed grapes that were shipped to customers around the country with a warning notice, which read: "Warning. Do not place this wine brick in one gallon of water, stir and let sit in warm temperatures for 10 days, or it might ferment and turn into wine."

I saw some funny looking buildings while driving through the valley.

Those were probably "yurts", round tent-like structures based on the dwellings used by Mongolian nomads.

The Mexican farmworkers who care for the vines throughout the year, and pick the grapes at harvest, are the unsung heroes of the Napa Valley wine industry. Housing in the valley is an ongoing problem, since the valley is an area where there is far more demand for housing than there is a supply.

A number of farmworker camps are scattered throughout the valley, run by both individual growers and wineries as well as by county organizations. These are to house the 2,000 or so temporary farmworkers who come to the valley each year for harvest.

Patterned after the original dwellings of Mongolian nomads, these yurts provide housing for farmworkers during harvest.

One of the most unusual farmworker camps was established in 2000. Thirteen Mongolian-style yurts, made in Oregon, were purchased by the Napa Valley Housing Authority, and erected by volunteers on local government-owned property. Workers sleep in the smaller ones, and the two larger ones are used for dining and community activities.

The yurts are taken down at the end of harvest, and erected again for the next harvest.

The industry has also built a permanent farmworker camp on eight acres of land near St. Helena donated by vintner Joseph Phelps. It was paid for by a tax on grapes initiated by Napa Valley grapegrowers themselves.

The complex includes two dormitory buildings, each with 15 two-person rooms, totaling 60 rooms, a multipurpose building with a kitchen and laundry, and staff quarters. It is more than just farmworker housing because it serves as a model for environmentally responsible, cost-saving construction.

The walls, floors, building pad and roadway were all constructed from earth removed in the excavation of wine caves throughout the county. The building technique is *rammed earth*, pioneered by a local Napa company, Rammed Earth Works (www.rammedearthworks.com).

The design of the building eliminates the need for conventional air conditioning, and uses radiant heating, with solar-heated water circulating through pipes in the floor.

Water use is kept to a minimum with low-flow fixtures, rainwater collection and graywater recycling. Wastewater is treated in engineered wetlands, and then used to irrigate gardens and landscaping.

Wine Stuff

WINE FACTS, STATISTICS AND TRIVIA

Age of vine before producing useful grapes
3 years

Age of vine before full production   5 years

Productive lifetime of a vine   30-35 years—Although the quality can remain good, the yield begins to decrease after that

Grape clusters in bottle	5-6
Grapes in a bottle	500-600
Clusters on a vine	40
Grapes in a cluster	75-100
Grape clusters in one glass of wine	1
Vines per acre	400
Pounds of grapes produced by one vine	8-12
Tons per acre	5 (average—can vary greatly)
Gallons of wine per ton of grapes	120
Gallons of wine per acre	800
Barrels per acre	13.5
Bottles per vine	10
Bottles per ton	500—700
Bottles per acre	4,000
Cases per barrel	24.6
Glasses per acre	16,000
Glasses in a bottle	5-6
Bottles per 60 gallon barrel	300

Calories in a 5 ounce glass of dry wine
100-125

Fat in a 5 ounce glass of dry wine 0

Carbohydrates in a 5 ounce glass of dry wine 1-2

Cost of acre of new vineyard in Napa Valley $120,000 (some existing property has been sold for $300,000 an acre)

Cost of French oak barrel $600-850

Cost of American oak barrel $300-550

Average age of a French oak tree used to make barrels 170 years

Number of years an oak barrel is used
5-8

Number of vineyard acres in Napa County (2000) 40,016 (out of a total of 485,120 acres in the entire county)—less than 8% of total land area

Number of vineyard acres placed in Land Trust never to be developed
More than 10,000

Most popular varietals in Napa Valley (in order of popularity)

1. Cabernet Sauvignon
2. Chardonnay
3. Merlot
4. Pinot Noir
5. Zinfandel
6. Sauvignon Blanc

Proportion of total value at harvest of red varietals compared to white
Nearly 3:1

Number of wineries in Napa Valley
Approximately 250

Number of wineries in Napa Valley built since 1966 243

Number of people/companies owning Napa Valley vineyards
More than 1000

Number of people directly employed in Napa Valley wine industry (wineries, vineyards, vineyard/winery services)
More than 8,000

Number of people directly employed in Napa Valley wine industry and resulting hospitality industry
More than 15,000

Year grapes first planted in Napa Valley
1838 (by George Yount)

First winery built in Napa Valley after Prohibition Stony Hill (1951)

First large winery built in Napa Valley after Prohibition
Robert Mondavi (1966)

Biggest Napa Valley crop before grapes
Prunes

Largest corporate owner of vineyards in Napa Valley
Diageo (British corporation)

Largest private owner of vineyards in Napa Valley
Andrew Beckstoffer (Beckstoffer Vineyards, St. Helena)

Number of cases of Napa Valley wine produced annually
6 million+ (1998)

Gross revenue from sales of that wine
$1 billion+ (1998)

Ranking of United States in world wine production (1999)
4th—533,596,000 gallons (behind France, Italy and Spain)

Ranking of United States in world wine acreage (1999)
4th—905,000 acres

Ranking of United States in world wide consumption (1999)
3rd—552,763,000 gallons

Percentage of U.S. wine made in California
90%

Percentage of California wine made in Napa Valley 4%

Average annual wine consumption of French per capita

15.81 gallons

Average annual wine consumption of Germans per capita

6.05 gallons

Average annual wine consumption of Canadians per capita

2.01 gallons

Average annual soft drink consumption of Americans per capita

55 gallons

Average annual beer consumption of Americans per capita

22 gallons

Average annual coffee consumption of Americans per capita

11 gallons

Cost of attending Napa Valley Wine Auction in 2002

$2,500/couple

Money raised by Napa Valley Wine Auction in 2002

$6.12 million

Money given by Napa Valley Wine Auction to local charities in 2002.

$5.8 million

Money given by Napa Valley Wine Auction to local charities since 1981.

More than $42 million

YOU CAN HAVE NAPA VALLEY WINE SHIPPED HOME. MAYBE.

One of the pleasures of visiting the Napa Valley is finding special wines and having them shipped to your home. However, many states currently prohibit you from purchasing wine directly from out-of-state wineries and having it shipped to you.

Thanks to Free The Grapes! for the information below which was current at press time, but is subject to change. It is provided as a guide and not as legal advice. The

sales room staff at the wineries will be able to tell you if they can currently ship to your state.

States that prohibit wine shipments currently include: Alabama, Arkansas, Delaware, Florida (felony), Indiana, Kansas, Kentucky (felony), Maine, Maryland, Massachusetts, Michigan, Mississippi, New Jersey, New York, Ohio, Oklahoma, Pennsylvania, South Dakota, Tennessee (felony), Utah, Vermont.

Note: This information, provided courtesy of *Free the Grapes!*, is subject to change. It is provided as a guide and not as legal advice. The sales room staff at all Napa Valley wineries will be able to tell you if they can currently ship to your state.

If your state's laws prohibit you from having Napa Valley wine delivered to your home, and you'd like to help change that, visit Free The Grapes! at www.freethegrapes.org.

WINE SHIPPERS

If you buy a few bottles at various wineries, you can consolidate them and ship them all at once from these businesses.

Buffalo's Shipping Post

2471 Solano Ave. Napa, CA 94558
707.226.7942
www.nfx.net/~buffalo/

Stagecoach Express

3377 Solano Ave. Napa CA 94558
707.257.1888 Fax: 707.257.1891
www.stagecoachexpress.com

DIRECTIONS: In the Vallergas/Redwood Plaza just off Highway 29 and Redwood Road. Open Monday-Friday 9 a.m. to 6 p.m. Saturday 10 a.m.-4 p.m. Sunday by appointment

WINE STORAGE

If wineries or shipping firms are unable to ship to your state, and you are serious about wine, you might consider using a local wine storage facility. Since it is in California, wineries can ship to the storage facility and your wine will be stored there. You can make your own arrangements to have wine shipped from your storage locker to your home as you need it. Facilities offer secure, temperature and humidity-controlled wine storage lockers of various sizes.

55 Degrees

1210 Church Street St. Helena CA 94574
707.963.5513
www.fiftyfivedegrees.com

Napa Valley Wine Storage

1135 Golden Gate Drive   Napa CA 94558
707.265.9990
www.napavalleywinestorage.com

Napa Wine Lockers

736 California Boulevard   Napa CA 94559
707.257.2903
www.napawinelockers.com

WINEMAKING CLASSES

Would you like to make wine yourself? Most winemakers in the Napa Valley have attended one of these schools, usually U.C. Davis due to its convenient location.

University of California, Davis – Department of Viticulture and Enology

http://wineserver.ucdavis.edu

Offers Bachelor of Science degree in Viticulture & Enology, and Bachelor of Science in Fermentation Science. Also a Master of Science in Viticulture & Enology.

California State University, Fresno – Department of Viticulture and Enology

http://cast.csufresno.edu/ve/

Offers Bachelor of Science degree in Viticulture or Enology, and Master of Science in Viticulture & Enology.

U.C. Davis, University Extension – Winemaking Classes

www.universityextension.ucdavis.edu/winemaking/

Offers courses in viticulture and enology, wine appreciation, and winemaking business.

HOME WINEMAKING

Making Table Wine at Home

http://wineserver.ucdavis.edu/WineGrape/Homewine/

The Home Winemakers Manual

http://home.att.net/~lumeisenman/

You can also visit www.homewine.com for ideas, inspiration and sources of Napa Valley grapes.

WINE APPRECIATION CLASSES

If you'd just like to learn more about wine and how to enjoy it, check with your local wine shop, adult school or community college to see if there are wine appreciation classes in your area. You might also consider the online classes from Wine Spectator Magazine: www.winespectatorschool.com.

WINE BLENDING AND TASTING KIT

Bourassa Vineyards in the Napa Valley sells a kit that you can use to host a wine blending/tasting party, or a blind wine tasting party. It includes step-by-step instructions and all the materials you'll need (except the wine) for blending and tasting.

Bourassa Vineyards

3212 Jefferson Street #394
Napa CA 94558
800.499.2366
www.bourassavineyards.com
www.wineblending.com

WINE PUBLICATIONS

Consumer

Wine Enthusiast Magazine

www.winemag.com

Wine Spectator Magazine
www.winespectator.com

WineAnswers.com
www.wineanswers.com

An online service of the Wine Market Council that provides comprehensive information on wine.

Wine Country Living (lifestyle)
www.winecountryliving.net

Dan Berger on Wine
www.creators.com/lifestyle_show.cfm?columns Name=dbe

A weekly column on wine. Berger offers knowledgeable, no-nonsense commentary on worldwide wines. If it isn't in your local newspaper, you can read it at the above web address.

Wine Industry

Practical Winery and Vineyard
www.practicalvineyard.com

Vineyard & Winery Management
www.vwm-online.com

Wine Business Monthly / Wine Business Insider
www.winebusiness.com

Wines and Vines
www.winesandvines.com

WINE STOCKS

Interested in owning stock in a Napa Valley winery? A few wineries in the Napa Valley are publicly-owned, although most of these are owned by non-California corporations.

Allied Domecq - ALLD
www.allieddomecqplc.com

An English company that owns Mumm Napa Valley (www.mummnapavalley.com) and William Hill Winery (www.williamhill.com).

Chalone Wine Group - CHLN
www.chalonewinegroup.com

A California company that owns Acacia Winery (www.acaciawinery.com).

Diageo – DEO
www.diageo.com

An English company that owns Beaulieu Vineyard (www.bv-wine.com) and Sterling Vineyard (www.sterlingvyds.com) through its UDV Guinness subsidiary.

Foster's Group – FGL
www.fostersgroup.com

An Australian company that owns Beringer Blass Wine Estates (www.beringerblass.com) which owns Beringer Vineyards (www.beringer.com), St. Clement Vineyards (www.stclement.com), and Stags' Leap Winery (www.stagsleapwinery.com).

LVMH Moet Hennessy Louis Vuitton – LVMH
www.lvmh.com

A French company that owns Domaine Chandon (www.dchandon.com) and has a majority interest in Newton Vineyards.

Robert Mondavi – MOND
www.mondavi.com

A California company that owns Robert Mondavi Winery (www.robertmondaviwinery.com) and 50% of Opus One (www.opusonewines.com).

Constellation Brands – STZ
www.constellationbrands.com

A U.S. company that owns Franciscan Oakville Estate (www.franciscan.com) and Mt. Veeder Winery (www.mtveeder.com).

UST – UST

www.ustshareholder.com

A U.S. company that owns Stimson Lane (www.stimsonlane.com) which owns Conn Creek Winery (www.conn-creek.com) and Villa Mt. Eden (www.villamteden.com).

Wine Industry Addresses

We've included this list so you can track down a favorite winery. Not all of these wineries have tours or onsite sales. In fact, most don't. (The major ones that do allow you to drop in are listed in our *Town* sections.)

Some wineries have such limited production that they are not interested in any visitors. Most that are interested can have visits by appointment only. (This is due to the county's attempts to minimize automobile traffic in many areas.)

Most small, out-of-the-way, family-owned wineries give tours only by appointment. These are the wineries that can be the most interesting, and that will give you a chance to actually talk with the winemaker himself.

To visit these wineries, call in advance. While you may be able to set up an appointment the same day, or the next day if you're spending the night in the valley, you're better off phoning before you even come to the valley.

This also works even for the larger wineries that give public tours. You might have your local wine shop call the winery and tell them you're a special customer who would like a private tour.

Wine Organizations

Association of African American Vintners
www.aaavintners.org

California Association of Winegrape Growers
www.cawg.org

Congressional Wine Caucus
www.house.gov/radanovich/wine/

Family Winemakers of California
www.familywinemakers.org

Napa County Farm Bureau
www.napafarmbureau.org

Napa Sustainable Winegrowing Group
www.nswg.org

Napa Valley Grape Growers Association
www.napagrowers.org

Napa Valley Vintners Association
www.napavintners.com

Wine America (American Vintners Association)
www.americanwineries.org

Wine Institute of California
wineinstitute.org

Regional Associations in Napa Valley

Carneros Quality Alliance
www.carneros.com

Mount Veeder Appellation
www.mountveederwines.com

Oakville Winegrowers
www.oakvillewinegrowers.org

Rutherford Dust Society
www.rutherforddust.org

Silverado Trail Wineries Association
www.silveradotrail.com

Stags Leap District Winegrowers
www.stagsleapdistrict.com

Napa Valley Winery List

Acacia Winery

2750 Las Amigas Road, Napa
707.226.9991
www.acaciawinery.com

Aetna Springs Cellars

7227 Pope Valley Road., Pope Valley 707.965.2675
www.aetnaspringscellars.com

Alatera Vineyards

2170 Hoffman Lane.,
Yountville
707.944.4005

Aloise Francisco Vineyards

1054 Bayview Avenue., Napa
707.252.4005

Altamura Winery

4240 Silverado Trail., Napa
707.253.2000
www.altamura.com

Amici Cellars

1109 Hudson Street St. Helena
707.967.9560
www.amicicellars.com

Amizetta Vineyards Winery

1099 Greenfield Rd, St. Helena
707.963.1460
www.amizetta.com

S. Anderson Vineyard

1473 Yountville Crossroad
Yountville 707.944.8642
www.4bubbly.com

Anderson's Conn Valley Vineyards

680 Rossi Road., St. Helena
707.963.8600

Andretti Winery

4162 Big Ranch Road Napa
707.255.3524
www.andrettiwinery.com

Araujo Estate Wines

2155 Picket Road, Calistoga
707.942.6061
www.araujoestatewines.com

Arroyo Winery

2361 Greenwood Avenue,
Calistoga 707.942.6995

Artesa

1345 Henry Road Napa
707.224.1668
www.artesawinery.com

Astrale e Terra

5017 Silverado Trail Napa
707.253.7643
www.astraleeterra.com

Atlas Peak Vineyads

3700 Soda Canyon Road.,
Napa
707.252.7971
www.atlaspeak.com

Azalea Springs

4301 Azalea Springs Way,
Calistoga 707.942.4811

Ballentine Vineyards and Winery

2820 N. St Helena Highway
St. Helena 707.963.7919
www.ballentinevineyards.com

Barlow Vineyards

4411 Silverado Trail,
Calistoga, CA 94515
707.942.8742
www.barlowvineyards.com

Barnett Vineyards

4070 Spring Mountain Road.,
St. Helena 707.963.0109
www.barnettvineyards.com

Bayview Cellars

1202 Main Street, Napa
707.255.8544
www.bayviewine.com

Beaucanon

1695 South St. Helena Hwy.
St. Helena 707.967.3520

Beaulieu Vineyard

1960 St. Helena Hwy.
Rutherford
707.967.5411
www.bv-wine.com

Bell Wine Cellars

6200 Washington Street
Yountville 707.944.1673
www.bellwine.com

Benessere Vineyards

1010 Big Tree Road St. Helena
707.963.5853
www.benesserevineyards.com

Beringer Vineryards

2000 Main Street St. Helena
707.963.4812
www.beringer.com

Bernard Pradel Cellars

2100 Hoffmann Lane
Yountville
707.944.8720

Bighorn Cellars

1085 Atlas Peak Road Napa
707.224.6565

Bouchaine Vineyards

1075 Buchli Station Road.,
Napa
707.252.9065
www.bouchaine.com

Buehler Vineyards
820 Greenfield Road., St.
Helena
707.963.2155
www.buehlervineyards.com

Burgess Cellars
1108 Deer Park Road., St.
Helena 707.963.4766
www.burgesscellars.com

Cain Vineyards & Winery
3800 Langtry Road., St.
Helena
707.963.1616
www.cainfive.com

Cakebread Cellars
8300 St. Helena Hwy.,
Rutherford
707.963.5221
www.cakebread.com

Calafia Cellars
629 Fulton Lane., St. Helena
707.963.5221

Cardinale Winery
7585 St. Helena Highway
Oakville 707.944.2807
www.cardinale.com

Carneros Creek Winery
1285 Dealy Lane., Napa
707.253.9463
www.carneros-creek.com

Carver Sutro Wine
3106 Palisades Road
Calistoga CA 94515
707.942.1029
www.carversutro.com

Casa Nuestra Winery
3451 Silverado Trail., N., St.
Helena 707.963.5783
www.casanuestra.com

Caymus Vineyards
8700 Sage Canyon Creek
Road., St.Helena
707.967.3010
www.caymus.com

Chappellet Vineyard
1581 Sage Canyon Road., St.
Helena 707.963.7136
www.chappellet.com

Charbay Winery & Distillery
4001 Spring Mountain Road,
St. Helena 707.963.9327
www.charbay.com

Charles Krug Winery
2800 St. Helena Hwy North
St. Helena
707.963.2761
www.charleskrug.com

Chateau Boswell
3468 Silverado Trail., St.
Helena
707.963.5472

Chateau Chevre Winery
2030 Hoffmann Lane.,
Yountville
707.944.2184

Chateau L'Ego
www.westsong.com/chateau

Chateau Montelena Winery
1429 Tubbs Lane., Calistoga
707.942.5105
www.chateaumontelena.com

Chateau Potelle
3875 Mount Veeder Road.,
Napa
707.255.9440
www.chateaupotelle.com

Chateau Woltner
3500 Silverado Trail., St.
Helena
707.963.1744

Chiles Valley Wineyard
2676 Lower Chiles Valley
Road., St. Helena
707.963.7294

Chimney Rock Winery
5350 Silverado Trail., Napa
707.257.2641
www.chimneyrock.com

Clos Du Val Wine Co., Ltd
5330 Silverado. Trail., Napa
707.259.2220
www.closduval.com

Clos Pegase Winery
1060 Dunaweal Lane.,
Calistoga
707.942.4981
www.clospegase.com

Colgin Cellars
7830-40 St. Helena Hwy
Oakille
707.524.4445

Conn Creek Winery
8711 Silverado Trail., St.
Helena
707.963.5133
www.conncreek.com

Corison Winery
987 St. Helena Highway St.
Helena 707.963.0826
www.corisonwinery.com

Corley Family Napa Valley
4242 Big Ranch Road, Napa
707.253.2802
www.corleyfamilynapavalley.com

Cosentino Winery

7415 St. Helena Hwy,
Yountville
707.944.1220
www.cosentinowinery.com

Costello Vineyards Winery

1200 Orchard Avenue, Napa
707.252.8483

Crichton Hall

1150 Darms Lane Napa
707.224.4200

Cuvaison Winery

4550 Silverado Trail.,
Calistoga
707.942.6266
www.cuvaison.com

D.R. Stephens Estate

1860 Howell Mountain Road
St. Helena
415.781.8000

Dalla Valle Vineyards

7776 Silverado Trail.,
Yountville
707.944.2676

Dariloush Winery

4240 Silverado Trail Napa
707.257.2345
www.darioush.com

David Arthur Vineyards

1521 Sage Canyon Road, St.
Helena
707.963.5190
www.davidarthur.com

Deer Park Winery

1000 Deer Park Road., Deer
Park
707.963.5411
www.deerparkwinery.com

Diamond Creek Vineyards

1500 Diamond Mountain
Road.,Calistoga
707.942.6926
www.diamondcreekvine-
yards.com

Diamond Mountain Vineyard

2121 Diamond Mountain
Road., Calistoga
707.942.0707

Domain Hill & Mayes

1775 Lincoln Avenue, Napa
707.224.6565

Domain Carneros by Taittinger

1240 Duhig Road., Napa
707.257.0101
www.domainecarneros.com

Domaine Chandon

California Drive., Yountville
707.944.2280
www.chandon.com

Domaine Montreax

4101 Big Ranch Road., Napa
707.252.9380

Domaine Napa Winery

1155 Mee Lane., St. Helena
707.963.1666

Dominus Estate

2570 Napanook Road.,
Yountville
707.944.8954
www.dominusestate.com

Duckhorn Vineyards

3027 Silverado Trail. N, St.
Helena 707.963.7108
www.duckhorn.com

Dunn Vineyards

805 White Cottage Road.,
Angwin 707.965.3642

Dutch Henry Winery

4300 Silverado Trail Calistoga
707.942.5771
www.dutchhenry.com

Eagle and Rose Estate

1844 Pope Canyon Road
Pope Valley 707.965.9463
www.eagleandrose.com

Edgewood Estates

401 St. Helena Hwy St.
Helena
707.963.2335

Ehlers Grove Winery

3222 Ehlers Lane., St. Helena
707.963.3200
www.ehlersgrove.com

Eisele V & L Family Estate

3080 Lower Chiles Valley
Road., St. Helena
707.965.2260
www.volkereiselevineyard.com

El Molino Winery

P.O Box 306, St. Helena
707.963.3632

Elkhorn Peak Cellars

200 Polson Road., Napa
707.255.0504
www.elkhornpeakcellars.com

Elyse Wine Cellars

PO Box 83, Rutherford
707.963.5496

Emilio's Terrace

1496 Walnut Drive Oakville
707.944.2193
www.etvine.com

Etude Wines

1250 Cuttings Wharf Road,
Napa
707.257.5300

Far Niente Winery
P.O. Box 327, Oakville
707.944.2861
www.farniente.com

Farella-Park Vineyards
PO Box 5217, Napa
707.254.9489

Flora Springs Wine Co.
1978 W. Zinfandel Lane., St.
Helena 707.963.5711
www.florasprings.com

Folie a Deux
3070 N. St. Helena Hwy., St.
Helena 707.963.1160

Forest Hill Vineyard
P.O. Box 96 St. Helena
707.963.7229

Franciscan Oakville Estate
1178 Calleron Road.,
Rutherford
707.963.7111
www.franciscan.com

Frank Family Vineyards
1091 Larkmead Lane St.
Helena
707.942.859

Franus Wine Company
2055 Hoffman Lane Yountville
707.945.0542
www.franuswine.com

Frazier
40 Lupine Hill Road Napa
707.255.3444
www.frazierwinery.com

Freemark Abbey Winery
3022 North St. Helena Hwy.
St. Helena 707.963.9694
www.freemarkabbey.com

Frisinger Cellars
2277 Dry Creek Road., Napa
707.255.3749

Frog's Leap Winery
8815 Conn Creek Road.,
Rutherford 707.963.4704
www.frogsleap.com

Galleron
PO Box 2 Rutherford
707.265.6552
www.galleronwine.com

Girard Winery
7717 Silverado Trail. Oakville
707.944.8577

Goosecross Cellars
1119 State Lane., Yountville
707.944.1986
www.goosecross.com

Grace Family Vineyards
1210 Rockland Drive., St.
Helena
707.963.0808

Graeser Winery
255 Petrified Forest Road.,
Calistoga 707.942.4437
www.graeserwinery.com

Green & Red Vineyard
3208 Chiles Pope Valley
Road., St. Helena
707.965.2346
www.greenandred.com

Grgich Hlls Cellar
1829 St. Helena Hwy.,
Rutherford
707.963.2784
www.grgich.com

Groth Vineyards & Winery
750 Oakville Cross Road.,
Oakville 707.944.0290

Guilliams Vineyards
3851 Spring Mountain Road
St. Helena 707.963.9059

Gustavo Thrace Winery
1146 First Street. Napa
707.257.6796
www.gustavothrace.com

Hagafen Cellars
PO Box 3035, Napa
707.252.0781
www.hagafen.com

Hakusan Sake Gardens
1 Executive Way, Napa
707.258.6160
www.hakusan.com

Hall
401 St. Helena Highway
South
St. Helena CA 94574
707.967.2620
www.hallwines.com

Hanso-Hsieh Vineyard
1019 Dry Creek Road., Napa
707.257.2632

Harlan Estate Winery
PO Box 352, Oakville
707.944.1441
www.harlanestate.com

Harrison Vineyards
1527 Sage Canyon Road.,
St.Helena 707.963.8271
www.harrisonvineyards.com

Hartwell Vineyards
5795 Silverado Trail., Napa
707.255.4269
www.hartwellvineyards.com

Havens Wine Cellars

2055 Hoffman Lane.,
Yountville
707.945.0921
www.havenswine.com

Heitz Wine Cellar

500 Taplin Road, St. Helena
707.963.3542
www.heitzcellar.com

Helena View Johnston
Vineyards

3500 Highway 128 Calistoga
707.942.4956

Hendry Winery

3104 Redwood Road Napa
707.226.2130

Hess Collection

4411 Redwood Road., Napa
707.255.1144
www.hesscollection.com

Honig Cellars

850 Rutherford Road.,
Rutherford
707.963.5618
www.honigwines.com

Jarvis Vineyards

2970 Monticello Road., Napa
707.255.5280
www.jarviswines.com

Joel Gott

1458 Lincoln Ave. Railcar #15
Calistoga 707.942.1109

Jones Family Vineyards

7830-40 St. Helena Highway
Oakville 707.942.0467
www.joneswine.com

Joseph Phelps Vineyards

200 Taplin Road., St. Helena
707.963.2745
www.jpvwines.com

Joya Wine Company

880 Vallejo Street., Napa
707.245.9548

Karl Lawrence Cellars

4541 Monticello Road., Napa
707.255.2843
www.karllawrence.com

Kate's Vineyard

5211 Big Ranch Road Napa
707.255.2644

Kathryn Hall Vineyards

60 Auberge Road Rutherford
707.967.0700 800.688.4255
www.kathrynhallvineyards.com

Kelham MacLean Winery

360 Zinfandel Lane St Helena
707.963.2000
www.kelhammaclean.com

Kent Rasmussen Winery

1001 Silverado Trail St.
Helena
707.963.5667

Kirkland Ranch Winery

1 Kirkland Ranch Road Napa
707.254.9100
www.kirklandranchwinery.com

Laird Family Estate

5055 Solano Avenue Napa
707.257.0360
www.lairdfamilyestate.com

Lail Vineyards

320 Stone Ridge Road
Angwin
707.963.3329
www.lailvineyards.com

Lan Vieille Montagne

3851 Spring Mountain Road.,
St. Helena 707.963.9059

Lakespring Winery

2055 Hoffman Lane.,
Yountville
707.944.2475

Lamborn Family Vineyards

2075 Summit Lake Drive,
Angwin
707.965.2811
www.lamborn.com

Lang & Reed Wine Company

PO Box 662 St. Helena
707.963.7547

Larkmead Kornell Champagne
Cellars

1091 Larkmead Lane., St.
Helena
707.942.0859

Larkmead Vineyards

1145 Larkmead Lane.,
Calistoga
707.942.6605
www.larkmead.com

Liparita Cellars

410 La Fata Street #200 St.
Helena 707.963.2775
www.liparita.com

Livingston-Moffett Wines

1895 Cabernet Lane, St.
Helena
707.963.2120
www.livingstonwines.com

Lokoya

7600 St. Helena Highway
Oakville 707.944.2807
www.lokoya.com

Long Meadow Ranch

1775 Whitehall Lane St.
Helena
707.963.4555
www.longmeadowranch.com

Lorenza-Lake Winery

1764 Scott Street St. Helena
707.963.8593
www.blockheadia.com

Louis M. Martini Winery

St. Helena Hwy., St. Helena
707.963.2736
www.louismartini.com

Luna Vineyards

2921 Silverado Trail Napa
707.255.5862
www.lunavineyards.com

Lynch Knoll

3305 North St. Helena
Highway Oakville
650.948.1344

Madonna Estate (Mont St.
John)

5400 Old Sonoma Road Napa
707.255.8864
www.madonnaestate.com

Mario Perelli-Minetti Winery

1443 Silverado Trail, St.
Helena
707.963.8762

Markham Vineyards

2812 N. St. Helena Hwy St.
Helena 707.963.5292
www.markhamvineyards.com

Marston Family Vineyards

3600 White Sulphur Springs
Road St. Helena
415.931.0443

Mayacamus Vineyards

1155 Lokoya Road., Napa
707.224.4030
www.mayacamas.com

Merryvale Vineyards

1000 Main, St. Helena
707.963.7777
www.merryvale.com

Milat Vineyards

1091 St. Helena Hwy., St.
Helena
707.963.0758
www.milat.com

Miner Family Winery

7850 Silverado Trail Oakville
707.944.9500
www.minerwines.com

Monticello Brothers

707.255.9100

Monticello Vineyards

4242 Big Ranch Road., Napa
707.253.2802
www.corleyfamilynapavalley.com

Montreaux

4242 Big Ranch Road., Napa
707.252.9380

Moon Vineyard

3315 Sonoma Highway, Napa
707.226.2642

Moss Creek Winery

6015 Steele Canyon Road.,
Napa
707.252.1295

Mt. Veeder Winery &
Vineyards

1999 Mt. Veeder Road., Napa
707.224.4039
www.mtveeder.com

Mumm Napa Valley

8445 Silverado Trail., Napa
800.686.6272
www.mummnapavalley.com

Napa Cellars

7481 St. Helena Highway
Yountville 707.944.2565
www.napacellars.com

Napa Valley Vintners
Association

PO Box 141, St. Helena
707.963.0148
www.napavintners.com

Napa Wine Company

1133 Oakville Cross Road.,
Oakville 707.944.1710
www.napawineco.com

Newlan Vineyards & Winery

5225 Solano Avenue., Napa
707.257.2399
www.kovesnewlanwine.com

Newton Vineyard

2555 Madrone Avenue, St.
Helena 707.963.9000

Nichelini Winery

2950 Sage Canyon Road., St.
Helena 707.963.0717
www.nicheliniwinery.com

Nickel and Nickel

8164 St. Helena Highway,
Oakville
707.944.0693
www.nickelandnickel.com

Niebaum-Coppola Estate
Winery

PO Box 208, Rutherford
707.963.9435
www.niebaum-coppola.com

Oakford Vineyards

PO Box 150, Oakville
707.945.0445
www.oakfordvineyards.com

Oakville Ranch Vineyards

7781 Silverado Trail, Napa
415.284.1620

Oliver Caldwell Cellars

3480 St. Helena Highway St.
Helena 707.963.2037

One Vineyard

3268 Ehlers Lane St. Helena
707.963.1123

Opus One Winery

7900 St. Helena Highway
Oakville 707.944.9442
www.opusonewinery.com

Origin-Napa

PO Box 670, St. Helena
707.963.6134
www.originnapa.com

Pahlmeyer

PO Box 2410, Napa
707.255.2321
www.pahlmeyer.com

Paoletti Estates Winery

4801 Silverado Trail Calistoga
707.942.0689
www.giannipaoletti.com

Paradigm Winery

683 Dwyer Road Oakville
707.944.1683
www.paradigmwinery.com

Peju Province

8466 St. Helena., Hwy
Rutherford 707.963.3600
www.peju.com

Perez and Sons Vineyards

707.963.8002

Philip Togni Vineyard

3780 Spring Mountain Road.,
St.Helena 707.963.3731

Phoenix Vineyards

3175 Dry Creek Road Napa
707.255.1971
www.phoenixvineyards.com

Pillar Rock Vineyard

6110 Silverado Trail Yountville
630.293.1175
www.pillarrockvineyard.com

Pine Ridge Winery

5901 Silverado Trail. Napa
707.252.9777
www.pineridgewinery.com

Plam Vineyards

6200 Washington Street,
Yountville 707.944.1102
www.plam.com

Plumpjack Winery

620 Oakville Cross Road
Oakville
707.945.1220
www.plumpjack.com

Pope Valley Cellars

6613 Pope Valley Road., Pope
Valley 707.965.1438

Prager Winery & Port Works

1281 Lewelling Lane., St.
Helena
707.963.7678
www.pragerport.com

Pride Mountain Vineyards

Spring Mountain Road., St.
Helena 707.963.4949
www.pridewines.com

Quintessa

PO Box 407, Rutherford
707.963.7111
www.quintessa.com

Raymond Vineyard & Cellar

849 Zinfandel Lane, St.
Helena
707.963.3141
www.raymondwine.com

Regusci Winery

5584 Silverado Trail Napa
707.254.0403
www.regusciwinery.com

Reid Family Vineyard

www.jkirkwood.com

Reverie on Diamond Mountain

1520 Diamond Mountain
Road Calistoga 707.942.6800
www.reveriewine.com

Ristow Estate

5040 Silverado Trail Napa
415.931.5405
www.ristowestate.com

Ritchie Creek Vineyard

4024 Spring Mountain Road.,
St. Helena 707.963.4661
www.ritchiecreek.com

Robert Biale Vineyards

707.257.7555

Robert Craig Wine Cellars

830 School Road #14 Napa
707.252.2250
www.robertcraigwine.com

Robert Keenan Winery

3660 Spring Mountain Road.,
St. Helena 707.963.9177

Robert Mondavi Winery

7801 St. Helena Hwy.,
Oakville
707.226.1335
www.robertmondavi.com

Robert Pecota Winery

P.O Box 303, Calistoga
707.942.6625
www.robertpecotawinery.com

Robert Sinskey Vineyards

6320 Silverado Trail, Yountville
707.944.9090
www.robertsinskey.com

Rombauer Vineyards

3522 Silverado Trail, St.
Helena
707.967.5120
www.rombauervineyards.com

Round Hill Vineyards

1680 Silverado Trail., St.
Helena
707.963.9503
www.roundhillwines.com

Rudd Estate

500 Oakville Cross Road
Oakville
707.944.8577

Rustridge Winery

2910 Lower Chiles Valley
Road., St. Helena
707.965.2871
www.rustridge.com/winery

Rutherford Grove Winery

1673 St. Helena Highway
Rutherford 707.963.0544
www.rutherfordgrove.com

Rutherford Hill Winery

200 Rutherford Hill Road.,
Rutherford 707.963.7194
www.rutherfordhill.com

Saintsbury

1500 Los Carneros Ave.,
Napa
707.252.0592
www.saintsbury.com

San Pietro Vara Vineyard &
Wine Company

1171 Tubbs Lane., Calistoga
707.942.0937

Sawyer Cellars

8350 St. Helena Highway
Rutherford 707.963.1980
www.sawyercellars.com

Schrader Cellars

2921 Silverado Trail Napa
707.942.1212

Schramsberg Vineyards

Schramsberg Road., Calistoga
707.942.4558
www.schramsberg.com

Schweiger Vineyards & Winery

4015 Spring Mountain Road
St. Helena 707.963.7980

Screaming Eagle Winery

7557 Silverado Trail Oakville
707.944.0749
www.screamingeagle.com

Seavey Vineyards

1310 Conn Valley Road, St.
Helena 707.963.8339
www.seaveyvineyard.com

Sequoia Grove Vineyards

8338 South St. Helena Hwy.,
Rutherford 707.944.2945
www.sequoiagrove.com

Selene Wines

PO Box 3131 Napa
707.258.8119
www.selenewines.com

Shafer Vineyards

6145 Silverado Trail. Napa
707.944.2877
www.shafervineyards.com

Showket-Awni Wines

Oakville
707.944.9553
wwwshowketvineyards.com

Shypoke Vineyard

4170 St. Helena Highway
Calistoga
707.942.0420
www.shypoke.com

Signorello Vineyards

4500 Silverado Trail, Napa
707.255.5990
www.signorellovineyards.com

Silver Oak Cellars

915 Oakville Cross Road.,
Oakville 707.944.8808
www.silveroak.com

Silverado Hill Cellars

3103 Silverado Trail., Napa
707.253.9306

Silverado Vineyards

6121 Silverado Trail., Napa
707.257.1770
www.silveradovineyards.com

Silver Rose Winery

400 Silverado Trail Calistoga
707.942.9581
www.silverrosewinery.com

Sky Vineyards

Napa 707.935.1391
www.skyvineyards.com

Smith-Madrone Vineyards

4022 Spring Mountain Road.,
St. Helena 707.963.2283

Spottswoode Winery

1902 Madrone Avenue St. Helena 707.963.0134
www.spottswoode.com

Spring Mountain Vineyard

2805 Spring Mountain Road. St. Helena 707.967.4188
www.springmtn.com

St. Andrews Winery

2921 Silverado Trail., Napa 707.259.2200

St. Clement Vineyards

2867 St. Helena Hwy., 707.963.7221
www.stclement.com

St. Supery Wine Discovery Center & Winery

8440 St. Helena Hwy., Rutherford 707.963.4507
www.stsupery.com

Stag's Leap Wine Cellars

5766 Silverado Trail, Napa 707.944.2020
www.stagsleapwinecellars.com

Stag's Leap Winery

6150 Silverado Trail, Napa 707.944.1303
www.stagsleap.com

Staglin Family Vineyard

P.O. Box 680, Rutherford 707.963.1749
www.staglin.com

Star Hill Winery

1075 Shadybrook Lane., Napa 707.255.1957
www.starhill.com

Steltzner

5998 Silverado Trail, Napa 707.252.7272
www.steltzner.com

Sterling Vineyards

1111 Dunaweal Lane., Calistoga 707.942.3344
www.sterlingvyds.com

Stonegate Winery

1183 Dunaweal Lane., Calistoga 707.942.6500
www.stonegatewinery.com

Stonehedge Winery

401 South St. Helena Highway St. Helena 323.780.5929

Stony Hill Vineyard

PO Box 308 St. Helena CA 94574 707.963.2636
www.stonyhillvineyard.com

Storybook Mountain Winery

3835 Hwy. 128, Calistoga 707.942.5310
www.storybookwines.com

Strack Vineyard

4120 St. Helena Hwy., Napa 707.224.5100

Stratford Winery

1472 Railroad Avenue, St. Helena 707.963.3200

Streblow Vineyards

1455 Summit Lake Drive, Angwin 707.963.5892

Sullivan Vineyards Winery

1090 Galleron Road., Rutherford 707.963.9646
www.sullivanwine.com

Summers Winery

1171 Tubbs Lane Calistoga 707.942.5508
www.sumwines.com

Summit Lake Vineyards & Winery

2000 Summit Lake Drive, Angwin 707.965.2488

Sutter Home Winery

277 St. Helena Hwy., St. Helena 707.963.3104
www.sutterhome.com

Swanson Vineyards

1271 Manley Lane,Rutherford 707.944.1642
www.swansonvineyards.com

Tongi Philip Vineyard

3780 Spring Mountain Road., St. Helena 707.963.3731

Trinchero Family Estates (See Sutter Home)

Traulsen Vineyards

2250 Lake Country Hwy., Calistoga 707.942.0283

Trefethen Veneyards

1160 Oak Knoll Ave, Napa 707.255.7700
www.trefethen.com

Truchard Vineyards

3234 Old Sonoma Road., Napa 707.253.7153

Tudal Winery
1015 Big Tree Road., St. Helena
707.963.3947
www.tudalwinery.com

Tulocay Winery
1426 Coombsville Road., Napa
707.255.4064
www.tulocay.com

Turley Wine Cellars
3358 St. Helena Hwy., St. Helena
707.963.0940
www.turleywinecellars.com

Turnbull Wine Cellars
8210 St. Helena Hwy., Oakville
707.963.5839

V. Sattui Winery
South St. Helena Hwy., St. Helena 707.963.7774
www.vsattui.com

Van Asperen Vineyards
1680 Silverado Trail St. Helena
707.968.3200
www.vanasperen.com

Van Der Heyden Vineyards & Winery
4057 Silverado Trail., Napa
707.259.9473
www.vanderheydenvine-yards.com

Venge Vineyards
7802 Money Rd., Oakville
707.944.1305

Viader Vineyards
1120 Deer Park Road., Deer Park
707.963.3816
www.viader.com

Vigil Vineyards
3340 Highway 128 Calistoga
707.942.2900
www.vigilwine.com

Villa Andriana
1171 Tubbs Lane Calistoga
707.942.5508

Villa Encinal
620 Oakville Cross Road, Oakville 707.944.1465

Villa Helena Winery
1455 Inglewood Ave, St. Helena
707.963.4334
www.wineweb.com/villahele-na.html

Villa Mt. Eden Winery
PO Box 350, St. Helena
707.944.2414
www.villamteden.com

Vincent Arroyo Winery
2361 Greenwood Avenue, Calistoga 707.942.6995

Vine Cliff Winery
7400 Silverado Trail., Yountville
707.944.1364
www.vinecliff.com

Vineyard 29
2929 Highway 29 North St. Helena 707.963.9292

Volker Eisele Family Estate
3080 Lower Chiles Valley Road., St. Helena
707.965.2260
www.volkereiselevineyard.com

Von Strasser Winery
1510 Diamond Mountain Road., Calistoga
707.942.0930
www.vonstrasser.com

W Winery
1001 Silverado Trail St. Helena
707.259.2800

Wermuth Winery
3942 Silverado Trail., Calistoga
707.942.5924

Whitehall Lane Winery
1563.S St. Helena Hwy., St Helena 707.963.9454

Whitford Cellars
4047 East 3d Avenue, Napa
707.257.7065

William Hill Winery
1761 Atlas Peak Road, Napa
707.224.4477
www.williamhill.com

Winter Creek Winery
PO Box 2847, Napa
707.252.8677

Woltner Estates Winery
150 White Cottage Road. South, Angwin 707.965.2445

Yverdon Vineyards
3787 Spring Mtn. Road., St. Helena 707.963.4270

Zahtila Vineyards

2250 Lake County Road
Calistoga 707.942.9251
www.zahtilavineyards.com

ZD Wines

8383 Silverado Trail, Napa
707.963.5188
www.zdwine.com

Local Information

Napa County Zip Codes

American Canyon	94503
Angwin	94508
Calistoga	94515
Deer Park	94576
Napa	94558
	94559
	94581
Oakville	94562
Pope Valley	94567
Rutherford	94573
St. Helena	94574
Yountville	94599

Telephone Prefixes

American Canyon	552
Angwin	965
Calistoga	942
Deer Park	963
Napa	224, 226, 251, 252, 253, 254, 255, 257, 258, 259
Oakville	944
Pope Valley	965
Rutherford	963
St. Helena	963, 967
Yountville	944

Telephone Calls

Emergency number (fire, police, ambulance) is 911.

Area code for the Napa Valley is 707.

California is -8 hours Universal Time (-7 during Daylight Savings Time in the summer).

Call operator ("00") for assistance.

To call a telephone number in another area code in the United States or Canada, dial 1, the area code, and the number.

To place international calls, dial 011, the country code, the city code, and the number.

Local Governments

Napa County League of Governments
www.nclog.org

Countywide community development strategy

County of Napa
1195 Third St. Napa CA 94559
707.253.4421
www.mynapa.info

City of Napa
955 School St. Napa CA 94559
707. 257.9503
www.cityofnapa.org
Napa Police Department—257.9223
Environmental Health—253.4471
Building Department—257.9540
Housing Authority—257.9543
Animal Control—253.4381
Fire Prevention—257.9590
Public Works Department—257.9520
Community Resources—257.9529

Bay Area Air Quality Management District—1.800.334.6367

Napa Sanitation District—258.6000

Napa Garbage Service - 255-5200

City of American Canyon
2185 Elliott Drive American Canyon CA 94503
707.647.4360
www.ci.american-canyon.ca.us

City of Calistoga

1232 Washington St. Calistoga CA 94515
707.942.2754
www.ci.calistoga.ca.us

City of St. Helena

1480 Main St. St. Helena CA 94574
707.967.2792
www.ci.st-helena.ca.us

Town of Yountville

6550 Yount St. Yountville CA 94599
707.944.8851

Congressman Mike Thompson

1040 Main Street, Suite 101,
Napa CA 94559
707.226.9898
www.house.gov/mthompson/

State Senator Wesley Chesbro

1040 Main Street, Suite 205,
Napa CA 94559
707.224.1990
www.sen.ca.gov/chesbro/

Assemblymember Pat Wiggins

1040 Main Street, Suite 101,
Napa CA 94559
707.258.8007
democrats.assembly.ca.gov/members/a07/

Political Parties

Napa County Democratic Central Committee

707.257.7165
mmillermrpjd@netscape.net

Napa County Greens

707.257.1166
napa@cagreens.org

Libertarian Party of Napa County

707.224.5535
www.napa.ca.lp.org

Napa County Republican Central Committee

707.224.2432
www.napagop.org

Superior Court of California, County of Napa

www.napacourt.com

Environmental Organizations

Napa-Solano Audubon Society

www.napasolanoaudubon.org

Napa Group of the Sierra Club

www.redwood.sierraclub.org/napa

Napa Valley Chapter, California Native Plant Society

www.ncfaa.com/skyline/cnps.htm

Get a Grip on Growth

www.westsong.com/ggg

Friends of the Napa River

www.friendsofthenapariver.org

Land Trust of Napa County

www.napalandtrust.org

Napa County Resource Conservation District

www.naparcd.org

Flood Control Project

A voter-approved flood control project is underway which will revitalize the Napa River and prevent flooding of homes and businesses. Information on the project and its ongoing effect on travel in the city of Napa is available online.

Napa Flood District
www.napaflooddistrict.org

Current Traffic Information
www.napatraffic.info

Flood Emergencies

Until the flood control project is completed, there is still a danger of flooding throughout the valley during heavy wintertime storms.

WEB SITES

Napa River Levels
www.mynapa.info/content/eoc/CurrentRiver.asp

County Road Conditions
www.mynapa.info/content/eoc/currentroad.asp

PHONE NUMBERS

Do NOT use 911 for information requests. Please reserve that number for actual emergencies.

Federal Emergency Management Agency (FEMA) – 800.462.9029. Residents and business owners can call FEMA for applications for assistance.

Napa County Road Conditions – 707.259.8304. Recorded message. Latest information available.

County of Napa Public Information Line – 707.259.8303. Live information on flood status available 24 hours a day during emergencies.

City of Napa Flood Information Line – 707.258.7813. Recorded message on flood status in English and Spanish from Public Information Office.

City of Napa Public Information Office – 707.258.7817. Live person.

Other Cities – Contact them at their main phone number (see above under Local Governments).

PG&E 24-hour Emergency and Customer Service – 800.743.5000

PG&E 24-hour Power Outage Hotline – 800.743.5002

Pacific Bell Repair Service – 611

Napa City Sewer – 707.258.6014 (24-Hour emergency number)

KVON 1440 AM/KVYN 99.3 FM Radio – 707.252.1440. Both stations maintain round-the-clock coverage. Listeners can call to report news. If KVON doesn't work, it probably means their transmitter is flooded out. Switch over to KVYN.

Volunteer Center of Napa County – 707.252.6222. Coordinates emergency volunteer services. Call if you'd like to help.

American Red Cross
Napa - 707.257.2900
St. Helena - 707.963.2717

Transportation Information – Call 511 toll-free from anywhere in Bay Area. Complete Bay Area public and private transportation information.

Napa County Humane Society – 707.255.8118. For missing or injured pets, or pet evacuation information.

Evacuation Shelters
For more information on shelters, contact the
Red Cross at the above numbers.

Calistoga - Napa County Fairgrounds
Napa - First United Methodist Church, 625
Randolph
Napa - Napa Seventh-Day Adventist Church,
1105 G Street (near Brown St.)
St. Helena - St. Helena High School
Yountville - Yountville Community Hall

Earthquakes

Since we're in California, we have earthquakes. We in the Napa Valley have been
fortunate over the years. We've sustained
minimal damage from large quakes that
have inflicted heavy damage in many other
parts of the San Francisco Bay Area. The
localized Yountville earthquake in 2000 had
a magnitude of 5.2. Most of the effects were
actually in Napa, where 25 people were
injured, including two critically. Damage
estimates were as high as $50 million.

And more will happen. According to a
report by the United States Geological
Survey, the Rodgers Creek-Hayward Fault
system (to the west of the Napa Valley) has
27% odds for one or more magnitude 6.7
or greater earthquakes from 2003 to 2032.
The Concord-Green Valley Fault system (to
the east) has only a 4.7% probability in the
same time period. No estimate has been
made for the West Napa Fault, which runs
through the center of the lower part of the
Napa Valley.

So it's best for everyone living in
Earthquake Country to be familiar with
quakes and how to prepare for, and deal
with, them. Here are websites with up-to-
date information.

Recent Earthquakes in California

http://quake.usgs.gov/recenteqs/latest.htm

Recent Earthquakes in San Francisco Bay
Area

http://quake.usgs.gov/recenteqs/Maps/San_Fra
ncisco.html

Shaking Amplification Potential of
Neighborhood Areas in City of Napa
www.abag.ca.gov/bayarea/eqmaps/gif11/napa-
mate.gif

Estimated Shaking Intensity for an
Earthquake of Magnitude 6.5 on the West
Napa Fault

In Napa
www.abag.ca.gov/bayarea/eqmaps/gif99/napana
pm.gif

Estimates Very Strong, Violent, and Very
Violent throughout most of Napa.

In Yountville
www.abag.ca.gov/bayarea/eqmaps/gif99/youn-
napm.gif

Estimates Very Strong throughout Yountville.

Estimated Shaking Intensity for an
Earthquake of Magnitude 6.7 on the
Concord-Green Valley Fault

In Napa
www.abag.ca.gov/bayarea/eqmaps/gif99/napac-
cgm.gif

Estimates Strong and Very Strong throughout
Napa.

Hazard maps for other Napa Valley towns can
be found at
www.abag.ca.gov/bayarea/eqmaps/pickcity.html

Association of Bay Area Governments (ABAG)
Earthquake Maps and Information

http://quake.abag.ca.gov/

Detailed information on all aspects of earthquakes, including things you can do before,
during and after.

Public School Districts

Napa County Office of Education

2121 Imola Avenue Napa CA 94559
707.253.6810
www.ncoe.k12.ca.us

Calistoga Joint Unified School District

1327 Berry St. Calistoga CA 94515
707.942.4703
www.calistoga.k12.ca.us

Howell Mountain School District

525 White Cottage Road Angwin CA 94508
707.965.2423
www.napanet.net/~hms

Napa Valley Unified School District (Napa, American Canyon, Yountville)

2425 Jefferson St. Napa CA 94558
707.253.3715
www.nvusd.k12.ca.us

Pope Valley Unified School District

6200 Pope Valley Road Pope Valley CA 94567
707.965.2402
www.popevalley.k12.napa.ca.us

St. Helena Unified School District

465 Main St. St. Helena CA 94574
707.967.2708
www.sthelena.k12.ca.us

Napa Valley College

2277 Napa-Vallejo Highway
Napa CA 94559
707.253.3000
www.napavalley.edu

Community Education

Napa Valley Adult School

1600 Lincoln Avenue
Napa CA 94558
707.253.3594
www.adulted.nvusd.k12.ca.us/
Offers evening and weekend classes in the city of Napa.

Napa Valley College

227 Napa-Vallejo Highway
Napa CA 94558
707.253.3000
www.napacommunityed.org/

Upvalley Campus
1088 College Avenue
St. Helena CA 94574
707.967.2900
Offers evening and weekend classes on a wide variety of subjects in St. Helena and Napa.

Napa Parks and Recreation

1100 West Street
Napa Ca 94559
707.257.9529
www.naparec.com
Offers recreation and special interest classes for adults and kids.

For a complete list of public and private school web sites, see
www.westsong.com/schools

Public Libraries

Napa City-County Library (Napa, Yountville, American Canyon, Calistoga)

www.mynapa.info/Library/

St. Helena Public Library

www.shpl.org/

Napa Neighbor

www.napavintners.com/community/napa_neigh bor.html

Napa Neighbor is a program of the Napa Valley Vintners Association. Many members of the Vintners Association offer special discounts, tours and complimentary wine tastings to you as a resident of the county—and sometimes to your guest as well. Just show your driver's license, if asked. Go to the web site to see a complete list of current winery members of the Napa Neighbors program.

Community-Supported Agriculture (CSA)

Local farms supported by subscribers that weekly receive boxes of (usually organic) fruits and vegetables. Costs vary (as do the size of the boxes) and range from $13 to $25 a week.

Riverdog Farm

PO Box 42 Guinda CA 95637
916.796.3802 Fax: 530.796.2222
riverdog@yolo.com

A 70-acre CSA organic farm in Guinda in Yolo County that has been delivering fresh produce to the Napa Valley since 1994. In fact they started in the valley. Deliver on Tuesdays, 51 weeks a year, to three locations in Napa, as well as Yountville, Oakville and St. Helena.

Organic Abundance (Organic Food Delivery)

Napa CA
707.251.5500
www.organicabundance.com

Regional organic produce delivered weekly or bimonthly to your home in Carneros,

Napa, Yountville, Oakville, Rutherford or St. Helena.

Health Food Stores

The valley has no large natural food store with an extensive produce section, but there are several health food stores with a good range of packaged foods, vitamins, minerals and other nutritional supplements. Several of them also have a limited amount of produce. You'll also find organic packaged food and produce sections at almost all of the valley's supermarkets.

Optimum Foods

633 Trancas Street, Napa CA 94558
707.224.1514
www.napanet.net/~optimum/

Nature Select Foods

1080 Main Street, St. Helena CA 94574
707.967.8545

Includes a juice bar.

Home Restaurant Delivery

Tired of pizza and Chinese food? Many Napa Valley restaurants, including some of its very finest, let you pick up food and take it home. In addition, here are two unique places in Napa where you can pick up quick Italian food to eat at home. And one service that will even pick up restaurant meals for you.

Depot Hotel Italian Dinners

806 Fourth St. Napa
707.252.4477

The hotel's long gone but the restaurant remains, and has been there since 1925. It's on the east side of Soscol Avenue just south of Third St., in back of the used car lot. Bring your own pot and take home pasta, including ravioli and malfatti. Bring plates and they'll load them up with your choices from their dinner menu, at menu prices. Just go around to the back door.

Lawler's Liquors

2232 Jefferson Napa
707.226.9311

A liquor store with a kitchen selling malfatti, ravioli, salad and French bread. Bring a container or they'll sell you a cheap plastic one.

Dine-in Deliveries Napa Valley

707.258.2833 Fax: 707.258.2847
www.dineinnapavalley.com

Meals from local restaurants delivered to your home, office or hotel room in Napa and Yountville.

Personal Chefs

If you don't want to cook *or* have restaurant food, there's a third option. A personal chef will work with you to develop a menu plan, then do all the shopping, cooking and cleanup. All you do when you come home from work is take a full meal out of the refrigerator or freezer, heat it and eat it. You get exactly the foods you like, in your own home. And there's no corkage fee.

Chef Lynn Martinez

707.554.1674

Chef Paul Obranovich

707.255.4100

Emergency Information

Emergency Phone Number

(Fire, police, ambulance)
Dial 911

Poison Control Center

800.523.2222

Hospitals/Medical Facilities

Queen of the Valley Hospital

1000 Trancas St. Napa CA 94558
707.252.4411
Emergency Room: 707.257.4038
www.thequeen.org

Kaiser Permanente (members only)

3285 Claremont Way Napa CA 94558
707.258.2500
Clinic only . No emergency room

St. Helena Hospital

PO Box 250 650 Sanitarium Road
Deer Park, CA 94576
707.963.3611
Emergency Room: 707.963.6425
www.sthelenahospital.org

Pharmacies

CALISTOGA

Silverado Pharmacy

1348 Lincoln Ave.
707.942.5115

ST. HELENA

Smith's St. Helena Pharmacy

1390 Railroad Ave. (Safeway Plaza)
707.963.2794

Vasconi Drugs

1381 Main Street
707.963.1444

NAPA

Family Drug

1805 Old Sonoma Road (corner of Jefferson Ave.)
707.224.7807

Long's Drugs

Three locations in Napa, all along Trancas Street at the north end of town.

3670 Bel Aire Plaza 707.255.2625
675 Trancas 707.252.4644
1558 Trancas 707.253.7906

Napa Valley Pharmacy

980 Trancas St. (in front of Queen of the Valley Hospital)
707.224.7887

Newspapers

Calistoga Tribune (weekly)

Mud City Weekender
1360 Lincoln Avenue Calistoga CA 94515
707.942.5181
calistogatribune@aol.com

Angwin Reporter (online only)

www.angwinreporter.com

Napa Sentinel (weekly)

1627 Lincoln Avenue Napa CA 94558
707.257.6272
www.napasentinel.com

Napa Valley Register (daily)

1615 Second St. Napa CA 94559
707.226.3711
www.napanews.com

St. Helena Star (weekly)

1328 Main Street St. Helena CA 94574
707.963.2731
www.sthelenastar.com

Weekly Calistogan (weekly)

1328 Main St. St. Helena, CA 94574
707.942.6242
www.weeklycalistogan.com

Yountville Sun (weekly)

6795 Washington St. Yountville CA 94599
707.944.5676

Radio Stations

KVON - 1440 AM (local news and weather)

www.kvon.com

KVYN - 99.3 FM (music)

www.kvyn.com

Television Stations

COMMERCIAL

There are no local commercial television stations. Main Bay Area stations are channels 3 (NBC), 5 (CBS) and 7 (ABC). PBS stations are Channels 9 and 22.

COMMUNITY

Napa Channel 28

Public Access TV
707.257.0574
www.channel28.org

Cable TV

Comcast

2260 Brown St.
Napa CA 94558
800.945.2288

Serves all cities in Napa County.

Babysitters

Bonded babysitters in your hotel room. Also for weddings and corporate events.

Cristie's

707.257.3748
www.cristies.com

Nannies of the Valley

707.251.8035
www.nanniesofthevalley.com

Petsitters

Even if you don't live in the Napa Valley, you might need a pet sitter. These services can come to your hotel or vacation home and look after Fido (or Fluffy). They can also care for your pet at their own facilities if you're just in the valley for the day. Contact them also for current information on hotels and inns that are dog-friendly.

Paws, Claws, Feathers and Fins
707.226.2805

Pet Buddy's
707.252.9506

Purr-Fect Pet Sitter and More
707.255-5294

Wine Country Pet Resort
1199 Cuttings Wharf Road
Napa CA 94559
707.252.7877
winecntrykennel@aol.com

Day boarding as well as overnight and long-term.

NOTES

Relocating to the Napa Valley

Whether you're moving your family or your entire company to the valley, here is some useful contact information.

Economic Development

Napa Valley Economic Development Corporation

433 Soscol Avenue, Suite B131
Napa, CA 94559
707.253.3212
www.nvedc.org

Chambers of Commerce

American Canyon Chamber of Commerce

3429 Broadway, Ste. C-1
American Canyon, CA. 94503
707.552.3650
www.amcanchamber.org

Calistoga Chamber of Commerce

1458 Lincoln Ave #9 Calistoga, CA 94515
707.942.6333 Fax 707.942.9287
www.calistogafun.com

Napa Chamber of Commerce

1556 First St. Napa CA 94559
707.226.7455
www.napachamber.org

The Napa Chamber offers a Relocation packet for $15 that includes maps, a business directory, and information on events, real estate, movers, education, employers, and much more.

St. Helena Chamber of Commerce

1010 Main Street Suite A
St. Helena CA 94574
707.963.4456 800.799.6456
www.sthelena.com

Yountville Chamber of Commerce

6516 Yount St. Yountville CA 94599
707.944.0904
www.yountville.com

Schools

The Napa Valley has a number of public school districts, with the largest covering Napa, Yountville and American Canyon. St. Helena and Calistoga have their own districts. The valley also offers private schools, religious as well as secular such as Montessori and Waldorf. Napa Valley College in Napa is a two-year community college and Pacific Union College in Angwin is operated by the Seventh Day Adventist church.

For a complete list of school web pages, see www.westsong.com/schools

Non-Profit Organizations

Community Foundation of the Napa Valley

www.cfnv.org

Napa County Hispanic Network

http://www.hispanicnetworkonline.com/

Napa Valley Coalition of Non Profits

1040 Main Street, Suite 305
Napa CA 94559
707.252.6301
www.napanonprofitcoalition.org

Over 70 agencies focusing on health and human services.

Real Estate

For a list of web pages for real estate agents and brokers, see
www.westsong.com/realestate

Cost of Real Estate

Looking for an inexpensive little country place in the wine country for a weekend home? Try the Napa Valley, where there's a home for every price range—as long as your price range starts around $400,000.

The median price for a home in Napa County is $420,000. Most new housing in the city of Napa starts at $500,000, but many new subdivisions are starting at $800,000. Housing is generally more expensive upvalley. Here are some current examples.

If you'd like a little something upvalley with vineyards, consider a 1,400 sq. ft. country house with 2 bedrooms, one bath, good views of the hills, a small farmworker's house and seven acres of award-winning Chardonnay. Take it away at $1.8 million.

Or perhaps you'd like a 1,700 sq. ft. home on 2.5 acres, secluded, good views, and an elegant 1,000 sq. ft. guest house. No vineyards, so it's only $1.1 million.

For something a little nicer, consider a 3,200 sq. ft. farmhouse built in 1910, a guest studio, a 1,500 sq. ft. caretaker's house, 15 acres already planted to a Bordeaux varietal, and 40 acres that can be planted, for a total of 160 acres. A steal at $5.9 million.

To turn unplanted land into vineyards will cost anywhere from $35-70,000 an acre, depending on the terrain. While you're waiting five years for those grapes to reach full maturity and produce money, you can build your own home, which these days can cost around $200-$250 per square foot. That's for a modest custom home. A high-end home could be as much as $600-$700 sq. ft., including such things as permitting and landscaping.

Just want a simple vineyard that's already producing? In the valley floor, that can be as much as $200,000 an acre for a well-known vineyard. It's cheaper on the hillsides; maybe only $125,00 an acre

Napa Valley Trivia

Napa Valley Movies

Napa Valley Film Commission

707.226.7459
sales@napavalley.org

Provides assistance to scouts and production companies, whether for feature-length films, TV or commercials.

The following movies were filmed in, or connected with, the Napa Valley)

Apocalypse Now (1979)

Director: Francis Ford Coppola (owner of Niebaum-Coppola Winery in Rutherford)

Marlon Brando, Robert Duvall, Martin Sheen, Sam Bottoms, Laurence Fishburne, Dennis Hopper, Harrison Ford.

Some exterior shots were done in the valley, particularly on the boat travelling upriver. Also, a former Napa High student reports that "The sound effects were done at Memorial Stadium using Napa High School students. We did a lot of yelling as a group for the riot scene with the USO. Several students were then kept after the group was released and were taped running on the steps and the grass with and without shoes."

The Bachelor, The (2002) (TV)

One full episode of this reality series.

Black Rain (1989)

Michael Douglas, Andy Garcia, Kate Capshaw.

Catholic School (1999)

Short documentary filmed at St. John's Catholic School in Napa

Deadly Harvest (1972) (TV)

Richard Boone, Michael Constantine, Patty Duke. Exterior scenes at a house just north of Yountville.

Dying Young (1991)

Julia Roberts, Colleen Dewhurst, Ellen Burstyn.

Encore! Encore! (1998) (TV)

Short-lived series starring Nathan Lane

Falconcrest (1981-1990) (TV)

Exterior winery shots filmed at Spring Mountain Winery in St. Helena and other locations throughout the valley.

Gates of Heaven (1978)

Documentary on *Bubbling Well Pet Memorial Park*, located just outside Napa.

Howard the Duck (1986)

Some scenes filmed at a now torn-down "restaurant" on the Carneros Highway just outside Napa.

Wells Fargo (1937)

Joel McCrea, Johnnie Mack Brown, Lloyd Nolan, Robert Cummings

Hunters Are For Killing (1970) (TV)

Martin Balsam, Melvyn Douglas, Suzanne Pleshette, Burt Reynolds, Larry Storch

Jack (1996)

Scene shot at St. Helena Elementary School

Killer Bees (1974) (TV)

Gloria Swanson, Kate Jackson.

Moonraker (1979)

Roger Moore.

Mumford (1999)

Scene shot in downtown St. Helena

My Old Man's Place (1972)

Once an Eagle (1976) (miniseries)

Pollyanna (1960)

Jane Wyman, Richard Egan, Karl Malden, Adolphe Menjou, Agnes Moorehead, Hayley Mills.

Shoot The Moon (1982)

Albert Finney, Diane Keaton.

They Knew What They Wanted (1940)

Tom Ewell, Charles Laughton, Carole Lombard, Karl Malden.

The Parent Trap (1998)

Portions were filmed at the Staglin Family Vineyard in Rutherford.

The Unholy Wife (1957)

Rod Steiger, Marie Windsor, Diana Dors.

This Earth is Mine (1959)

Rock Hudson, Jean Simmons, Claude Rains, Dorothy McGuire.

A Walk in the Clouds (1995)

Keanu Reeves, Anthony Quinn.

Extensive Napa Valley locations including: Mount Veeder Winery, Napa; Mayacamas Winery, Napa; Beringer Vineyards, St. Helena; Charles Krug Winery, St. Helena; Duckhorn Vineyards, St. Helena.

Wild in the Country (1961)

Elvis Presley, Tuesday Weld, John Ireland, Hope Lange, Gary Lockwood.

Bigfoot

Even Bigfoot allegedly visits the Napa Valley. The large, hairy creature, also known as a *Sasquatach* or *Yeti*, was reportedly seen a number of times in the Pope Valley area over the period 1978-1989.

Bigfoot was occasionally observed running in the distance. Other incidents involved footprints, screams and smells. It was described as about seven feet tall and covered head-to-toe with grayish-brown hair. One resident even stated that one "had tried to enter their house but was frightened away with a gun blast."

Sightings usually occurred in early evenings, but sometimes in the early morning just before daybreak.

Boysenberries

Boysenberries, a hybrid of blackberries, were developed in the 1920s in the Napa Valley by Rudolf Boysen. They were later popularized by Walter Knott at his farm stand in Buena Park, California that eventually became known as *Knott's Berry Farm*.

Invention of Loudspeaker

Edwin Pridham and Peter Jensen moved to Napa in 1911 and set up a research lab. They invented the "Magnavox" loudspeaker, the first public address system. Their first public demonstration was in San Francisco's Golden Gate Park on December 10, 1915. On December 25, they played music to a crowd of 100,000 people in front of San Francisco City Hall. Their Magnavox company gained national attention when they provided loudspeakers for a

1919 speech in San Diego by President Woodrow Wilson.

Tribute in downtown Napa's Dwight Murray Plaza to the inventors of the loudspeaker.

Mary Ellen Pleasant

Mary Ellen Pleasant is perhaps better known as "Mammy Pleasant", but it was a name she detested. She was born a slave in Georgia some time between 1814 and 1817, the illegitimate daughter of an enslaved Vodou priestess from Haiti and a Virginia governor's son, John Pleasants. She was bought out of slavery by a planter and indentured for nine years as a store clerk with abolitionist Quakers in Massachusetts.

Around 1841 she married a wealthy mulatto merchant/contractor from Ohio and Philadelphia named James Smith, who was also a slave rescuer on the Underground Railroad. The two worked to help slaves flee to safety in Canada and safe states. Smith died in 1844, leaving her a $45,000

fortune and a plantation run by freedmen near Harper's Ferry, Virginia.

Because of slaver reaction to her own ongoing Underground Railroad activities, she was forced to flee to New Orleans in 1850 where she met the Vodou queen Marie Laveau, who trained her in how to "pressure the powerful to help the powerless" —blacks and poor women—gain rights and jobs. She then went to San Francisco, arriving in April 1852. Because she had no "freedom papers" she passed herself off as white, while she worked as a steward and cook in a white boardinghouse and invested in real estate and various business activities.

Mary Ellen Pleasant (1814?-1904)

Pleasant's training with Marie Laveau proved beneficial. Pleasant became so successful at leveraging social change that many called her San Francisco's "Black City Hall". Her activities and her money helped ex-slaves avoid extradition, start businesses and find employment in hotels, homes and on the steamships and railroads of California.

In 1858 she returned to the East, bought land to house escaped slaves, and aided abolitionist John Brown both with money and by riding in advance of his famous raid at Harper's Ferry encouraging slaves to join him.

She went back to San Francisco where her investments with an influential business partner helped her amass a joint fortune estimated at $30 million. She later led the Franchise League movement in San Francisco that earned blacks the right to testify in court, and to ride the trolleys. Her lawsuit in 1868 in San Francisco against the North Beach and Mission RailRoad was used as a precedent in 1982 to achieve contemporary civil rights.

Mary Ellen Pleasant died in San Francisco in 1904. Her body was taken by friends to Napa and buried in Tulocay Cemetery. On her tombstone is inscribed "the mother of civil rights in California."

For more information, incuding a book on Mary Ellen Pleasant by Susheel Bibbs, see http://hometown.aol.com/mepleasant.

POW Camp

At the end of World War II, a farm labor camp on the Silverado Trail was converted to a camp for German prisoners of war. The camp was established to provide agricultural labor as many of the usual farmworkers were away on duty with the military.

The POW camp was located north of Yountville on the east side of the Trail, where Rector Creek flows down from Rector Dam. The compound was surrounded by barbed wire, had lookout towers with machine-guns and searchlights, and was patrolled by heavily-armed guards. Every day, just after dawn, the prisoners were loaded into open trucks and taken to work in prune orchards and vineyards in the valley.

The first 250 German POWs did not arrive until August 14, 1945, over three months after the surrender of Germany, and the same day the Japanese agreed to unconditional surrender.

As an interesting sidenote, during the war German and Italian "enemy" aliens *and citizens* (All Japanese-Americans had been moved to camps east of the Sierra Mountains) were not allowed within a certain distance from the California coast. The line went approximately through the middle of the Napa Valley. The result was that one German-American resident of the valley, a baker, found his home on one side of the line and his bakery on another. After a number of confrontations, he was finally allowed to pass freely between his home and his workplace.

Shipbuilding During World War II

From 1940 to the end of the war, Basalt Rock Company's Steel Division built 115 barges and 40 other ships for the U. S. Navy. The shipyard was located south of the city of Napa on the Napa River, where Napa Pipe Corporation is located today. (You can see the facilities when looking north from the Butler Bridge, which carries Highway 29 over the river.) Ships were as large as 1,700 tons and included self-propelled freighters and fuel oil tankers. LSTs (tank landing ships) were also repaired at the shipyard.

Valleys of Napa County

You thought Napa County had only one valley? Guess again. How about 97? That's the count of valleys designated by the United States Geological Survey. Of course 73 of these are small enough to be called canyons, but that still leaves 24 full-fledged valleys.

Next time you're driving through Napa County, don't just visit the Napa Valley. Track down one of these other valleys, too. Some are easy to find. Others? Well, see for yourself.

Valley Name

American Canyon, Anderson Canyon, Apple Tree Canyon.

Bear Canyon, Bear Valley, Bell Canyon, Browns Valley, Brushy Canyon, Bull Canyon, Burrell Canyon, Butts Canyon.

Campbell Canyon, Capell Valley, Carneros Valley, Cedar Canyon, Cedar Valley, Cherry Valley, Chimney Canyon, Coleman Canyon, Congress Valley, Conn Valley.

Daglia Canyon, Dardon Canyon, Decke Canyon, Devils Canyon, Dutch Henry Canyon.

East Bull Canyon, East Chapman Canyon, East Mitchel Canyon, Elder Valley.

Fir Canyon, Foss Valley.

Gordon Valley, Gosling Canyon, Government Trail Canyon, Green Canyon.

Harris Canyon, Heath Canyon, Hoisting Works Canyon, Husman Canyon.

Italian Valley.

Jackson Canyon, Jameson Canyon, Jericho Canyon, Johnson Canyon.

Kidd Canyon, Kimball Canyon, Kortum Canyon, Kreuse Canyon.

Lion Canyon, Little Portuguese Canyon, Little Valley, Long Canyon, Lovall Valley.

Markley Canyon, Mill Valley, Milliken Canyon, Mysterious Valley.

Napa Valley, Negro Canyon.

Oil Well Canyon.

Pickle Canyon, Pope Valley, Portuguese Canyon, Pratt Valley.

Quarry Canyon.

Rector Canyon, Redwood Canyon, Right-Hand Canyon.

Sage Canyon, Segassia Canyon, Seventy Acre Canyon, Simmons Canyon, Snell Valley, Soda Canyon, Soda Valley, South Fork Tully Canyon, Spanish Valley, Spring Valley, Steel Canyon, Steele Canyon, Stone Trough Canyon, Sulphur Canyon, Swartz Canyon.

Tin Can Canyon, Toll Canyon, Tully Canyon.

Wallet Canyon, West Bull Canyon, West Chapman Canyon, West Mitchel Canyon, Wildcat Canyon, Wing Canyon, Wood Canyon, Wooden Valley, Wragg Canyon.

NOTES

Wedding Planning

If you're looking for somewhere to get married, you've come to the right place. Thousands of weddings are performed in the churches, hills and vineyards of this beautiful area.

The valley provides all the resources you'll need to launch your married life. Whether your entourage is two or 2,000, accommodations and services are available to make your wedding and reception a festive and memorable event.

Caterers can cater; hotels can lodge; limousines can transport; restaurants can provide nourishment; wineries can provide wine and settings; photographers can record with photos, film or video; travel agencies can get friends and relatives here and back home again; and of course ministers, priests, rabbis and justices of the peace can provide religious or secular ceremonies. And wedding organizers can organize the whole thing.

Oh yes, and masseuses, masseurs and other spa staff can help you recover from the ordeal.

We invite you to have your wedding in the Napa Valley. It worked for us.

NOTE: The Napa Chamber of Commerce offers a Wedding packet for $15 that includes maps, a visitor guide, magazines, and information on things to do, wedding services, coordinators, sites, lodging and much more. Contact them at 707.226.7455 or www.napachamber.org.

CAKES

Alexis Baking Company
1517 Third Street
Napa CA 94559
707.258.1827

Butter Cream Bakery
2297 Jefferson Street
Napa CA 94558
707.255.6700

Exquisite Desserts
Napa
707.251.8368
sherri@exquisitedesserts.com

Gillwood's Bakery
1320 First Street
Napa CA 94559
707.253.0409

Model Bakery
1357 Main Street
St. Helena CA 94574
707.963.8192

Schat's Bakkerij
1353 Lincoln Avenue
Calistoga CA 94515
707.942.0777
www.schats-bakery.com

Sweet Finale
1146 Main Street
Napa CA 94559
707.224.2444
www.sweetfinale.com

Sweetie Pies
520 Main Street
Napa CA 94559
707.257.8817
www.sweetiepies.com

CANDLES

Hurd Beeswax Candles
1255 Lincoln Avenue
Calistoga CA 94515
707.963.7211
www.hurdbeeswaxcandles.com

Napa Valley Candle Factory & Gift Shop
3037 California Blvd.
Napa CA 94558
707.255.0902

CATERERS

All Seasons
1400 Lincoln Avenue
Calistoga CA 94515
707.942.9111

Best Enterprises
Best BBQ Catering
PO Box 10489 Napa
707.952.5956
bestbbq@telocity.com

Melissa Teaff Catering
707.954.8160
www.melissateaffcatering.com

Michelle's Gourmet Catering
707.254.7071

Pairs Catering
707.942.5483

Napa Gardens
PO Box 2598
Yountville, CA 94599
707.945.0458

Piper Johnson Catering
2450 Foothill Boulevard #G
Calistoga CA 94515
707.942.5432

Wine Valley Catering
707.258.0403

FLOWERS

Beau Fleurs Flower Company
1006 First St.
Napa CA 94559
707.224.7993

Claudia "K" Florists & Gifts
1104 Adams Street
St. Helena CA 94574
707.963.3101

Garaventa's Florists & Gifts
851 Lincoln Avenue
Napa CA 94558
707.255.8878   800.826.7566

Karol Cummins Flowers
1794 Oak Street
Napa CA 94559
707.257.8189

Michael Holmes Designs
2292 Monticello Road
Napa CA 94558
707.226.3655

St. Helena Florist
1340 Railroad Avenue
St. Helena CA 94574
707.963.4048

Tesoro
649 Main Street
St. Helena CA 94574
707.963.3316
www.tessoroflowers.com

Wine Country Florist and Gift
4211 Solano Avenue
Napa CA 94558
707.224.0667

FORMAL WEAR

Craig Williamson Menswear
3204 Jefferson
Napa CA 94558
707.224.5284

Mario's Mens Clothing
1223 Main St.
St. Helena CA 94574
707.963.1603

President Tuxedo
1349 Napa Town Center
Napa CA 94559
707.224.1750

LOCATIONS

Also see our Lodging section for resorts, hotels and spas

di Rosa Preserve
5200 Carneros Highway
Napa CA 94559
707.226.5991

First Presbyterian Church
1333 Third Street
Napa CA 94559
707.224.8693

Napa Elks Lodge
2840 Soscol Avenue
Napa CA 94558
707.255.4522

Napa Valley Aloft
PO Box 2500
Yountville, CA 94599
707.944.8638

Napa Valley Balloons
6795 Washington Street
Yountville, CA 94599
800/253-2224

Napa Valley Exposition
575 Third Street
Napa CA 94559
707.253.4900

Unity in Napa Valley
1249 Coombs Street
Napa CA 94559
707.255.6881

Yountville Community Hall
6550 Yount Street
Yountville CA 94599
707.944.2959

MINISTERS

Minister Jacqueline
Non-Denominational Ordained Minister
PO Box 723
Calistoga CA 94515
707.355.0850
www.winecountryminister.com

MUSIC AND ENTERTAINMENT

California Music Express
707.257.1697

David Auerbach
PO Box 2117
Napa CA 94558
707.224.4222
Custom Music on Fifty Rare Instruments

Fran Fanelli
202 Manor Ct.
American Canyon, CA 94589
707.557-2758

Harp music for all occasions

Napa Valley Musicians
www.napamusic.com

North Bay Entertainment
5 Financial Plaza, Suite 120
Napa CA 94558
707.224.0241
Music, Magic & Mime

OmniMod DJ Service
Napa
707.257.1206
www.napanet.net/~omnimod

Phoenix Entertainment
PO Box 55
Calistoga CA 94515
707.942.9058

PARTY SERVICES

Napa Valley Party Services
365 La Fata Street
St. Helena CA 94574
707.963.8001

Wine Country Party
1924 Yajome Street
Napa CA 94559
707.252.0711

PHOTOGRAPHERS

Art & Clarity
707.257.1166 800.776.7468
www.artclarity.com

Berdon Photography
PO Box 5147
Napa CA 94581
707.252.3076

Blain Ross Productions
2560 Jefferson Street
Napa, CA. 94558
707.226.7769

Bruce Miller Photography
1732 Jefferson Suite 10
Napa CA 94559
707.253.9205

**C&C TV Productions
(Video)**
321 Kingsly Lane
American Canyon, CA 94589
707.557.8548

CAV Media (Video)
1125 Lincoln Avenue
Napa CA 94558
707.255.9467

Creative Focus
2422 Rigdon Street
Napa CA 94558
707.255.3550

Donna Ghiringhelli
707.226.6820

Donna Olmstead
707.251.5725
www.napaphotos.com/olm-
stead.html

Eyeris Photographic
1406 Third St. #1
Napa, Ca 94559
707 254 7659

"I Do" Photography
707.258.0526

Jaeger Photographics
1222 Darling St.
Napa CA 94558
707.265.9001

Jane Russon Photography
PO Box 884
Napa CA 94559
707.253.9080

Leigh Milleur Photography
PO Box 322
Calistoga CA 94515
707.942.5259
www.napavalleyphotography.com

Lightworks Photography
1725 Third Street
Napa CA 94559
707.252.4172

**Margretha Lane
Photography**
1545 Oak Street
Napa CA 94558
707.255.2234

Nanci Kerby
PO Box 283
Napa CA 94559
www.napaphotos.com/nker-
by.html

**Photographers of the Wine
Country**
www.napaphotos.com

Photos by Marissa
187 Kreuzer Lane
Napa CA 94558
707.253.8540

Rebecca Pronchick
707.253.8733
www.napaphotos.com/becca.
html

Saribalis-Cole Photography
707.226.5101

PRINTING AND
ENGRAVING

Napa Printing & Graphics
1701 Soscol Avenue
Napa CA 94559
707.257.6555

Prints Charming
1303 First Street
Napa CA 94559
707.257.3646

Silverado Engraving
PO Box 5786
Napa CA 94581
707.257.0236

Sir Speedy Printing Center
PO Box 6977
Napa CA 94581
707.252.0383

TOUR/EVENT
ORGANIZERS

**Apples & Oranges Event
Planning**
707.254.8980

Wine & Dine Tours
P.O. Box 513
St. Helena CA 94574
707.963.8930 800.WINETOUR

WEBSITES

WeddingGuest.com
PO Box 4133
Napa, CA 94558
www.weddingguest.com

Custom wedding websites

WEDDING CONSULTANTS, ORGANIZERS AND OFFICIANTS

Affectionate Arrangements

1149 Rancho Drive
Napa CA 94558
707.253.7026

All Great Occasions

P. O. Box 419
Napa CA 94559
707.258.8006
Email: kbailey@napanet.net

Apples & Oranges Event Planning

707.254.8980

The Main Event

PO Box 3827
Napa CA 94558
707.253.8160

Napa Valley Weddings— Caroline Templeton

PO Box 6376
Napa CA 94581
707.224.1824
jctempleton@csi.com

Personalized Weddings by Kim

PO Box 6492
Napa CA 94581
707.253.1492

Shirley Tedeschi— Weddings and Events Consultant

P.O. Box 54
Rutherford, CA 94573
707.963.8447

Steven Russon— Wedding Officiant

707.224.8177

Wedding Ministries/Enchanting Elopements

3416 Yount Avenue
Napa CA 94558
707.252.1156

Weddings by Darlene

1357 Napa Town Center
Napa CA 94559
707.255.4161

Wine Country Weddings

6795 Washington Street
Yountville, CA 94599
707.945.1314

California State Historical Landmarks

Courtesy of the Office of Historic Preservation - California Department of Parks and Recreation
http://ohp.parks.ca.gov

No. 359 **OLD BALE MILL** - This historic gristmill was erected by Dr. E.T. Bale, grantee of Carne Humana Rancho, in 1846. The mill, with surrounding land, was deeded to the Native Sons of the Golden West by Mrs. W. W. Lyman, and was restored through the efforts of the Native Son Parlors of Napa County.

LOCATION: Bale Grist Mill State Historic Park, Hwy 29, 3369 N St. Helena Hwy, 3 mi NW of St. Helena

No. 547 **CHILES MILL** - Joseph Ballinger Chiles, who first came to California in 1841, erected the mill on Rancho Catacula 1845-56. The first American flour mill in Northern California, it was still in use in the 1880s. Chiles served as a vice president of the Society of California Pioneers, 1850-53.

LOCATION: SW corner on hillside, Chiles and Pope Rd and Lower Chiles Valley Rd, 3.6 mi N on Hwy 128, Chiles Valley

No. 563 **CHARLES KRUG WINERY** - Founded in 1861 by Charles Krug (1825-1892), this is the oldest operating winery in Napa Valley. The pioneer winemaker of this world-famous region, Krug made the first commercial wine in Napa County at Napa in 1858.

LOCATION: Krug Ranch, 2800 Main St, St. Helena

No. 564 **GEORGE YOUNT BLOCK-HOUSE** - In this vicinity stood the log block-house constructed in 1836 by George Calvert Yount, pioneer settler in Napa County. Nearby was his adobe house, built in 1837, and across the bridge were his grist and saw mills, erected before 1845. Born in North Carolina in 1794, Yount was a trapper, rancher, and miller. He became grantee of the Rancho Caymus and La Jota. He died in Yountville in 1865.

LOCATION: NE corner of Cook Rd and Yount Mill Rd, 1 mi N of Yountville

No. 565 **PETER LASSEN GRAVE** - In memory of Peter Lassen, the pioneer who was killed by the Indians April 27, 1859, at 66 years of age.

LOCATION: 2550 Wingfield Rd via Richmond Rd, 5 mi SE of Susanville

No. 682 **SITE OF YORK'S CABIN, CALISTOGA** - Among the first houses in this area was John York's log cabin, constructed in October 1845. Rebuilt as part of the home of the Kortum family, it was used as a residence until razed in 1930. Nearby was the cabin of David Hudson, also built in October 1845. Calistoga was named by Samuel Brannan.

LOCATION: SW corner Hwy 29 (Foothill Blvd) and Lincoln Ave, Calistoga

No. 683 **SITE OF HUDSON CABIN, CALISTOGA** - David Hudson was one of the early pioneers who helped develop the upper portion of Napa Valley by purchasing land, clearing it, and planting crops and building homes. Hudson built his cabin in October 1845.

LOCATION: NE corner of Hwy 29 (Foothill Blvd) and Lincoln Ave, Calistoga

No. 684 **SAM BRANNAN STORE, CALIS-TOGA** - Sam Brannan arrived in Napa Valley in the late 1850s and purchased a square mile of land at the foot of Mount St. Helena. This is the store he built, in which he made $50,000 in one year.

LOCATION: NW corner of Wappo Ave and Grant St, 203 Wapoo Ave, Calistoga

No. 685 **SAM BRANNAN COTTAGE, CALISTOGA** - Sam Brannan arrived in Napa Valley in the late 1850s with the dream of making it the "Saratoga of California." In 1866 cottages were built and palm trees planted in preparation for the grand opening of the resort. This is the only cottage still standing.

LOCATION: 1311 Washington St, Calistoga

No. 686 **SITE OF KELSEY HOUSE, CAL-ISTOGA** - Nancy Kelsey arrived in California in 1841 with the Bidwell-Bartleson party and settled with her family south of present-day Calistoga. Now the hearthstone is all that can be seen of the house. The property is owned by the Rockstrohs.

LOCATION: 500 ft NW of intersection of State Hwy 29 and Diamond Mtn Rd, 1.1 mi S of Calistoga

No. 687 **NAPA VALLEY RAILROAD DEPOT, CALISTOGA** - The Napa Valley Railroad depot, now the Southern Pacific depot, was built in 1868. Its roundhouse across Lincoln Avenue is gone. On its first trip, this railroad brought people to Calistoga for the elaborate opening of Brannan's summer resort in October 1868.

LOCATION: 1458 Lincoln Ave, Calistoga

No. 693 **GRAVE OF GEORGE C. YOUNT** - George Calvert Yount (1794-1865) was the first United States citizen to be ceded a Spanish land grant in Napa Valley (1836).

Skilled hunter, frontiersman, craftsman, and farmer, he was the true embodiment of all the finest qualities of an advancing civilization blending with the existing primitive culture. Friend to all, this kindly host of Caymus Rancho encouraged sturdy American pioneers to establish ranches in this area, so it was well populated before the gold rush.

LOCATION: George C. Yount Pioneer Cemetery, Lincoln and Jackson Sts, Yountville

No. 710 **ROBERT LOUIS STEVENSON STATE PARK** - In the spring of 1880, Robert Louis Stevenson brought his bride to Silverado. He and Fannie Osbourne Stevenson lived here from May 19 until July, while he gathered the notes for Silverado Squatters.

LOCATION: Hwy 29 (P.M. 45.5), 75 mi NE of Calistoga

No. 814 **BERINGER BROTHERS WINERY** - Built by Frederick and Jacob Beringer, natives of Mainz, Germany, this winery has the unique distinction of never having ceased operations since its founding in 1876. Here, in the European tradition, were dug underground wine tunnels hundreds of feet in length. These maintain a constant temperature of 58 degrees, a factor considered necessary in the maturing and aging of fine wines.

LOCATION: 2000 Main St, St. Helena

No. 828 **VETERANS HOME OF CALI-FORNIA** - This home for California's aged and disabled veterans was established in 1884 by Mexican War veterans and members of the Grand Army of the Republic. In January 1897, the Veterans Home Association deeded the home and its 910 acres of land to the state, which has since maintained it.

LOCATION: SW corner of California Dr and Hwy 29, Yountville

No. 878 **FIRST PRESBYTERIAN CHURCH BUILDING** - Designed by pioneer architects R. H. Daley and Theodore Eisen, this church is an outstanding example of late Victorian Gothic architectural styling. It is the best surviving example in this region of the early works associated with Eisen, who later became an important Southern California architect. The church has been in continuous use since its construction in 1874, longest pastorates were those of Richard Wylie and Erwin Bollinger.

LOCATION: 1333-3rd St between Randolph and Franklin Sts, Napa

No. 939 **TWENTIETH CENTURY FOLK ART ENVIRONMENTS (THEMATIC) - LITTO** - This is one of California's exceptional Twentieth Century Folk Art Environments. Over a period of 30 years, Emanuele "Litto" Damonte (1896-1985), with the help of his neighbors, collected more than 2,000 hubcaps. All around Hubcap Ranch are constructions and arrangements of hubcaps, bottles, and pulltops that proclaim that "Litto, the Pope Valley Hubcap King," was here.

LOCATION: 6654 Pope Valley Rd (P.M. 14.3), 2.1 mi NW of Pope Valley

NOTES

History of Napa County

Courtesy of the Napa County Historical Society,
1219 First Street, Napa CA 94559
(in the Goodman Building)
707.224.1739

2000 B.C. - 1823 A.D.

The Wappo Indians are the sole inhabitants of the Napa Valley.

1823

DON FRANCIS CASTRO and Father JOSE ALTIMURA, under an armed escort led by JOSE SANCHEZ, are the first Europeans to explore the Napa Valley.

182?

Sometime during this decade, GUY FLING becomes the first American to explore the Napa Valley.

1829

KIT CARSON enters the Napa Valley while on a hunting trip.

1831

GUY FLING leads Napa County's first settler, GEORGE C. YOUNT, into the Napa Valley.

1836

The first treaty between the natives and the Mexicans is negotiated.

GEORGE C. YOUNT is awarded the first land grant in the Napa Valley, Rancho Caymus. YOUNT built the area's first permanent dwelling, a wooden blockhouse.

1837

DR. EDWIN TURNER BALE (Bale Mill) arrives in California from England.

1838

A smallpox epidemic rages through Napa County, killing hundreds of Wappo Indians.

1839

Dr. Bale marries MARIA IGNACIA SOBERANES, niece of General Mariano Vallejo.

1840

CAYETANO JUAREZ builds two adobes on his Rancho Tulucay and moves his family from Sonoma to Napa Valley.

1841

DR. EDWIN TURNER BALE becomes a citizen of Mexico and is granted Rancho Carne Humana, which comprises the land between present-day Rutherford and Calistoga.

1844

Colonel JOSEPH B. CHILES, who guided one of the earliest immigrant trains to California, is granted Rancho Catacula in the Napa Valley.

The first landing of a ship in what will become Napa City. The ship is called the Sacramento.

1846

The Bale Grist Mill is completed.

COLONEL JAMES CLYMAN, mountain man, arrives in the Napa Valley with his wife, HANNAH and the REASON P. TUCKER family. When DONNER (of the Donner Party) refused to listen to CLYMAN about the danger of following the planned shortcut, CLYMAN and TUCKER came by the longer established trail.

Reason P. Tucker leads one of the relief parties when the Donner Party becomes trapped in a Sierra snowfall. Other Napa settlers aid in rescuing the survivors.

John C. Fremont camps in Sacramento. He is bound for Sonoma to revolt against Mexican rule. In Napa he is joined by John Grigsby, William Hargrave, David Hudson, Harrison Pierce, Elias Barnett, Nathan Coombs and Benjamin and Samuel Kelsey. Two days later, Nancy Kelsey (the first white woman to enter California over the Sierras) travels to Sonoma on horseback with her small infants, following her husband, Benjamin.

The Bear Flag Rebellion takes place in Sonoma and the Bear Flag party is formed.

The California Republic, with the Bear Flag as its symbol, comes to an end in less than sixty days, when California becomes a territory of the United States.

1847

The Town of Napa is founded by NATHAN COOMBS. The townsite is surveyed by James M. Hudspeth. At the time there are only the two adobe homes of CAYETANO JUAREZ and Nicholas Higuera in the area.

Napa's first structure, a saloon, is built by HARRISON PIERCE. a former miller at Bales Mill.

1848

The first general store is built in Napa township by JOSEPH P. THOMPSON, followed closely by a second general store built by GEN. MARIANO VALLEJO and his son-in-law, JOHN FRISBIE.

JAMES MARSHALL discovers gold at Sutter's Mill in Sacramento. Napa City is deserted as residents flocked to the mines. Most of the valley farmers stay on their land.

1849

Napa County is formed as one of California's original counties.

DOCTOR EDWARD TURNER BALE dies on 9 October.

The first school (the second private school in California) is opened in the Napa Valley near Bale's Mill. The teacher is the widowed and orphaned SARAH GRAVES FOSDICK, a survivor of the DONNER Party. She has been brought to Napa Valley by her rescuer, REASON P. TUCKER.

1850

The Dolphin is the first steamship to navigate the Napa River.

The first election in Napa County is held. The officers of the new government are: Judge, JOHN E. STARK; Coroner, FLORENTINE E. KELLOGG; Surveyor, J. E. BROWN; Sheriff, N. Mckimmey; Treasurer, RALPH KILBURN.

1852

JACOB SCHRAM buys hillside property just south of Calistoga and plants Napa County's first hillside vineyard. He hires Chinese workers to plant and cultivate the vines under the supervision of his wife, ANNA, while he continues his trade as a barber in Calistoga and White Sulphur Springs.

1853-1865

A drought strikes the Napa Valley.

1853

The newly elected board of supervisors, JOHN HAMILTON, JESSE WHILTON, and FLORENTINE A. KELLOGG, holds its first meeting in the town of Napa on 6 December.

The townships of Napa, Yount and Hot Springs are created.

The community of St Helena is established.

Napa Valley's first church building is erected on property owned by Florentine Kellogg. It is Methodist in denomination and is called The White Church after ASA WHITE, a friend of KELLOGG's and the man who delivers the first sermon.

1856

The *Napa County Reporter* opens its doors as the county's first newspaper. The first edition is printed on 4 July by ALEXANDER J. COX, editor and proprietor.

1858

A silver rush occurs in Napa County, and the mining era begins.

The first Catholic Church erected in Napa Valley, St John the Baptist, is dedicated by ARCHBISHOP ALLEMANY on 6 November.

CHARLES KRUG produces 1,200 gallons of wine in the Napa Valley using a small cider press.

A telegraph line between Vallejo and Napa is laid.

The first bank is established by J. H. GOODMAN.

The Methodist Episcopal Church is built at 2nd and Randolph on land donated by NATHAN COOMBS.

1859

SAM BRANNAN purchases land in the upper Napa Valley; the purchase includes the land on which Calistoga will be developed.

Tulocay Cemetery is established on 48 and 4/5 acres given by DON CAYETANO JUAREZ.

1860

CHARLES KRUG marries DR. BALE'S daughter, CAROLINE. KRUG plants grapes on land just north of St. Helena, on land that had been CAROLINE'S dowry.

The Napa Collegiate Institute opens, the forerunner of the University of the Pacific in Stockton.

  Cinnabar (mercury ore) is discovered in the Mayacamas range northwest of Calistoga, by J. Cyrus and A. J. Bailey.

1861

The Phoenix Mining Company is organized to extract mercury from cinnabar.

A severe winter hits the Napa Valley exterminating most of the area's cattle herds.

1863

The *Napa Register* begins publication.

1864

The Napa Valley Railroad begins operation. The track runs from Vallejo to Calistoga, making stops at Napa, Yountville, Oakville, Rutherford, Bello, St. Helena, Barro, Bale

An early steam train in the Napa Valley, date unknown. Photo courtesy of Napa County Historical Society.

and Walnut Grove. When the passengers debark at the end of the line, Mount St. Helena rises majestically before them.

Napa County becomes one of California's leading quicksilver (mercury) producers.

1865

GEORGE YOUNT, Napa County's first Anglo settler, dies at his home at Caymus Ranch on 5 Oct.1866.

JOHN LAWLEY begins his toll road from Calistoga over Mount St. Helena to Lake County.

1867

The telegraph line to Napa is extended from Napa to Calistoga.

The Napa City Gas Light Company is incorporated to provide lighting on the streets of Napa; Napa becomes the tenth city in California to be lit by gas.

1869

F. A. Sawyer establishes Sawyer Tanning Company as a wool pullery. A year later his father, B. F. Sawyer leaves Newport, New Hampshire, comes west and goes into business with his son.

1870

The first library in Napa is opened by the Napa Library Association. It holds 1000 volumes.

1872

The Town of Napa is incorporated.

1873

The Seventh Day Adventist Church is organized in Napa.

1874

The Town of Napa is reincorporated as the City of Napa.

The First Presbyterian Church is erected on land donated by NATHAN COOMBS.

The *St. Helena Star* is founded.

EADWEARD MUYBRIDGE, the "Father of the Motion Picture", is tried in the City of Napa for the murder of his wife's lover. He is acquitted.

1875

The St. Helena Viticultural Club is organized with CHARLES KRUG as its first president.

1876

The Napa State Asylum for the Insane receives its first patients.

1877

The Calistogan is founded.

JACOB and FREDERICK BERINGER establish the Beringer Bros. Winery.

1878

The St. Helena Sanitarium is founded by W. A. PRATT, a member of the Seventh Day Adventist faith. Natural healing is stressed.

Frederick Beringer, cofounder of Beringer Vineyards. Photo courtesy of Wine Institute.

Jacob Beringer, cofounder of Beringer Vineyards in 1876. Photo courtesy of Wine Institute.

1879

The Bale Grist Mill grinds grain with its 36-foot waterwheel for the last time.

1880

At 9:20 a.m. on 23 May, ROBERT LOUIS STEVENSON and FANNIE VANDERGIFF OSBOURNE board the Napa Valley Railroad day coach in Vallejo and begin the forty-two mile journey to Calistoga. They spend their unconventional honeymoon in a rustic, abandoned shack at the defunct Silverado Mine. They make friends with JACOB SCHRAM and ANNA, his wife, visiting them at their secluded vineyard home, and tasting all eighteen wines produced by the Schrams.

1881

COLONEL JAMES CLYMAN, aged 88, dies and is buried in the Tulocay Cemetery in Napa.

1883

Silverado Squatters and *Treasure Island* by ROBERT LOUIS STEVENSON is published. The road to the SCHRAM's Vineyard is described in the former, Mount St Helena is Treasure Island's Spyglass Hill and JOHN SILVERADO is the inspiration for Long John Silver.

The Napa City Water Company is founded by SAMUEL HOLDEN.

CAYETANO JUAREZ dies and is buried in the Tulocay Cemetery on land he had donated to the City of Napa.

1884

The San Francisco Chapter of the Grand Army of the Republic (GAR) establishes the Veteran's Home. The facilities consist of a kitchen, a dining room, living quarters, sick wards, an office and a chapel.

1885

Southern Pacific Railroad takes over operation of Napa Valley's railroad.

1888

The Palisades Mine begins operation.

1891

CHARLES KRUG dies.

1893

Half of the vineyards in the Napa Valley become infested with the root louse, phylloxera.

County's first high school opens in the St Helena Presbyterian Church.

1894

St. Helena Library opens.

1897

The State of California assumes administration of the California Veteran's Home.

Napa High School is constructed.

Last public hanging in California is at Napa Courthouse. Billie Roe is hanged for the 1891 murder in Napa of Lucina Greenwood.

1901

On May 2, the Goodman Library is opened on property gifted by GEORGE E. GOODMAN. He had been Napa County Treasurer from 1861-1870.

1902

The Calistoga Free Public Library opens.

The Napa Valley Railroad Company, an electric railroad, is incorporated and provides service from Benicia to Calistoga.

1903

The Napa Glove Factory is organized. It is the largest glove factory west of Chicago.

1909

500,000 fruit and nut trees are established in the valley by this date.

Pacific Union College, formerly established in Healdsburg, is moved to Angwin. The dedication of the grounds of the accredited four-year liberal arts institution is held on 29 September.

1910

The Shurtleff Hospital, Napa City's first hospital, opens. It is named after DR. BENJAMIN SHURTLEFF.

1915

The loudspeaker is invented in Napa by EDWIN PRIDHAM and PETER JENSEN while they are working to improve the telephone receiver.

1916

The County Library System is established to service outlying communities who have no libraries.

1917

BRUCE LAND of Napa becomes the first Napa County resident drafted in World War I.

A second hospital, the Francis Hospital, is built in Napa.

1920

Prohibition becomes law. Many Napa Valley wineries go out of business.

The Shurtleff and the Francis hospitals are replaced by the Victory Memorial Hospital.

1922

The LAWLEY toll road is purchased by the county. It becomes State Highway 29.

1923

The construction of Millikan Dam is begun.

Calistoga High School opens.

1924

The Napa State Asylum for the Insane is renamed Napa State Hospital.

GIUSEPPE MUSANTE first bottles water. His company will be the forerunner of the Calistoga Mineral Water Company.

1929

Passenger train service ends in the Napa Valley.

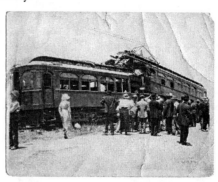

While this wasn't the reason train service in the valley ended, it shows things didn't always go smoothly. Date unknown. Courtesy of Napa County Historical Society.

A hospital is built on the grounds of the Veteran's Home.

1932

The Christian Brothers move their novitiate and winemaking operation to the Napa Valley.

1933

Prohibition is repealed.

1939

By this date the Sawyer Tanning Company of Napa is the largest tannery west of the Mississippi.

1942

Basalt Rock Company of Napa launches two U. S. Navy tankers on the Napa River.

1948

Conn Dam is completed.

1950'S

Controversial plans announced to flood the Berryessa Valley and community of Monticello as part of the Bureau of

Recreation State Water Project. Lake Berryessa is to be used as a recreation area.

1953

5,500,000 gallons of wine are produced in the Napa Valley.

1958

Queen of the Valley Hospital replaces Victory Memorial Hospital.

1963

Over 500,000 people visit the Napa Valley's wineries.

1968

The Calistoga Soaring Center opens.

The County Board of Supervisors create agricultural preserve zoning restrictions.

1974

The Napa Valley Genealogical and Biographical Society is formed. A library is established and quarters are rented to house the collection.

1976-1977

A severe drought strikes the Napa Valley (and all of California). Water rationing takes place in several of the county's communities.

1980

Voters approve Measure A saving agriculture by restricting residential growth in the unincorporated areas to 1% a year.

1981

The Calistoga Mineral Water Company is purchased by the French firm, Perrier.

Atlas Peak fire consumes 23,600 acres, leading to $36 million in property loss and destroys 31 residences and 36 outbuildings.

1983

Over 400,000 people tour the Christian Brothers Greystone Winery.

1985

The seventieth anniversary of the invention of the loudspeaker in Napa is celebrated.

The *Napa Valley Times* issues its inaugural edition on July 25.

The premiere edition of the *Napa Sentinel* is published on September 20.

The Napa Valley Wine Train begins its first run in December.

1986

In mid-February, continuous rain floods valley communities and inundates the vineyards, about a decade after the area experienced a severe drought.

A temporary shelter is provided for the homeless in the Presbyterian Church gym. The Napa Valley Shelter Project is formed in the fall of the year.

1988-1991

After an historic fundraising effort, the Napa Valley Genealogical and Biographical Society closes escrow on a property located on Menlo Avenue at California in Napa. On 1 April, the Napa Valley Genealogical Library opens for researchers.

1996

The New Technology High school opens in Napa with 130 students. This unique school is established to respond to the challenges to the educational system as the 21st century approached.

1997

Napa City celebrates 150 years of existence.

Sawyers of Napa announces that they are quitting their tannery business after 128 years in Napa.

2000

Historic Hatt Building is renovated and opens as Napa River Inn.

Concerns about Glassy-Winged Sharp-shooter launch county-wide protection efforts.

2001

Copia—the American Center for Wine, Food and the Arts—opens.

2002

Historic Napa Valley Opera House reopens and presents its first performance in 88 years.

2004?

Uptown Theater scheduled to reopen, restored to its 1930s grandeur with 1000 seats and an art-deco decor.

Napa County Statistics

Population

City of Napa	72,585
City of American Canyon	9,774
City of Calistoga	5,190
City of St. Helena	5,950
Town of Yountville	2,916
Unincorporated	27,864
Total County	124,279

Highest Point
Sugarloaf Mountain   2,988 feet high

Largest Lake
Lake Berryessa   21 miles long

Borders
Mayacamas Mountains (western)
Vaca Range (eastern)

Population, percent change, 1990 to 2000:	+12.2%
Persons under 5 years old, percent, 2000:	6.1%
Persons under 18 years old, percent, 2000:	24.1%
Persons 65 years old and over, percent, 2000:	15.4%
White persons, percent, 2000:	80.0%
Black or African American persons, percent, 2000:	1.3%
American Indian and Alaska Native persons, percent, 2000:	0.8%
Asian persons, percent, 2000:	3.0%
Native Hawaiian and Other Pacific Islander, percent, 2000:	0.2%
Persons reporting some other race, percent, 2000:	10.9%
Persons reporting two or more races, percent, 2000:	3.7%
Female population, percent, 2000:	50.1%
Male population, percent, 2000:	49.9%
Persons of Hispanic or Latino origin, percent, 2000:	23.7%
White persons, not of Hispanic/Latino origin, percent, 2000:	69.1%
High school graduates, persons 25 years and over, 1990:	60,710
College graduates, persons 25 years and over, 1990:	16,773
Housing units, 2000:	48,554
Homeownership rate, 2000:	65.1%

Households, 2000:   45,402

Persons per household, 2000:   2.62

Households with persons under 18 years, percent, 2000:   34.4%

Median household money income, 1997 model-based estimate: $44,667

Persons below poverty, percent, 1997 model-based estimate: 8.8%

Children below poverty, percent, 1997 model-based estimate: 14.4%

Business

Private nonfarm establishments with paid employees, 1998:   3,537

Private nonfarm employment, 1998:   47,205

Private nonfarm employment, percent change 1990-1998:   31.3%

Nonemployer establishments, 1997   7,974

Retail sales, 1997:   952,590,000

Retail sales per capita, 1997: $8,077

Minority-owned firms, 1992:   863

Women-owned firms, 1992:   3,454

Housing units authorized by building permits, 1999:   713

Local government employment—full-time equivalent, 1997: 4,263

Geography

Land area, 2000:   754 square miles

Land area: 485,120 acres

Acres of vineyards: 40,000 (approx.)

Persons per square mile, 2000:   164.8

1351 Lounge 61, 142
1801 Inn 97
55 Degrees 185

A

ABC Transport Express 2
Above the West Ballooning 134
Acacia Winery 22
Adagio Inn 100
Adobe House Restaurant 25
Adventures Aloft 134
Aetna Springs Cellars 82
Aetna Springs Golf Course 82, 131
Aging, Wine 166
Airport Shuttles 2
Airport, Angwin 81
Airports 2
Alex's Restaurant 72
Alexis Baking Company & Café 26
All Seasons Bistro, Wine Bar
    and Wine Shop 72
Allegria 26
Alliance Wine Tours 106
Alpacas of Napa Valley 26
Ambrose Bierce B&B 100
American Canyon Attractions 21
American Canyon Online 16
American Center for Wine,
    Food and the Arts 26
American Indian Trading
    Company 73
American Safari Cruises 3
Amtrak 3
Ana's Cantina 142
Andretti Winery 26
Andretti, Mario 26
Anette's Chocolate & Ice
    Cream Factory 26
Angèle Restaurant 26
Angels Are Inn 94
Angwin Airport 81
Angwin Attractions 81
Anheuser-Busch Brewery 90
Antidote 61
Antique Fair 115
Antique Tours Limousine
    Service 7
Antiques 115
Appellation vs. Viticultural Area 157
Appellations and American
    Viticultural Areas (AVAs) 156
April in Carneros 120
Arbor Guest House 97
Archery 128
Aroma Wheel 170
Art Galleries 115
Art on Main 115
Artesa Winery 23
Artful Eye 115
Artisan Wine Tasting 62
Arts and Entertainment 118
Arts Council of Napa Valley 118

B

Babysitters 207
Back Label 160
Back Room Wines 26
Baking Mixes 110
Bale Grist Mill State Historic
    Park 62
Ballentine Vineyards and
    Winery 62
Balloon Aviation of Napa
    Valley 134
Balloons Above the Valley 134
Balloons, Hot Air 133
Barrels 160
Bartels Ranch & Country Inn 100
Bastille Day Celebration 121
Bay Area Ridge Trail 132
Bay Leaf Restaurant 27
Beaded Nomad 27
Bear Flag Inn 94
Beaulieu Vineyard 58
Beazley House 98
Bed and Breakfast Inns 94
Beef 111
Beer 111
Belle Arti 27
Berger, Dan 170
Beringer Vineyards 62
Best Time to Visit 10
Bicycle Rentals 129
Bicycle Shops 129
Bicycling 128
Big Paw Grub 113
Bigfoot 212
Biking, Mountain 147
Bistro Don Giovanni 27
Bistro Jeanty 50
Black Tie Taxi 7
Blackbird Inn 98
Blanket Wrap 105
Blue Heron Gallery 115
Blue Violet Mansion 98
Boating 127, 129
Bombay Bistro 27
Bonaventura Balloon
    Company 134
Bookends Book Store 116
Books, Best on the Napa
    Valley 15
Bookstores 116
Bordeaux House 102
Bosko's Trattoria 73
Bothé-Napa Valley State Park
    73, 137
Bottle Sizes 157
Bouchaine 23
Bouchon 51
Bouchon Bakery 51

Auberge du Soleil 85
Audubon Society 200
Automobile Rental 7

Bounty Hunter Rare Wine &
    Provisions 27
Bourassa Vineyards 185
Boysenberries 212
Brambles, The 94
Brannan Cottage Inn 94
Brannan's 73
Bridgeford Flying Services 28
Brix 51
Brown Estate Vineyards 83
Bubbling Well Pet Memorial
    Park 28
Buckhorn Grill 28
Budo, Restaurant 44
Buffalo's Shipping Post 184
Bureau of Reclamation Lake
    Berryessa Field Office 83
Burgess Cellars 81
Burgundy House 102
Bus 3
Butter Cream Bakery 28
Bylund House 100

C

Ca'toga Galleria d'Arte 80, 115
Cable TV 207
Café 29 62
Café Society 28
Caffe Cicero 29
Cakebread Cellars 59
California Native Plant Society 200
California Wine Tours 7
Calistoga Attractions 72
Calistoga Bookstore 116
Calistoga Country Lodge 94
Calistoga Depot 73
Calistoga Inn 73
Calistoga Inn Restaurant 73, 141
Calistoga Mineral Water
    Company 74
Calistoga Oasis Spa 105
Calistoga Pack Goats 74
Calistoga Pottery 115
Calistoga Ranch 74
Calistoga Roastery 74
Calistoga Spa Hot Springs 105
Calistoga Village Inn & Spa 74, 105
Calistoga Wayside Inn 95
Calistoga Wine Stop 74
Calpine Geothermal Visitor
    Center 90
CalTrans 6
Cameo Cinema 62
Camp Napa Culinary 110
Camping 135
Candlelight Inn 98
Canoeing 134
Cantinetta at Tra Vigne 63
Cardinale Winery 56
Carlin Cottages 95
Carneros Attractions 22
Carneros Inn 23

Carneros Lodge 24
Carols in the Caves 120
Carpenter, Hugh 110
CasaLana 95, 110
Castle in the Clouds 102
Catacula Lake Winery 83
Caves, Wine 167
Cedar Gables Inn 98
Cedar Street Spa 106
Celadon 29
Cemetery, Tulocay 47
Chablis Inn 29
Chajo Fine Art Furnishings 115
Chamber Music in the Napa
    Valley 121
Chambers of Commerce 209
Chappellet Vineyard 85
Charbay Winery and Distillery 63
Charles Krug Winery 63
Chardonnay Golf Club 131
Charles Krug Winery 63
Chateau de Vie 95
Chateau Hotel and Conference
    Center 29
Checkers 74
Cheese 111
Chiarello, Michael 68
Chien Blanc Lodging 95
Child, Julia 30, 35
Chiles Valley 82
Chimney Rock Winery 85
Chocolate 111
Christian Brothers Retreat &
    Conference Center 29
Christmas Tree Farms 117
Christopher's Inn 95
Churchill Manor 98
Cindy's Backstreet Kitchen 63
Cinedome 8 29
Cinnamon Bear 100
Clarification, Wine 166
Classic Limousine 7
Climate 11
Clos Du Val Wine Co 85
Clos Pegase Wine/Art Culture 121
Clos Pegase Winery 74
Cole's Chop House 29
Comfort Inn 21
Community Education 203
Community Foundation of the
    Napa Valley 209
Community-Supported
    Agriculture (CSA) 204
Compadres Bar & Grill 51
Conaway, James 15
Conference Facilities 107
Conn Creek Winery 85
Cooking Classes 110
Copia 30
Copperfield's Books 117
Coppola, Francis Ford 48, 59
Corison Winery 64
Corks 158
Corkscrew collection 64

Corporate Tour Planning 106
Cosentino Winery 51
Cottage Grove Inn 95
Crazy Creek Soaring 91
Crop Production 156
Cruise Ships 3
Cruise West 3
Crush 121
Crush 29 75
Crush and the Making of Wine
    164
Cucina à la Carte 51
Cuisine, Napa Valley 109
Culinary Institute of America at
    Greystone 64
Culver Mansion 95
Cuttings Wharf Road 90
Cuvaison Winery 85
Czech Inn 95

D

Darioush Winery 85
Daughters Inn 98
Dean and Deluca 64
Del Dotto Wine Caves and
    Tasting Room 30
Democrats 200
Department of Fish and Game 130
Depot Hotel Italian Dinners 204
Destination: Napa Valley Tours 106
Di Rosa Art & Nature Preserve 24
Di Rosa, Rene 24
Diamond Mountain Stables 133
Dine-in Deliveries Napa Valley 205
Disc Golf 130
Domaine Carneros Winery 24
Domaine Chandon Bastille
    Day Celebration 121
Domaine Chandon Winery &
    Restaurant 51
Downtown Joe's 30
Downtown Napa Walking Tour 143
Downtown Trolley 30
Dr. Wilkinson's Hot Springs 81
Drama 118
Dreamweavers Theatre 31
Driving Tips 5
Duckhorn Vineyards 86
Dutch Henry Winery 86

E

Eagle & Rose Inn 100
Eagle and Rose Residence Inn 64
Eagle and Rose Winery 82
Earthquakes 202
Economic Development 209
Education 203
Eisele Family Estate 83
El Bonita Motel 64
Elms, The 96
Elmshaven 81
Embassy Suites 31

Emergency Information 205
Enoteca Wine Shop 75
Entertainment 118
Environmental Organizations 200
Erika's Hillside B&B 100
Esperya 7
Esquisse Winery and
    Vineyards 64
Essential Wine Tasting Guide 171
Etude Wines 24
Evans Airporter 2
Events 120

F

Factory Outlets 37
Falconcrest. 70
Family Farms 111
Fanny's 96
Fans in Vineyards 180
FAQ, Wine 178
Far Niente Winery 56
Farmers Markets 110
Fermentation 165
Ferry 2
Festival Of Lights 121
Film Festival, Wine Country 125
Fine Arts 118
First Presbyterian Church 31
Fishing 130
Five-One-One 6
Flat Iron Grill 75
Flea Market, Napa-Vallejo 38
Flood Control Construction 7
Flood Control Project 200
Flood Emergencies 201
Flora Springs Tasting Room 65
Foil, Wine Bottle 158
Folie à Deux 65
Food Products 112
Foothill Café 31
Foothill House 96
Forest Manor 94
Forni-Brown Gardens 111
Franciscan Oakville Estate 65
Freemark Abbey 65
French Laundry Restaurant 52
Friends of the Napa River 200
Frog Hollow House 98
Frog's Leap Winery 59
Front Label 159
Fujiya Restaurant 32
Fumé Bistro & Bar 32

G

Gamble Ranch 111
Garnett Creek Inn 96
Gay Information 141
Genova Delicatessen 32
Geocaching 130
Gerhard's Napa Valley
    Sausage 114
Get a Grip on Growth 200

Gillwood's Restaurant (St. Helena) 65
Gillwoods Restaurant (Napa) 32
Giugni & Son Grocery Company 65
Glass Gallery 115
Glass Mountain Inn 101
Glassy-Winged Sharpshooter 163
Glossary of Wine Terms 171
Goat's Leap Cheese 111
Goats, Calistoga Pack 74
Golden Haven Spa Hot Springs Resort 75
Golf 131
Gondola Servizio 32
Goosecross Cellars 52
Gordon's Café and Wine Bar 52
Governments 199
Graeser Winery 75
Grapeseed Oil 112
Grapevines 161
Green Valley Café 65
Greenfield Winery 21
Greens 200
Greyhound Bus 3
Greystone 72
Grgich Hills Cellar 59
Grgich, Miljenko 59, 151
Group Outings 7

H

Hacienda Guest House 96
Hagafen Cellars 86
Hakusan Sake Gardens 32
Hall 66
Hans Fahden Vineyards 76
Harms Vineyard and Lavender Fields 117
Harvest 121
Harvest Inn 66
Harvest Statistics 156
Havens Wine Cellars 52
Hawthorn Inn & Suites 33
Health Food Stores 204
Health Spa Napa Valley 106
Heitz Cellars 66
Helicopter 2
Hennessey House 99
Henry Joseph Gallery 116
Henry's 33
Hess Collection Winery 33
Highway 29 89
Hiking 132
Hillcrest Country Inn 96
Hilltop House B&B 101
Hillview Country Inn 99
Hilton Garden Inn Napa 33
Historical Landmarks 221
History of Napa County 223
History of the Napa Valley 9
Hoffmann Farm 111
Holiday House 96

Home Restaurant Delivery 204
Home Winemakers Classic 121
Home Winemaking 185
Honey 112
Horse Camping 102, 133
Horseback Riding 133
Hospitals 205
Hot Air Balloons 133
Hotel d'Amici 96
Hotel St. Helena 66
Hotels 93
Huether, Gordon 23
Hurd Beeswax Candles 76
Hurley's Restaurant 52
Hydro Bar and Grill 76, 141

I

I. Wolk Gallery 116
Imani Gallery 116
In-N-Out Burger 34
Indian Springs Resort 76
Ink House, The 101
Inn at Southbridge 66
Inn at the Vines 33
Inn of Imagination 99
Inn on Randolph 99
Inns 93
Iris Gardens 122
It's-It Ice Cream 112

J

Jarvis Conservatory 34
Jarvis Vineyards 34
Jellies 112
Jelly Belly 91
Jessel Gallery 116
John Muir Inn 34
Jonesy's Famous Steak House 34
Joseph Phelps Vineyards 87
Julia's Kitchen 35
JV Wine & Spirits 35

K

Kayaking 134
Keller, Thomas 52
Kelley's "No Bad Days" Café 35
Kids' Favorites 140
Kirkland Ranch Winery 35
Kosher Wines 162

L

La Belle Epoque 99
La Boucane 35
La Chaumiere 96
La Fleur 101
La Toque 59
Label, Wine Bottle 159, 160
Labyrinth at the Methodist Church 36
Laird Family Estate 36
Lake Berryessa Marina Resort 83

Lake Berryessa Attractions 83
Lamb 112
Land Trust Hikes 121
Land Trust of Napa County 200
Larkmead Country Inn 96
Lavender 117
Lavender Hill Spa 106
Lawler's Liquors 205
Lee Youngman Galleries 116
Libertarian Party of Napa County 200
Libraries 203
Limousine Services 7
Lincoln Avenue Spa 106
Linen 118
Litto's Hubcap Ranch 82
Lodging Reservations 93
Loudspeaker, Invention of 212
Louis M. Martini Winery 66

M

Madonna Estate Winery 24
Magical Moonshine Puppet Theater 121
Main Street Books 117
Mammy Pleasant 213
Marchiori, Carlo 80
Marina, Napa Valley 25
Marine World, Six Flags 91
Market Restaurant 66
Markham Vineyards 67
Markley Cove Boat Rentals 84
Marshall's Farm Honey 21
Martini House 67
Martini Winery 66
Massage 105
Mayacamas Ranch 76
McClelland - Priest B&B Inn 99
Meadowlark Country House 96
Meadowood Resort 86
Medical Facilities 205
Meeting Facilities 107
Merryvale Wineyards 67
Microbreweries 111
Milat Vineyards 67
Milliken Creek Inn 99
Miner Family Vineyards 86
Mineral Baths 104
Misto Restaurant 36
Model Bakery 68
Mondavi Winery 57
Mondavi, Margrit Biever 30, 39
Mondavi, Robert 30, 57
Mont St. John 24
Monticello Vineyards 36
Moore's Landing 25
Mora Lane 96
Most Visited Attractions 11
Motels 93
Mount St. Helena 9
Mount View Hotel & Spa 77
Mount View Spa 105

Mountain Biking 147
Mountain Home Ranch 77
Mountain Men 121
Movies 119
Movies, Napa Valley 211
Mt. St. Helena Golf Course 131
Mud Baths 104
Mumm Napa Valley 86
Murals 36, 119
Museums 118
Music 118
Musicians 119
Mustard Festival, Napa Valley 123
Mustard's Grill 53

N

Nance's Hot Springs 77
Napa Attractions 25
Napa Book Tree 117
Napa Cellars 56
Napa County AVAs 157
Napa County Democratic
  Central Committee 200
Napa County Fair 122
Napa County Greens 200
Napa County Hispanic
  Network 209
Napa County Historical
  Society 37, 223
Napa County Iris Gardens 122
Napa County Landmarks 146
Napa County Republican
  Central Committee 200
Napa County Resource
  Conservation District 200
Napa County Transportation
  Planning Agency 6
Napa Downtown Association 146
Napa Firefighters Museum 37
Napa General Store 37
Napa Golf Course 131
Napa Group of the Sierra Club 200
Napa Inn, The 99
Napa Life 16
Napa Mill 37
Napa Neighbor 204
Napa Premium Outlets 37
Napa River 8, 127
Napa River Adventures 37
Napa River Ecological Reserve 53
Napa River Inn 38
Napa River Trail 133
Napa Riverfront District 38
Napa Sentinel 16
Napa Sierra Club 133
Napa State Hospital 38
Napa Town & Country Fair 122
Napa Valley Winery List 188
Napa Valley Academy Awards
  Benefit 122
Napa Valley Airport 2
Napa Valley Balloons 134

Napa Valley Christmas Tree
  Farm 117
Napa Valley Classic 122
Napa Valley Coalition of Non
  Profits 210
Napa Valley Coffee Roasting
  Company 38, 68
Napa Valley College 203
Napa Valley College Theatre 122
Napa Valley Conference and
  Visitors Bureau 38
Napa Valley Cooking School 110
Napa Valley Country Club 131
Napa Valley Drifters 134
Napa Valley Economic
  Development Corporation 209
Napa Valley Emporium 39
Napa Valley Exposition 39
Napa Valley Film Commission 211
Napa Valley Fly Fishermen 130
Napa Valley Free-Range Beef 111
Napa Valley Grapevine Wreath
  Company 59
Napa Valley Grille 53
Napa Valley Jazz Festival 122
Napa Valley Lamb Company 112
Napa Valley Lavender
  Company 117
Napa Valley Linen Company 118
Napa Valley Lodge 53
Napa Valley Marathon 122
Napa Valley Marina 25
Napa Valley Marriott 39
Napa Valley Model Railroad
  Club 122
Napa Valley Museum 54
Napa Valley Mustard Festival 123
Napa Valley Naturals 112
Napa Valley Off-Road Tours 7
Napa Valley Olive Oil
  Manufacturing Company 68
Napa Valley Online 15
Napa Valley Opera House 39
Napa Valley Orchids 118
Napa Valley Ovens 77
Napa Valley Pantry 110
Napa Valley Redwood Inn 39
Napa Valley Register 16
Napa Valley Repertory Theatre 123
Napa Valley Shakespeare
  Festival 123
Napa Valley Soap Company 118
Napa Valley Spanish Villa Inn 101
Napa Valley Symphony 123
Napa Valley Traditions 39
Napa Valley Trail Rides 40
Napa Valley Travelodge 40
Napa Valley Trolley Systems 77
Napa Valley Wine & Cigar 40
Napa Valley Wine Auction 123
Napa Valley Wine Festival 124
Napa Valley Wine Hardware 68
Napa Valley Wine Jelly 112

Napa Valley Wine Library 68
Napa Valley Wine Library
  Tasting 124
Napa Valley Wine Storage 185
Napa Valley Wine Train 40
Napa Valley.com 15
Napa Wine Company 56
Napa Wine Lockers 185
Napa Wine Merchants 40
Napa Winery Shuttle 7
Napa-Solano Audubon Society
  200
Napa-Sonoma Wine Country
  Visitors Center 21
Napa-Vallejo Flea Market and
  Auction 38
NapaNuts 113
NapaStyle 68
Native Plant Society 200
Nature Select Foods 204
Neighborhood, The 41
Nest 56
New Technology High School 41
Newspapers 206
Nichelini Winery 83
Nickel and Nickel 57
Nicola's Delicatessen &
  Pizzeria 77
Niebaum-Coppola Winery 59
Night Life 141
Non-Profit Organizations 209
North Bay Entertainment 119
North Bay Unity League 141
North Light Gallery 116
Nuts 113

O

O'Rear, Charles 16
Oak Knoll Inn 99
Oak Shores Park 84
Oakville Attractions 56
Oakville Grocery 57
Oakwood 97
Oat Hill Mine Trail 77
Off the Preserve! 42
Old Faithful Geyser 78
Old World Inn 99
Oleander House 102
Oliver House 101
Olive Oil 113
Oliver House 101
Omega 3 Seafoods 42
Omi's Farm 111
Open Studios 124
Opera House, Napa Valley 39
Optimum Foods 204
Opus One Winery 57
Orchids 118
Organic Abundance 204
Organic Vineyards 161
Organic Wines 162
Osprey Seafood Market 42
Oxbow School 42

P

Pacific Blues 54
Pacific Union College 82
Pacific Union College
    Bookstore 117
Paint Your World 42
Paintball Jungle 22
Palisades Market 78
Paris Tasting 151
Parks and Camping 135
Pasta Prego 43
Pawlcyn, Cindy 63
Pearl 43
Peju Province 60
Pére Jeanty 54
Perfect Purée of Napa Valley 113
Personal Chefs 205
Peterson Family Christmas
    Tree Farm 117
Petit Logis 102
Petrified Forest 78
Petsitters 207
Pharmacies 205
Phelps Vineyards 87
Photo Opportunities 15
Piatti Ristorante 54
Piccolino's Italian Café 43
Picnicking 138
Pierce's Disease 163
Pilar 43
Pine Ridge Winery 87
Pink Mansion, The 97
Pizza Azzurro 43
Pizzeria Tra Vigne 68
Pleasant, Mary Ellen 213
Political Parties 200
Pope Valley 82
Pope Valley Winery 82
Population 215
Post-Fermentation 166
Posticino 43
Prager Ports and Wines 68
Prager Winery B & B 101
Prisoner of War Camp 214
Private Preserve 179
Pronunciation, Wine Varietal 171
Provenance Vineyards 60
Public School Districts 203
Publications, Wine 185
Punt 158
Puppet Theater, Magical
    Moonshine 121
Purees 113
Putah Creek Resort 84

Q

Quail Mountain 97
Quail Ridge Reserve 84
Questions & Answers, Wine 178
Quintessa 87

R

Radio Stations 206
Rainfall, Average 12
Raku Ceramics 116
Rammed Earth Works 182
Ranch Market Too! 54
Ranches 94
Rancho Caymus Inn 60
Rancho Gordo 112
Rancho Monticello Resort 103
Raspberry's Art Glass 116
Raymond & Company
    Cheesemongers 68
Raymond Vineyard & Cellar 69
Real Estate 210
Recreational Vehicle Camping 103
Red Hen Antiques 43, 115
Red Hen Cantina 44
Red Rock Café and Catering 44
Red Wines 153
Redwood Inn, Napa Valley 39
Regusci Winery 87
Relocating to the Valley 209
Republicans 200
Resorts 93
Restaurant Budo 44
Restaurante La Strada 22
Retreats 93
Reynolds Family Winery 87
Ridge Trail, Bay Area 132
Ristorante Allegria 44
River City 44, 141
River Terrace Inn 44
RiverBend Hotel 44
Riverdog Farm 204
Robert Craig Wine Cellars
    Tasting Room 44
Robert Louis Stevenson State
    Park 78, 138
Robert Mondavi Summer
    Festival 124
Robert Mondavi Winery 57
Robert Sinskey Vineyards 87
Roman Spa Hot Springs 106
Romantic Tips 140
Rombauer Vineyards 87
Roses 163
ROTO Beverage 114
Ruffino's 45
Rustridge Bed & Breakfast Inn 100
RustRidge Winery 83
Rutherford Attractions 58
Rutherford Gardens 60
Rutherford Grill 60
Rutherford Hill Winery 87

S

Safari West 91
Saintsbury 25
Saketini Asian Diner and
    Lounge 45
Salute Santé Grapeseed Oil 112

Salvestrin Estate Vineyard &
    Winery 69
San Francisco Bay Trail 132
Sattui Winery 71
Sausage 114
Sawyer Cellars 61
Scarlett's Country Inn 97
Scenic Drives 89
Schat's Bakkerij 79
Schools 209
Schramsberg Vineyards 79
Scott Courtyard 97
Seasons of the Vineyard 164
Seguin Moreau Napa
    Cooperage 45
Sequoia Grove Vineyards 61
Settling, Wine 166
Shackford's Kitchen Store and
    More 45
Shady Oaks Country Inn 101
Shafer Vineyards 88
Shakespeare Festival, Napa
    Valley 123
Sharpsteen Museum 79
Shipbuilding During WWII 214
Shopping 114
Sierra Club 200
Silver Oak Cellars 58
Silver Rose Inn 106
Silverado Archery Club 128
Silverado Brewing Company 69
Silverado Country Club and
    Resort 88
Silverado Museum 69
Silverado Trail Attractions 84
Silverado Vineyards 88
Sinskey Vineyards 87
Six Flags Marine World 91
Skyhill Napa Valley Farms 111
Skyline Wilderness Park 45, 103
Slow Food 114
Smith's Mount St. Helena
    Trout Farm 92
Soap 118
Society for Creative
    Anachronism 125
Soda Canyon Store 88
Spanish Flat Resort 84
Sparkling Wine 166
Sparrow Lane 114
Spas 103
Spirits In Stone 70, 116
Spot, The 70
Spring Mountain Vineyard 70
St. Clement Vineyards 69
St. Helena Attractions 61
St. Helena Olive Oil Company 61
St. Helena Premium Outlets 69
St. Helena Star 16
St. Helena Wine Center 69
St. Helena Wine Merchants 70
St. Supéry Vineyard & Winery 61
Stag's Leap Wine Cellars 88

Stagecoach Express 184
Stahlecker House 100
State Parks 137
Statistics, Napa County 215
Steele Park Resort 84
Sterling Vineyards 79
Stevenson Manor Inn 97
Stevenson, Robert Louis 69,
   78, 79, 138
Stewart's Farm 112
Stocks, Wine 186
Sulfites 159
Sunny Acres 101
Sunshine Foods 70
Superior Court of California,
   County of Napa 200
Sustainable Winegrowing
   162
Sutter Home Winery 70
Sweeney's Sport Store 130
Sweet Finale 47
Sweetie Pies 47
Symphony on the River
   Festival 125

T

Taco Trucks 47
Tall Timbers Chalet 100
Tasting Bars 19
Tasting on Main 71
Tasting Wine 169
Taxi Cabernet 7
Taxis 7
Taylor's Refresher 71
Telephone Prefixes 199
Television Stations 206
Temperatures, Average 12
Terminology, Wine 171
Terra 71
The Spot 70
Timothy, Brother 64
Tour Ideas 16
Tour Planning 106
Towns and Regions 21
Tra Vigne Restaurant 71
Trader Joe's 47
Traffic Information 6
Trailside Inn 97
Train 3
Traintown 92
Transportation 6
Treasures of Tibet 80
Triangular Test 170
Trinchero Family Estates 70
Triple S Ranch 80
Triple S Restaurant 80
Trivia, Napa Valley 211
Tulocay Cemetery 47
Turnbull Wine Cellars 58
Tuscany 48
Twin Pine Casino 92

U

Uptown Theater 48
Uva Trattoria Italiana 48

V

V. Sattui Winery 71
Vallerga's Market 48
Valley Men Who Cook 125
Valleys of Napa County 215
Varietal Pronunciations 171
Vegetarian Restaurants 109
Veranda Club Spa 54
Veterans Home Fourth Of July
   Fireworks 125
Veterans Home of California 55
Victorian Holiday Candlelight
   Tour 125
Villa Ca'toga 80
Villa Corona 48
Villa Romano 49
Villagio Inn & Spa 55
Vine Village 113
Vinegar 114
Vineyard, In the 161
Vineyard Country Inn 101
Vineyard Outlet 49
Vintage 1870 55
Vintage 1870 Wine Cellar 55
Vintage Inn 55
Vintner's Collective 49
Vintner's Golf Club 131
Viticultural Areas 156
Volker Eisele Family Estate 83
Von Strasser Winery 80

W

Walking Tour of Napa 143
Wappo Bar & Bistro 80
Washington Street Lodging 97
Water Skiing 134
Weather Report 12
Websites 15
Wedding Planning 217
Weekly Calistogan 16
White Barn 125
White Sulphur Springs Retreat
   & Conference Center 71
White Wine Fermentation 165
White Wines 152
Whitehall Lane Winery 72
Wilkinson's Hot Springs 81
Willi's Water Ski Center 134
Wine 151
Wine & Dine Tours 106
Wine and Crafts Faire 125
Wine Appreciation Classes 185
Wine Auction, Napa Valley 123
Wine Bars 19
Wine Blending/Tasting Kit 185
Wine Bottle "Package" 157
Wine Caves 167

Wine Country Concierge 106
Wine Country Film Festival 125
Wine Country Helicopters 2
Wine Country Inn 101
Wine Country Kitchens 112
Wine Country Victorian &
   Cottages 102
Wine Facts, Statistics and
   Trivia 182
Wine Garage 81
Wine Garden Food and Wine
   Bar 55
Wine Industry Addresses 187
Wine Library Tasting 124
Wine Library, Napa Valley 68
Wine Organizations 187
Wine Plane 49
Wine Prism 171
Wine Publications 185
Wine Shippers 184
Wine Spectator Greystone
   Restaurant 72
Wine Stocks 186
Wine Storage 184
Wine Tasting 169
Wine Tasting Tools 170
Wine Train 40
Wine Valley Lodge 49
Wine Varietal Basics 152
Wine Way Inn 97
Winemaking Classes 185
Wineries of Napa Valley 50
Winery List 188
Winery Shuttle 7
Winiarski, Warren 88, 151

Y

Yount Mill Road 90
Yountville Attractions 50
Yountville Inn 55
Yountville Park 56
Yurts 182

Z

ZD Wines 89
Zinfandel Inn 102
Zinsvalley Restaurant 50
Zip Codes 199
ZuZu 50

Order More Copies
of This Book

Online
On the web at: www.napavalleybooks.com
Pay with a credit card or your PayPal account.

By mail
Send a check payable to Westsong Publishing to:
Napa Valley Book
PO Box 2254
Napa CA 94558

Book is $16.95 plus shipping.
(Please add 7.75% sales tax ($1.32) if book is shipped to a California address).

Shipping by air
U.S:$4.00 for first book and $2.00 for each additional book.
International: $9.00 for first book and $5.00 for each additional book.

Quantity Purchases
Contact us at nvbook@westsong.com for information about quantity orders. We can produce special front cover imprints with your company logo or sales message.

Or Buy the eBook

The ebook version of The Napa Valley Book is in .PDF format, suitable for your home computer or PDA. It has more than 100 color photographs, a table of contents with hyperlinks, and more than 700 active hyperlinks to Napa Valley websites. Put it on your desktop computer, laptop or PDA.

For more information on buying and immediately downloading the ebook, go to
www.napavalleybooks.com